Dear Anne,

I hope this book provides inspiration and ideas! Your skills in architecture and caregiving and horticulture combine into horticultural therapy in a beautiful way! I hope you enjoy this lovely book — full of research, documentation and evidence-based design.

Warmly,

Julia

P.S. Thank you again for all of your loving work with Mom. She loves your cooking and is thriving under your care.

Therapeutic Landscapes

Therapeutic Landscapes

An Evidence-Based Approach to Designing
Healing Gardens and Restorative Outdoor Spaces

CLARE COOPER MARCUS

NAOMI A. SACHS

WILEY

Library of Congress Cataloging-in-Publication Data:

Marcus, Clare Cooper.
    Therapeutic landscapes : an evidence-based approach to designing healing gardens and restorative outdoor spaces/Clare Cooper Marcus, Naomi Sachs.
        pages cm
    Includes index.
    ISBN 978-1-118-23191-3 (cloth); ISBN 978-1-118-41940-3 (ebk); ISBN 978-1-118-42110-9 (ebk)
    1. Medical geography. 2. Landscapes—Therapeutic use. 3. Landscape architecture—Therapeutic use. 4. Evidence-based design.   I. Sachs, Naomi, 1968- II. Title.
    RA792.M335 2014
    614.4'2—dc23
                                                                                                    2013007059
Printed in the United States of America
10 9 8 7 6 5 4 3 2 1

Contents

Foreword   vii

Acknowledgments   ix

ONE
Introduction   1

TWO
History of Hospital Outdoor Space   6

THREE
Theory, Research, and Design
Implications   14

FOUR
Types and Locations of Therapeutic
Landscapes in Healthcare   36

FIVE
The Participatory Design Process   47
Teresia Hazen

SIX
General Design Guidelines for Healthcare
Facilities   56

SEVEN
Children's Hospital Gardens   91

EIGHT
Gardens for Cancer Patients   115

NINE
Gardens for the Frail Elderly   129

TEN
Gardens for People with Alzheimer's and
Other Dementias   148

ELEVEN
Hospice Gardens   165

TWELVE
Gardens for Mental and Behavioral Health
Facilities   179

THIRTEEN
Gardens for Veterans and Active Service
Personnel   206

FOURTEEN
Rehabilitation Gardens   222

FIFTEEN
Restorative Gardens in Public Spaces   235

SIXTEEN
Horticultural Therapy and Healthcare
Garden Design   250
Teresia Hazen

SEVENTEEN
Planting and Maintaining Therapeutic
Gardens   261
Marni Barnes

EIGHTEEN
Therapeutic Landscapes and
Sustainability   288

NINETEEN
The Business Case and Funding for
Therapeutic Gardens   298

TWENTY
Evaluation of Therapeutic Gardens   308

INDEX   317

Foreword

The publication of this important book could not be more timely, given the great wave of healthcare facility construction and renovation overtaking the United States and other countries. Healthcare environments are changing and responding to trends and challenges as varied as new payment policies that reward quality and satisfaction, the growing importance of ambulatory care and rehabilitation, rising acuity levels of hospital inpatients, and rapid growth in the number of frail elderly and those with Alzheimer's disease or other forms of dementia. The fast-evolving character of healthcare underscores the need to rethink the design of care environments and to create better facilities that prominently include gardens designed in evidence-informed ways to reduce stress, improve satisfaction and clinical outcomes, and enhance sustainability.

The interdisciplinary field of evidence-based design (EBD) has developed over the past twenty-five years in response to the need for sound knowledge to help guide healthcare design that improves care quality, outcomes, and cost-effectiveness. It makes solid sense to use the best available evidence when creating a new, long-lived healthcare environment on which so many will depend. Although the quality and amount of EBD research has rapidly increased, most studies address issues linked to the architecture and interior design of hospitals—the effects of single versus multibed patient rooms on infection transmission, for example. A smaller but growing body of EBD research has examined the influences of gardens and nature views on quality of care and outcomes in healthcare facilities. This book provides an up-to-date account of the research and theory on the effects of nature and excels in extracting and clearly explaining the design implications. Readers will gain a great deal of evidence-informed knowledge and insight concerning what garden design approaches work and which are not effective in improving healthcare quality.

It has been fifteen years since publication of the landmark volume edited by Clare Cooper Marcus and Marni Barnes, *Healing Gardens: Therapeutic Benefits and Design Recommendations*. Compared to that 1999 work, this new book by Marcus and Naomi A. Sachs contains much fresh material, based on recent research, plus a wealth of new knowledge derived from evaluations of several innovative and successful therapeutic gardens created in recent years by landscape architects and healthcare providers. The book

begins by surveying the history of hospital outdoor space, provides a chapter covering research and theory, and follows with chapters on types and locations of therapeutic spaces in healthcare, and general design guidelines relevant across different categories of medical facilities.

Each of the following chapters focuses on a garden category designed for specific patients or user groups: gardens for children's hospitals, for example; for patients with cancer; for persons with Alzheimer's; and for mental and behavioral health facilities. These chapters present case studies of exemplary real-world gardens, accompanied by instructive and interesting insights obtained from postoccupancy assessments giving balanced views concerning strengths and weaknesses of the settings. Each chapter reviews research relevant to the specific user group and discusses design guidelines adjusted to meet their particular therapeutic needs. These chapters are superbly illustrated. A few examples of the many outstanding gardens featured: the Olson Family Garden at St. Louis Children's Hospital, Alnarp Rehabilitation Garden in Sweden, and the internationally renowned Oregon Burn Center Garden at Legacy Emanuel Medical Center in Portland. Additionally, this is the first book on healing gardens with chapters on planting design and maintenance, horticultural therapy, sustainability, gardens for veterans, restorative spaces in public spaces, and the business case for healing gardens, including funding strategies.

A theme running through the book is that a participatory design process is vital to creating a successful therapeutic garden. This critical topic is the focus of a noteworthy chapter by Teresia Hazen, which describes the participatory process developed at Legacy Health in Portland, Oregon, and used to create several successful gardens at Legacy medical centers. The Legacy process begins with the premise that there is no one-size-fits-all garden design adequate to meeting the needs of varied types of patients, their families, and associated clinicians. The Legacy process instead tailors the design of each garden to ensure it directly and effectively serves the therapeutic needs of a particular category of patients (for example, stroke patients, burns cases) and their families and healthcare team.

More than any other previous book, *Therapeutic Landscapes* provides research-grounded yet user-friendly information that will enable readers to successfully design, fund, and build healthcare facilities that provide beneficial access to nature for patients, visitors, and staff. This book will be an indispensable resource for healthcare designers and horticultural therapists. It will also be of great value for healthcare administrators, facility managers, facility developers, and many therapists and other clinicians. The knowledge and lessons it offers will be critically important for increasing the quality and success of any healthcare project that provides gardens or other forms of access to nature.

Roger S. Ulrich, PhD, EDAC

Acknowledgments

We are deeply grateful to the many people who helped make this book a reality. We thank two colleagues who generously contributed their time and expertise by writing chapters: Teresia Hazen of Legacy Health in Portland, Oregon, who wrote chapters 5, "The Participatory Design Process," and 16, "Horticultural Therapy and Healthcare Garden Design"; and Marni Barnes of Deva Designs in Palo Alto, California, who wrote chapter 17, "Planting and Maintaining Therapeutic Gardens."

We greatly appreciate those colleagues who wrote or contributed to individual case studies of exemplary restorative landscapes that they designed, studied, or helped facilitate. These include Chris Garcia and Shelagh Smith (chapter 9); Chris Garcia (chapter 11); Jessy Bergeman, Victoria L. Lygum, and Ulrika K. Stigsdotter (chapter 12); Brian Bainnson (chapter 13); and Jeffrey Smith, Patty Cassidy, Kevin Aust, and David Kamp (chapter 15).

As we wrote about the business case for healing gardens and funding considerations, we asked a variety of colleagues for their experiences and drew upon their responses. For useful insights we want to thank: Brian Bainnson, Carter van Dyke, Becky Feasby, Bob Golde, Teresia Hazen, Rob Hoover, Kirk Hines, David Kamp, Deborah LeFrank, Connie Roy-Fisher, Alberto Salvatore, Jeffrey Smith, Jerry Smith, Lisa Waisath, and Daniel Winterbottom.

We greatly appreciate those colleagues who took the time to read and give valuable feedback on drafts of various chapters and case studies. These include Janet Brown, Barbara Kreski, Deborah LeFrank, Steve Mitrione, Connie Roy-Fisher, Zofia Rybkowski, Alberto Salvatore, Amy Wagenfeld, James Westwater, and Russell Wilson.

We asked colleagues for images or site plans of projects they had designed, studied, or photographed that we might include in the book, and we had an overwhelming response. We offer our thanks to the many individuals and firms who replied: Lena Welen Andersson, Kevin Aust/AECOM, Angela Milewski/BHA Design, Brian Bainnson/Quatrefoil, Marni Barnes/Deva Designs, Tom Benjamin/Wellnesscapes, Jessy Bergeman, Melissa Bierman/Legacy Health, Beverly Brown/Nazareth College, Renata Brown/Cleveland Botanical Garden, Laura Blackwell/The Plaza at Twin Rivers, Sabrina Buttitta/Plant Connection, Patrick Carey/Greenroofs.com, Jack Carman/Design for Generations, Sharon Coates/Zaretsky Associates, Tara Graham Cochrane/Design Well, Nilda Cosco/Natural Learning Initiative, Brenna Costello/SmithGroup JJR, Bob Cunningham/Arcadia Studio, Sharon Danks/Bay Tree Design, Leah Diehl/University of Florida, Henry Domke/Henry Domke Fine Art, Mark Epstein/Hafs-Epstein, Julie Evans/The Fockele Garden Company, Terri Evans/Shepley Bulfinch, Lesley Fleming, Gwenn Fried/NYU Langone Medical Center, Chris Garcia/San Diego Botanic Garden, Charlotte Grant, Teresia Hazen/Legacy Health, Ella Hilker/Haverefugiet, Kirk Hines/Wesley Woods-Emory Healthcare, Sonja Johansson/Johansson Design Collaborative, Bryan Johns/Clarke-Lindsey Village, Jennifer Jones/Carol R. Johnson Associates, Kenneth Helphand/University of Oregon, David Kamp/Dirtworks, Lydia Kimball/Mahan Rykiel Associates, Barbara Kreski/Chicago Botanic Garden, Kurisu International, Deborah LeFrank/LeFrank and Associates, Kun Hyang Lee/Asia Pacific Association of Therapeutic Horticulture, Victoria Linn Lygum, Laurel Macdonald/Macdonald Environmental Planning, Beth Matlock/Living Art Designs, Randall Metz/Grissim Metz Andriese Associates, Maja Steen Moller, Jim Mumford/Good Earth Plants, Dorinda Wolfe Murray/Independent Gardening Ltd., Upali Nanda, Danna Olsen/University of Wisconsin–Madison, Samira Pasha/Perkins+Will, Annie Pollock/Arterre Landscape Design, Mary Poole/Christian Care Community, Robert Rensel/Cleveland Botanical Garden, Annette Ridenour/Aesthetics Inc., Susan Rodiek/Texas A&M University, Geoff Roehll/Hitchcock Design Group, Connie Roy-Fisher/Studio Sprout, Alberto Salvatore/Salvatore Associates, Jan Satterthwaite/VireO Design Studio, Herb Schaal, FASLA, Becky Hoerr and Peter Schaudt/Hoerr Schaudt Landscape Architects, Giulo Senes/University of Milan, Mike Shriver/National AIDS Memorial Grove, Erin Smith/Just in Time Therapy, Jeffrey Smith/Professional Engineering Associates, Shelagh Smith/Vancouver General Hospital, Rick Spalenka/RGS Designs, Diana Spellman/Spellman Brady, Ulrika Karlsson Stigsdotter/University of Copenhagen, Tim Sturdy/Mainzeal, Christine Ten Eyck/Ten Eyck Landscape Architects, Nissa Tupper/HGA Architects and Engineers, Martha Tyson/Upland Design, Roger Ulrich/Chalmers University, Carter van Dyke/Carter van Dyke Associates, Lori Vierow/Planning Resources Inc., Amy Wagenfeld/Western Michigan University, Gary Wangler/St. Louis Children's Hospital, Keith Watson/Gardening Leave, Steven Wells/Austin Health Royal Talbot Rehabilitation

Center, Daniel Winterbottom/University of Washington, Mary Wyatt/TKF Foundation/Open Spaces Sacred Places. We extend a special thank you to Henry Domke of www.henrydomke.com for his generosity in letting us use his nature photographs.

We are grateful to all of the members of the Therapeutic Landscapes Network who submitted images, stories, and ideas as we were developing the themes encompassed in this book.

We want to thank two people who were invaluable in helping us get the manuscript into shape: Janine Baer, for computer assistance; and Laura Leone, who tirelessly checked and organized references.

Thank you to Ian Muise, Rowena Philbeck, and Sheetal Goyal Rakesh at Texas A&M University's Technical Reference Center for technical support.

We are deeply grateful to the following people at John Wiley and Sons: Margaret Cummins, Senior Editor, encouraged us from the very beginning to undertake this book and guided us through the process with a firm but gentle and competent hand; Mike New, Editorial Assistant, for his invaluable help with organizing images and permissions; David Sassian, Senior Production Editor, for his excellent production skills.

Finally, some personal thanks. Clare wishes to thank her family—her children Lucy Marcus and Jason Cooper Marcus, daughter-in-law Angela Laffan, and grandsons Myles and Remington Marcus—who understood her passion for this work and gave her unfailing support and love. Her thanks go also to many friends, as well as her family, who rallied around when she broke her right (dominant) arm during the process of completing the book. Naomi wishes to thank her best friend, James Westwater, for his tremendous support—including insistence on healthy eating, sleeping, and spending time in nature ("Remember, this is what you're writing about!"); Agnes and Boo for making her take them on daily walks and providing healthy doses of positive distraction; and her parents, Benjamin and Jacqueline Sachs and mum-in-law, Nedra Westwater, for their love and encouragement.

CHAPTER 1

Introduction

> Having spent many weeks in the hospital left an indelible imprint on the way I experience pain, suffering, and loss within the recognized healthcare environment. Surely this fear and anxiety that one feels in this controlled and somewhat clinical building can leave one feeling more vulnerable, fragile, and scared. Just by being outside and with nature, to smell and touch the plants, reduced the depression and dread. I think more positive thoughts, am hopeful, and if I cry I feel the plants understand and do not judge or cringe.
>
> Mariane Wheatley-Miller, personal communication, 2013

HOSPITALS AND OTHER HEALTHCARE FACILI-TIES are some of the most difficult places for people to be. Regardless of the physical setting, they are almost invariably environments where people face a high degree of stress. Patients may be experiencing physical or emotional pain; visitors, in an alien and, for many, a threatening environment, are worried about a loved one or close friend. Healthcare providers, in many cases dealing with life and death on a daily basis, are under an enormous amount of pressure. Their hours are long and their workload is taxing.

Since the mid-1990s there has been an increasing emphasis on a patient-centered approach in healthcare and a growing understanding of the importance of evidence-based design (Cama 2009; Frampton, Gilpin, and Charmel 2003). Hospital interiors have largely changed from the white, clinical settings of decades ago to more colorful—sometimes even hotel-like—environments. Nursing homes, renamed assisted-living facilities, have largely left behind their depressing reputation and are being reborn as warm, homelike settings. The environmental needs of specific patients, such as those with Alzheimer's disease, are increasingly understood. In short, there has been a revolution in the provision of healthcare and the recognition that the physical environment matters to people's health and well-being and that the health and well-being of the whole person needs to be addressed rather than just the disease.

Along with these beneficial changes to healthcare buildings, there has been a growing recognition that the whole environment—including outdoor space—matters (fig. 1.1). A significant body of research confirms and sheds new light on what many people have known intuitively: that connection with nature is beneficial—even vital—for health. Walking in the woods, sitting on a park bench, tending the soil in one's garden, and even watching the colors and movements of nature from indoors are all passive and active ways to connect with the natural world. They awaken our senses, encourage physical movement and exercise, facilitate social connection, reduce stress and depression, and elicit positive physiological and psychological response. Healthcare facilities—from hospitals to specialized medical settings to assisted-living and retirement communities—are striving to incorporate specially designed outdoor spaces that can support the health and well-being of patients, residents, visitors, and staff (fig. 1.2).

Professional magazines are increasingly mentioning praiseworthy hospitals with healing gardens or views to nature. Excellent books have been published recently that focus specifically on healthcare outdoor space (Rodiek and Schwarz 2006, 2007; Pollock and Marshall 2012). However, it is rare that journals and magazines read by designers review such books or feature articles on healthcare outdoor space. Sadly, excellent books and monographs on healthcare building design often pay scant attention to outdoor spaces. Building plans are depicted with white expanses around them as if they are floating in space.

While the evidence for the importance of access to nature is there—and growing—the actual provision of appropriate outdoor space in healthcare facilities is often less than adequate, with limited "green nature," unmet needs for privacy and "getting away," even poor provision of the most basic needs, such as ease of access, comfortable seating, safe walking surfaces, protection from the sun, and so on.

1.1 The trend toward patient-centered care continues to grow. Healthcare facilities such as the Northeast Georgia Medical Center, in Gainesville, incorporate restorative gardens into the master plans from the beginning of the design process. The Wilheit-Keys Peace Garden offers physical access to nature outside of the building and visual access from inside. Designer: The Fockele Garden Company.
Copyright, The Fockele Garden Company

The goal of this book is to focus critical attention on healthcare outdoor space, to emphasize the importance of evidence-based design, to highlight exemplary case studies, and to present research-based guidelines to inform clients and designers of restorative outdoor spaces. The aim is to address two key groups of readers: the clients and funders of healing spaces and the designers (principally landscape architects) who will translate client needs into an actual environment. If clients and funders understand more about the requirements and goals of a healing garden, they can more easily communicate with the designer. If designers understand more about the research on which to base their decisions, they are more likely to meet the goals of their clients—those who provide the funding and the users who will eventually benefit from the garden (fig. 1.3).

With an audience of two quite different sets of "actors," it is inevitable that some parts of this book will speak more to one than the other. For example, some sections of the chapter on planting and maintenance may be basic knowledge for an experienced landscape architect but new and useful information for a client. The detailed design guidelines are principally aimed at the practicing designer and may be of less importance to the client or philanthropic donor. Chapters on horticultural therapy and participatory design may provide new information for many readers. The case studies of exemplary gardens throughout document existing best practices and will, the authors hope, inspire anyone using this book.

The core of the book consists of the general design guidelines presented in chapter 6. These are research-informed recommendations that need to be followed in any kind of healthcare outdoor space, whether it is a courtyard or a roof garden, whether it is at an acute-care hospital or a residential

1.3 Native plantings at Kent Hospital in Warwick, Rhode Island, create a beautiful entrance. Designer: Wellnesscapes.
Photo courtesy of Thomas Benjamin, Wellnesscapes.com, on behalf of Kent Hospital

facility for the frail elderly. Beyond these basic guidelines, specific guidelines must also be followed for certain patient groups. These are explained in chapters 7 through 14—gardens for ill children, those with cancer, the mentally ill, Alzheimer's

patients, the frail elderly, returning veterans, rehabilitation patients, and those in hospice.

Different terms have emerged to refer to outdoor spaces in healthcare, and two different types can be recognized. A healing, therapeutic, or restorative garden (these terms are used interchangeably in this book) is one that users, whether residents or visitors, experience any way they want: to sit, walk, look, listen, talk, meditate, take a nap, explore. Therapeutic benefits are derived from just being *in* the garden. No staff is necessary, except for maintenance. Such a garden might be found at an inpatient acute-care hospital, a residential facility for the frail elderly, a hospice, or an outpatient clinic.

In an enabling garden, by contrast, activities are led by a professional horticultural therapist (HT), occupational therapist (OT), physical therapist (PT), and other allied professionals in collaboration with other clinical staff. The HT might engage recovering stroke victims in weeding, watering, and repotting plants; the PT or OT might help someone with a broken limb by encouraging reaching, grasping, and exercising. Therapeutic benefits are derived from hands-on activities and exercise in the garden (fig. 1.4). Such a garden

1.4 A veteran transplants seedlings into a larger pot at Gardening Leave in Auchincruive, Scotland.
Courtesy of Gardening Leave Limited

1.5 Great spangled fritillary on butterfly weed.
Photo from www.henrydomke.com.

is likely to be found at a rehabilitation hospital, some mental and behavioral health facilities, and some children's hospitals.

For the purposes of this book, "nature" is defined quite broadly, and while largely referring to vegetation, it also refers to wildlife, water, stone, the weather, sky, clouds, wind, and sun. "Access to nature" includes actual passive and active, indoor and outdoor engagement with nature through any or all of the senses (fig. 1.5).

Indoor contact with nature can include looking out at nature through a window; viewing nature imagery (still and moving pictures); seeing, touching, and smelling indoor vegetation; and hearing nature's sounds through an open window or through sound recordings (birds, water, and the like).

1.6 The Elizabeth and Nona Evans Restorative Garden at the Cleveland Botanical Garden in Cleveland, Ohio, provides opportunities for passive and active connection with nature. Designer: Dirtworks, PC
Courtesy of Dirtworks, PC; photo by Bruce Buck

1.7 Echinacea flower detail.
Photo from www.henrydomke.com

Outdoor contact with nature is likely to engage more than one of the senses and can range from passive to active: sitting just outside the entry of a building, taking a stroll, stopping to look at, touch, or smell plant material, engaging in physical or occupational therapy, gardening, watering plants, taking a brisk walk for exercise, jogging, or engaging in team sports (fig. 1.6).

The word "garden" will be used throughout the book to refer to any designed outdoor space with predominant greenery, even though the term has slightly different meanings in different English-speaking countries. For example, in the United Kingdom it refers to the whole of a defined and designed cultivated space that is predominantly green, whereas in the United States it tends to refer to a planting bed, such as a flower garden (fig. 1.7).

"Healthcare facilities" are defined as places where people receive medical care. These include—but are not limited to—inpatient and outpatient facilities, acute-care general hospitals, rehabilitation hospitals, psychiatric hospitals, children's hospitals, veteran's hospitals, specialty hospitals and clinics (cancer, kidney dialysis, mental health, etc.), hospice, residential and outpatient facilities for those with special needs (the frail elderly, Alzheimer's patients, the mentally ill, battered women).

References

Cama, R. 2009. *Evidence-Based Healthcare Design.* Hoboken, NJ: John Wiley and Sons.

Frampton, S., B. L. Gilpin, and P. A. Charmel, eds. 2003. *Putting Patients First: Designing and Practicing Patient-Centered Care.* San Francisco: Jossey-Bass.

Pollock, A., and M. Marshall, eds. 2012. *Designing Outdoor Spaces for People with Dementia.* Sydney, Australia: Hammond Press.

Rodiek, S., and B. Schwarz, eds. 2006. *The Role of the Outdoors in Residential Environments for Aging.* New York: Haworth Press.

———, eds. 2007. *Outdoor Environments for People with Dementia.* New York: Haworth Press.

CHAPTER 2

History of Hospital Outdoor Space

THE HISTORY OF HOSPITALS AND HEALING PLACES goes back many centuries. At one time nature was seen as intrinsic to healing, but this important connection was largely lost by the twentieth century. Now, however, it is being rediscovered, in the form of healing gardens and therapeutic landscapes in healthcare settings.

One of the first healing places for which we have evidence was the Aesclipion at Epidaurus in ancient Greece—one of a network of healing places functioning from the fourth century BCE to the sixth century CE. Natural spring water was used in cleansing rituals; a library, museum, theater, marketplace, and groves of trees provided for people's entertainment as they waited until the auguries were favorable and they could enter the most important building, the *abaton* (Gesler 2003). Here, dream-healing took place, for it was believed that when people were asleep, the soul left the body and could communicate with the gods. Sleeping patients received prescribed cures from the god Asclepius, and when they awoke, his injunctions were administered by physician-priests (ibid.).

Among the first hospitals as we know them were Roman military hospitals with naturally lit and cross-ventilated wards separated from each other to avoid cross-infection, although this was long before any understanding of germ theory (Heathcote 2010). Throughout the Middle Ages in Western Europe, monastic hospices and infirmaries cared for pilgrims and others who were sick as part of the Christian obligation to offer charity and show mercy to the poor. A major figure in this era was Hildegard von Bingen, a remarkable twelfth-century German mystic, theologian, and medical practitioner who—along with Hippocrates—did not imagine the body as a machine or disease as a mechanical breakdown. She embraced the concept of greenness, or *viriditas*, gleaned from the practical concerns of gardening. Just as plants put forth leaves, flowers, and fruit, so the human body has the power to grow, give birth, and heal (Sweet 2012).

Monastic settings were the first instances where a garden, usually enclosed by an arcaded cloister, was specifically incorporated as part of a healing environment (fig. 2.1). Bernard of Clairvaux (1090–1153) wrote of the intentions of this space at the hospice at Clairvaux, France: "Within this enclosure many and various trees . . . make a veritable grove which lying next to the cells of those who are ill, lightens with no little solace the infirmities of the brethren, while it offers to those who are strolling about, a spacious walk. . . . The sick man sits upon the green lawn. . . . He is secure, hidden, shaded from the heat of the day . . . for the comfort of his pain, all kinds of grasses are fragrant in his nostrils. The lovely green of herb and tree nourishes his eyes. . . . The choir of painted birds caresses his ears. . . ." (Gerlach-Spriggs, Kaufman, and Warner 1998, 9). This passage indicates the remarkable intuitive insights of early Christian leaders regarding the significance of sensory awakening in nature as a component of healing, an understanding that was for a long time lost, and only now, almost a thousand years later, is being rediscovered.

As monasticism declined in the fourteenth and fifteenth centuries, care of the sick fell to civic and ecclesiastical authorities. Within the Roman Catholic tradition, one of the primary design requirements of a hospital was the provision of long wards, where the priest celebrating Mass could be seen from every bed. The influential Ospedale Maggiore of Milan (1458), for example, was built in a cruciform plan with windows so high that no one could see the formal gardens outside (Thompson and Golden 1975, 31).

Some hospitals continued the courtyard-garden tradition exemplified in the monastic cloister gardens. The English hospital and prison reformer John Howard (1726–90) reported hospitals in Marseilles, Pisa, Constantinople, Trieste, Vienna, and Florence that had gardens where patients could see through windows and doorways, and where convalescing patients could stroll (Warner 1995, 18) (fig. 2.2).

In England, by the seventeenth century, wealthy merchants and philanthropic nobility were willing their grand homes and grounds to act as hospitals. Soon architects were building hospitals in the style of grand houses, such as Christopher Wren's Royal Chelsea Hospital in London with its spacious lawns and courtyards (Darton 1996, 91). But for most, the hospital was still a refuge of last resort. Birth, sickness, convalescence, and death were mostly experienced at home (ibid., 70).

Among the first set of recommendations for hospital garden design were those written by the German horticultural theorist Christian Cay Lorenz at the end of the eighteenth

2.1 Medieval hospital garden (now part of a hotel), Santiago de Compostela, Spain.
Photo by Clare Cooper Marcus

2.2 Eighteenth-century hospital courtyard (now part of the Danish Museum of Design), Copenhagen, Denmark.
Photo by Clare Cooper Marcus

century: "The garden should be directly connected to the hospital. . . . A view from the window into blooming and happy scenes will invigorate the patient . . . [and] encourages patients to take a walk. . . . The plantings should wind along dry paths, which offer benches. . . . The spaces between could have beautiful lawns and colorful flower beds. . . . Noisy brooks could run through flowery fields. . . . A hospital garden should have everything to enjoy nature and to promote a healthy life" (Warner 1995). These suggestions uncannily foreshadow the findings of researchers in the late-twentieth century who offered credible empirical evidence that viewing or being in nature reduces stress (see chapter 3).

The next major shift in hospital design and the provision of outdoor space was the development of the pavilion hospital. In Western Europe, the seventeenth century saw an emphasis on the systematic collection of data on births and deaths and the careful observation of patients in hospitals. New hospital designs paid special attention to hygiene and ventilation, since it was then believed that infections were spread by noxious vapors or miasmas in the air emanating from swamps, stagnant water, and rotting waste. For example, a new hospital in Edinburgh constructed in 1729 was built in a U-shape on a hill to catch the air and sun, and two acres were set aside for a garden (Gerlach-Spriggs, Kaufman, and Warner 1998, 15).

Pavilion-style hospitals comprised two- and three-story buildings linked by a continuous colonnade, and narrow wards with large windows that enhanced ventilation. Between the wards were courtyards and gardens, which began to be reconsidered as important components of the healing environment. Several influential hospitals designed in this style included St. Thomas' Hospital in London, the rebuilt Hôtel Dieu in Paris, and several naval and military hospitals built at the height of Britain's imperial power.

Florence Nightingale, British nurse and public health reformer, enthusiastically endorsed these new hygienic hospital plans, which became the predominant form in the nineteenth and early-twentieth centuries. Having cared for the wounded during the Crimean War (1854–56), Nightingale observed unexpected differences in mortality experienced by soldiers treated in tents and temporary buildings and those treated in conventional hospitals. She proposed that high mortality rates in hospitals could be solved through a combination of design, sanitation, and quality care. At the Scutari military hospital near Constantinople, she succeeded in reducing the death rate from cholera and dysentery from 42 percent to 2 percent through hygiene and careful nursing practice (Darton 1996, 93).

In one of her influential publications she wrote: "Second only to fresh air . . . I should be inclined to rank light in importance for the sick. Direct sunlight, not only daylight, is necessary for speedy recovery, . . . being able to see out of the window instead of looking at a dead wall; the bright colors of flowers, . . . being able to read in bed by the light of the window. . . . It is generally said the effect is upon the mind. Perhaps so, but it is not less so upon the body on that account" (Warner 1995, 24) (fig. 2.3). Her insights marked a significant important return to an understanding that mind and body are intertwined and must be treated as one. With the study of anatomy in the Renaissance, when the dissection of cadavers revealed "no spirit inside the body," that understanding had been discredited.

The rise of Romanticism prompted a reconsideration of the role of nature in bodily and spiritual restoration. Writers such as Rousseau and Goethe extolled the powers of nature

2.3 A typical narrow, well-lit ward of a nineteenth-century pavilion-style hospital.
Photo by Clare Cooper Marcus

to foster contemplation and an emotional connection with spirit. The landed gentry created landscapes that mimicked nature. Cities built parks for the physical and mental health of their residents. It was during this period that there was a dramatic reemergence of nature as part of the restorative environment, particularly in the treatment of the mentally ill.

Rethinking the treatment of the mentally ill began at the hospital at Zaragosa, Spain, founded in 1409. Instead of patients being confined and punished, as was the custom at the time, they followed a simple daily routine of communal meals, household chores, and work in vegetable gardens, vineyards, orchards, and on a farm (Warner 1995, 17). This method of socializing patients became known in the nineteenth century as the "moral treatment," and was enthusiastically endorsed by the reformers Dr. Phillippe Pinel in France and William Tuke in England.

In 1792 William Tuke and the Society of Friends established The Retreat on the outskirts of the English city of York. Here, in a radical new approach to treatment, the mentally ill were treated with gentleness and kindness instead of being chained down and beaten like prisoners. Access to landscaped grounds became part of the treatment; it was believed that the mentally ill could not cope with city environments and could only recover in peaceful natural surroundings. The grounds also protected patients from being perused by the curious and served as a space for gardening and farming.

The philosophy behind these new kinds of hospitals spread to North America. The first such hospital in the United States was the Friends Asylum in Philadelphia founded in 1813. By the 1820s, asylums with natural landscaped grounds had opened in Boston and New York. The American landscape architect Andrew Jackson Downing wrote in 1848: "Many a fine intellect, overtasked and wrecked in the too ardent pursuit of power and wealth, is fondly courted back to reason and more quiet joys by the dusky, cool walks on the asylum" (Schuyler 1999, 79).

By the 1850s, it was accepted professional orthodoxy that a naturalistic landscape had a direct role in the treatment of the mentally ill and that the mind and body must be treated together. Views onto greenery were believed to "soothe shattered nerves," while exercise and gardening were employed to restore bodily health.

The principal proponent of this restorative landscape approach in the United States was Dr. Thomas Kirkbride, who in 1851 was invited by his peers to compose a set of "propositions on the structure and arrangement of asylums" (what we would now term design guidelines). In these he proposed that asylums should be located in the countryside not less than two miles from a large city; that they have at least one hundred acres of land, or half an acre per patient; of this, at least fifty acres should be dedicated to gardens and pleasure grounds; and that wards for "the most excited class" of patients should have large windows and pleasant views. The "Kirkbride Plan" was unanimously endorsed by his peers, and by 1900, asylums built on these propositions had been created in twenty-eight states.

But paralleling this development, immigration and urban poverty in US cities mushroomed. Asylum wards soon became overcrowded, the humane treatment of patients declined, and asylums became the last resort for hopeless cases. While some of the early influential models are still in operation—for example, the Retreat at York, England, and the Friends Hospital, Philadelphia—and their beautiful landscaped grounds remain, twentieth-century labor unions opposed the policy of engaging patients in farm and garden work. Apart from occasional horticultural therapy programs, the grounds are now primarily used for passive enjoyment.

By the 1850s, the centuries-old belief that disease was spread by noxious-smelling miasmas began to be questioned. A turning point was Dr. John Snow's investigation of a cholera epidemic in London, where he traced deaths from the disease to drinking polluted water from the Broad Street pump (Johnson 2006). Although this was the beginning of an understanding of germ theory, it was not until Scottish surgeon Joseph Lister's discovery of sepsis and French chemist Louis Pasteur's discovery of bacteria in the 1860s that it was fully accepted. This radically changed the rules of hospital design (Heathcote 2010). Since the spread of germs could

now be contained by antiseptics and basic hygiene, physical separation as in the pavilion hospital was no longer necessary, though many have remained in operation up to the present time (fig. 2.4).

Land-consuming low-rise pavilion hospitals began to be replaced by highly functional compact "monoblock" and high-rise hospitals, where design was concerned with efficiency and infection control; illness was treated with the help of antibiotics, pain killers, anesthesia, and improved surgical techniques; emotions were now studied in psychology, the physical body in anatomy and medicine, thus severing any lingering belief in the mind-body connection; outdoor space was relegated to parking lots and delivery ramps; gardens disappeared, and glimpses of nature were restricted to token areas of landscaping at the main entrance. Traditional styles were thrown out in favor of the International Style, and many new urban hospitals came to resemble office blocks and corporate headquarters. Even the sanitarium, where tuberculosis had been treated with ample exposure to sunlight, fresh air, and spacious grounds, now fell into disuse as drugs were found to treat the disease. Two kinds of healthcare facility did not succumb to this loss of a connection with nature: the hospice and the nursing home. For residents and patients in these facilities, the emphasis was, and is, on care rather than cure. The buildings are often designed at a domestic scale, echoing images of home—one element of which is the garden.

Alongside the proliferation of large medical centers, several professions arose that heralded a resurgence of interest in the garden. Occupational and physical therapy (OT and PT) came into prominence in the treatment of veterans returning from World War I. By the end of the twentieth century, rehabilitation hospitals (and the rehab wards of acute-care hospitals) often included a garden or outdoor area where patients could work with physical therapists in a more normalized setting than the hospital interior.

After World War II, horticultural therapy came into prominence as a subset of occupational therapy, using gardening as a means of restoring both physical and mental health. Degree programs in this profession were established, and indoor and outdoor gardening programs were instituted in veterans hospitals, psychiatric facilities, chronic-care facilities, and rehabilitation hospitals. Trained professionals work with the clinical staff to facilitate the recovery of patients who have experienced posttraumatic stress disorder, traumas, strokes, brain injuries, and other forms of mobility impairment (see chapters 14 and 16). These professionals work as well in prisons and geriatric facilities.

2.4 Nineteenth-century pavilion-style hospital, Edinburgh Royal Infirmary (now converted to apartments), Edinburgh, Scotland.
Photo by Clare Cooper Marcus

By the latter decades of the twentieth century, a number of changes in society signaled the emergence of what has become known as patient-centered care. The general public began to take an interest in health and wellness, recognizing the importance of diet and exercise rather than focusing on illness and disease. There was a growing interest in alternative or complementary medicine. Tools became available to research the mind-body connection. Healthcare designers and administrators began to recognize the physical environment of the hospital as an important component in a competitive market place and strived to create more patient-friendly settings.

One of the signature events in the development of patient-centered care was the emergence of the Planetree model in the early 1980s. In the mid-1970s, San Francisco resident

Angelica Thieriot was hospitalized with a life-threatening condition. Although the best of Western medicine was available, little attention was paid to her emotional, social, and spiritual needs (Frampton, Gilpin, and Charmel 2003, xxvii). Motivated by this negative experience, Thieriot founded the nonprofit organization Planetree in 1978, its name taken from the plane tree under which Hippocrates taught his students.

The entire hospital experience was evaluated from the perspective of the patient. A consumer health resource center was opened in San Francisco in 1981. In 1985 a patient-oriented thirteen-bed model hospital unit at Pacific Presbyterian Medical Center in San Francisco was designed by University of California professor Roslyn Lindheim (ibid., xxix). The emphasis was on organizational and physical changes meant to create more healing environments. Organizational changes included unrestricted visiting hours, permitting children and pets to visit, and encouraging family members to stay overnight and to cook food for the patient. Physical changes included a homelike decor; naturalizing the interior environment with plants, fish tanks, and so on; connecting the interior environment to the outdoors by providing views to attractive outdoor spaces; and stressing the importance of healing gardens for patients, family members, and staff (ibid., 237). For example, the waiting area for ambulatory surgery and endoscopy at Lakeland Hospital in Niles, Michigan was "designed to focus the attention of patients and families toward the calming and peaceful view provided by the natural setting of the St. Joseph River . . . as they mentally prepare for their procedure" (ibid., 171). For the first time since the clearly articulated value of nature in the treatment of the mentally ill in the nineteenth century, the Planetree model brought nature and gardens back into focus as important elements of a healing environment and a healthy workplace.

In the 1990s, the Eden Alternative was another innovation emphasizing nature as a component of healing. Shocked by the institutional environment of a nursing home they had been hired to administer, Dr. William Thomas and his wife, Judy Myers-Thomas, instituted a philosophy of creating more homelike settings by bringing in plants and animals (dogs, cats, birds, fish) and encouraging children to visit. After these cultural and environmental changes were made, remarkable changes were noted in the residents in terms of alertness, happiness, and reduced rates of mortality. The staff and administrators of many nursing homes have now been trained in this approach, and more than three hundred facilities have been "Edenized" in the United States, Canada, Europe, and Australia.

Less well known in North America than in Western Europe is anthroposophy—the healing philosophy of Rudolf Steiner (1861–1925), who argued that all healthcare buildings should have the physical and spiritual health of their users at their core (Heathcote 2010). This is best exemplified at the Vidar Clinic, designed by Erik Asmussen in Järna, Sweden, near Stockholm, where a simple organic plan built around a green courtyard eschews the straight corridors and square windows of contemporary hospitals.

Paralleling the incorporation of Planetree elements in hospitals and the Eden Alternative philosophy in nursing homes, academic research began to provide sound scientific evidence for the importance of nature and gardens in the healing process. The initial work in this area appeared in Roger Ulrich's

2.5 The presence of a healing garden is becoming more common in American healthcare facilities.
Photo by Clare Cooper Marcus

(1984) much-cited article "View through a Window May Influence Recovery from Surgery." With access to the medical records of patients who were recovering from surgery, Ulrich found that those who had views onto trees asked for less high-dose pain medication, called the nurse less often, and went home sooner than those who looked out onto a brick wall. This study was followed by many others (reviewed in chapter 3) that have provided strong scientific evidence for something most people would intuitively expect to be true—that moving from a difficult or frightening situation into a garden or a natural landscape results in a reduction in stress. The medical world began to take note and realize that trees and gardens in healthcare were not just cosmetic niceties. They could actually affect the bottom line.

Psychologists began to experiment with nature imagery and found that having subjects *imagine* themselves in a restorative, natural environment also had a stress-reducing effect. Blue Shield of California gave surgery patients audio compact discs that helped them imagine being in a natural setting, and this along with breathing exercises and music resulted in shorter hospital stays and lower drug costs. For the price of a $17 CD, Blue Shield saved on average $2,000 per surgery patient. Kaiser Permanente, the large HMO, now gives free imagery CDs to all surgery patients.

From the mid-1990s, healing gardens began to appear in hospitals, chronic-care facilities, hospices, and senior communities (fig. 2.5). The annual conference of the American Society of Landscape Architects began to add a preconference workshop or tour on healing garden design. In 1999 the award-winning organization and website Therapeutic Landscapes Network (www.healinglandscapes.org) was founded to provide information and connect those interested in this new emerging field. In 2003 the School of the Chicago Botanic Garden inaugurated an annual postgraduate certificate program in healthcare garden design, which now draws students from all over North America as well as from overseas.

The early healing gardens tended to be in acute-care general hospitals serving a variety of patients as well as staff and visitors. Designers, who often look to precedents to guide their work, drew upon metaphors; regional attributes; and historical, cultural, and domestic precedents, as well as envelope-pushing "artistic statements." Some of these resulted in successful restorative landscapes; others did not. A promising new direction beginning in the early years of the twenty-first century saw medical diagnosis treated seriously as a design precedent. The garden began to be seen as a means of treatment, and spaces were created for specific patient populations with contributions to the design process from clinical staff, current and former patients, and family members. Such gardens include those for patients with cancer, HIV/AIDS, psychiatric problems, burns, and Alzheimer's disease and other forms of dementia, as well as gardens for distinct age groups such as children and the frail elderly.

Despite the growing interest in providing healing gardens, many designers (and their fee-paying clients) knew little about the published research or how to translate this into design programs. This gap began to be filled by the almost simultaneous publication of three important books: *The Healing Landscape: Therapeutic Outdoor Environments* by Martha Tyson (1998), *Restorative Gardens: The Healing Landscape* by Nancy Gerlach-Spriggs, Richard E. Kaufman, and Sam Bass Warner Jr. (1998), and *Healing Gardens: Therapeutic Benefits and Design Recommendations*, edited by Clare Cooper Marcus and Marni Barnes (1999). A further significant step in the communication of research on the importance of nature was the production of a set of three award-wining DVDs entitled *Access to Nature for Older Adults* (Rodiek 2009).

As the impetus to recognize nature as a component of healing has gained ground, a number of official bodies began to draft mandatory and/or voluntary guidelines for the incorporation of access to nature as an element in hospital design. The 2014 *Guidelines for Design and Construction of Health Care Facilities* will include "Access to Nature" as one of eight key elements in the physical environment component of the Environment of Care. LEED for Healthcare and the Sustainable Sites Initiative (SITES) now award credits and provide guidelines for visual and physical access to nature and natural light. In the UK, the National Health Service is working to incorporate access to nature into the design of its health facilities.

The growing interest in the importance of gardens in the medical world has been paralleled by many other segments of society's reawakening to the beneficial aspects of connecting with nature. Writers within the deep ecology and eco-feminist movements have passionately argued the need for our working in partnership with nature for our very survival (Roszak, Gomes, and Kanner 1995; Roszak 1992; Macy and Johnstone 2012; Macy 1991; McKibben 1986, 2010). In his book *The Spell of the Sensuous*, eco-philosopher David Abram (1996) maintains that nature speaks to us through all our senses in a different way from how we communicate with each other. Publication of Richard Louv's (2008) book—*Last Child in the Woods: Saving Our Children from Nature Deficit Disorder*—and the inauguration of the website www.childandnature.org have resulted in a large wave of interest from parents, teachers, and others as to how they can bring nature back into children's lives. Louv's (2012) follow-up book *The Nature Principle* argued for the importance of nature in the lives of everyone. In the field of psychotherapy, in books such as Linda Buzzell and Craig Chalquist's (2009) *Ecotherapy: Healing with Nature in Mind* and Craig Chalquist's (2007) *Terrapsychology: Reengaging the Soul of Place*, a small but vocal group of eco-psychologists have called for the recognition that our separation from nature has led to significant mental health consequences and that great benefits can come from wilderness trips, conducting therapy in nature, and encouraging clients to explore the sense of place where they live. While gardening has long been the number one American pastime in terms of dollars spent, a burgeoning interest in home-grown food has resulted in long waiting lists for plots in urban community gardens.

Thus, in the millennia since the healing center at Epidaurus in ancient Greece, we have come full circle—back to an understanding of the mind-body connection and the significance of nature in the healing process. What is needed now are the tools to assist the sponsors and designers of contemporary healing gardens so that these spaces meet their full potential of being truly restorative landscapes.

References

Abram, D. 1996. *The Spell of the Sensuous: Perception and Language in a More-Than-Human World*. New York: Vintage Books.

Buzzell, L., and C. Chalquist. 2009. *Ecotherapy: Healing with Nature in Mind*. San Francisco: Sierra Club Books.

Chalquist, C. 2007. *Terrapsychology: Reengaging the Soul of Place*. New Orleans, LA: Spring Journal Books.

Cooper Marcus, C., and M. Barnes, eds. 1999. *Healing Gardens: Therapeutic Benefits and Design Recommendations*. New York: John Wiley and Sons.

Darton, E. 1996. "The Evolution of the Hospital." *Metropolis*, October: 67–97.

Frampton, S., L. Gilpin, and P. A. Charmel. 2003. *Putting Patients First: Designing and Practicing Patient-Centered Care*. San Francisco: Jossey-Bass.

Gerlach-Spriggs, N., R. E. Kaufman, and S. B. Warner, Jr. 1998. *Restorative Gardens: The Healing Landscape*. New Haven: Yale University Press.

Gesler, W. M. 2003. *Healing Places*. Lanham, MD: Rothman and Littlefield.

Heathcote, E. 2010. "Architecture and Health." Pp. 52–93 in *The Architecture of Hope: Maggie's Cancer Caring Centres*, edited by C. Jencks and E. Heathcote. London: Frances Lincoln Ltd.

Johnson, S. 2006. *The Ghost Map: The Story of London's Most Terrifying Epidemic and How It Changed Science, Cities, and the Modern World*. New York: Riverhead Books.

Louv, R. 2008. *Last Child in the Woods: Saving Our Children from Nature-Deficit Disorder*. New York: Algonquin Books of Chapel Hill.

———. 2012. *The Nature Principle: Reconnecting with Life in a Virtual Age*. New York: Algonquin Books of Chapel Hill.

Macy, J. 1991. *World as Lover, World as Self: Courage for Global Justice and Ecological Renewal*. Berkeley, CA: Parallax Press.

Macy, J., and C. Johnstone. 2012. *Active Hope: How to Face the Mess We're in without Going Crazy*. Novato, CA: New World Library.

McKibben, B. 1986. *The End of Nature*. New York: Random House.

———. 2010. *Eaarth: Making a Life on a Tough New Planet*. New York: Times Books.

Rodiek, S. 2009. *Access to Nature for Older Adults*. Three-part DVD series. College Station, TX: Center for Health Systems & Design, Texas A&M University.

Roszak, T. 1992. *The Voice of the Earth: An Exploration of Ecopsychology*. Grand Rapids, MI: Phanes Press, Inc.

Roszak, T., M. E. Gomes, and A. D. Kanner. 1995. *Ecopsychology: Restoring the Earth, Healing the Mind*. New York: Sierra Club Books.

Schuyler, D. 1999. *Apostle of Taste: Andrew Jackson Downing, 1815–1852*. Baltimore, MD: John Hopkins University Press.

Sweet, V. 2012. *God's Hotel: A Doctor, a Hospital, and a Pilgrimage to the Heart of Medicine*. New York: Riverhead Books.

Thompson, J. D., and G. Golden. 1975. *The Hospital: A Social and Architectural History*. New Haven: Yale University Press.

Tyson, M. 1998. *The Healing Landscape: Therapeutic Outdoor Environments*. New York: McGraw Hill.

Ulrich, R. S. 1984. "View through a Window May Influence Recovery from Surgery." *Science* 224: 420–21.

Warner, S. B., Jr. 1995. "Restorative Gardens: Recovering Some Human Wisdom for Modern Design" (unpublished manuscript).

CHAPTER 3

Theory, Research, and Design Implications

The View through a Window

In the late 1970s, environmental psychologist Roger Ulrich began to research the emotional and physiological effects of environmental aesthetics on a population that experiences a great deal of emotional duress: hospital patients. He was one of the first researchers to study and publish quantitative evidence on the effects of access to nature in the healthcare setting. His "View through a Window May Influence Recovery from Surgery," published in *Science* in 1984, became the seminal argument for access to nature in healthcare facilities. Ulrich compared the recovery records of gall bladder surgery patients who had a bedside window view of trees with those of patients who had a view of a brick wall. The outcomes data revealed that patients with the nature view had shorter hospital stays (7.96 days, compared with 8.70 days), suffered fewer postsurgical complications, needed fewer doses of potent narcotic pain medication, and received more positive written comments in their medical records from staff (e.g., "patient is in good spirits"). Patients in the wall view group, on the other hand, had more negative evaluative comments ("patient is upset," "needs much encouragement"). Medical and social science researchers have replicated Ulrich's study many times, and it has continued to hold up (Marberry 2010) (fig. 3.1).

Ulrich's study, cited in thousands of publications—from books to scholarly journals to newspaper and magazine articles—was, and continues to be, significant for two reasons. First, it demonstrated to the medical community—using the same empirical, quantitative methods that they used and respected—that the physical environment, and specifically views of nature, had a measurable positive effect on patient health. Second, it established a business case for providing access to nature. All of the improved health outcomes for patients—duration of hospital stay, amount of pain medication, degree of strain on nursing staff, and level of patient satisfaction—translated directly to potential cost savings. (For further discussion, see chapter 19.)

This chapter focuses on theory and research that underpin the provision and evidence-informed design of gardens and other natural settings in healthcare facilities. A significant body of research, using a broad array methodologies and populations, and looking at a variety of health outcomes, confirms and sheds new light on what many people have known intuitively: that connection with nature is beneficial—even vital—for human health and well-being. The research discussed in this chapter is only a small percentage of the literature on the positive benefits of contact with nature. The chapter is not intended as a literature review, but rather as an introduction and overview of the theory and research on the physical design of nature settings in healthcare facilities.

The Importance of Research

Why do we need research to tell us what we think we already we know?

Research informs design

If the goal of good healthcare design is to promote optimal health and well-being for patients, visitors, and staff, then it must be based on the best information available. Research aids in good decision making about what to do and, just as importantly, what *not* to do. While research can be a useful tool for any design work, it is essential in environments where people are emotionally and physically vulnerable. The most frequently cited part of the Hippocratic Oath reads, "I will prescribe regimens for the good of my patients according to my ability and my judgment and *never do harm* to anyone" (Edelstein 1943). Ideally, everyone working in the healthcare realm—staff, administrators, designers, etc.—would abide by this oath in their practice. Intuition and personal preferences are not enough. Ulrich (1999, 65) states, "Some designers may unwittingly create gardens containing negative distractions if they focus exclusively on design qualities that please their personal aesthetic tastes. . . . Further, the types and styles of environmental design

3.1 Even a simple view of grass and trees can promote health and healing.
Photo from www.henrydomke.com

and art that many designers and artists personally prefer can be those that elicit distinctly negative reactions from the public."

Winston and Cupchik (1992) found that artists and experienced art viewers preferred work that was more intellectually challenging or emotionally provocative than that preferred by the general public. In a study of the preferences of three hundred randomly selected hospital inpatients, Carpman and Grant (1993) found a consistent preference for nature images and a dislike of abstract art. Nanda, Eisen, and Baladandayuthapani (2008) found that people's art preferences varied significantly between hospital patients and people with art or design backgrounds. While patients preferred images with nature and realistic content, the designers tended to prefer abstract or stylized content.

These and many other studies support the appropriateness of nature and representative nature content (art and design) in hospitals, and they also underscore the need to focus on the specific needs of the end user.

> Regardless of whether a garden might garner praise in professional design journals as "good" design, the environment will qualify as bad or failed design in healthcare terms if it is found to produce negative reactions. These points imply that the use of the term 'healing' in the context of healthcare gardens ethically obligates the garden designer to subordinate or align his or her personal tastes to the paramount objective of creating a user-centered, supportive environment. (Ulrich 1999, 30)

Research makes the case for good design

Great strides have been made in the acceptance of the built environment's powerful effect on people's health, but throughout most of the twentieth century, gardens were thought to be—by most architects as well as healthcare providers—unnecessary amenities. In a budget-conscious era when every dollar counts, and in healthcare facilities where funding and space are at a premium, the benefits of contact with nature through gardens and other landscapes has to be proven. Any design decisions made for an existing or a new facility will need to be well supported. Research—especially if it clearly demonstrates potential improvements in health for patients and staff and/or a healthy bottom line for the facility—can be an effective tool in convincing even the most skeptical decision makers.

Research informs policy

Laws and regulations governing facility design and construction rarely change without a good reason—in other words, without strong evidence. For example, the American Society for Healthcare Engineering (ASHE) of the American Hospital Association publishes the *Guidelines for Design and Construction of Health Care Facilities*, a document used by Authorities Having Jurisdiction (AHJs) as a basis to review and approve the designs for any proposed renovations to existing or new healthcare facility construction. Any changes to the document, published every four years, must be proposed and then accepted by the Federal Guidelines Regulations Commission. Changes with the strongest evidence are the most likely to be adopted (FGI 2013).

Evidence-Based Design

Using the best possible research to inform design is referred to as evidence-based design (EBD). The need for this approach in healthcare became clear when a report in 2000 from the Institute of Medicine revealed that medical errors were involved in 98,000 hospital deaths a year. In the same year, the Centers for Disease Control reported that the annual cost of hospital-acquired infections for the United States was estimated to be $5 billion (Ulrich et al. 2008). In a review of the literature on evidence-based healthcare design, Ulrich et al. (ibid., 62) stated, "hospital-acquired infections and medical errors are among the leading causes of death in the United States, each killing more people than automobile accidents, breast cancer, or acquired immune deficiency syndrome (AIDS)." Industry professionals realized that to the extent that the physical environment may contribute to—or ameliorate, or even prevent—such problems, design decisions had to be based on sound empirical evidence.

EBD evolved from other disciplines that use research to guide decisions, most notably evidence-based medicine, which integrates clinical expertise with the best available evidence from systematic research. Healthcare architect and researcher/scholar Kirk Hamilton sought to formalize the concept of EBD. His definition states, "Evidence-based design is a process for the conscientious, explicit, and judicious use of current best evidence from research and practice in making critical decisions, together with an informed client, about the design of each individual and unique project" (Stichler and Hamilton 2008, 3). Hamilton's definition is important because it stresses that research, or evidence, is not just to be found in published work. Evidence-based healthcare design is still a relatively new field with many gaps in the literature. For any design, "on-the-ground" site-specific and user-specific research is essential. There is no one-size-fits-all.

The Center for Health Design (2008, 4) has simplified Hamilton's definition to "the process for basing decisions about the built environment on credible research to achieve the best possible outcomes." "Outcomes" are defined as measures of a person's condition (health, well-being, satisfaction) or indicators of healthcare quality. Measures include observable clinical signs or medical measures (e.g., blood pressure, heart rate, length of stay), subjective measures (reported pain and mood levels, satisfaction with environment or service,

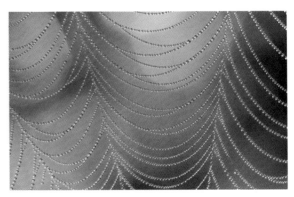

3.2 Examining the minutiae of the natural world may reduce stress by distracting a person from worrisome thoughts.
Photo from www.henrydomke.com

etc.), and economic measures (cost of patient care, recruitment or hiring costs of staff, etc.) (Ulrich 1999) (fig. 3.2).

A current limitation of EBD practice is its emphasis on quantitative methods, particularly randomized control trials (RCTs). This type of research is still considered the gold standard in the medical field, and thus healthcare designers strive to fit that paradigm. Yet the evidence-based medicine framework of strictly controlled laboratory experiments with as few variables as possible is not always the best fit (and is often impossible) in settings that involve human beings and natural environments. There are signs that a broader approach of "mixed methods" research, with evidence gathered from many different sources and using many different methodologies (including qualitative and quantitative), is beginning to be embraced as more realistic and productive. This approach can help to support, refute, or call other evidence into question, thereby creating a picture that has greater dimension and, thus, potential for successful design.

In Australia, Singapore, the United Kingdom, and several provinces of Canada, an architect cannot apply to design a hospital unless he or she is qualified in EBD. In the United States this is true for the design of military hospitals, and is increasingly encouraged in all healthcare design with the establishment of the Evidence-based Design Accreditation and Certification (EDAC) through the Center for Health Design (Ulrich 2011).

Research on Benefits of Nature Exposure

In a literature review of more than four hundred peer-reviewed articles on evidence-based healthcare design, Ulrich et al. (2008, 108) reported relationships between design strategies or environmental interventions and healthcare outcomes. In two categories—reduced pain and reduced patient stress—"especially strong evidence" indicated a link between access to nature and health outcomes. Research reviewed also indicated a link between access to nature and reduced depression, reduced length of stay, increased patient satisfaction, decreased staff stress, and increased satisfaction.

Virtual nature, real nature

Identifying empirical evidence from any sort of physical environmental factors, such as wall color, spatial configuration, or quantity of beds to a room, is challenging because of the number of variables. With nature, the variables are myriad and difficult to control as they shift, sometimes from moment to moment. To date, most research on preferences and outcomes has been conducted using simulations of nature, such as pictures or videos, to reduce the number of variables. Some studies indicate that research using simulated nature produces results that can be considered reliable because they are similar enough to research involving actual nature (Hull and Stewart 1992; Nanda, Eisen, and Baladandayuthapani 2008; Taylor, Zube, and Sell 1987). While this research is valuable for showing that nature is beneficial (and sometimes for showing *how* it is beneficial), the question then arises: If simulated views of nature are effective in promoting health, then why do we even need real nature?

Art on the walls is certainly less expensive to install and maintain than a living garden. However, some research indicates a progressive improvement in outcomes, beginning with still pictures of nature (as opposed to pictures of urban scenes, abstract views, or no pictures), then moving images, then views of real nature, and, finally, passively or actively engaging with real nature. A study by Friedman, Freier, and Kahn (2004) found that a real-time streaming image of nature on a plasma screen television improved psychological well-being, cognitive functioning, social connectedness, and connections with nature, implying that a moving image may be more beneficial than a still image. A study by Kahn et al. (2008) compared the effects on recovery of three views from an office space—an outdoor scene through a window, the same scene on a plasma television screen, and a blank wall. After experiencing mild stress, the subjects' heart rate recovery was more rapid when they looked out of a window rather than at the plasma screen or a blank wall.

Studies that look at other sensory exposure, such as scent, or combined sensory experiences, suggest that while pictures of nature are an important component of the environment of care, they cannot be a substitute for real nature views

3.3 Fragrant plants in a healthcare garden elicit the attention of two senior residents. Scent is the strongest memory trigger.
Courtesy of Studio Sprout; photo by Michiko Kurisu

and therapeutic gardens (fig. 3.3). The neuroscientist Esther Sternberg suggests that part of nature's benefit is derived from the multitude of simultaneous positive sensory experiences (Sachs 2009; Sternberg 2010). A study by Kline (2009) on the ability of nature-related stimuli to promote relief from acute pain found that the combination of nature views and sounds was more effective in reducing pain than either type of stimulus used alone. A study by Diette et al. (2003) found that the patients undergoing a painful bronchoscopy who were shown views of simulated nature and heard sounds of a bubbling brook before and during the procedure had a 50 percent increase in self-reported "very good" or "excellent" pain control as compared to the control patients. Perhaps the reason that contact with nature is so difficult to measure is precisely the reason why, or even how, it is beneficial (fig. 3.4).

Scent, "forest bathing," and "green exercise"

The preference for and benefits from nature extend beyond the visual realm. Hyun-Ju, Fujii, and Cho (2010) studied cerebral and autonomic nervous system activity and self-reported mental function in male subjects as they inhaled the natural scent of pine needles. Cerebral activity was activated in the feeling, judgment, and motor areas of the frontal lobe, as well as in the memory area in the temporal lobe. Self-reports also indicated increased vigor and decreased confusion. Fujita, Miyoshi, and Watanabe (2010) found that "green odor" (a 50:50 mixture of trans-2-hexenal and cis-3-hexenol) reduced maternal stress as well as prenatal stress in these mothers' offspring. Watanabe et al. (2011) found that green odor not only had a therapeutic but also a potentially preventive effect on depressive-like states in rats. Oka et al. (2008)

3.4 A naturalistic stream at McKee Medical Center, a cancer treatment center in Loveland, Colorado, provides a multisensory experience for garden visitors. Designer: BHA Design.
Courtesy of BHA Design; photo by Jerod Huwa

found that green odor attenuated stress responses of systolic and diastolic blood pressure in humans.

Shinrin-yoku, which translates roughly as "forest bathing," was originally introduced by the Forest Agency of Japan to promote walking and health. It has since become a popular practice. A study by Li et al. (2007) found that "green exercise"—physical movement in a natural setting—increased the activity of natural killer (NK) cells, a part of the immune system that fights cancer. This, in turn, helps to boost stress resistance. Li attributes some of the stress reduction to the presence of phytoncides (wood essential oils), antimicrobial volatile organic compounds emitted from trees to protect them from rotting and insects. Li et al. (2008) compared the effects of walking in a forest with walking in a city. A high concentration of phytoncides was detected in forest air; in contrast, almost none were present in the city air. The study found that only the forest walking increased NK activity and number and decreased the concentration of adrenaline

(a stress indicator) in urine. The effects of the forest walks were found to last at least seven days. A larger-scale study by Park et al. (2010) of 260 people at twenty-four sites across Japan found that the average concentration of salivary cortisol, an indicator of stress, was 13.4 percent lower in people who walked in and viewed a forest area than in people performing a similar activity in urban settings.

Research on green exercise is not limited to Japan. In a UK study of more than 1,850 participants, researchers found that people who took part in walks in a country park with woodlands, grasslands, and lakes had significantly better mood and self-esteem outcomes than those who walked for the same amount of time in an indoor shopping mall. For example, 92 percent of the park walkers reported a decrease in depression, whereas 22 percent of mall walkers actually reported an increase in depression (Mind 2007). A study in the United States by Berman, Jonides, and Kaplan (2008) focused on outcomes of memory performance and attention

3.5 Whitman Walker AIDS Clinic, Arlington, Virginia. The healing garden behind the clinic, open to the public, by encourages outdoor exercise.

Photo by Dave Harp, courtesy of TKF Foundation

exposure had 84 percent fewer hip fractures than those not regularly exposed to sunlight. Sunlight exposure in children can help to prevent rickets and, possibly, myopia (Bowcott 2010; McBrien, Morgan, and Mutti 2008). Active interaction with nature—gardening or yard work, for example—has additional benefits. A study by Turner et al. (2002) found that women fifty years of age and older who gardened or did yard work at least once a week had higher bone density readings than those who performed other types of exercise, including jogging, swimming, and aerobics. (See chapter 16 for further discussion of research related to active nature engagement.) Some research on rats has found that *Mycobacterium vaccae*, a bacterium commonly found in soil, triggers the release of serotonin, a hormone that decreases anxiety and depression, elevates mood, and improves cognitive function (Jenks and Matthews 2010; Lowry et al. 2007). While this study has yet to be conducted with humans, the findings have intriguing implications for how active engagement with soil and other natural materials could play a more direct physiological role in people's health.

Nature and the city

There is considerable evidence of preference for, and improved health outcomes in, environments that are nature-dominated rather than heavily urban. An early study by Ulrich (1979) found that students who were experiencing stress due to a final exam had greater restoration (reduction in negative feelings such as fear and anger/aggression and improvement in positive feelings) when they viewed slides of plant-dominated nature settings versus urban scenes without nature. Honeyman (1992) replicated the study with the addition of urban scenes with vegetation, finding that urban scenes with vegetation had a greater restorative effect than those without. Moore (1981–82) found that prison inmates with cells looking out onto the interior courtyard (half of the study group) had a 24 percent higher frequency of sick call visits than those with a window view of rolling farmland and trees. A later study by West (1985) found similar results. In a study involving patients and visitors at a Michigan hospital, Reizenstein and Grant (1981) found that people consistently preferred scenes with a higher number of trees. As the number of trees increased, the ratings increased. "Trees were seen as a source of visual interest as well as a source of beauty, shade, and color. The absence of plantings was characterized as "bare" and "boring" by some respondents" (Carpman and Grant 1993, 202). Cooper Marcus and Barnes (1995) found that of 143 patients, visitors,

span. Researchers compared people who walked for one hour in nature—including in the winter—versus in a city environment, finding a 20 percent improvement in both memory and attention span. Berman noted, "People don't have to enjoy the walk to get the benefits. We found the same benefits when it was 80 degrees and sunny over the summer as when the temperatures dropped to 25 degrees in January. The only difference was that the participants enjoyed the walks more in the spring and summer than in the dead of winter" (Louv 2011, 29) (fig. 3.5).

Being outdoors in sunlight is important for the body's production of vitamin D, which is critical for bone health (fig. 3.6). A study by Sato et al. (2003) found that elderly stroke patients who received as little as fifteen minutes per day of sunlight

3.6 Residents in a high-rise retirement community enjoy the plants in the Clare Tower rooftop garden, Chicago, Illinois. Designer: Hoerr Schaudt Landscape Architects.
Photo by Scott Shigley

and staff interviewed at four hospitals with gardens in Northern California, two-thirds of the respondents mentioned trees, flowers, and plants as characteristics of the garden that were helpful to them. More than half mentioned other positive sensory experiences such as pleasant sounds, smells, the feel of the sun, and fresh air. Nakamura and Fujii (1992) recorded brain wave activity with an electroencephalogram (EEG) while persons were seated in a real outdoor setting and viewed a hedge of greenery, a concrete fence with dimensions similar to the hedge, or a mixed condition with part greenery and part concrete. According to the EEG data, the greenery elicited relaxation, while the concrete elicited stress responses (fig. 3.7).

As reported above, nature sounds have been found to be restorative. In turn, urban sounds tend to have a negative

3.7a A "before" picture of the courtyard at the Austin Health's Royal Talbot Rehabilitation Centre in Melbourne, Australia.
Photo by Steven Wells

impact. This may be heightened in places where people expect to "be in nature" but are interrupted by reminders of the city. Cooper Marcus and Barnes (1995) found that users of hospital gardens reacted negatively to incongruent urban noises such as air conditioners, street traffic, and overhead traffic (airplanes, helicopters). Mace, Bell, and Loomis (1999) studied subjects who were exposed to congruent nature sounds (birds, water, breezes) and the incongruent urban sound of helicopter noise while they viewed nature scenes. Even low-level helicopter noise significantly reduced the restorative effects of viewing nature scenes. These findings provide strong implications for the siting and design of gardens in healthcare facilities. Nature sounds should be maximized and urban sounds, including ambulances, air conditioners, and street traffic, should be minimized through the siting of the facility or garden, or with design interventions such as water that masks unpleasant noises.

The presence of live plants in schools, hospitals, and offices has been shown to increase health, concentration, productivity, and satisfaction (Dravigne et al. 2008; Randall et al. 1992; Leather et al. 1998). Wells (2000), among others, found a significant correlation between children's access to greenery and green space and increased levels of cognitive functioning. A series of studies by Andrea Faber Taylor, Frances Kuo, and Bill Sullivan at the University of Illinois Landscape and

3.7b The redesigned courtyard at the Austin Health 's Royal Talbot Rehabilitation Centre in Melbourne, Australia, offers far more sensory interest for people viewing and being in the garden.
Photo by Steven Wells

Human Health Laboratory demonstrated the positive effects of trees and other nearby nature on both children and adults in urban environments. Children with attention deficit-hyperactivity disorder (ADHD) exhibited fewer symptoms after even as little as twenty minutes in natural settings. After time spent in a more urban setting, the children did not display the same level of benefit (Faber Taylor and Kuo 2009). In a study at a Chicago public housing development, Faber Taylor, Kuo, and Sullivan (2002) found that girls who lived in closer proximity to greener nature views exhibited higher levels of self-discipline than those in housing that was nearly identical but lacking nature views and access.

Proximity to nature, especially trees, was also found to have a beneficial effect on the amount of domestic violence in Chicago public housing households (Kuo and Sullivan 2001a), women's ability to cope with major life issues (Kuo 2001), and amount of inner city crime (Kuo and Sullivan, 2001b). Bell, Wilson, and Liu (2008) found in a two-year study of 3,800 children in inner city neighborhoods that the greener the neighborhood was, the lower the body mass index (BMI) was. Higher greenness was also associated with lower odds of children's and youth's increasing their BMI scores over two years. Studies such as these have attracted national attention. Public health advocates such as Dannenberg, Frumkin, and Jackson (2011) argue that access to nature is a major public health issue that must be addressed not just with individual grassroots efforts but on a larger policy level as well (fig. 3.8).

Theoretical and Philosophical Underpinnings

Why are people attracted to nature? Why do they prefer and benefit more from nature over urban settings or indoor environments devoid of plants? Answers to these questions can facilitate an understanding of the research described above

3.8 Children grow herbs and vegetables on the rooftop garden at the Gary Comer Youth Center in Chicago, Illinois. Designer: Hoerr Schaudt Landscape Architects.
Photo by Scott Shigley

and can also guide decisions about what types of settings and elements within those settings will be most beneficial.

Biophilia

The social psychologist Erich Fromm coined the term *biophilia*, which he defined as "the passionate love of life and all that is alive" (Fromm 1973, 365) and "love for humanity and nature" (Fromm 1997, 101). The word derives from the Latin *bio* (life) and *philia* (attraction). The opposite of biophilia is generally accepted to be "biophobia," literally "fear of life," and has been defined as the fear of living things such as snakes and spiders, for example (Ulrich 1993). Most people, however, attribute the term *biophilia* to the biologist Edward O. Wilson. In *The Biophilia Hypothesis*, Wilson stated, "Biophilia, if it exists, and I believe it exists, is the innately emotional affiliation of

3.9 Butterfly release in the Olson Family Garden at St. Louis Children's Hospital.
Photo by Gary Wangler

human beings to other living organisms. Innate means hereditary and hence part of ultimate human nature" (Kellert and Wilson 1993, 31) (fig. 3.9).

Prospect-refuge theory

Geographer Jay Appleton's theory of environmental aesthetics—most often referred to as "prospect-refuge theory"—is based on an adaptive-evolutionary perspective. In *The Experience of Landscape*, Appleton (1975) proposed that people's aesthetic preferences in art, and in the landscape, derive from perceptions of what is needed for survival. Despite the fact that humans are, by and large, no longer hunter-gatherers, they still respond positively to settings and elements (shelter, safety, food, water, light, air) that would have enabled their early ancestors' survival. Likewise, humans intuitively avoid environments, things, and situations (hazards) that appear to threaten survival. Thus, the ability to *see* with a clear view (prospect) from a safe vantage point *without being seen* (refuge) and *without potential danger* (hazard) is most comfortable, and thus most preferred. Research across many different countries and cultures has validated Appleton's theory. Looking out from a safe vantage point over a savannah landscape appears to be almost universally preferred, be it dotted with oaks, acacia, or other species, as in a pastoral park, or the grid of trees at the World Trade Center Memorial (Balling and Falk 1982; Heerwagen and Gregory 2008; Orians 1980; Ulrich 1993) (fig. 3.10).

It is notable that people who are ill or fatigued prefer a higher percentage of refuge. Additionally, teenagers tend to prefer more prospect (to see *and* be seen) than refuge; and women tend to prefer more refuge than men (Heerwagen and Gregory 2008). In terms of healthcare garden design, this theory points to the need for plentiful settings where a person

3.10 A savannah-type setting of open grassland with scattered trees is a universally preferred landscape.
Photo from www.henrydomke.com

can feel secure, with ample protection at his or her back and a clear view forward.

Heerwagen and Orians (1993) discuss "environmental habitability cues" and identify four key components of environments that provide what enables people to survive and thrive: resource availability, shelter, hazard cues, and wayfinding. Human response is not just response to the things themselves, but also to their symbolic meaning. Relating this to landscape preferences that can inform design, people are attracted to water elements because of an innate dependence on water for survival, on elements of shelter and refuge because they were once needed as protection from predators, and on ease of wayfinding to allow easy movement from place to place.

Stress: The "fight or flight" response

At an early evolutionary stage, humans developed what Walter Cannon described as the "fight-or-flight response" (Cannon 1932). When faced, for example, with a saber-toothed tiger, an individual had to choose whether to flee the situation or fight the attacker. The body, via the sympathetic nervous system and the endocrine system, surged with adrenalin that enabled both (fig. 3.11). In contemporary times people still face stressful, though less often life-threatening, situations (traffic jams and workplace issues, for example) that elevate stress hormones such as cortisol. Though no longer in mortal danger, the body response is the same. The experience becomes more exaggerated—and in cases of chronic illness, more prolonged—in a healthcare setting. Thus, identifying environmental factors that ameliorate stress can help improve outcomes. Ulrich (1993, 32) defines stress as "the process of responding to events and environmental

3.11 This ferruginous hawk will prompt a fight-or-flight response in many animals. Snakes, spiders, mice, and other creatures provoke a similar response in humans.
Photo from www.henrydomke.com

features that are challenging, demanding, or threatening to well-being." Stress has multiple negative short- and long-term consequences that affect the body physically and emotionally. Among other short-term outcomes, stress disturbs sleep, increases feelings of isolation and depression, elevates heart rate and blood pressure, reduces the body's ability to make antibodies, weakens the immune system, and prolongs wound healing. While stress is harmful in and of itself, it (especially long-term, chronic stress) it can also contribute to negative health outcomes such as coronary heart disease, cancer, type 2 diabetes, and depression. Additionally, stress increases behaviors—such as smoking, alcohol consumption, and poor eating and exercise habits—that contribute to many chronic diseases (Taylor 2012; Selhub and Logan 2012; Sternberg 2010; Ulrich 1999). Much of the research related to gardens in healthcare focuses on restoration from stress. Two of the most relevant theories—and related design implications—are Roger Ulrich's stress reduction theory and Rachel and Stephen Kaplan's attention restoration theory.

Stress reduction theory

Roger Ulrich's (1999) *Theory of Supportive Gardens* emphasizes positive health outcomes through stress reduction for two primary reasons. First, most people who are sick, or who are caring for the sick, experience stress. As contact with nature has been shown to reduce stress, then gardens in healthcare facilities make good sense. Second, many people—most who are not aware of the "evidence"—seek out nature-dominated settings to reduce stress (Francis and Cooper Marcus 1991, 1992). That stress is a pervasive, well-documented, and important health-related problem in hospitals implies major significance for the finding that restoration is the key benefit motivating persons to use gardens in healthcare facilities (Ulrich 1999). There is ample evidence to indicate that (1) a sense of control, (2) social support, (3) physical movement and exercise, and (4) positive natural distractions all help to reduce stress. To the extent that a restorative garden is designed to support these four factors, Ulrich argues, they will have beneficial effects on stress reduction.

Although security and a *sense* of security are not one of the four factors listed, Ulrich asserts that both are essential backdrops for all four of the other conditions.

1. Sense of control (actual and perceived) and access to privacy

Research by Evans and Cohen (1987), Glass and Singer (1972), and others has shown that people who feel a sense of control experience less stress, are better able to cope when faced with stress, and are healthier than people who experience a loss or lack of control. People who are sick are often stripped of control—of their own body; of what they wear (e.g., hospital gowns); of what they are and are not allowed to do, eat, and drink; of what others can do to them (e.g., frequent blood draws); and of their physical environment (temperature, sound). Lack of a sense of control, including lack of privacy (Proshansky, Ittelson, and Rivlin 1975), can have deleterious effects, causing greater stress and adversely affecting outcomes.

A garden can play an important role in providing a sense of control by allowing people a temporary means of mental or physical escape from a stressful environment and situation. The escape can be passive—for example, looking out a window at a nice view—or active, such as going outside for a walk. In some cases, simply the awareness of a garden (the ability to escape), even if people cannot or do not visit it regularly, can be enough to relieve stress (Ulrich and Addoms 1981) (fig. 3.12).

Design considerations for sense of control

For a garden to foster restoration by providing a sense of control, people must know that it exists; they must be able to get to and into it easily; and they must be able to use it as they choose. Thus a garden should be visible from a main entry or other gathering/ waiting areas (cafeteria, waiting rooms, etc.), have proper way-finding signage from areas where it is not visible, be open either all of the time or at regular hours, and provide various opportunities for enjoyment. Visual and auditory privacy are essential. If treatment or patient rooms look into a garden, all users (those within the building and those within the garden) must be considered. People sometimes go outside because it is the only place they can go to be alone or with a loved one or colleague. Marcus and Barnes (1995) found that people often sought out gardens for privacy or to be alone. A garden with a number of different spaces, and several different types of spaces, prevents overcrowding and allows people to choose where they want to be in any given situation. Choices within the garden of places to wander (choice of destination, easy or more challenging pathway, etc.), things to look at, and places to sit (sun or shade, private or more open, near the building or far away) all facilitate a sense of control. Staff and long-term-care residents who are included in the design process often feel a sense of empowerment that then fosters a greater sense of ownership, and even stewardship, of the garden (Francis 1989; Hester 1984; Ware 1994).

2. Social support

A significant body of research correlates social support with good health. According to Ulrich (1999, 42), "People who

3.12 These chairs are light enough to be moved around, allowing people to choose where to sit and what to look at—alone or in a group, in the sun or in shade. Don Allen Memorial Garden, Sharp Mesa Vista Hospital, San Diego, California. Designer: Schmidt Design Group.
Photo by Naomi Sachs

3.13 A cancer support group meets in a garden shelter at The Gathering Place, Beachwood, Ohio.
Photo by Chris Garcia

receive higher levels of social support are usually less stressed and have better health status than persons who are more socially isolated. . . . Low social support may be as great a risk factor in mortality as is cigarette smoking." Ulrich defines social support as the emotional, material, and/or physical aid and caring that a person receives from one or more other individuals. It can manifest in many ways, including expressing to someone that he or she is cared about; encouraging a person to express feelings or beliefs; giving someone a sense of belonging to a social group or network; and providing tangible assistance. Research findings have revealed that higher levels of social support, and lower levels of perceived loneliness and isolation, improve recovery (fig. 3.13).

Design considerations for social support
Gardens and parks outside of the healthcare setting have been documented as places that facilitate social interaction. Research on public parks has shown that design, such as location and configuration of seating, can influence whether

and how spaces are used (Cooper Marcus and Francis 1990). Gardens within healthcare facilities can provide the same benefits. A variety of spaces allows for a variety of interaction. Seats that face each other, or that can be moved to face each other, allow two or three people to talk. Bigger spaces are also important for accommodating larger groups of visitors and staff for unplanned and programmed activities and gatherings. In some cultures, a patient is visited by his or her large immediate or extended family. Some of the design considerations listed under "Sense of control" also apply to "Social support," including providing areas for privacy and locating gardens near gathering areas such as waiting rooms and cafeterias.

3. Physical movement and exercise
The physical and emotional benefits of exercise are well documented and are important in the siting and design of gardens. Ulrich's (1999, 48) theory of supportive garden design places emphasis on the ability for even mild movement and exercise to reduce stress, including depression (fig. 3.14).

Design considerations for physical exercise
A garden (indoors or out), or a view to a garden, can serve as motivation for a patient to get out of bed or walk down a corridor or venture outdoors. Even for patients not well enough to go outside, just the journey to a window overlooking a garden provides an opportunity for movement. Within a garden or other outdoor space, incentives and opportunities for exercise can be provided with walking loops of varying lengths—perhaps within a courtyard and also around the facility or campus—and of varying levels of difficulty; a destination such as a gazebo or special view; and interesting things to see and do throughout the garden. Places for children, especially well siblings, to run around and blow off steam reduce their own and their parents' stress level (see chapter 7). Places for games—a bocce court, a miniature golf course, perhaps even a ball court—provide more structured opportunities for exercise as well as social interaction. Rehabilitation gardens are designed so that physical therapists and other allied professionals, such as occupational and horticultural therapists, can work outdoors with patients recovering, for example, from a stroke or head injury (see chapter 14).

4. Natural distractions (positive distraction through contact with nature)
"A positive distraction is an environmental feature or situation that promotes an improved emotional state in the perceiver,

3.14 A walking loop around a lake with a fountain at McKay Dee Hospital, Ogden, Utah, provides the opportunity for gentle or more vigorous exercise. Designer: Office of James Burnett.
Photo by Chris Garcia

may block or reduce worrisome thoughts, and fosters beneficial changes in physiological systems such as lowered blood pressure and stress hormones" (Ulrich 1999, 49). Along with laughter, music, art, and companion animals, nature has been found to be one of the best forms of positive distraction. In a healthcare environment where situations and procedures are often stressful, frightening, or painful, positive distraction is extremely important (fig. 3.15).

Design considerations for nature distraction

A garden in a healthcare facility should feel like a garden, with as many opportunities to engage with nature as possible. People venture outside to escape, literally and figuratively, the sights, smells, and sounds encountered within the building. A healthcare garden should serve as a contrast, a place of respite, a breath of fresh air. Based on their own research as well as others', Cooper Marcus and Barnes (1999) recommend a ratio of

3.15 The Garden of Healing and Renewal in Clarkston, Michigan—a healthcare garden open to the surrounding community—is lush with varied plantings, places to walk, and places to sit. Designer: Professional Engineering Associates.
Copyright Jeffrey T. Smith

approximately 30 percent hardscape (paving, walls, etc.) to 70 percent vegetation.

Attention restoration theory

Whereas Ulrich's research and grounded theory has focused on stress reduction, especially for patients in healthcare settings, Stephen and Rachel Kaplan have focused on attention restoration. The Kaplans' *attention restoration theory* (ART) identified two interrelated systems (Kaplan 1995; Kaplan and Kaplan 1989). *Directed attention* involves concentration on a specific, often difficult or stressful task (e.g., taking a test, performing an operation, walking down a busy city street) that simultaneously requires blocking out distracting sensory stimuli. Prolonged periods of directed attention without restoration lead to mental, and even physical, fatigue. Prolonged mental fatigue can result in an increase in irritability, impatience, unhappiness, and even hostility. Furthermore, mental fatigue can lower an individual's proper judgment and ability to concentrate, thus increasing the potential for errors. Restoration from mental fatigue caused by prolonged directed attention is essential. The Kaplans' theory proposes that certain environments, including nature, are particularly effective at fostering recovery. Part of the restoration comes from *indirect attention*, or *involuntary attention*, a term first coined by William James in 1892 to define a form of

attention that does not require effort and thus restores mental fatigue. The Kaplans also use the terms *fascination* and *soft fascination* to refer to this restorative state. Although the Kaplans' early work focused on people's experience in wilderness environments, Rachel Kaplan asserted that any sort of "nearby nature"—"whether experienced directly or inadvertently—can contribute to well-being. Tending houseplants, the view of a tree from a window, gardening, street trees, planters with flowers at bus stops . . . , there are so many ways that the natural world may benefit people" (Louv 2011, 29).

The Kaplans identify four characteristics of restorative settings: being away, extent, fascination, and compatibility. For the greatest restoration, all of these elements must be in play together (Kaplan, Kaplan, and Ryan 1998):

1. *Being away:* Escape or withdrawal from the source of fatigue or stress. Being away can be physical, from traveling deep into a wild forest to stepping outside for a breath of fresh air; visual, such as looking out a window or even at a picture; or mental, such as imagining a place one wants to be. However, merely being away is not enough. "Extent," or where one escapes to, is also important.

2. *Extent:* A space with enough scope to allow someone to feel that they are away, in "a whole different world." A place—either physical or in the mind's eye—that is large or detailed

enough to invite exploration. Such a place should also engender fascination.

3. *Fascination:* A setting, or thing, that is interesting enough to hold one's attention. "Fascination derives not only from interesting things or places, but also from processes such as thinking, doing, and wondering. . . . Nature is well endowed with objects of fascination in flora, fauna, water, and the endless play of light. People also tend to be fascinated with natural processes such as growth, succession, predation, and even survival itself" (Kaplan, Kaplan, and Ryan 1998, 20) (fig.3.16).

4. *Compatibility:* A situation in which one's inclinations are compatible with one's environmental circumstances. For example, a desire be alone in a quiet place and finding a garden bench tucked away in a corner. An example of incompatibility might be one's desire to go outside not being met due to bad weather, locked doors, or institutional policy.

Design considerations for ART

The Kaplans' research has found the following four factors to be high in preference and thus most likely to facilitate attention restoration (Kaplan, Kaplan, and Ryan 1998). There are clear implications in all of these for the design of a restorative outdoor space.

1. *Coherence:* A setting that is orderly and organized into clear areas so that people can easily see and make sense of a place.

2. *Complexity:* A rich setting with many opportunities for sensory engagement. A coherent setting can and should be complex. The two are not mutually exclusive. For example, a garden can have a clear layout but be rich with trees, shrubs, flowers, places to sit, and paths to wander.

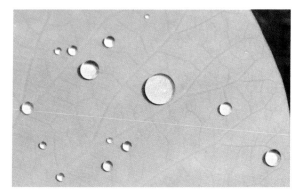

3.16 These water drops on a lotus leaf can elicit fascination.
Photo from www.henrydomke.com

3. *Legibility:* A distinct setting that has one or more memorable components—something that helps someone remember the place and also allows them to navigate easily through the space.

4. *Mystery:* A setting where one feels compelled to explore and discover. Curving pathways, vegetation that partly obscures what is coming next—a glimpse of something that engages the visitor and draws him or her forward.

It could be argued that ART plays its greatest role in places of work, learning, and general living (cities, neighborhoods). When applied to healthcare, attention restoration through nature contact may be most beneficial to staff who must focus on difficult, taxing activities for much of the workday. From a safety perspective, the need for attention restoration for staff is paramount in helping to reduce the likelihood of medical errors. In a study by Pati, Harvey, and Barach (2008), nurses with a view through a window onto a nature scene exhibited less stress and fatigue, and a stronger ability to concentrate and focus on tasks, than those with no view or a nonnature view. A study by Cooper Marcus and Barnes (1995) found that nurses and other healthcare staff were often the primary users of gardens and other types of outdoor spaces in hospitals. Especially in acute-care general hospitals, patients are often not in the hospital long enough, or they are not well enough, to go outside. Getting outdoors was viewed by staff as an important means of escaping, physically and emotionally, from demanding and stressful work (fig. 3.17).

In her research, Barnes (1994) investigated where people go when they are seeking solace outdoors. Subjects described helpful aspects of their chosen environments, and commonalities were found between those sites that were selected in natural areas and those in built environments. These common aspects were assessed in light of previous work in the fields of environmental psychology and medicine, resulting in a theory of healing meditation as cued by the environment. Four phases of this process were identified: (1) moving away: a separation or opening to allow movement away from an unproductive perspective or mood; (2) sensory awakening: release from focus-directed attention providing support for more basic involuntary and effortless thought processes; (3) reconnecting with self: quiet reflection and/or cathartic release; (4) spiritual attunement: inner trust and a sense of well-being derived from awareness of the transcendent and connection to the universal. This theoretical analysis provides a framework for guidelines in the creation of therapeutic landscapes, which Barnes (1994; 1999; 2002) presented in her work.

3.17 A nurse takes a break in the sun in the Meditation Garden at Banner Gateway Medical Center, Gilbert, Arizona. Even short periods of time in nature can reduce stress and facilitate restoration.
Photo by Clare Cooper Marcus

Other Pertinent Theories for Evidence-Based Healthcare Design

Emotional congruence theory

An individual's emotional state has a profound effect on his or her experience of a place or thing. Niedenthal et al. (1994) proposed that how a person feels at any given time influences what and how she or he sees. This is called emotional congruence theory. If someone is happy, they see the world "through rose-colored glasses"; they notice and appreciate attractive scenes and elements and can more easily overlook something that is unattractive. In the same way, someone who is stressed or depressed may look at the same scene and see something entirely different, noticing more things that are ugly, and perhaps that even appear threatening. "Evidence suggests that fear promotes

processing of the fearful, sadness the sad, and happiness the happy" (Ulrich 1999, 66). In a series of studies on patient reactions to abstract art and nature art, Ulrich and colleagues found that patients had stronger positive physiological and self-reported reactions to unambiguous nature art. The opposite was true with the abstract art: patients elicited strong negative reactions, even including attacking the work. When patient reactions were compared with staff in a psychiatric facility, the same artwork often triggered quite different responses. For example, with one abstract piece that somewhat resembled apple cores, one nurse said "I think it's fun. Whimsical. I'd like to have it in my home." Two patient comments included "Charred skulls. Drops of blood are flying" and "Wounded people. They're in pain and crying out" (Ulrich 1999, 67). These reactions strongly suggest the different mind-set of people who are emotionally and/or physically compromised, as well as the need for sensitive designers who listen and respond appropriately to their clients' needs. Related to the theory of emotional congruence is what the authors refer to as the "aesthetic placebo."

The aesthetic placebo

Healthcare design research has confirmed what people in industries such as hotels, restaurants, casinos, offices, and retail stores have known for a long time—that how a place *looks* affects how people *feel*, and can also affect how they *behave*. An attractive, well-designed, and well-maintained healing environment reassures a person that she or he will be given an equally high level of attention and care. A facility's physical attractiveness, both indoors and out, has been directly linked to stress reduction, patient satisfaction, and perceived quality of care (Becker, Sweeney, and Parsons 2008; Dijkstra, Pieterse, and Pruyn 2008). In *Healing Spaces: The Science and Place of Well-Being*, the neuroscientist Esther Sternberg (2010) discusses a "placebo effect" in relation to human responses to aesthetics. Expectation plays a pivotal role in the placebo effect: "When you feel better because you believe that something will heal you—whether that something is a drug, an action, a person, a procedure, or a place—you are experiencing the placebo effect" (Sternberg 2010, 191). Perhaps another reason that gardens are restorative in a healthcare setting has to do with preconceptions. Many people have had negative experiences with healthcare institutions. Even without a direct experience, the majority of people fear sickness, pain, and death, all of which occur in healthcare facilities—even those that are beautifully designed. On the other hand, most people have had positive experiences, and thus have positive associations, with natural or garden settings. In addition to the biophilic influence, people seek nature because it is familiar; they associate it with refuge, health, and well-being. In two studies by Francis and Cooper Marcus (1991, 1992), a high percentage of architecture and landscape architecture students, when asked about where they went when they felt sad or upset, responded that they sought out places in nature. A follow-up study with people from the general population by Barnes (1994) confirmed these findings (fig. 3.18).

Nature and pleasure

Most of the research conducted to date has focused on stress reduction and attention restoration—in other words, the ability of nature to restore the body to a healthy state or to ameliorate an unhealthy state. However, scientific advances such as the ability to view and measure the brain's neurological functions are allowing scientists to see that nature can actively

3.18 Viewing natural scenes such as sanderlings on a beach activates brain cells that evoke pleasure and help reduce stress.
Photo from www.henrydomke.com

promote health and pleasure—and how it does so. When people go to the park, or lie on the grass looking up at the clouds and the leaves, or garden in their backyard, the initial thought is not usually, "I must reduce my stress level, so I will engage in this stress-reducing activity in nature." They do so because it brings pleasure—it makes them feel good. One could argue that these are two sides of the same coin. What brings pleasure reduces stress. What reduces stress brings relief, which could be thought of as a form of pleasure. In discussing this idea, Sternberg describes research by Professor Irving Biederman at the University of Southern California, who found that "when people view scenes that are universally preferred—a beautiful vista, a sunset, a grove of trees—the nerve cells in that opiate-rich pathway become active. It is as if when you're looking at a beautiful scene, your own brain gives you a morphine high! Not only that, but as color, depth, and movement are added to the scene, more and more waves of nerve cells become active farther along this opiate-rich gradient" (Sternberg 2010, 33). Research using EEG readings has identified that people's contact with animals not only reduces stress reactivity and improves immune system function, it also increases the production of oxytocin. Oxytocin, often referred to as the "love hormone" or the "cuddle hormone," is actually a hormone-like peptide that is critical for social (such as mother-infant) bonding and empathy (Selhub and Logan 2012). A study by Weinstein, Przybylski, and Ryan (2009) found that when people viewed images of nature as opposed to urban scenes, they were inclined to be more social, more caring towards others, more community-oriented, and more generous (see also Mapes 2009). It may well be that contact with nature—Wilson's theory of biophilia—affects humans more profoundly than had been previously imagined.

More research needs to be conducted on the salutogenic—health-*promoting*—effects of nature in healthcare settings, offices, schools, neighborhoods, large urban areas, and so on. Howard Frumkin (2008, 113) states, "We probably need to learn to measure positive outcomes and not just negative outcomes—health and well-being, and not just pathology—a challenge for both psychology and medicine." There has been much talk in the past few years about "salutogenic design"—design that, like preventive medicine, promotes health rather than trying to heal what has already been broken (Antonovsky 1979; Dilani 2011). The medical field has begun to adopt a biopsychosocial model, in which mind and body are viewed as inextricably linked, rather than the biomedical model, in which the body takes precedence over the mind/thoughts/emotion (Taylor 2012). These changing views are encouraging for designers who seek to integrate patient-, family-, and community-centered care into design.

Next Steps

At a recent research conference in Sweden, the running joke about EBD was, "My mother could have told you that." This is often also the case with good design. Common sense, intuition, and communicating with one's client can bring excellent results. However, to "do no harm" and provide the best quality of care for patients, visitors, and staff, evidence-based—or evidence-informed—design is critical. This chapter has covered much of the research, as well as foundational theoretical and philosophical concepts, that inform many of the guidelines in this book. More research is needed, as this relatively new field still has gaps. Even when more of those gaps are filled, there will always be questions that must be addressed without available published evidence—hence the need for direct communication and multidisciplinary participation throughout the design process.

References

Antonovsky, A. 1979. *Health, Stress and Coping.* San Francisco: Jossey-Bass.

Appleton, J. 1975. *The Experience of Landscape.* New York: John Wiley and Sons.

Balling, J. D., and J. H. Falk. 1982. "Development of Visual Preference for Natural Environments." *Environment and Behavior* 14 (1): 15–28.

Barnes, M. 1994. "A Study of the Process of Emotional Healing in Outdoor Spaces and the Concomitant Landscape Design Implications." Master of landscape architecture thesis, University of California, Berkeley.

———. 1999. "Environmental Cues and Emotional Restoration." Pp. 92–100 in *Towards a New Millennium in People Plant Relationships*, edited by M. Burchett, J. Tarran, and R. Wood. Sydney: University of Technology, Sydney, Australia.

———. 2002. "The Role of Perception in the Designing of Outdoor Environments." Pp. 135–40 in *Interaction by Design: Bringing People and Plants Together for Health and Well-Being*, edited by C. Shoemaker. New York: John Wiley and Sons.

Becker, F., B. Sweeney, and K. Parsons. 2008. "Ambulatory Facility Design and Patients' Perceptions of Healthcare Quality." *Health Environments Research and Design Journal* 1 (4): 35–54.

Bell, J. F., J. S. Wilson, and G. C. Liu. 2008. "Neighborhood Greenness and 2-Year Changes in Body Mass Index of Children and Youth." *American Journal of Preventative Medicine* 35 (6): 547–53.

Berman, M. G., J. Jonides, and S. Kaplan. 2008. "The Cognitive Benefits of Interacting with Nature." *Psychological Science* 19 (12): 1207–12.

Bowcott, O. 2010. "Rickets Warning from Doctors as Vitamin D Deficiency Widens." *The Guardian*, January 21. www.guardian.co.uk/society/2010/jan/22/sharp-rise-vitamin-a-deficiency.

Cannon, W. B. 1932. *The Wisdom of the Body.* New York: Norton.

Carpman, J. R., and M. A. Grant. 1993. *Design that Cares: Planning Health Facilities for Patients and Visitors.* Washington, DC: American Hospital Association.

Center for Health Design. 2008. *An Introduction to Evidence-Based Design.* EDAC study guide No. 1. Concord, CA: The Center for Health Design.

Cooper Marcus, C., and M. Barnes. 1995. *Gardens in Healthcare Facilities: Uses, Therapeutic Benefits, and Design Recommendations.* Concord, CA: Center for Health Design.

Cooper Marcus, C., and M. Barnes, eds. 1999. *Healing Gardens: Therapeutic Benefits and Design Recommendations.* New York: John Wiley and Sons.

Cooper Marcus, C., and C. Francis. 1990. *People Places: Design Guidelines for Urban Open Space.* New York: Van Nostrand Reinhold.

Dannenberg, A. L., H. Frumkin, and R. J. Jackson. 2011. *Making Healthy Places: Designing and Building for Health, Well-Being, and Sustainability.* Washington, DC: Island Press.

Diette, G. B., N. Lechtzin, E. Haponik, A. Devrotes, and H. R. Rubin. 2003. "Distraction Therapy with Nature Sights and Sounds Reduces Pain during Flexible Bronchoscopy: A Complementary Approach to Routine Analgesia." *CHEST* 123 (3): 941–48.

Dijkstra, K., M. E. Pieterse, and A. Pruyn. 2008. "Stress-reducing Effects of Indoor Plants in the Built Healthcare Environment:

The Mediating Role of Perceived Attractiveness." *Preventive Medicine* 47 (3): 279–83.

Dilani, A. 2011. "Salutogenic Design for Public Health Promotion and Prevention." Paper presented at the Design and Health World Congress, Boston, July 7.

Dravigne, A., T. Waliczek, R. Lineberger, and J. Zajicek. 2008. "The Effect of Live Plants and Window Views of Green Spaces on Employee Perceptions of Job Satisfaction." *HortScience* 41 (1): 183–87.

Edelstein, L. 1943. *The Hippocratic Oath: Text, Translation, and Interpretation*. Baltimore, MD: John Hopkins University Press.

Evans, G. W., and S. Cohen. 1987. "Environmental Stress." Pp. 571–610 in *Handbook of Environmental Psychology*, edited by D. Stokols and I. Altman. New York: John Wiley and Sons.

Faber Taylor, A., and F. E. Kuo. 2009. "Children with Attention Deficits Concentrate Better after Walk in the Park." *Journal of Attention Disorders* 12 (5): 402–09.

Faber Taylor, A., F. E. Kuo, and W. C. Sullivan. 2002. "Views of Nature and Self-Discipline: Evidence from Inner City Children." *Journal of Environmental Psychology* 22 (1–2): 49–63.

FGI (Facility Guidelines Institute). 2013. "Home." Facility Guidelines Institute. www.fgiguidelines.org/.

Francis, M. 1989. "Control as a Dimension of Public-Space Quality." Pp. 147–72 in *Human Behavior and Environment: Advances in Theory and Research, Vol. 10: Public Places and Spaces*, edited by I. Altman and E. H. Zube. New York: Plenum.

Francis, C., and C. Cooper Marcus. 1991. "Places People Take Their Problems." *Proceedings of Annual Conference of Environmental Design and Research Association* 22: 178–84.

———. 1992. "Restorative Places: Environment and Emotional Well-Being." *Proceedings of Annual Conference of Environmental Design Research Association* 23.

Friedman, B., N. G. Freier, and P. H. Kahn, Jr. 2004. "Office Window of the Future? Two Case Studies of an Augmented Window." *Extended Abstracts of CHI 2004 Conference on Human Factors in Computing Systems*, April 24–29.

Fromm, E. 1973. *The Anatomy of Human Destructiveness*. New York: Henry Holt and Company.

———. 1997. *On Being Human*. London: The Continuum International Publishing Group Ltd.

Frumkin, H. 2008. "Nature Contact and Human Health: Building the Evidence Base." Pp. 107–18 in *Biophilic Design*, edited by S. Kellert, J. Heerwagen, and J. Mador. Hoboken, NJ: John Wiley and Sons.

Fujita, S., S. Ueki, M. Miyoshi, and T. Watanabe. 2010. "'Green Odor' Inhalation by Stressed Rat Dams Reduces Behavioral and Neuroendocrine Signs of Prenatal Stress in the Offspring." *Hormones and Behavior* 58: 264–72.

Glass, D. C., and J. E. Singer. 1972. *Urban Stress: Experiments on Noise and Social Stressors*. New York: Academic Press.

Heerwagen, J. H., and B. Gregory. 2008. "Biophilia and Sensory Aesthetics." Pp. 227–41 in *Biophilic Design*, edited by S. Kellert, J. Heerwagen, and J. Mador. Hoboken, NJ: John Wiley and Sons.

Heerwagen, J. H., and G. H. Orians. 1993. "Humans, Habitats and Aesthetics." Pp. 139–72 in *The Biophilia Hypothesis*, edited by S. Kellert and E. O Wilson. Washington, DC: Island Press.

Hester, R. T. 1984. *Planning Neighborhood Space with People*. 2nd ed. New York: Van Nostrand Reinhold.

Honeyman, M. C. 1992. "Vegetation and Stress: A Comparison Study of Varying Amounts of Vegetation in Countryside and Urban Scenes." Pp. 143–45 in *The Role of Horticulture in Human Well-Being and Social Development: A National Symposium*, edited by D. Relf. Portland, OR: Timber Press.

Hull, R. B., and W. P. Stewart. 1992. "Validity of Photo-Based Scenic Beauty Judgments." *Journal of Environmental Psychology* 12: 101–14.

Hyun-Ju, J., E. Fujii, and T.-D. Cho. 2010. "An Experimental Study of Physiological and Psychological Effects of Pine Scent." *Journal of Korean Institute of Landscape Architecture* 38 (4): 1–10.

Institute of Medicine. 2000. *To Err is Human: Building a Safer Health System*. Washington, DC: Institute of Medicine.

Jenks, S. M., and D. Matthews. 2010. "Ingestion of Mycobacterium Vaccae Influences Learning and Anxiety in Mice." Paper presented at the Annual Animal Behavior Society Meeting, William and Mary College, Williamsburg, Virginia, July 25–30.

Kahn, P. H. Jr., B. Friedman, B. Gill, J. Hagma, R. L. Severson, N. G. Freier, E. N. Feldman, S. Carrère, and A. Stolyar. 2008. "A Plasma Display Window?—The Shifting Baseline Problem in a Technologically Mediated Natural World." *Journal of Environmental Psychology* 28 (2): 192–99.

Kaplan, R., and S. Kaplan. 1989. *Experience of Nature: A Psychological Perspective*. New York: Cambridge University Press.

Kaplan, R., S. Kaplan, and R. L. Ryan. 1998. *With People in Mind*. Washington, DC: Island Press.

Kaplan, S. 1995. "The Restorative Benefits of Nature: Toward an Integrative Framework." *Journal of Environmental Psychology* 15: 169–82.

Kellert, S., and E. O. Wilson. 1993. *The Biophilia Hypothesis*. Washington, DC: Island Press.

Kline, G. A. 2009. "Does a View of Nature Promote Relief from Acute Pain?" *Journal of Holistic Nursing* 27 (3): 159–66.

Kuo, F. E. 2001. "Coping with Poverty: Impacts of Environment and Attention in the Inner City." *Environment and Behavior* 33 (1): 5–34.

Kuo, F. E., and W. C. Sullivan. 2001a. "Environment and Crime in the Inner City: Does Vegetation Reduce Crime?" *Environment and Behavior* 33 (3): 343–67.

———. 2001b. "Aggression and Violence in the Inner City: Impacts of Environment via Mental Fatigue." *Environment and Behavior* 33 (4): 543–71.

Leather, P. J., M. Pyrgas, D. Beale, and C. Lawrence. 1998. "Windows in the Workplace: Sunlight, View and Occupational Stress." *Environment and Behavior* 30 (6): 739–63.

Li, Q., K. Morimoto, M. Kobayashi, H. Inagaki, M. Katsumata, Y. Hirata, K. Hirata, H. Suzuki, Y. J. Li, Y. Wakayama, T. Kawada, B. J. Park, T. Ohira, N. Matsui, T. Kagawa, Y. Miyazaki, and A. M. Krensky. 2008. "Visiting a Forest, but Not a City, Increases Human Natural Killer Activity and Expression of Anti-Cancer Proteins." *International Journal of Immunopathology and Pharmacology* 21 (1): 117–27.

Li, Q., K. Morimoto, A. Nakadai, H. Inagaki, M. Katsumata, T. Shimizu, Y. Hirata, K. Hirata, H. Suzuki, Y. Miyazaki, T. Kagawa, Y. Koyama, T. Ohira, N. Takayama, A. M. Krensky, and T. Kawada. 2007. "Forest Bathing Enhances Human Natural Killer Activity and Expression of Anti-Cancer Proteins. *International Journal of Immunopathology and Pharmacology* 20: 3–8.

Louv, R. 2011. *The Nature Principle: Human Restoration and the End of Nature-Deficit Disorder*. Chapel Hill, NC: Algonquin Books.

Lowry, C. A., J. H. Hollis, A. de Vries, B. Pan, L. R. Brunet, J. R. Hunt, J. F. Paton, E. van Kampen, D. M. Knight, A. K. Evans, G. A. Rook, and S. L. Lightman. 2007. "Identification of an Immune-Responsive Mesolimbocortical Serotonergic System: Potential Role in Regulation of Emotional Behavior." *Neuroscience* 146 (2): 756–72.

Mace, B. L., P. A. Bell, and R. J. Loomis. 1999. "Aesthetic, Affective, and Cognitive Effects of Noise and Natural Landscape Assessment." *Society and Natural Resources* 12 (3): 225–42.

Marberry, S. O. 2010. "A Conversation with Roger Ulrich." *Healthcare Design*, November 1. www.healthcaredesignmaga zine.com/article/conversation-roger-ulrich?page=show.

McBrien, N. A., I. G. Morgan, and D. O. Mutti. 2009. "What's Hot in Myopia Research—The 12th International Myopia Conference, Australia, July 2008." *Optometry and Vision Science* 86 (1): 2–3.

Mind. 2007. *Ecotherapy—The Green Agenda for Mental Health*. London: Mind Publications. www.mind.org.uk/ assets/0000/2138/ecotherapy_report.pdf.

Moore, E. 1981–1982. "A Prison Environment's Effect on Health Care Service Demands." *Journal of Environmental Systems* 11: 17–34.

Nakamura, R., and E. Fujii. 1990. "Studies of the Characteristics of the Electroencephalogram when Observing Potted Plants: Pelargonium Hortorum "Sprinter Red" and Begonia Evansiana." *Technical Bulletin of the Faculty of Horticulture of Chiba University* 43: 177–83.

———. 1992. "A Comparative Study of the Characteristics of the Electroencephalogram when Observing a Hedge and a Concrete Block Fence." *Journal of the Japanese Institute of Landscape Architects* 55: 139–44.

Nanda, U., C. M. Chanaud, L. Brown, R. Hart, and K. Hathorn. 2009. "Pediatric Art Preferences: Countering the 'One-Size-Fits-All' Approach." *Health Environments Research and Design Journal* 2 (4): 46–61.

Nanda, U., S. Eisen, and V. Baladandayuthapani. 2008. "Undertaking an Art Survey to Compare Patient Versus Student Art Preferences." *Environment and Behavior* 40 (2): 269–301.

Niedenthal, P. M., M. B. Setterlund, and D. E. Jones. 1994. "Emotional Organization of Perceptual Memory." Pp. 87–113 in *The Heart's Eye: Emotional Influences in Perception and Attention*, edited by P. M. Niedenthal and S. Kitayama. New York: Academic Press.

Oka, T., S. Hayashida, Y. Kaneda, M. Takenaga, Y. Tamagawa, S. Tsuji, and A. Hatanaka. 2008. "Green Odor Attenuates a Cold Pressor Test-Induced Cardiovascular Response in Healthy Adults." *BioPsychoSocial Medicine* 2: 2.

Orians, G. H. 1980. "Habitat Selection: General Theory and Applications to Human Behavior." Pp. 49–63 in *The Evolution of Human Social Behavior*, edited by J. S. Lockhard. New York: Elsevier North-Holland.

Park, B. J., Y. Tsunetsugu, T. Kasetani, T. Kagawa, and Y. Miyazaki. 2010. "The Physiological Effects of Shinrin-Yoku (Taking in the Forest Atmosphere or Forest Bathing): Evidence from Field Experiments in 24 Forests across Japan." *Environmental Health and Preventive Medicine* 15 (1): 18–26.

Pati, D., T. Harvey, and P. Barach. 2008. "Relationships between Exterior Views and Nurse Stress: An Exploratory Examination." *Health Environments Research and Design Journal* 1 (2): 27–38.

Proshansky, W. M., W. H. Ittelson, and L. G. Rivlin. 1970. "Freedom of Choice and Behavior in a Physical Setting." Pp. 173–183 in *Environmental Psychology: Man and His Physical Setting*, edited by H. M. Proshansky, W. H. Ittelson, and L. G. Rivlin. New York: Holt, Rinehart, and Winston.

Randall, K., C. A. Shoemaker, D. Relf, and E. S. Geller. 1992. "Effects of Plantscapes in an Office Environment on Worker Satisfaction." Pp. 106–9 in *Role of Horticulture in Human Well-Being and Social Development*, edited by D. Relf. Arlington, VA: Timber Press.

Reizenstein, J. E., and M. A. Grant. 1981. "Patient and Visitor Preferences for Outdoor Courtyard Design." Unpublished research report #10, Patient and Visitor Participation Project, Office of Hospital Planning, Research and Development, University of Michigan, Ann Arbor.

Sachs, N. A. 2009. "Interview with Dr. Esther Sternberg, Author of Healing Spaces: The Science of Place and Well-Being." *Therapeutic Landscapes Network*, September 16. www.heal-inglandscapes.org/blog/2009/09/interview-with-dr-esther-sternberg-author-of-healing-spaces-the-science-of-place-and-well-being/.

Sato, Y., N. Metoki, J. Iwamoto, and K. Satoh. 2003. "Amelioration of Osteoporosis and Hypovitaminosis D by Sunlight Exposure in Stroke Patients." *Neurology* 61: 338–42.

Selhub, E. M., and A. C. Logan. 2012. *Your Brain on Nature.* Hoboken, NJ: John Wiley and Sons.

Sternberg, E. M. 2010. *Healing Spaces: The Science and Place of Well-Being.* Cambridge, MA: Harvard University Press.

Stichler, J. F., and D. K. Hamilton. 2008. "Evidence-based Design: What is It?" *Health Environments Research and Design* 1(2): 3–4.

Taylor, J. G., E. H. Zube, and J. L. Sell. 1987. "Landscape Assessment and Perception Research Methods." Pp. 361–93 in *Methods in Environmental and Behavioral Research*, edited by R. B. Brechtel, R. Marans, and W. Michelson. New York: Van Nostrand.

Taylor, S. E. 2012. *Health Psychology.* 8th ed. New York, NY: McGraw-Hill.

Turner, L. W., M. A. Bass, L. Ting, and B. Brown. 2002. "Influence of Yard Work and Weight Training on Bone Mineral Density among Older U.S. Women." *Journal of Women and Aging* 14 (3–4): 139–48.

Ulrich, R. S. 1979. "Visual Landscapes and Psychological Well-Being." *Landscape Research* 4: 17–19.

———. 1984. "View through a Window May Influence Recovery from Surgery." *Science* 224 (4647): 420–21.

———. 1993. "Biophilia, Biophobia, and Natural Landscapes." Pp. 74–137 in *The Biophilia Hypothesis*, edited by S. Kellert and E. O Wilson. Washington, DC: Island Press.

———. 1999. "Effects of Gardens on Health Outcomes: Theory and Research." Pp. 27–86 in *Healing Gardens: Therapeutic Benefits and Design Recommendations*, edited by C. Cooper Marcus and M. Barnes. New York: John Wiley and Sons.

———. 2011. "Evidence Based Design Practices." Lecture presented at the Healthcare Garden Design Certification Program, Chicago Botanic Garden, May 4.

Ulrich, R. S., and D. L. Addoms. 1981. "Psychological and Recreational Benefits of a Residential Park." *Journal of Leisure Research* 13: 43–65.

Ulrich, R. S., C. Zimring, X. Zhu, J. DuBose, H.-B. Seo, Y.-S. Choi, X. Quan, and A. Joseph. 2008. "A Review of the Research Literature on Evidence-Based Healthcare Design." *Health Environments Research and Design* 1 (3): 61–125.

Ware, C. 1994. "Designing and Building Healing Gardens at Health Care Facilities." Sacramento, CA: Spink Corp.

Watanabe, T., M. Fujihara, E. Murakami, M. Miyoshi, Y. Tanaka, S. Koba, and H. Tachibana. 2011. "Green Odor and Depressive-Like State in Rats: Toward an Evidence-Based Alternative Medicine?" *Behavioural Brain Research* 224 (2): 290–96.

Wells, N. M. 2000. "At Home with Nature: Effects of Greenness on Children's Cognitive Functioning." *Environment and Behavior* 32: 775–95.

West, M. J. 1985. "Landscape Views and Stress Response in a Prison Environment." Unpublished master's thesis, Department of Landscape Architecture, University of Washington, Seattle.

Winston, A. S., and G. C. Cupchik. 1992. "The Evaluation of High Art and Popular Art by Naïve and Experienced Viewers." *Visual Arts Research* 18: 1–14.

CHAPTER 4

Types and Locations of Therapeutic Landscapes in Healthcare

WHERE MIGHT AN ATTRACTIVE RESTORATIVE outdoor space in a healthcare facility be located, whether or not it is designated as a healing garden? What kind of form might it take?

These are questions that are bound to emerge as healthcare administrators, clinical staff, and designers consider the provision of green space in a new or renovated facility. The following brief typology, or "menu," of possible locations and forms was assembled from field notes taken on visits to more than one hundred hospitals and other healthcare facilities during the period 1995–2012 in the US, Canada, Australia, Denmark, Sweden, and the UK. When published literature is sparse, there is no substitute for analytical fieldwork.

The types of locations described below range from the most spacious to the smallest and least accessible. After a definition of each, some possible advantages and disadvantages are listed. Case studies of garden spaces in many of these locations appear in chapter 4 of C. Cooper Marcus and M. Barnes (eds.), *Healing Gardens: Therapeutic Benefits and Design Recommendations* (Wiley, 1999).

Extensive Landscaped Grounds

Where a number of healthcare buildings are positioned on a large greenfield site, thoughtful site planning can ensure that areas between buildings are not just leftover spaces but are planned from the start as useful therapeutic spaces.

Advantages

- Can be developed as outdoor walking routes between buildings, as settings for outdoor eating or waiting, and as exercise spaces for patients, visitors, and staff.

- In senior housing, if developed with looped walking routes and adequate resting places, can provide a setting that will encourage exercise.

- With thoughtful planting, can visually tie together a variety of buildings into a campus-like setting.

- Can potentially be developed into a variety of landscapes from manicured lawns and flower beds to natural woodland or meadow.

- If accessible to the general public, can create a sense that the facility is part of the community.

Disadvantages

- Maintenance of spacious green areas may be costly.

- If the outdoor space is developed in a piecemeal fashion, the relationship between spaces, as well as interior-exterior connections, may lack cohesiveness.

- May serve as a "reserve" for future expansion of the facility and eventually be built over.

- Unless detailed correctly for the intended users, it can become a "green desert," rarely used and perceived as wasted space.

Borrowed Landscape

Views from a healthcare facility onto natural landscapes, a greenway, a city park, and the like can provide positive distractions for patients, residents, and staff. Where a new or remodeled facility abuts a potential borrowed landscape, it is very important that windows from patient/resident rooms, waiting rooms, and single-loaded corridors are positioned to take advantage of these views.

Advantages

- Green outlook is provided with no expense of land acquisition or maintenance to the healthcare facility.

- Wildlife or people using the space may provide a pleasing diversion for those looking out.

- An experience of nature is close at hand, even in inclement weather.

- Views out are complemented by daylight coming in.

- Can provide a useful orientation element to assist in wayfinding.

Disadvantages

- Unless designated as a park or greenbelt, the space may eventually be built over.

- If ambulatory access to the space is not possible, may be frustrating to some people.

Nature and Fitness Trails

Although a rare amenity in a hospital setting or residential facility, an accessible nature or fitness trail can provide a welcome outdoor experience, especially for staff on their lunch hour, ambulatory patients, residents, and visitors taking a family member on an outing. Some healthcare facilities use graphic signs to designate a walking route via public sidewalks or pathways around a building, through the campus, or to another destination such as nearby woods, wetlands, and so on (fig. 4.1).

Advantages

- Exercise is an important component of stress reduction and sometimes people will only take a walk when encouraged to do so. A walking path with signs and crosswalks that forms a loop around a facility may prompt staff on a break to get outside and walk.

- Can take advantage of the natural landscape close to a facility when it is located in an out-of-town setting.

4.1 A fitness trail that encircles the Royal Edinburgh Infirmary, Edinburgh, Scotland, is used by staff on breaks, including nurses on the night shift who need respite from working in the intensive care unit.
Photo by Clare Cooper Marcus

- May provide an educational and community resource.

- The route doesn't necessarily need much space or capital outlay when using established sidewalks and pathways.

Disadvantages

- If the route is predominantly alongside traffic and/or parking, some potential users may be put off by the less-than-aesthetic setting.

- Not as usable by frail elderly or in-patients as a courtyard or front porch outdoor space.

- Depending on the climate, may not be usable all year.

- Location away from the facility may raise issues of safety and supervision.

- Unless seating is provided at regular intervals for taking a rest, trail use will be limited to those who are physically fit.

- Unless well signed from a well-used interior space (or mentioned in printed orientation material), this amenity may be unknown and/or underused.

Landscaped Setback

An area of green—usually a lawn—separating a building from adjacent streets, often required by zoning regulations.

Advantages

- May provide a familiar, comforting image evoking a sense of the front lawn of a home.

- Can provide passersby with a green "buffer," enhancing the appearance of a possibly institutional-looking building.

- Provides offices or rooms at the front of the building with some privacy from passing vehicular and pedestrian traffic.

- If designed well for sitting and conversing, may provide an appreciated, usable outdoor space.

Disadvantages

- A space akin to a residential front yard is often not intended for use, and its lack of seating, pathways, and so on may be frustrating for staff or visitors who want to use it, especially if this is the only available outdoor space (fig. 4.2).

4.2 A landscaped setback, while providing a green setting for a hospital, is often wasted space in terms of use and costly in terms of maintenance. With the addition of accessible paths and seating, this space could be transformed into an attractive place of respite at a facility where there are few other usable outdoor areas.
Photo by Clare Cooper Marcus

- If the integration of landscaped setback and vehicular and pedestrian approaches is not carefully thought through, the result may be a confusing approach to the building.

- When quite extensive in size, this space is often intended for future expansion of the facility.

Front Porch

A largely hard-surfaced area at the main entrance to a building is reminiscent of the front porch of a house, though obviously larger.

Advantages

- Provides a visual cue to the main entrance analogous to the front porch of a house.

- Overhang or porte-cochère may scale down the size of the building.

- Sensitively located seating provides an amenity for those waiting to be picked up, waiting for a bus, or just watching the world go by. A setting especially favored in senior housing.

Disadvantages

- May be overused—creating congestion—if it is the only outdoor seating area provided.

- May be underused if main access to the facility is via parking under the building or from an adjacent parking garage.

- May be confusing if vehicular and pedestrian needs are not sensitively integrated, or when the main entrance to a hospital and the emergency entrance are located next to each other.

- May raise the conflict of people smoking just outside the entry—an unpleasant experience for many who are traversing the space.

Entry Garden

An entry garden is a landscaped area close to the building entrance that, unlike a front porch, is a green space with a garden image and, unlike a landscaped setback, is designed and detailed for use (fig. 4.3).

Advantages

- Garden is visible and accessible from a well-used entry point.

- Makes aesthetic use of part of the site that might otherwise have been paved for parking.

4.3 A garden near a hospital entrance can provide a place for ambulatory patients to get outside, for people waiting for a taxi, or for staff taking a quick break. In senior housing it is often favored as a place to "watch the world go by."
Photo by Clare Cooper Marcus

- Provides a pleasing "garden" image on entering a hospital or senior living environment.

- Allows use by ambulatory inpatients or elderly residents who want to watch the world go by.

- May successfully double as a public park, and costs of maintenance devolve onto a city department.

- In a facility for seniors, will often prove the most popular area for sitting outdoors.

Disadvantages

- Without sensitive planting, may be too exposed to nearby parking and entry road.

- Depending on the garden's size and location, may impede access to the main entrance.

- Space for garden may have to compete with parking.

- High visibility of space may deter inpatients in hospital garb, or some seniors concerned about security, from using the space.

Backyard Garden

This kind of garden is characterized by its location—at the back of a building—rather than anything to do with its intrinsic design.

Advantages

- Depending on the adjacent uses, it can provide a quiet green space in contrast to the busier locations of a front porch or front entry garden.

- When appropriately landscaped, those in a senior living facility or at a hospice may find it a pleasing reminder of the backyard they used to have at home.

Disadvantages

- Unless clearly visible from a well-used common space, or well signed, people may not know it is there—especially those who only visit the facility occasionally.

- If adjacent uses at the back include parking or streets, the need for a quiet setting may not be met.

- If the facility is for dementia residents or psychiatric inpatients, the boundaries of such a garden must be carefully designed and disguised to prevent attempts at escape.

A "Tucked Away" Garden

A space set away from the building(s) and sometimes separated from it by an access road, parking area, or service entry, for example.

Advantages

- Can make good use of otherwise "leftover" space on the site.

- A short walk to the garden can provide a welcome separation from activities in the building and provide a sense of getting away.

Disadvantages

- Without good signage or visibility, may be sparsely used except by those who know about it.

- In senior facilities, unlikely to be used if it is difficult to access.

Courtyard

These are spaces—usually square or rectangular in form—that form voids in a building complex, often incorporated to bring daylight into the facility. They often have building walls and windows on four sides; sometimes, an L-shaped building encloses a courtyard with garden boundaries forming the other two sides. In a hospital setting, a courtyard should ideally be immediately visible or apparent upon entering the building so that visitors and patients know that it is there. The courtyard is one of the oldest forms of built space and has the potential to provide potent feelings of safety, shelter, retreat, and focus.

Advantages

- Semiprivate and surrounded by the building it serves. A particular advantage in a facility for residents or inpatients who need a high degree of security (for example, a psychiatric unit or Alzheimer's facility).

- Brings light into the core of a building.

- Depending on its location, it may be easily viewed and accessed (fig. 4.4).

- When a cafeteria occupies one or more sides of the courtyard, it can function as an outdoor eating place.

- Adjacent buildings may shield the space from the wind and provide needed shade.

- Space is likely to be experienced as human scale if the surrounding buildings are not too high.

- Views into a courtyard can provide useful wayfinding cues for people passing by in an adjacent corridor, particularly if the planting includes some unique features

- A courtyard can provide attractive views from windows of offices or patient rooms adjacent to the space.

Disadvantages

- Depending on its size, location, and design, a courtyard can create a "fishbowl" effect, and thus few people will use it, as they may feel on display.

- If lacking an adequate buffer—planting or structural—adjacent rooms may need to keep their blinds drawn for privacy. HIPAA regulations would likely preclude the use of a courtyard in these circumstances.

- Annoying sounds may intrude into adjacent rooms or from rooms into the courtyard.

- Courtyards are often the location for noisy HVAC units.

- If many courtyards are provided—principally for reasons of natural daylight and cross-ventilation—there may not be the budget to keep them all well maintained and some may be kept locked.

- Most courtyards are too small to provide adequate space for exercise.

4.4 A courtyard at a regional medical center in Illinois that is fully visible from the main waiting area. A receptionist offers pagers to visitors who wish to use the courtyard garden while they wait to be called to an appointment.
Photo by Clare Cooper Marcus

- Depending on the size and season, and the height of adjacent buildings, the space may be too shady and cold for comfortable use.

The Hole-in-a-Donut Garden

This is a variation of a courtyard garden, but larger and subtly different. Rather than a void "punched out" of a building (the courtyard), in this case the buildings in a facility are grouped in a rough circle around an outdoor space developed as a garden.

Advantages

- Many windows provide views into the green space, not only ensuring that people know that it is there but also enhancing wayfinding.

- In a large complex, the quickest route from one building or department to another may be through the central green space, thus ensuring that many people (particularly staff) are exposed to greenery during their daily routines.

- Where the buildings completely enclose the garden, it provides a place of privacy and security, particularly appropriate in a unit for those with dementia or inpatient psychiatric patients.

Disadvantages

- Where patient rooms are at grade and there is insufficient privacy between their windows and those using the garden, HIPAA regulations are likely to be violated and use of the garden compromised. (Other disadvantages are comparable to those listed under "Courtyards," above.)

Plaza

Plaza spaces are outdoor areas that are predominantly hard-surfaced, but often furnished for use. They may include trees, shrubs, or flowers in planters, benches, as well as lighting. The overall image is not of a green space but of a paved hard-surface area.

Advantages

- Low plant maintenance and irrigation costs.

- A small place can be designed for relatively heavy use.

- Depending on the paving details, patients using wheelchairs, walkers, or crutches may be able to move easily in this space.

Disadvantages

- May have few of the qualities that many people perceive as therapeutic in outdoor spaces—an overall green and/or colorful setting, a garden or oasis feel.

- May evoke the image of a shopping mall or corporate office plaza rather than a space for peaceful, stress-reducing, passive enjoyment.

- Reflected heat from hard surfaces may be a deterrent to use.

- Light-colored paved surfaces may create a glare problem, especially for the elderly and patients on certain medications.

- If paving has expansion joints wider than one-eighth inch, may preclude use by those using walkers or pulling IV-poles, since the wheels may become trapped.

- Predominance of hard surfaces may convey a cold, hard image.

Roof Garden

A garden space developed on all or part of the top of a building.

Advantages

- Can provide an oasis space in a high-density setting where none is available at grade.

- Captures space that might otherwise be unused.

- Private and secure for people in the facility; it is unlikely that people just walking by would access or use the space.

- As long as it is adequately designed for safety, can provide an appropriate outdoor space for those patients (e.g., psychiatric inpatients) or long-term residents (e.g., those with dementia) who require a high degree of security.

- Has the potential for expansive views to the surrounding urban or natural landscape, providing a positive distraction and feelings of visual escape (fig. 4.5).

Disadvantages

- Structural limitations may preclude the use of large trees, water features, or planting areas that create heavy loads.

- In a hospital setting, critical facilities beneath the roof—for example, a surgery suite—may preclude the development of a roof garden for fear of eventual leakage.

- A roof is highly exposed to the elements and may be windier than spaces at ground level, or enclosed courtyards.

- Depending on the orientation and height of any adjacent buildings that create shadows, temperatures may be uncomfortably hot or cold.

- Heating/air conditioning units often vent on roofs, creating intrusive mechanical sounds.

- Unless well signed, visitors and patients may not know of its existence.

Roof Terrace

Unlike a roof garden, which is located on *top* of a building, a roof terrace is usually on the side of a building, forming a long narrow "balcony" to that building, with the outdoor space positioned on the roof of an adjacent, lower building.

Advantages

- Captures space that might otherwise go unused.

- There is a potential for expansive views beyond the facility, providing a sense of visual escape.

- Planting on the inner, building edge of the terrace can provide an attractive green outlook from adjacent rooms and create a privacy barrier between those in the building and those using the terrace.

- A linear form creates a potential space for exercise.

- When the terrace is located off a main foyer or waiting area, no signage is needed to make its existence known, and those in the waiting area can experience a green outlook and views beyond.

4.5 Roof garden at Clare Tower, a high-rise residence for older adults in Chicago, Illinois. Designer: Hoerr Schaudt Landscape Architects.
Photo courtesy of Hoerr Schaudt

Disadvantages

- The function of space(s) underneath the terrace may preclude part or all of terrace from being developed as a usable landscaped space.

- Since large trees are likely precluded for structural reasons, the space may lack necessary shade.

- Depending on its location, the terrace may be too exposed—too hot, cold, or windy.

- Unless carefully designed, a terrace may intrude on the privacy of people in adjacent rooms and its use precluded under HIPAA regulations.

A Peripheral Garden

Where space is limited, a narrow green space can entirely encircles a building like a belt, with several access points to it from the building.

Advantages

- If well detailed and accessible from several exits from the building, this can form at attractive garden walk, especially for staff on breaks.

- May encourage needed exercise in a senior facility, since the green space is easily accessible and those using it can return to the building before completing the entire loop if they are tired or need to access a toilet, for example.

- In a hospice or acute-care facility, the garden walk can provide an attractive respite for family members or a setting where they can take an inpatient for a brief outing.

- Potentially provides a green outlook from all the windows in the facility (fig. 4.6).

Disadvantages

- May not provide the sense of "getting away" from a building that can be experienced in a larger garden.

4.6 A walking path through a peripheral garden encircles the San Diego Hospice, in San Diego, California. The path is accessible from the building at many points.
Photo by Clare Cooper Marcus

• Depending on the nature of the adjacent uses to this garden walk, it may not provide a sufficient respite experience.

Atrium Garden

In latitudes where the climate precludes sitting or strolling outdoors during much of the year, an indoor garden—heated or air-conditioned—can provide an attractive substitute. Numbers of medical facilities in very hot regions (e.g., Florida and the southern United States), or very cold regions (Canada, Scandinavia) incorporate a glass-roofed solarium or atrium furnished with appropriate trees, plants, and seating (fig. 4.7).

Advantages

• Simulates an "outdoor" green experience, even during times of inclement weather.

• Provides a space that is undoubtedly part of the territory of the facility and is secure.

• Space is usually very visible and accessible.

• Depending on the size of the space, the height of plant materials can provide a green outlook from rooms above grade.

• Interior of building can be flooded with daylight.

Disadvantages

• Heating or cooling of the space increases energy costs.

• Indoor plants may need special care or entail high maintenance and replacement costs.

• Difficult growing conditions may lead to use of artificial plants, which may lessen their effect on stress reduction.

• May raise concerns about infection control.

Viewing Garden

With space and budget limitations, some facilities may incorporate a small garden that cannot be entered but can be viewed from inside the building.

4.7 An indoor garden at the Cardiovascular Center, University of Michigan, Ann Arbor, Michigan. Designer: Shepley Bulfinch.
Photo courtesy of Shepley Bulfinch

Advantages

- Brings light into the building interior.

- Introduces views onto greenery from adjacent sitting and circulation spaces.

- Those viewing the greenery from indoor seating are sheltered from the rain or snow or are in a needed heated or air-conditioned space.

- There are likely to be lower maintenance costs, compared with accessible and used spaces.

Disadvantages

- Nature elements cannot be viewed up close, touched, or smelled, thus their multisensory qualities are diminished.

- Water features or birds—if present—cannot be heard.

- Those who might want to cannot walk, stroll, or sit in the garden.

CHAPTER 5

The Participatory Design Process

Teresia Hazen

Coordinator of Therapeutic Gardens, Legacy Health, Portland, Oregon

THIS CHAPTER EXAMINES EVIDENCE AND best practices in order to promote a participatory design process for creating garden environments that support and encourage treatment therapies, care of patients, and restorative engagement opportunities for patients, visitors, and employees. A participatory design process developed at Legacy Health, Portland, Oregon (the Therapeutic Garden Design Team Process), has proven to be effective and has served as a model for many other healthcare facilities in the United States and internationally. Developed and used for over twenty years, this is only one of several models available to design teams. Many agencies start with some of these proven concepts and create successful hybrid models for each unique setting. Though this process is used here for the design of specific therapeutic gardens, it could potentially be used on a larger scale for the overall site planning and design of an entire healthcare facility. Case studies based on the process are presented at the end of the chapter.

> Healthcare has changed significantly in recent years: more admissions are short-term, many operations can be performed on an out-patient basis, increased attention is being given to preventive medicine, and there is additional need for ambulatory centers rather than private rooms. In today's medical thinking, it is vitally important to consider the patient's total well-being, that is, the physical, intellectual, emotional, and social needs of the patient. One of the goals of the design process should be to provide an environment which supports and encourages the treatment, therapy, and care of patients. Such an environment can be designed if all the users (that is, the patients and personnel) have a genuine participation in the planning and design process. The environment must also support the interdisciplinary work of the staff: medical, nursing, administrative, psychologists, sociologists, and educators. (Ericksen 2002).

Dr. Bradley E. Karlin states: "At a new inpatient psychiatry building, the Veterans Affairs Palo Alto Health Care System, we were active members of the design team model and provided extensive clinical input to the design process. We subscribe to a patient-centered, inclusive approach to design and treatment" (Karlin and Zeiss 2006).

Healthcare personnel are key to successful design processes. The National Health Service (NHS) of the UK outlines a wide-ranging body of research pointing to staff satisfaction and associated benefits having a close association with how employees feel about their employer and, particularly, their sense of engagement with their work place. Engagement is seen as going beyond involvement to capture "the hearts and minds" of staff, with benefits to the organization (NHS Employers 2008).

Participatory design is an approach to design that actively involves all stakeholders (e.g., employees, partners, customers, citizens, and end users) in the design process to help ensure that the product designed meets their needs and is usable. The term is used in a variety of fields—urban design, architecture, landscape architecture, and medicine, for example—as a way of creating environments that are more responsive and appropriate to their inhabitants' and users' cultural, emotional, spiritual, and practical needs. It is one approach to placemaking and has been used in many settings and at various scales.

Evidence-based studies support the participatory process. Although it is more complex to orchestrate a participatory design process than it is to have a few decision makers, some significant benefits can result (Carpman and Grant 1993). One-size-fits-all rarely provides a very good fit. A better fit requires accommodating the many ways in which people differ. Genuine participation needs to start early and reach the diverse segments of the population. The format for getting feedback has to be friendly and appropriate. Soliciting local involvement needs to be an ongoing part of management (Kaplan and Kaplan 1998).

Carpman and Grant (1993) identify several significant benefits of inclusive participation in the design process:

1. Helping to clarify design objectives

2. Lowering construction costs by avoiding errors

3. Stimulating positive behavior and attitudes

4. Creating a sense of community

5. Creating a marketing strategy

Legacy Health Overview

Legacy Health (Legacy) is a nonprofit health system with six hospitals and more than fifty clinics with 2,500 physicians serving on the medical staff. Employees numbering 9,000 provide services around the clock. A Level I trauma center is located on the Emanuel Medical Center campus. Across the system, the average length of stay is 4.45 days.

Marie Valleroy, MD, physiatrist, summarizes the garden design process: "Our therapeutic gardens and HT [horticultural therapy] program at Legacy use an approach steeped in one of the traditions of rehabilitation: the interdisciplinary team meeting. Bringing interested and involved rehabilitationists together with designers and architects around the issues and goals of a given therapeutic garden space has been highly effective. Patients, family members, and volunteers, as part of the team, are key to the process and sources of user input. By drawing from these diverse and complementary sources, the team increases the versatility and power of the garden."

Purpose of Legacy Health therapeutic gardens

The goals of Legacy Health are that gardens in their hospitals and clinical units will:

1. Provide a therapeutic garden setting to support clinical programs and patient goals related to therapies (physical, occupational, speech, recreational, horticultural, and mental health), nursing, social services, child life, spiritual care, other clinical services, and patients' personal needs and goals. Legacy names this therapeutic intervention of the garden, *garden-enriched care* (GEC). Legacy Research Institute's director of clinical research, Alar Mirka, MD, PhD, developed this term in 2012 while leading a research grant writing team.

2. Offer supportive, restorative environments for patients, families, visitors, and staff.

3. Provide a setting for movement and mild exercise such as walking and wheeling in nature.

4. Provide environmental, horticulture, and gardening education, thus promoting thoughtful care of the environment.

Design process

Hospital vice president of operations Bryce Helgerson explains the process: A critical piece of the design team process is bringing together members of the healthcare team who understand the clinical needs of the patient and blend them with the needs of the staff, volunteers, and families. By having this cross section of members, the team achieved a successful outcome that not only provides a beautiful environment, but one with a function that meets the needs of these various groups. A key in achieving this reality is to establish up-front goals and to brainstorm as a team. Early in Legacy's design experience, the team intuitively developed a process that supports the use of valuable staff time, involves appropriate users, and achieves desired results. A description of this process is the focus of this chapter.

Organizing Staff to Conceptualize Needs

Institutionally, this process at Legacy is called the Therapeutic Garden Design Team Process. A format of three one-hour meetings is understood, accepted, and practiced with effective results and is considered to be one of the agency's best practices.

Unit directors and managers initiate potential therapeutic garden projects as part of the therapeutic program. Unit managers collaborate with the coordinator of therapeutic gardens (coordinator) to select appropriate members for the design team. The design team consists of ten to fifteen members and includes adequate staff and diversity of users to achieve desired results. The unit manager and coordinator of therapeutic gardens select team members. For example, the team for the Oregon Burn Center garden included the landscape architect, the coordinator of therapeutic gardens, the unit manager, the medical director, an occupational therapist, a social worker, a nurse, three former patients, a former patient's wife, three horticultural therapy interns, and one staff member each from facilities management and grounds. The involvement of facilities management and grounds staff early on is essential to the ongoing support and care of the hospital outdoor spaces (Cooper Marcus and Barnes 1999).

Design team members commit to participating in these three one-hour meetings. They understand how their consistent presence lends the needed continuity to effective and efficient work processes, the needed product, and the best aspirations of teamwork. Design team meetings drive all design work and occur immediately after the site is selected.

5.1 Meeting no. 1: Brainstorming the main issues regarding the design of a new garden at Legacy Health, Portland, Oregon.
Courtesy Legacy Health

Design team meeting no. 1

Legacy participants' comments reflect appreciation for the consideration shown for their time with respect to meetings that start and end as scheduled. The agenda is sent to participants in advance of the meeting. The meeting opens with introductions around the table, allowing all participants to share their role with the unit and passion about the task at hand (fig. 5.1).

The unit manager or director then reviews the task, which may sound something like "to create a beautiful garden to serve our programs, patients, families, and staff." The educational component at each of the three meetings helps members develop background and skills to help educate other staff and community members, which in turn translates into a broad base of staff and community support, including financial and in-kind resources and the recruitment of garden volunteers. Next, brainstorming guidelines are reviewed and members describe activities and programs that would take place in the garden, needs of patients and the unit, and needs of families, visitors, and staff. Specific garden elements to support patients, visitors, and staff are discussed, and the coordinator directs specific questions to cue team members as needed. Participants readily initiate questions, comments, opinions, hopes, and dreams for the garden. Brainstorming usually requires twenty to thirty minutes. Some of the fifty-nine items from team brainstorming for the Oregon Burn Center Garden, for example, were as follows:

- Shade is critical; pergolas, arbors, canopies
- Garden storage/maintenance shed
- Tables for wheelchairs

- Four to five small group areas for families
- Smooth paths for IV poles
- Make it beautiful like the Children's Garden
- Reduce glare from the brick walls, glass, and concrete
- Design for optimal patient view out the window with optimal privacy in-room
- Drought-tolerant, disease-resistant plantings

The session ends with the coordinator reviewing the accomplishments of the meeting and presenting an overview of the next steps. The landscape architect will present a conceptual design to the team at meeting number two.

At the conclusion of meeting number one, a team member described the power of the meeting: "The first healing garden design team meeting was short and to the point, plus being fun, friendly, and very productive. The brainstorming session was inclusive and totally without value judgment of ideas. This sparked creative thinking. I loved being a part of it and look forward to the next session" (Barbara Reader, volunteer, family member of a frequent patient, passionate gardener, and healing garden advocate; pers. comm.). Research on participation points to participants' sense of accomplishment, joy in learning new things, pride in contributing to the appearance of their neighborhoods, and feeling that the enormity of environmental degradation need not be so inevitable (Kaplan and Kaplan 1998). Participation in the design team at Legacy frequently leads to staff involvement in volunteer maintenance tasks in the garden as well as referring family and friends for this service role.

Design team meeting no. 2

The meeting begins with an introductions activity around the group. The American Horticultural Therapy Association (AHTA) Therapeutic Garden Characteristics are introduced (see chapter 16). The anticipation of the conceptual design creates excitement. The landscape architect then presents alternate designs to the group, explaining how brainstorming needs have been met. Throughout the presentation, the landscape architect and the coordinator encourage discussion and questions. The group reviews the brainstorming list from the minutes of meeting number one, to be sure priorities are met.

Meeting number two accomplishments are reviewed by the coordinator, and the task for the final meeting is reviewed. Members are advised that in meeting number three the landscape architect will present a revised and more detailed conceptual plan to the team.

5.2 At meeting no. 2, two or three concept plans prepared by the landscape architect are discussed with the design team. At meeting no. 3, a final concept plan is presented.
Courtesy of Legacy Health

The team sets the final meeting date for three to four weeks later. Team members will continue the evaluation process with peers and relay that information to the coordinator, who communicates with the landscape architect (fig. 5.2).

Design team meeting no. 3

The meeting opens with an introductions activity. The educational component for this meeting may be a case study of a patient's experience with one of the gardens or research studies to support gardens in healthcare.

The final presentation by the landscape architect begins with the unveiling of the design boards of the conceptual and elevation drawings of the new garden design. The landscape architect and the coordinator jointly lead this presentation to explain and support the needs as identified by the various user groups. Team members review the plan and check it for elements and features essential to the clinical unit goals.

The coordinator thanks everyone for their participation and reviews the charge and the accomplishments. This therapeutic garden design team has completed its work. Staff, families, and patients typically describe feeling honored to participate in the Legacy design team process. Their comments reflect how they are convinced by the demonstrated results of prior teams and also by the work of their team.

The next step is for the coordinator and the unit manager to present the project to the hospital administration for final approval. The administration then forwards the project to Legacy Foundation for fund development.

Benefits of the Design Team Process

A number of conditions are needed to achieve maximum benefits from participation:

1. A healthcare organization that promotes the satisfaction and morale of staff and that understands and values the participatory design process

2. A designer who places high value on the satisfaction of users' needs and who is skilled in the participatory process

3. Staff and other users who are willing to contribute time, expertise, and enthusiasm to the process

4. A skilled and experienced leader who can guide the process (Sommer 1983; Carpman and Grant 1993)

Landscape architect Brian Bainnson explains how he places high value on users' needs:

> I try to take an open approach to the design of healthcare gardens. It is important for me to come to the initial meeting with no preconceived notion of what the garden might look like, what materials, forms, and design elements that it will contain. This allows me to listen and find inspiration in the design from the design team and the site. When institutions are looking to select a designer, they need to understand that some designers approach a project as a way to further their own agenda. The designer's ability to be able to listen and work collaboratively is as much a design skill as knowing how to mix colors and textures of plants to achieve a pleasing end. Ego needs to be left at the door, and the designer needs to embrace the possibilities of collaborative design.
>
> With that being said, it is important to select a designer with a strong aesthetic so that they can create a unified design that can hold the sometimes disparate elements of a healthcare garden together. The designer must also possess good technical skills and understand the complexities of design and construction while knowing when and who needs to be involved in the design and engineering of the project. (Brian Bainnson, pers. comm., 2011.)

Staff groups at Legacy are sensitive to their achievements, engagement, and how they make a difference. Vi Hansen, a licensed clinical social worker, first participated in a design team in 1996 and describes the process:

> The design process for our therapeutic gardens reflected a holistic approach to care by emphasizing interdisciplinary participation in the planning phase. The process included three one-hour planning sessions that focused on specific goals, objectives and timelines. Staff with expertise in various clinical areas shared their

knowledge about specific needs of patients, families, and staff that had implications for design. This input was incorporated into the final design as a way of maximizing use and potential clinical benefits of the therapeutic garden. The process ensured that everyone was on board and had a vested interest in the outcome. (Vi Hansen, pers. comm., 2011.)

Nathan Kemalyn, MD, of the Oregon Burn Center (OBC), participated in the design team for his unit's garden in 2002. He acknowledges the remarkable needs of burn patients and their families:

These clients as well as the unit staff represent diverse users. The nature of burn injury and of burn care brings caregivers and patients into a durable relationship that exemplifies the value of teamwork. Patients, family, caregivers, and public supporters of the burn center all have perspectives, contributions, and needs that must be in alignment for ideal teamwork to occur in the therapeutic environment. It makes intuitive sense that a therapeutic garden that will be a part of the burn care environment should reflect the best aspirations of teamwork in its design and execution.

Burn patients have specific physical limitations as they work through their acute care. Beginning with their first conscious awareness, they can participate in the therapeutic garden by simply seeing it from their ICU bed. As they progress from critical care to acute care, rehabilitation, and discharge, the garden will be present as a medium with which they can interact in an evolving way as their bodies heal. For staff members, families, and friends, the burden of caring for painful, life threatening, and disfiguring wounds can be mitigated by opportunities to retreat from the battle, experience solitude, and receive new energy from the encounter with nature in the garden.

Dr. Kemalyan concludes,

The garden is an example of continual growth and regeneration; a perfect metaphor for the work occurring within the OBC. It can be a reflection of our collective hope for recovery of the whole individual in body, mind and spirit. Taking a collective approach to the garden's design promises to bind us together in its use as a restorative tool in our work. (Nathan Kemalyan, in the Case Statement for the Oregon Burn Center Garden, Emanuel Medical Center Foundation, 2002)

Environmental psychologists Rachel and Stephen Kaplan (1998) note: "The intended users often have a great deal to contribute to the planning, design, and management of their environment. Participation can lead to unique solutions that speak to local needs and fit the local context. Genuine impact can lead to greater sense of ownership, stewardship, and community. People are sensitive to signs of making a difference."

Legacy understands the benefits of the participatory design process. The process, first developed in 1991, allows for design development from the bottom up instead of the top down. Legacy selects landscape architects who place high value on the satisfaction of users' needs. These landscape architects must be knowledgeable, receptive, and highly skilled in user participation promotion.

Legacy design team members are eager to contribute time, effort, expertise, and enthusiasm to the process. Lastly, a skilled, experienced participation leader to guide the process is essential to team satisfaction and exemplary team and product results. One team member stated: "Thank you for inviting me to participate in your process to create another wonderful healing nature space." The best aspirations of teamwork are reflected in the versatility and power of the garden as a tool in the care Legacy provides.

The following case studies were modeled on the Legacy process. These professionals (an HT and landscape architects) previously participated in Legacy projects. They describe how they used elements of the model and made adjustments for their unique project, team, and setting.

CASE STUDY

Chilgok County Geriatric Hospital, Chilgok, South Korea

At Chilgok County Geriatric Hospital, horticultural therapist Kun Hyang Lee spearheaded the garden design team process. Garden goals included (1) enhancing the environment of care and support therapeutic programs, and (2) increasing client, visitor, staff, and community involvement.

Design team members included the chairman of the board and hospital staff, including maintenance staff, doctors, and nurses. Local people who work in horticulture participated with the staff of Chilgok County Agricultural Technology Service Center. Architects, landscape architects, and the horticultural therapist were present (fig. 5.3).

Meeting number one began with introductions. Education about the benefits of therapeutic gardens was followed by the therapeutic garden characteristics. Lee states,

5.3 Kun Hyang Lee, horticultural therapist, describes the benefits of therapeutic gardens to staff at Chilgok Country Geriatric Hospital, Chilgok, South Korea.
Courtesy Kun Hyang

This meeting was a very good opportunity to get together for planning a therapeutic garden in a hospital. Since there are not many therapeutic gardens in hospitals in Korea, I think this was a meaningful start and a good example for Korea's healthcare settings. The staff of the hospital did not know much about therapeutic gardens before the education session. However, staff could talk about the benefits of gardens for themselves and patients in the hospital after the education session. I feel that time for education during the meeting was very important.

Lee gives several observations about the activities:

The chairman of the board was interested in benefits for the local community through building the garden in the hospital. It was good to show pictures of well-designed therapeutic gardens as examples. It helped the people in the meeting understand and then to develop their ideas about what they wanted in their hospital garden.

Meeting number two opened with introductions, followed by discussion of therapeutic garden characteristics with an activity, followed by images of therapeutic gardens in the United States. The landscape architect gave an overview of the setting, which was followed by brainstorming the needs for the garden. Lastly, each participant completed a therapeutic garden survey, consisting of twenty questions about the garden design and preferred activities.

Lee shared other insights from this meeting:

Since the chairman of the board gathered more garden team members from the local community, there were several new members in the second meeting. I needed to give a brief presentation about the therapeutic garden characteristics focusing more on explaining benefits for seniors. After two education sessions, team members shared more questions and opinions about the garden design and activities.

Lee was able to adjust the process she learned as a Legacy HT intern and to make it work in planning sessions for a garden to serve geriatric clients in South Korea.

CASE STUDY

Returning Heroes Home Healing Garden, Warrior and Family Support Center, Brooks Army Medical Center, San Antonio, Texas

Brian Bainnson, a landscape architect with twenty-five years of experience and most recently fifteen years specializing in healthcare gardens, guided development at The Warrior and Family Support Center at Brooks Army Medical Center. The new Returning Heroes Home Healing Garden in San Antonio encompasses 20,000 square feet. The Warrior and Family Support Center provides services to soldiers and their families that complement the care they are receiving at the medical center. They may receive job training and job-placement services, family and individual counseling, and a range of recreational and social activities.

Bainnson notes that as the project was designed on a fast track without the opportunity for a normal design process, he needed to conducted telephone interviews with key personnel who would be using the garden. Once the design concepts were completed, a site visit was conducted at which he had an opportunity to meet individually with facility staff, including many of the therapists who work with soldiers. The director of nursing, an occupational therapist, a physical therapist, a social worker, a landscape architect, and others formed the design team. Design goals included creating a garden where severely wounded soldiers would engage in therapies and independent activities to assist in their rehabilitation process. Time was also spent meeting with soldiers and their families to hear their personal stories of survival and recovery, all of which helped craft the design.

Completed, the garden is now used for both passive and active therapeutic activities for individuals and small and large groups. It is a place in which soldiers can feel safe and where they can be with their families and experience normalizing activities. Bainnson knew that the dialogue with therapists, managers, and patients and their families was essential to creating a healing environment of care for all who would use the Returning Heroes Home Healing Garden. In reflecting on this project, he notes that he learned powerful new lessons from each team member and the setting. (For a case study of this garden, see chapter 13).

Harrison Medical Center, Bremerton, Washington

This project features the work of landscape architect Mark Epstein of Seattle, Washington. Under Epstein's direction, Harrison Medical Center in Bremerton formulated plans for an oncology healing garden. The design process started in June 2010, was delayed for a year, and concluded in 2011. Construction was completed in the fall of 2012. For this 2,400-square-foot garden, the design team included the foundation director, oncology managers, occupational and physical therapists, complementary therapists, spiritual caregivers, infection control specialists, the facilities director, the family of a former patient, the architect, volunteers, a community member, and the landscape architect.

Goals for the design:

1. Restoration from stress of hospital environment
2. Setting for PT, OT, and speech therapy
3. Setting for hospital public functions
4. Model for future therapeutic gardens at other organization facilities

Populations served:

1. Acute-care oncology staff, patients, and visiting families
2. Radiation-treatment patients and families

Notable in this project was an attempt to negotiate the installation of the garden by working with a contractor to value-engineer the design to keep the project within budget. This resulted in several design changes and challenges to maintaining therapeutic elements in the garden plan.

Epstein notes that he is still learning lessons from this project and shares two: The educational component at the first design team meeting is essential to retaining therapeutic design elements as the design process evolves. At Harrison, pressures to change or modify the design that would have reduced the therapeutic benefits came from the passage of time (the project was stalled for a year), the introduction of outside potential donors and artists, and a hospital project manager who was not present at the design team meetings. The educational component allowed these pressures to be deflected by the project proponents.

Epstein feels that guiding and engaging design team members, resolving complex issues, and ensuring the understanding of the many entities involved kept this project focused and moving forward. This helped team members hold the vision and maintain continued support for the team's work to get desired results.

So, How Do We Start?

This is a question often asked by designers, therapists, philanthropists, fundraisers, medical directors, and program managers. The research studies, case examples, and content presented in this chapter are intended to guide and assist in the problem solving for a wide range of healthcare settings.

Key points for designers

- Have professional training, with several years of experience and successful project work in the specialty of healthcare gardens.

- Before any project, begin networking with therapists and other healthcare providers. Learn about treatment settings and therapists' skill sets. Schedule quarterly "meet and greets" to learn from healthcare professionals. Some firms hire wetland and traffic consultants; how about HT and therapeutic garden consultants, too?

- Meet with users alone or in small groups, over the phone, or by conference calls.

- Start discussions and take notes. Listen.

- Brainstorm. Listen.

- Ask probing questions. Avoid judgment. Listen.

- Respect budget and time constraints of the staff and medical unit.

- Avoid overdesigning and the resultant complexity and costs.

- Share and learn with other design and allied health professionals.

- Conduct presentations, write, publish, and share about your garden design team process experience.

Key points for the healthcare team

- Start the conversation. Is a therapeutic garden a priority in your patient care services?

- Discussions take time. Build consensus and support. It may take one, two, or more years to build and educate a support team.

- Who are your champions on the clinical, administration, and philanthropy teams? Champions are required.

- Use professional services. A horticultural or other professional therapist (trained in HT) with several years of experience, a record of successful program development, and strong leadership skills is essential.

- Select a designer with several years of experience in this specialty and a track record of successful collaborative work.

- Select a designer who is committed to meeting clinical program goals. No egos here!

- Select a garden design team of twelve to fifteen members. Brainstorming can be difficult with more than twenty people.

- Schedule three one-hour meetings. This team's work is concluded at the end of meeting number three.

- Plan to start small, maintain quality, and learn and grow in garden development across the healthcare campus.

- The foundation team directs the fundraising.

- Start construction after funds are raised.

In conclusion, essential for the successful creation of therapeutic gardens through a participatory process are:

- A healthcare organization that promotes the satisfaction and morale of staff and understands and values the participatory design process.

- A designer who places high value on the satisfaction of users' needs and who is skilled in the participatory process.

- Staff and other users who are willing to contribute time, expertise, and enthusiasm to the process.

- A skilled and experienced participatory process leader to guide the process.

While health and human services settings are complex, financially stressed, and ever changing, there are tools, processes, and many positive examples to help inspire development of successful gardens in healthcare. Effective participatory design processes and the best aspirations of teamwork are reflected in the versatility and power of the garden as a tool in the care provided.

References

Carpman, J. R., and M. A. Grant. 1993. *Design that Cares: Planning Health Facilities for Patients and Visitors.* Chicago: American Hospital Publishing.

Cooper Marcus, C., and M. Barnes, eds. 1999. *Healing Gardens: Therapeutic Benefits and Design Recommendations.* New York: John Wiley and Sons.

Ericksen, A. 2002. "Participatory Planning and Design of a New Children's Hospital." Stockholm: International Academy for Design and Health. http://www.designandhealth.com/uploaded/documents/Publications/Papers/Aase-Eriksen-WCDH2000.pdf.

Karlin, B. E., and R. A. Zeiss. 2006. "Best Practices: Environmental and Therapeutic Issues in Psychiatric Hospital Design." *Psychiatric Services* 57 (10): 1376–78.

Kaplan, R., and S. Kaplan. 1998. *With People in Mind: Design and Management of Everyday Nature.* Washington, DC: Island Press.

NHS Employers. 2008. *Briefing 50—Staff Engagement in the NHS.* London: NHS Employers.

Sommer, R. 1983. *Social Design: Creating Buildings with People in Mind.* Englewood Cliffs, NJ: Prentice Hall.

Additional Reading

Sanders, E., and P. J. Stappers. 2008. "Co-creation and the New Landscapes of Design." *CoDesign: International Journal of CoCreation in Design and the Arts* 4 (1): 5–18.

Shoemaker, C. 2002. *Interaction by Design: Bringing People and Plants Together for Health and Well-Being*. Ames, IA: Iowa State Press.

Simson, S., and M. Straus, eds. 1998. *Horticulture as Therapy: Principles and Practices*. Binghamton, NY: Haworth Press.

CHAPTER 6

General Design Guidelines for Healthcare Facilities

THIS CHAPTER PROVIDES GENERAL DESIGN guidelines that are applicable to *all* therapeutic gardens and outdoor spaces in all categories of healthcare facilities. Subsequent chapters focus on facilities that serve specific populations (e.g., children, people with dementia, people with cancer). With the design of outdoor space at an acute-care hospital, serving a variety of patients, for example, only the general guidelines need to be consulted. For gardens that serve a specific patient group (e.g. those recovering from burns, those with Alzheimer's disease) guidelines that pertain to that population should be used (see chapters 7 through 14) *in addition* to these general guidelines. In a few cases, a guideline for a specific user group may conflict with a general guideline (e.g., in a garden for people with cancer, using scented plants is *not* advised). "Garden" and "outdoor space" are used in the singular, with the understanding (and hope) that a healthcare facility may provide more than one place where patients, visitors, and/or staff can connect with nature in meaningful ways. The term "landscape architect" (LA) includes landscape designers—those trained in the field but not certified by the Council of Landscape Architecture Registration Board (CLARB).

Most of the guidelines in this chapter are organized under either of two headings: "Required" or "Recommended." Those that are required are essential for the health and well-being of the users and may also have stronger support from research or good practice; those that are recommended have either less evidence to support them or, if there is a conflict of space or budget, are elements that are slightly less important. Guidelines are numbered for ease of reference. They are not necessarily listed in order of importance. Although repetition is avoided whenever possible, some guidelines are reiterated in subsequent chapters.

An important yet undefinable part of good design is the "magic," or inspiration, that pulls everything together and creates a space that becomes more than the sum of its parts. No guidelines can dictate this. It is up to the designer to tap into his or her sense of inspiration, empathy, and beauty for this intangible, unquantifiable, and yet essential ingredient. At the same time, it must be remembered that garden users whose health is compromised have very special needs.

The general design guidelines are organized in three sections:

A. Overarching design considerations—Apply to every component of all outdoor spaces. For example, in every facility, for every population, and for every specific physical design element, *safety, security, and privacy* must be addressed.

B. Programming and site planning considerations—Apply to the overall site and building(s), not just to individual outdoor spaces. These must be addressed early in the planning process, *before* design and detailing of the outdoor space begins.

C. Specific physical design guidelines for all therapeutic gardens—Apply to the physical components of a therapeutic garden, such as pathways, seating, planting, and the like.

Overarching Design Considerations

The following considerations apply to *every* component of *all* outdoor spaces.

Safety, security, and privacy

Outdoor spaces in healthcare facilities serve people who are in one way or another vulnerable. Just as a physician must "do no harm" under the Hippocratic oath, a designer must use a similar approach. All aspects of the outdoor space must ensure users' physical and emotional safety and security and must follow Health Insurance Portability and Accountability Act (HIPAA) protocol, just as any indoor space does. Although HIPAA is concerned primarily with the confidentiality of medical records, it also pertains to a patient's privacy within a consulting office or room and has implications for the placement of windows abutting communal space such as a garden.

Accessibility—ADA and Universal Design

All, or the majority of, outdoor spaces must conform at minimum to standards stipulated by the Americans with Disabilities Act (ADA). Furthermore, to enable safe and comfortable use for people regardless of age, ability, or preference, Universal Design (UD) principles should also be followed (see Erlandson 2008 and Sanford 2012). To create the safest and most positive experience, therapeutic gardens must go above and beyond what is legally required. For example, ADA-compliant door thresholds are often still too high for people using walking aids, wheelchairs, or IV poles to make the transition from indoors to outdoors. In some instances, especially when a garden is large enough to offer a variety of experiences (e.g., pathways to nearby woodlands), some exceptions may be made as long as the *majority* of usable spaces are compliant with the tenets of ADA and UD.

Physical and emotional comfort

Beyond being safe, all elements of the garden must be comfortable. The overall goal is to create an environment in which people feel nurtured and cared for. When people are physically and emotionally comfortable, they are likely to stay in a garden longer and benefit more from the experience. Design responses such as providing safe and comfortable places to walk and sit, creating opportunities for choice and a sense of control, enabling interaction with plants, and creating opportunities for social connection and support all facilitate physical and emotional comfort.

Positive distraction

One of the most important functions of outdoor space in a healthcare setting is to help users to "get away," both physically and emotionally, from an interior environment that may be alien, stressful, threatening, and intimidating. The garden itself, and as many elements within it as possible, should provide users with positive distractions (fig. 6.1).

Engagement with nature (biophilia)

Research has shown that connection to nature, especially in healthcare settings, is one of the most effective forms of

6.1 This prairie warbler in a cedar provides "biophilic" positive distraction as it delights the eyes and ears.
Photo from www.henrydomke.com

positive distraction. The deeper the connection to nature is, the greater the therapeutic benefits are. Plantings, natural materials, nature sounds, and the presence of water are all examples of biophilic positive distraction.

Maintenance and aesthetics

A garden and all of its components *must* be properly maintained. Broken or damaged elements such as pavement and seating, or poorly maintained plant material, can jeopardize user safety; shoddy maintenance also conveys the message that the institution "doesn't care" or is inept. A well-maintained garden, on the other hand, translates to patients, visitors, and staff that they are in an environment that supports health. Good design will always include a detailed maintenance plan and funding for ongoing care of all outdoor (as well as indoor green) spaces. See the chapter 17 for details and strategies on planting and maintenance.

Sustainability

Outdoor spaces that benefit people should also benefit the environment. Low-impact development and maintenance, ecological methods of stormwater management, and other strategies all contribute to the "triple bottom line" of social, environmental, and economic responsibility. Similar to a well-maintained garden conveying a message of care, an ecologically designed and stewarded landscape also sends a positive message (fig. 6.2). Refer to chapter 18 for more details as well as examples of built works.

Programming and Site Planning Considerations

Apply to the overall site and building, not just to individual outdoor spaces.

The following are not rigid guidelines, per se, but factors—both physical and programmatic—that will (or should) influence design.

Therapeutic gardens and other outdoor spaces function best as restorative environments when they are fully integrated into a facility's comprehensive design program from the earliest stages of the planning and design process, before design and detailing of each outdoor space begins. The two most important concepts are:

1. There is no "one size fits all." Each project is different. Site, context, programming, and other factors all directly affect design.

2. The overall "environment of care" (EOC) and all of its components must be considered simultaneously. The EOC concept is a systems thinking approach to addressing the total healthcare environment. This approach is scalable and can apply to a part of the healthcare system or to the system as a whole. The EOC includes six inextricably linked components: concepts, people, systems, layout/operation, physical environment, and implementation. Emphasis is on the relationship *between* things and not just the things themselves. In traditional design, the focus is on one component of the EOC—the physical environment. Other components are addressed by other professionals or clinical and operational leaders who rarely interact or understand the impact of their decisions on the other parts of the system. This fragmented, loosely related set of parts results in inefficiencies and mistakes or other undesirable and unintended consequences of decisions made without considering the relationships between components. With the EOC approach, all of the interwoven components are addressed simultaneously through the coordinated efforts of the design team, thus increasing the likelihood of positive outcomes (Salvatore 2003).

Other programming and site planning considerations include the following:

The interdisciplinary design team (IDT)

The IDT is defined as all of the stakeholders involved in the programming, design, construction, and ongoing management of a facility. It can include staff (from doctors to facilities personnel), administration including the board and the "C-suite," (CEO, COO, CFO), patients and their families, funders, designers, members of the community, and so on. The makeup, vision, and goals of the IDT will influence design. The IDT is essential in any healthcare garden design project to ensure that input from all of the stakeholders is included—so that everyone is "on the same page." In many cases, the best "research" or "evidence" that informs design comes from conversations with members of the IDT, especially the staff. They are often the most knowledgeable about the specific population for whom the facility or garden is being designed—who they are, what their needs are, potential challenges and obstacles, and so on. Listening and responding to the various stakeholders will not only inform design, it will also give them a sense of being a meaningful part of a project. Feelings of involvement and empowerment lead to a sense of stewardship that will continue long after the building phase has been completed. For more information on the participatory design process, see chapter 5.

6.2 Plantings at the Arizona Cancer Center in Tucson create a lush landscape while at the same time using native, drought-tolerant vegetation. Designer: Ten Eyck Landscape Architects.

Photo by Christine Ten Eyck

Evidence-based design (EBD)

Design functions most successfully when it is based on, or informed by, the best available research and evidence. If an EBD approach is used, researchers will be included on the IDT; existing evidence will be consulted to inform design; and new research will be incorporated into the project based on the goals and objectives. Researchers can assist in developing a design hypothesis and research strategy particular to the healthcare facility's vision for desired outcomes.

Composition and culture of the organization

Organizational composition (who makes up the healthcare facility) and culture—an organization's stated and unstated values, shared assumptions, policies and procedures, and official and informal organizational structure (Schein 1992)—can have a tremendous impact on design possibilities, process, execution, future use, and maintenance. Integrating access to nature and therapeutic gardens as a critical component of the overall healing environment will ideally have buy-in as early as possible from all stakeholders. A champion from senior administration can often streamline efforts for greatest success within a particular healthcare environment and culture.

Functional program

The functional requirements of a space—physical and programmatic—will (or should) form the basis of how that space is designed. The guidelines that follow below and in chapters 7 through 14 elaborate how functional needs should be addressed in any healthcare situation.

Patient or resident population

The needs of the people for whom the healthcare facility, and the garden, is specifically designed is one of the most critical factors. Many of the guidelines below address this concern.

Budget and funding

Available funding, and the source of the funds, plays a major role in up-front as well as maintenance costs. The development office should explore opportunities for philanthropy as early as possible in the design process. In some cases, design cannot begin until at least partial funding is obtained. See chapter 19 on funding for more information.

New construction vs. remodel

With new construction, the potential for incorporating meaningful access to nature is generally greater and easier than in a remodel situation. Remodels often pose challenges and the need for creative solutions such as rooftop gardens or carving out "extra" spaces within or surrounding the building. Remodeling also brings change—not always welcome—to an existing culture or the way things are done in a specific department, which may require education of staff to maximize the positive outcomes from the changes.

Geographic location

A site's specific location (country, region, site)—with factors such as amount of daylight throughout the year, climate,

orientation to sun and prevailing winds, and even the potential for natural disasters—influences design. Density is also significant. An urban site with no surrounding green space differs vastly from a greenfield site with opportunities to start from scratch or take advantage of nearby natural or cultural amenities. Even the definition of "nature" itself may need to be modified depending on cultural and regional differences, site, and availability of existing and potential nearby nature that is both visually and physically accessible. As one example, designers of a hospital remodel in a dense urban area may rely on natural light, views of sky, and indoor plants and images of nature within the building to provide "access to nature."

Programming and site planning guidelines

Required

1. **Consider the entire site as a healing environment**. From the moment patients see the healthcare facility and grounds, they should feel assured of the organization's commitment to their health and well-being. The parking lot, front entry, spaces between buildings, and individual courtyards should all convey a message of care for patients, visitors, and staff (fig. 6.3, fig. 6.4).

2. **Involve the landscape architect (LA) as part of the IDT from the beginning of the design process**. The LA's expertise is critical in general site planning, incorporating access to nature throughout the entire site, locating and orienting buildings, utilizing existing natural features, locating windows to maximize views, and siting gardens and courtyards.

3. **Use a landscape architect trained in therapeutic garden design**. Professionals trained in this specific area will have a greater knowledge of the research and precedents for implementing successful EBD. They will also be better equipped to work with the IDT and all of the project's stakeholders. Some landscape architects specialize even within healthcare design, focusing, for example, on gardens for children or people with dementia.

4. **Design for all patient types being served and for the needs of the most vulnerable population**. In a general healthcare setting (one that does not serve a specific patient population—for example, a general acute-care hospital), the outdoor environment must serve and benefit all

6.3 The green, shaded parking lot at San Diego Hospice, San Diego, California, provides physical comfort and emotional reassurance from the moment people arrive.
Photo by Naomi Sachs

6.4 Signage with planting makes a bright welcome at this hospital entry in California.
Photo by Clare Cooper Marcus

patients, as well as visitors and staff. In this case the design should first meet the needs of the most vulnerable populations (e.g., frail elderly, people with cognitive impairments, people who are immunocompromised but are still allowed to go outside).

5. **Design for health outcomes and for programs/activities that support the desired outcomes**. The design team should have a clear understanding of the desired health outcomes for garden users and also of programs and activities that may take place within the garden to support the outcomes. Is the garden meant solely for passive connection with nature, with the outcome of stress reduction and improved well-being? Is it also intended as a place for people to exercise or to participate in physical, occupational, and/or horticultural therapy? Will the garden be used for functions such as fundraisers and community events? These factors will all affect the siting and design of each space (fig. 6.5).

6. **Staff should be educated about the use and benefits** of the garden as well as in developing a protocol for patient use.

7. **For specific garden programs, use professionals appropriate for the design**. Occupational, physical, and other allied professional therapists will ideally always be involved on the IDT from the outset. When this is not the case, they should be brought in for the design of any garden space that is to have an active therapeutic component.

8. **Make every effort to provide at least one separate outdoor space that is only available to staff**. This space should be easily accessible from places where staff are most likely to take a break—lunchroom or employee dining room, for example. Because staff must be "on" for so much of the long workday, having a space where they do not have to see or interact with patients, residents, or visitors provides an essential restorative benefit. A separate garden also allows staff to meet with each other or talk on cell phones without disrupting patients or compromising privacy. In a large facility it is preferable to have several staff gardens in different locations since many staff have short breaks and do not have the time to walk far to take advantage of an outdoor space. When a separate garden is not possible, providing distinct "rooms" within a garden is all the more important to allow staff and patients/visitors to occupy separate spaces (fig. 6.6).

9. In addition to providing an outdoor space, explore opportunities to **incorporate nature indoors** through interior gardens, atria, and potted plants; views to existing nature or landscapes designed for the healthcare facility; nature art and sounds; and other "biophilic design" elements, such as natural materials and colors. All of these strategies provide benefits in addition to access to real nature, or when access to real nature is not possible (due to climate or weather conditions, patient health, or building/floor/room location) (fig. 6.7).

6.5 Occupational therapist Amy Wagenfeld works with a client in the garden. Occupational, physical, and horticultural therapists, as well as other allied professionals, should be involved in the design process from start to finish.
Courtesy of Studio Sprout; photo by Michiko Kurisu

10. Building design and garden location:

   a. **Design the building(s) so that the garden** (or the main garden, if there is more than one) **is prominently visible and accessible from the principal spaces used by the** **public inside the building** such as a lobby, waiting area, major corridor, or cafeteria (fig. 6.8).

   b. The **garden should be sited in a quiet location** to facilitate a sense of "being away." Avoid areas with

6.6 A separate garden enables staff to escape from the demands of work and from patients and visitors at the Oregon Burn Center Garden in Portland, Oregon. Designer: Quatrefoil, Inc.

Courtesy of Legacy Health

intrusive noises—such as those adjacent to traffic, loading docks, air conditioner units—that will disturb users' experience of the space as a natural, restorative environment. If such noises are unavoidable, minimize people's awareness of them through design (e.g., locating primary seating areas far away from noise or using features that mask the noise, such as a buffer wall or decorative water fountain) (fig. 6.9).

c. The **garden should not be located near food exhaust vents**. It should be **free of food or cooking odors**, as these detract from the natural aroma of plants and fresh air and may exacerbate nausea for people on certain medications.

d. In narrow **outdoor areas where windows are directly across from each other, the space should be at least thirty feet wide**. Care should be taken to **provide operable window coverings or one-way glass to protect privacy**. Where such a space is less than thirty feet wide, it may be necessary to design it as a **viewing garden**, to be looked into but not entered.

e. Where the outdoor space is limited in size, the **ratio of the height of the adjacent buildings to the width of the open space is critical**. Height-to-width ratios between 1:3 and 1:2 create a space that feels human scaled. It may also provide some shade in summer and some sun access in winter. A space that is experienced as a "light well" may

6.7 Indoor plants, gardens, and atria allow people to connect with nature at all times of the year regardless of weather or health status. The Thea and James Stoneman Healing Garden, an indoor garden at the Dana-Farber Cancer Institute, Yawkey Center for Cancer Care, Boston, Massachusetts. (See chapter 8 for a case study of this garden.) Designers: Carol R. Johnson Associates, Landscape architects; Zimmer Gunsul Frasca, Architects.

Copyright Carol R. Johnson Associates, Inc.

6.8 Sitting in the surgical intensive care unit waiting room at St. Anthony's Medical Center Heart and Surgical Pavilion, St. Louis, Missouri, feels almost like being in the garden. Project team: Interiors, Spellman Brady & Company; Architect, Cannon Design; Landscape architect, Austin Tao and Associates.
Photo by Debbie Franke

be in shade most of the time and raise issues of privacy for those in the space and those looking into it.

f. In all situations, **carefully analyze microclimate site conditions**, especially for the primary garden. Latitude and orientation will have a major effect on comfort and thus on use, as will factors such as glare and excessive heat from glass radiating from existing buildings on or adjacent to the site or from a proposed new building.

g. The primary therapeutic garden should receive a **minimum of approximately a half day (six hours) of sunlight**.

h. In a partially enclosed or courtyard garden, **building height should maximize solar access** in order to enable solar access.

i. The **primary garden should be sited to provide shelter** from prevailing winds in colder or temperate climates/seasons and to catch welcoming breezes in hot climates/seasons.

j. Regardless of garden location, the **main building entry should have a covered area with several comfortable benches or chairs** to allow protection from the elements while people wait outside. When possible, provide an **entry garden** (a garden adjacent to the main building entry), or garden elements such as potted plants, so that people feel welcome and can connect with nature immediately outside of the building.

Recommended

1. Especially in greenfield construction (new construction on an undeveloped site), **consider the site's existing positive**

6.9 This dramatic waterfall at the Edward Heart Hospital in Naperville, Illinois, successfully masks sounds from the hospital as well as nearby traffic and other noise. People sitting near the fountain can also feel that their conversations will not be overheard. Designer: Hitchcock Design Group.
Photo by Clare Cooper Marcus

6.10 The Illinois Cancer Center, Peoria, Illinois, was sited to take advantage of the existing natural scenery. The view from the treatment infusion area of a lush, green landscape benefits patients and staff. Interiors, Spellman Brady and Company; Architect, PSA Dewberry.
Photo by Debbie Franke

attributes such as views, vegetation (especially mature trees), and nearby features such as ponds, wetlands, and woods for visual and/or physical access (fig. 6.10).

2. **Provide more than one garden in more than one location**. For example, within one healthcare facility: an entry garden; a staff garden; a series of interior courtyard gardens; a patio with tables and chairs accessible from the cafeteria. Connecting some of these gardens with a **walking loop encourages physical activity** and enhances motivation to go exploring. Providing several outdoor spaces can maximize sun access at different times of the day. In the Northern Hemisphere, east-facing spaces are ideal for morning use, south-facing for use during most of the day, and west-facing for evening use in the summer. In the Southern Hemisphere, east-facing spaces are good for morning use and north-facing for most of the day.

3. **Provide more than one entrance to the garden**. A courtyard garden, for example, may be used as a pass-through for staff and/or visitors who might otherwise not have time to spend outdoors. Connecting a garden with internal circulation can also enhance walking loops (fig. 6.11).

4. **Provide balconies or terraces for patient or resident rooms**, especially if they can look out onto existing nature (mountains, woods, lake) or designed nature (garden or other landscape). In some cases, a balcony or terrace that does *not* overlook the primary therapeutic garden may be preferable, as it allows for greater privacy for both patients and garden users. This is especially important for staff gardens that need privacy.

5. **Design the building with operable windows** throughout or in some parts to allow in fresh air and nature sounds.

6.11 A nurse at the Jupiter Medical Center in Jupiter, Florida, can walk through the garden to get from one part of the building to another or to other buildings on campus. Designer: Studio Sprout.
Courtesy of Studio Sprout; photo by Connie Roy-Fisher

6.12 The Garden of Healing and Renewal in Clarkston, Michigan, serves the hospital and is also open to the community around the clock, 365 days a year. See the case study in chapter 15. Designer: Professional Engineering Associates.
Copyright Jeffrey T. Smith

Research has shown an increase in patient satisfaction when they can control their environment. This possibility will depend on state, local, or facility regulations and on the type of facility.

6. **Connect the garden to the larger community**, physically and programmatically, by providing physical access (through sidewalks, pathways, and other linkages) to nearby parks and shopping centers, and with events such as farmers markets, wellness classes, and community gatherings. See chapter 15 on healthcare facilities that connect to the community (fig. 6.12).

Specific Physical Design Guidelines for All Therapeutic Gardens

With any outdoor space in a healthcare setting, it is critical for designers to follow these guidelines. If the facility serves a specific population (say, cancer patients), the

following guidelines, as well as those appearing in chapters 7 through 15 pertaining to that specific patient group, should be followed.

General considerations

Required

1. The **garden should serve as a contrast to the indoor clinical setting**. In general, the more institutional and disconnected from nature the facility is indoors, the more important contact with nature and a general naturalistic feel is outdoors. **Consider overall layout** (e.g., curvilinear rather than rectilinear) **in addition to specific materials and plantings** (fig. 6.13).

2. **Ensure that the garden has sufficient shade, with opportunities for people to sit in sun or shade** at different times of the day and in different seasons of the year. People with certain medical conditions or on certain medications are required to stay out of the sun and will not use the garden unless they can find a place to sit in the shade. On the other hand, many visitors and staff like to step outside, even if only for a few minutes, to feel the warmth of the sun. In many climates, providing shade in hot weather (or sun in cold weather) extends the amount of time the garden can be used. Gardens are often

designed with trees as the primary source of shade. Thus, trees with the largest caliper should be specified to give maximum shade right away. Additional shade structures such as moveable umbrellas, soft or hard canopies, shade sails, gazebos, arbors, and pergolas serve as temporary or permanent elements (fig. 6.14).

3. **When a garden is not completely enclosed by the building(s), it should be adequately enclosed with fencing or a hedge**, for example. This is especially important where it abuts a road or parking. Parents need to feel assured that their children can play and not inadvertently stray out of the space (fig. 6.15).

4. Even if the garden is not completely bordered, it should **have a sense of physical enclosure** so that users experience security and privacy from what is happening outside the garden. A defined garden can also allow users to get away to a place separate from the building interior.

5. **Provide adequate wayfinding to and within the garden**. This is especially important when the garden is not immediately visible, such as with a rooftop garden, or in a building or on a campus where care delivery is spread out. Include information in staff and patient information packets and provide clear signage in multiple prominent locations

6.14 The Ulfelder Healing Garden at Massachusetts General Hospital in Boston, Massachusetts, is a rooftop garden. If not for the four feet of extra soil brought in to accommodate mature trees, this environment would have been too sunny and windy for use during much of the year. Designer: Halvorson Design Group.

Photo by Naomi Sachs

so that people are aware of the garden and can find it easily. Wayfinding within the garden can be accomplished with signage or with memorable features that are visible from most of the garden, such as a piece of artwork, a pavilion, or a gazebo (fig. 6.16).

6. **Emphasize a view that is attractive from the main garden entry**. This will entice people to explore the space and will also allow people who cannot venture far into the garden to still enjoy it.

7. Design the garden with a **legible layout that can be grasped from the main entry**.

8. **Provide a covered area and seating just outside the primary garden entrance** as a transition between indoors and outdoors (e.g., roof, canopy, or porch) to allow people to get a sense of the garden and the weather and to enable people to be outside even when they cannot or do not want to venture further. This transition area also allows people's eyes to adjust to changes in brightness (fig. 6.17).

6.16 This pergola announces the entrance to the healing garden at Advocate Hope Children's Hospital in Oak Lawn, Illinois. It also serves as a landmark for those within the garden, helping them find their way back to the entrance. Designer: Hitchcock Design Group.
Photo by Clare Cooper Marcus

6.15 This bright, sculptural fence at a children's garden at Rady Children's Hospital in San Diego, California, creates a whimsical enclosure.
Photo by Naomi Sachs

6.17 The garden on the third floor at Legacy Good Samaritan Hospital in Portland, Oregon, is visible through the window as one enters the intensive care unit (as seen here) and from within the patient rooms
Photo Courtesy of Legacy Health

6.18 The Rothschild Garden at a senior center in Evanston, Illinois, features two large raised beds and several benches along the perimeter pathway, with plantings of varying heights, forms, textures, and colors. The garden is visible through large glass windows along the hallways on all four sides of the building, bringing in natural light and providing views even when one is not outside.
Photo by Naomi Sachs

9. Create a number of **subspaces with different qualities** within the garden for people to choose from. This can foster a sense of control, and the spaces can provide settings for social support. Examples include spaces for one or two people and for a group, spaces that feel enclosed and secluded, and spaces that feel expansive and allow people to observe activity. These can be defined by planting, pathways, or structures. Seating arrangements should allow people in wheelchairs, on benches, or on chairs to easily have a conversation.

10. Design the garden, and elements in the garden, so that **wheeled mobility users or those on a gurney have an interesting sensory experience**—things to see, smell, touch, and hear at their level (fig. 6.18).

11. **Maintain an inclusive culture** to support all who use the healthcare services. If the majority of garden users are from a particular religious or cultural group, consider incorporating (as well as avoiding, when appropriate) design elements that have special significance for that group (fig. 6.19).

12. Smoking is now prohibited on most healthcare campuses. In facilities where this is not the case, **smoking must be prohibited in garden areas**. For other outdoor spaces where the facility's code does not dictate a minimum distance, smoking should not be permitted closer than 50 feet from a window or building entry. "No Smoking" signage should be attractive and discreet. In very limited instances, planned smoking areas are actually an important design element. "Going out for a smoke" may be the only motivation for a patient to get out of bed. In the process, the patient or resident gets exercise, a change of scenery, and an opportunity to connect socially with others. This is often the case in Veterans Administration (VA) and mental and behavioral health treatment facilities (see chapter 13).

Recommended

1. **Make provisions in the garden for bad weather and climatic extremes**. For example, a covered area enables people to be outdoors even in inclement weather; a buffer of wall or hedge shelters people from wind; heaters or fans warm or cool a space and extend the length of time people can use it (fig. 6.20).

2. **Create a sense of place** with plants, materials, and colors that reflect the geographic region.

3. **Provide a space and/or furniture that allows a person to lie down for a rest** (e.g., a lawn or a bench) (fig. 6.21).

6.19 This statue of Quan Yin, the goddess of compassion, is a place for people to leave offerings in the Chinese Garden, Liu Fang Yuan or Flowing Fragrance, at the Huntington Library in Pasadena, California. *Photo by Naomi Sachs*

6.20 This shady small porch with fans hanging from the ceiling adjoins the staff cafeteria at Jupiter Medical Center, Jupiter, Florida, enabling employees to be outside through much of the year, even in the rain and extreme heat. Designer: Studio Sprout. *Photo by Naomi Sachs*

4. Where appropriate, **incorporate views beyond the garden**. These can be supported by vegetative framing, location of pathways, and the placement of seating.

5. In a few places, **provide restful, naturalistic sounds** such as water and wind chimes. Pleasant sounds can sometimes mask unpleasant noises (a fountain masks the sound of nearby traffic, for example). Allow those who might be irritated by chimes, for example, or a particular water feature, to find a place out of earshot. Wind chimes should be located away from the building so they don't disrupt residents' sleep.

6. Where space permits, **provide an area such as a flat lawn or patio** large enough to be used for informal gatherings, group activities, recreation, or programmed events (fig. 6.22).

7. Spaces for exercise and therapy should be **located away from the main traffic areas** to give participants privacy. **Spaces for therapy should be located as close to the indoor therapy clinic**(s) as possible and should be designed by integrating elements that support physical, occupational, and speech therapies outdoors.

8. **Locate a destination point**—a pergola or gazebo, for instance—a short distance from the entrance to encourage people to move into the garden.

Visual access

Visual access to outdoor space, and especially to a therapeutic garden, is critical. People are much more likely to visit a garden that they can see. Furthermore, windows provide visual access to nature and natural light even when people cannot go outside (fig. 6.23).

6.21 Nurses take a much-needed break from work-related stress at Jupiter Medical Center in Jupiter, Florida. Designer: Studio Sprout.
Courtesy of Studio Sprout, photo by Connie Roy-Fisher

6.22 The small lawn in the Olson Family Garden at St. Louis Children's Hospital in St. Louis, Missouri, is used for many different activities—free play, picnics, and programmed events throughout the year. See chapter 7 for a case study of this garden. Designer: EDAW.
Photo by Gary Wanger

6.23 This naturalistic stream is visible through the glass doors and windows at the end of the hallway, as well as from a large waiting room. One nurse commented, "This is the first place I've worked where I felt like I'm outside in a garden all the time!" Smilow Cancer Hospital at Yale-New Haven Hospital, New Haven, Connecticut. Designer: Towers Golde. *Photo by Naomi Sachs*

Required

1. Ensure that the garden entrance is easy to see from inside and that doors are glass or have glass panels in or beside them that allow people to check out the garden and the weather before venturing outside (fig. 6.24).

2. Ensure that the garden can be, if necessary, **easily monitored by staff**.

3. **Orient windows and indoor seating to ensure that the garden can be easily viewed and enjoyed by people sitting inside**. Consider views of the garden from more than one location and from more than one level (waiting area, cafeteria, patient rooms, or staff break room).

4. In patient or resident rooms that overlook the garden or other views of nature, **windowsills should be above grade**,

6.24 The Meditation Garden at Banner Gateway Medical Center in Gilbert, Arizona, is easily visible through large glass doors and windows. The elegant etched sign on the door invites people outside.
Photo by Naomi Sachs

6.25 Even on a rainy day, patients can enjoy a view of the garden while lying in bed.
Photo by Naomi Sachs

and no more than 3 feet above the floor. When possible, these rooms should be **designed so that a patient can see out of the window while lying in bed** without having to turn his or her head to one side (fig. 6.25).

5. **Provide aesthetic lighting** that allows people to view the garden from indoors after dark (fig. 6.26).

Physical access

Gardens should be easy to get to and transitions between indoors and outdoors should be smooth.

Required

1. **Ensure that doors to the garden are easy to operate**, preferably with an automatic door opener. In assisted-living facilities where residents could reach outdoor areas using automatic door openers, they spent significantly more time walking outside than in facilities without them (Rodiek 2011). If automatic door openers are not an option, doors should be light enough to be easily opened and should close gradually to accommodate those who are moving slowly.

2. Provide **flat, smooth thresholds and entryways** to the garden for ease of those using wheeled mobility devices, walking aids, strollers, or IV poles. A multiregional study found that the amount of time spent outdoors by assisted-living residents nearly tripled where door thresholds were easier to cross (Rodiek and Lee 2009).

3. **Discuss with staff which patients or residents may be allowed to go out into the garden unsupervised** and under what circumstances. Educate visitors and families on the parameters for taking their loved ones out to the garden.

Recommended

1. **Keep doors to the garden unlocked at all times**. If this is not possible, keep the garden open at regular hours, with hours posted near the garden entrance.

2. Keep the garden **open in all weather and all seasons**.

3. Keep the garden **open at night**. See guidelines below for lighting.

4. Provide **signage at or near the garden entry** that invites people to use the space and offers pertinent information about it—hours/seasons that the garden is open, purpose of the garden, and a garden plan, for example (fig. 6.27).

6.26 The Scottsdale Healthcare Healing Garden in Scottsdale, Arizona, is open around the clock, 365 days a year. Attractive night lighting can be seen from the hospital entrance and main lobby, an invitation to enjoy the garden. Designers: Ten Eyck Landscape Architects, Gensler Architects. *Photo by Nick Merrick*

6.27 Clear, attractive signage at Edward Heart Hospital in Naperville, Illinois, lets people know that they may use the garden, and at what times. *Photo by Clare Cooper Marcus.*

5. Provide **clear signage about how doors open** and whether they open in or out. This reduces insecurity and confusion.

6. In areas with serious **insect problems**—mosquitoes, flies, or gnats—provide **screening around the entrance area**.

7. Consider giving patients and their families **restaurant beepers or a way to be texted on their cell phones** to inform them when it is time for their appointment or when loved ones are out of surgery.

Pathways
Required

1. The **primary pathway should be flat**, with no steps and a grade no greater than 2 percent.

2. Cross slopes on primary pathways should be **no greater than 2 percent**.

3. The **primary pathway should be at least 7 feet** wide and should have **passing areas/nodes every 25 feet**.

4. Provide **frequent and adequate resting spots**.

5. Provide **appropriate traction** on primary pathways to enable full, safe, and easy access to most of garden.

6. To prevent canes, crutches, wheels of IV poles, or spiky high heels from becoming trapped, ensure that **control joints on paving units and concrete are no wider than 1/8 inch** and without beveled or rounded edges.

7. Provide **curbs or raised edges along the primary path** to make navigating the garden safer for those using wheelchairs and walkers and to prevent washout from planting beds.

8. **Curvilinear pathways** are more easily navigable for people in wheelchairs and walkers. Because of their naturalistic form, they may also be visually preferable to straight paths with sharp corners (fig. 6.28).

9. **Minimize glare on all path surfaces**. Consider tinted concrete, stabilized decomposed granite, or something similar. Some populations—including people on certain medications, elderly people, and people with sensory challenges and traumatic brain injuries—are highly sensitive to glare.

10. **Minimize extreme contrasts of dark and light on the ground plane**. For example, arbors that cast dark, slatted shadows onto a pathway can cause "visual cliffing," a phenomenon in which dark areas of pavement are perceived as changes in grade such as steps or holes. Especially common with older

6.28 Anne's Garden at Northeast Georgia Medical Center, Gainesville, Georgia, comprises many components of a successful healing garden: a rich variety of plants and other sensory stimuli, including a water feature; a sense of enclosure; and curvilinear pathways of tinted concrete, with benches spaced at comfortable locations along the route. One would certainly experience a sense of "getting away" in this garden. Designer: The Fockele Garden Company.

Copyright The Fockele Garden Company

people and people with traumatic brain injury and other sensory processing disorders, cliffing is emotionally unsettling and can lead to falls as people try to step over or around the perceived grade change (fig. 6.29).

11. To mitigate the "fishbowl" effect, **ensure that pathways and plantings provide garden users adequate privacy** from windows looking onto the space.

12. Similarly, **provide adequate privacy for those inside rooms adjacent to the garden**. This is particularly important where patient or treatment room windows overlook the garden.

13. Organize pathways to guide people through the space in a way that provides a **variety of experiences** (enclosed and open, shady and sunny, or changing vistas, for example).

14. When designing bench pads next to paths, **provide enough space for a wheelchair user** in addition to the bench.

Recommended

1. If the garden is large enough, **maximize choices and opportunities to explore by providing a hierarchy of paths** that offer different routes, lengths, and destinations.

2. For **secondary pathways, consider providing increasing levels of difficulty** (with surface material or grade changes) to allow for exercise and a variety of experiences. Consult with

physical or occupational therapists on staff, as they know what their client population needs and is capable of.

3. In very large areas, **provide clear wayfinding signage** that enables users to find their way through the space and back to the building (fig. 6.30).

4. Consider **providing distance markers** along the pathway so that a person—for example, a staff member or someone recovering from surgery—can judge how far he or she walks each day (fig. 6.31).

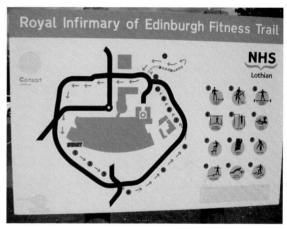

6.30 Fitness trail signage marks an exercise route around the medical buildings at the Royal Infirmary of Edinburgh, Edinburgh, Scotland. *Photo by Clare Cooper Marcus*

6.29 Shadows from the overhead trellises create strong contrasting lines that can be confusing. People with poor vision or sensory processing disorders often read them as changes in grade. *Photo by Clare Cooper Marcus*

6.31 The primary path in the garden at Randall Children's Hospital in Portland, Oregon, provides an easy gauge for people to measure walking distance. *Photo by Clare Cooper Marcus*

5. Where the site permits, **provide a pathway(s) that connects to natural (woodlands, wetlands, meadow) or built/cultural features** (other buildings on campus or a nearby downtown area) on or adjacent to the site. Ensure adequate signage at the beginning and end of all pathways, as well as along the way (fig. 6.32).

6. **Labyrinths** have become increasingly popular in healthcare settings. The classical labyrinth consists of a continuous path that winds in circles into a center and out again. This basic form dates from antiquity and is intended for contemplative walking. A labyrinth is sometimes erroneously referred to as a maze, which consists of a complex system of pathways between tall hedges, with the purpose of getting people lost. The aim of a maze is playful diversion, whereas the aim of the labyrinth was, and is, to offer the user a walking path of quiet reflection. Unless the garden is quite large, it is not advisable to include any form of labyrinth, since it takes up a large amount of (usually unsheltered) space and may be used only occasionally. However, if a labyrinth is being considered, the following guidelines should be used:

a. The classical labyrinth consists of eleven, seven, or five concentric circles. The path of the eleven-circuit labyrinth is 860 feet long and thus *should not* be considered for a healthcare garden. Walking that far would likely tax the energy of patients and the time of visitors or staff. The **seven- or five-circuit labyrinth is more appropriate**, both in terms of the length of the path and the overall area required.

b. People walking a labyrinth are in a contemplative, introspective mood and do not want to be stared at. **Site the labyrinth in a secluded location** out of sight of other garden users and nearby windows.

c. Since some people view the process of walking a labyrinth to be a spiritual experience, **site it where others will not be forced to walk across it** to get from one destination to another.

d. Since many people may be unfamiliar with the purpose of a labyrinth, provide **information nearby indicating how to walk the path** (fig. 6.33).

6.32 Healthcare facilities should take advantage of nearby amenities. A nature trail is accessible from Bremerton Naval Hospital in Bremerton, Washington.
Photo by Clare Cooper Marcus

6.33 This labyrinth at St. Joseph Memorial Hospital, Santa Rosa, California, is appropriate for a healthcare setting. The walking route is relatively short (seven-circuits), and vegetative screening and an absence of overlooking windows ensures privacy. A simple sign explains its use.
Photo by Clare Cooper Marcus.

Seating
Required

1. The **majority of seats should have backs and arms** to provide comfort and assist in sitting down and getting back up (fig. 6.34).

2. **Seating material should not retain excessive heat or cold** (as do, for example, steel, stone, plastic, and concrete), which would make it unpleasant or even dangerous in certain seasons and weather conditions. As most people associate wooden seating with a garden, this is often the best choice.

3. Especially in rainy climates, **seating should be designed so that it does not permit water to pool** and can easily be wiped dry after a rain shower.

4. **Seating materials should not produce glare**. Avoid aluminum, white, and other bright and reflective surfaces.

5. Provide some **moveable seating that is light enough to move yet sturdy enough to prevent tipping**. Moveable seating enables people to manipulate their surroundings, thus providing choice, a sense of control, and opportunities for socializing in small or large groups. Sturdiness is important for those experiencing weakness or lack of stability since they need to be able to move a chair but also feel secure that when they push up to standing the chair will not tip over.

6. Provide **seating options for a person alone, or for two or possibly three** people, in semiprivate locations. When, for example, someone receives a poor prognosis and wants to talk with a loved one, or a nurse is stressed from work and wants to eat lunch alone, semiprivate niches are much sought after and appreciated (fig. 6.35).

7. Provide **some seating for groups larger than two**, such as a combination of fixed and moveable seats that can be arranged for any size group. This can serve large groups of visitors or a staff group having an informal meeting outdoors (fig. 6.36).

8. Place the majority of **fixed seating with something—planting, a wall, or a hedge, for example—behind it**. The theory of "prospect and refuge" suggests that people feel most comfortable in this situation, possibly due to evolutionary memories of living on the protective forest edge and looking out over a savannah. (See chapter 3 for more details.)

9. Locate **seating at nodes no greater than twenty-five feet apart** along the main path system to allow people to rest.

6.34 Wooden benches with arms are comfortable and allow people who are unsteady to sit down and get up more easily. The design of the Wellspring line by Landscape Forms was based on research about what furniture would be safest and most comfortable for all users. Note that the seating is still light enough to move, allowing users control over their environment.
Photo by Clare Cooper Marcus

10. Provide **tables where people can eat lunch or do paperwork outdoors**. Provide some tables that are fixed and sturdy and some that are smaller and moveable. Include attractively accessible tables, and be sure to allow space for wheelchairs. Consider installing a table adjacent

6.35 Chairs for two in the Graham Garden at Saanich Community Hospital, Victoria, British Columbia. Designer: LeFrank & Associates.
Photo by Deborah LeFrank

to a seating wall and leaving one side open to accommodate wheelchairs (fig. 6.37).

Recommended

1. Ensure that the **near view from all seating is attractive and visually interesting** (planting or other landscape feature).

2. Provide a **variety of views**—up close and distant—from some seating areas (fig. 6.38; see also fig. 6.37).

3. Additionally, place some **seating where there is activity for people to watch**.

4. While fixed and moveable seating is essential, also consider providing **supplementary seating options** such as seat walls atop or next to raised beds.

5. Provide several **chaise longues**. Tired visitors or stressed staff find these especially relaxing for a rest or a nap (fig. 6.39).

6. Provide **durable, stain resistant cushions or fabric seats** for benches or chairs. If possible, store in an accessible waterproof container within or nearby the garden (fig. 6.40).

Planting

Below are a few general design guidelines related to planting design and material. Refer to chapter 17 for a more comprehensive list of guidelines.

6.36 A staff meeting takes place under an arbor at Jupiter Medical Center in Jupiter, Florida. Designer: Studio Sprout.
Courtesy of Studio Sprout; photo by Connie Roy-Fisher

6.37 A table in the courtyard at McKay Dee Hospital in Ogden, Utah, provides a restorative view of the fountain and park beyond. Designers: HKS Architects, Design West.
Photo by Chris Garcia

Required

1. **Provide a ratio of approximately 7:3 "softscape" (plants) to "hardscape" (paved ground plane, steps, walls).** This ensures that the overall image is of a garden rather than a predominantly hard-surfaced plaza. Research indicates that people gain emotional and physical benefit from viewing or being in nature-dominated spaces—even for as little as five to ten minutes (Ulrich 1999). Although there are various ways of calculating the proportion of green in a garden, probably the simplest is to consider the amount of planting at or near ground level— shrubs, herbaceous plants, groundcover, and grass (fig. 6.41).

2. Ensure that planting design and material **provide a rich, multisensory experience** (seasonal variety, color/texture combinations, fragrance, wildlife habitat) so that no matter the season or time of day, there is always something to engage a person's attention.

3. Incorporate **planting that offers "fascination" and sensory engagement**, such as ornamental grasses that move in the breeze, trees that create changing shade patterns or have interesting bark, or unusual flowers (fig. 6.42).

4. Utilize plant material to **shape space within the garden** by creating subspaces, canopies, and privacy screening.

5. Maximize the use of **low-maintenance and resilient plants**.

Recommended

1. Where possible, **incorporate mounded or sloped beds** that increase visibility from a seated or prone position.

6.40 Comfortable seats with cushions situated around a fountain and shaded by a large cloth canopy provide a relaxing outdoor setting for military personnel being treated at the Palo Alto Veterans Administration Hospital, Palo Alto, California.
Photo by Clare Cooper Marcus

6.38 The Thea and James Stoneman Healing Garden at the Dana-Farber Cancer Institute, Yawkey Center for Cancer Care, Boston, Massachusetts, has many views indoors within the atrium garden and also provides an expansive view of the Boston skyline. (See the case study in chapter 8 for more details.) Designers: Carol R. Johnson Associates Landscape Architects, Zimmer Gunsul Frasca, Architects.
Photo by Naomi Sachs

6.41 Research indicates that people gain emotional and physical benefit from viewing or being in nature-dominated spaces—even for as little as five to ten minutes. This garden is a good example of a plant-dominated landscape. For more information on the rain gardens and other green landscaping measures at Kent Hospital's Breast Center in Warwick, Rhode Island, see chapter 18. Designer: Thomas Benjamin, Wellnesscapes.
Photo courtesy of Thomas Benjamin, Wellnesscapes.com, on behalf of Kent Hospital

2. **Incorporate vegetation growing at multiple heights** (e.g., at grade, overhead vines and trees, hedges or planted walls, or raised beds) for a variety of sensory experience so that everyone has the opportunity to see, touch, smell, listen to, and even taste plants (fig. 6.43).

3. If structures around the garden are tall, **use trees that reduce the scale of buildings**. This will also ensure that **windows on upper floors have a view onto greenery**.

6.39 A playful set of chaises longues at the Women's Garden, Banner Gateway Medical Center in Phoenix, Arizona.
Photo by Naomi Sachs

6.42 Purple coneflower and native grasses delight the senses.
Photo from www.henrydomke.com

4. **Use plants from the local ecosystem** to reduce maintenance, provide a sense of place, and strengthen the emotional connection to the natural environment (fig. 6.44).

Utilities

Required

1. **Provide ample storage** for maintenance equipment in or very near the garden.

2. **Provide trash and recycling receptacles**, especially near benches and at the entrance. Receptacles should be attractive and must be emptied regularly.

3. **Provide hose bibs nearest areas that will require hand watering.** If watering is part of physical, occupational, horticultural, or other therapies, consult with staff therapists to determine locations.

4. **Provide at least one emergency phone** within the garden.

6.43 The healing garden at the Baltimore Washington Medical Center in Glen Burnie, Maryland, has many levels for people to enjoy, while at the same time providing a sense of safe enclosure. The garden is also viewable from the infusion therapy wing of the cancer center. Designer: Mahan Rykiel Associates, Inc.
Photos by Mitro Hood, courtesy of TKF Foundation

6.44 The yellow blossoms of *Hesperaloe* play off of the yellow fence screens in Scottsdale Healthcare Healing Garden in Scottsdale, Arizona. Designers: Ten Eyck Landscape Architects, Gensler Architects.
Photo by Bill Timmerman

6.45 Drinking fountains at the Chicago Botanic Garden in Glencoe, Illinois.
Photo by Naomi Sachs

6.46 Avoid water features that might be tempting to children when left unattended.
Photo by Naomi Sachs

Recommended

1. **Provide electrical outlets** and possibly an option for outdoor cooking, especially in areas designated for programmed activities.

2. **Provide universally accessible drinking fountains** in or close to the garden (fig. 6.45).

3. Ensure that **restrooms are located near the garden**.

Lighting

1. **Provide aesthetic lighting** that extends views to the garden, including from indoors, after dark.

2. **Ensure that all pathways are adequately and evenly illuminated** so that visitors can safely enjoy the garden at night.

3. **Ensure that lighting does not shine into patient or resident rooms**.

4. Ensure that all light fixtures, especially path lights and uplighting, are **not tripping hazards and will not shine into people's eyes** when they are in the garden.

5. Provide **electrical outlets adjacent to structures or trees** that could accommodate seasonal lighting.

Water features

Water features can be important components of a therapeutic garden. They provide positive distraction, something soothing or interesting to look at and listen to, a destination to aim for, an assist in wayfinding, and an attraction for wildlife.

Consider providing one, if not more. For all water features, consider the following:

1. Minimize slipping and tripping hazards by ensuring that **wind-borne spray does not make nearby pathways wet or impassible**.

2. **Address infection-control issues**. This is especially important for facilities serving patients who are immunocompromised (those undergoing chemotherapy and people with AIDS, for example). The landscape architect should **connect early with the infection-control officer and the facilities manager** to learn about regulations and protocol. *It is critical that all water features be designed and installed for easy routine maintenance*. A **reliable maintenance plan** must be in place. Fountains that **spray should be avoided**, as they are more likely to transmit airborne bacteria, such as *Legionella*. For more information about infection control, visit the Therapeutic Landscapes Network website at www.healinglandscapes.org.

3. **Consider a water feature's interactive potential—both welcome and unwelcome—in its design and location**. People (especially children) will want to interact with water (touch, put things into, climb into, play in). In some cases, this can be encouraged. In others, direct contact may be unsafe and/or impractical (fig. 6.46).

4. The water feature should **engage more than one sense** (sight, sound, and even touch, when appropriate) (fig. 6.47).

5. **Some seating should be located near the water feature** so that people can enjoy it up close (fig. 6.48).

6.47 A girl runs her hand along the waist-high water feature at the Coastal Maine Botanical Garden's Lerner Garden of the Five Senses, Boothbay, Maine. Designer: EDAW.
Copyright AECOM; photo by Dixi Carrillo

6. The **sound should have a calming or soothing effect**—for example, reminiscent of a natural feature such as a small creek or waterfall—rather than a potentially jarring effect (such as a loud, intermittent pulsing that can be irritating and has no counterpart in nature or a trickling that sounds like the flow of urine).

7. The water feature **should be attractive at all times of year**, including when it is empty. For cold climates, it should be pleasing to look at when the water is drained or frozen over.

In hot, dry climates, water shortages sometimes require decorative water features to be shut off. Malfunction or maintenance may also require the water feature to be shut off from time to time (fig. 6.49).

Other garden elements

All of the following are recommended rather than required. However, the best practices listed below should be adhered to for any of the features used.

6.49 This tiled fountain at Rady Children's Hospital in San Diego, California, is beautiful even without water.
Photo by Naomi Sachs

1. Incorporate one or more of the following **elements that allow people to actively engage with the garden**:

    a. **Fun or whimsical features** that may elicit a smile (fig. 6.50).

    b. **Plant labels with information** such as botanical (Latin) and common name, country of origin, historic use, and symbolism. Looking at plants and their labels provides a welcome distraction and encourages conversation. However, too many labels and other text (interpretive signage, donor

6.50 These cheerful, hand-painted rocks set in the planting bed are a sweet surprise to someone walking along the adjacent path.
Photo by Naomi Sachs

6.51 Plant labels provide information and a deeper engagement with the plants. They also often spark conversation. Chicago Botanic Garden, Glencoe, Illinois.
Photo by Naomi Sachs

6.52 At the Ulfelder Garden at Massachusetts General Hospital, Boston, Massachusetts, a pot full of small white river rocks stands at the garden entrance with a sign that reads "Touch Stones—Please take one with you." Visitors often take a stone and hold it while they are in the garden, and then take it with them when they leave. This is one of the most popular features of the garden, and the stones are replenished on a regular basis.
Courtesy of designcOnsulTation; photo by Amy Wagenfeld, PhD, OTR/L, CAPS

recognition, and the like) may intrude on people's sense of "getting away" through immersion in nature (fig. 6.51).

c. **Other educational or interpretive material**, such as a garden plan, or information about the history of the site or area. This information can be mounted within the garden, at the garden entrance, or on laminated pages as a guide.

d. **Features or materials that can be moved, manipulated, changed**, or perhaps even taken home. For example, small stones that can be balanced or a container where people are invited to place flowers or fallen leaves (fig. 6.52).

e. **Features that offer visiting children opportunities for exploration and play** ("rollable" slopes or "jumpable" rocks or ledges). Note that in healthcare facilities that do not specifically serve children, the degree of play allowed or encouraged will depend heavily on the population being served and the program of the garden.

f. A **visitors book** where people can record their feelings about the garden. Comments from visitor's books can also be a way for a facility to see people's positive feedback and are often useful in providing evidence to support the funding of continued maintenance, upgrades and additions, horticultural therapy staff, and even more gardens throughout the facility.

g. A **garden journal** that could be sold in the gift shop for journaling, learning about plants, or reflection.

2. **For four-season interest, consider other elements in addition to plantings** (e.g., brightly colored benches, mosaic tiles, pots, or lighting). This is especially important in climates where plants go dormant and there is not much to see during winter months (fig. 6.53).

3. **To recognize donors, provide unobtrusive opportunities** within the garden or indoors near the entry to the garden.

4. With all artwork, including sculpture, **avoid cognitively dissonant or ambiguous works**. People experiencing stress tend to project their negative feelings onto other people or objects in the environment (for more on emotional congruence, see chapter 3). An ambiguous piece of art may be interpreted in a quite different way than the artist intended. Abstract, challenging, and ambiguous artwork that may be appropriate in a museum or gallery is not appropriate in a healthcare environment. Representational art and work that is appropriate to the culture or region are preferable (fig. 6.54 and fig. 6.55).

6.53 This tiled wall in the Healing Garden at St. Joseph Memorial Hospital, Santa Rosa, California, provides visual and tactile interest, even when plants are dormant or not flowering.

Photo by Clare Cooper Marcus

6.54 Sculptures, seating, and any other structures in the garden should be carefully thought through. These seals were installed at a children's garden where they beg to be touched and played on. However. . .

6.55 . . . they become too hot in the sun!

Photos by Naomi Sachs

6.56 Every opportunity should be provided to enable patients, visitors, and staff to connect with nature. Our biophilic selves find joy and solace in the connection with other living things.
Photo from www.henrydomke.com

5. Provide **opportunities to observe wildlife** (fish ponds or plants that attract butterflies, for example). Note that birds and birdsong will naturally come into the garden, but due to infection-control issues, birds should not be actively encouraged (through feeders, birdhouses, and birdbaths) into outdoor spaces of, for example, acute-care hospitals.

They are appropriate in others settings, such as facilities for the frail elderly, for those with Alzheimer's and other forms of dementia, and hospice facilities. Designers should work with the infection-control officer and facilities manager to determine design options and maintenance strategies (fig. 6.56).

References

Cooper Marcus, C., and M. Barnes, eds. 1999. *Healing Gardens: Therapeutic Benefits and Design Recommendations*. New York: John Wiley and Sons.

Erlandson, R. F. 2008. *Universal and Accessible Design for Products, Services, and Processes*. Boca Raton, FL: CRC Press.

Rodiek, S. 2011. "Increasing Physical Activity through Access to Nature." Presented at Environments for Aging annual conference, March 21, Atlanta, GA.

Rodiek, S., and C. Lee. 2009. "Elderly Care: Increasing Outdoor Usage in Residential Facilities." *World Health Design*. www .worldhealthdesign.com/External-space-Increasing-outdoor-usage-in-facilities-for-older-adults.aspx.

Salvatore, A. (2003). "Changing the Standards." *Interiors and Sources*, 7: 82–84.

Sanford, J. A. 2012. *Universal Design as a Rehabilitation Strategy*. New York: Springer Publishing Company.

Schein, E. H. 1992. *Organizational Culture and Leadership*. 2nd ed. San Francisco: Jossey-Bass.

Ulrich, R. S. 1999. "Effects of Gardens on Health Outcomes: Theory and Research." Pp. 27–86 in *Healing Gardens: Therapeutic Benefits and Design Recommendations*, edited by C. Cooper Marcus and M. Barnes. New York: John Wiley and Sons.

CHAPTER 7

Children's Hospital Gardens

Research

The research summarized in chapter 3 illustrating positive health outcomes from contact with nature can also be inferred to be applicable to children. The potential benefits to a sick child of going outdoors include getting away from the hospital interior, feeling fresh air and sunshine, hearing birds and water, experiencing greater freedom and a sense of control in a more familiar environment, relating to staff and family in a more relaxed way, perhaps interacting with a favorite pet brought from home, and potentially feeling less anxiety, stress, and pain (fig. 7.1).

This chapter will discuss the positive effects of gardens at children's hospitals, beginning with summaries of postoccupancy evaluations (POEs) at children's hospitals in San Diego, California; St. Louis, Missouri; and three cities in Texas.

The **Leichtag Family Healing Garden** at San Diego Children's Hospital (now known as Rady Children's Hospital) is a 40 × 100 foot garden that was completed in 1997. The garden features a large sculpted metal dinosaur at the entrance, a ceramic tile sea-horse fountain, a wall with glass insets representing the signs of the zodiac, a 14-foot-tall windmill with birds that "fly" within the structure, and a shadow wall incorporating cutouts of animals. Flowers and plants were selected for their medicinal values, and the garden is enclosed by curvilinear, brightly colored walls. Ground surfaces include small "islands" of grass surrounded by concentric ovals of concrete in shades of teal, green, and blue reminiscent of the ocean. Ceramic sea creatures decorate the walls, and the overall feel is that of a Southern California beach scene. The garden is in a slightly out of the way location at the back of the hospital.

During a POE that included thirty-two hours of observation, two hundred people were recorded using the garden (Whitehouse et al. 2001). Most were families who relaxed while their children explored the garden. The majority appeared to be healthy, active siblings of patients, or were outpatients themselves. Staff used the garden on breaks and on rare occasions brought children to the garden. Surprisingly, nearly half of all users spent less than five minutes there. This seemed to be due in part to the lack of interesting, interactive

things for children to do, and in part due to lack of shade. Interviews revealed that adult users would have liked more trees, greenery, and shade, while two-thirds of children wanted "more things to do." Indeed, while the colorful aesthetic initially attracted children, after they had examined and touched the fountain (a favorite feature), many craved a more structured play area. Very few hospitalized children were brought to the garden because most were too sick. Some of the staff who worked with bereaved families or emotionally disturbed children commented on the need for more places of privacy or refuge (fig. 7.2).

However, the majority of adults interviewed endorsed going to the garden to rest and get away from stress, and 90 percent reported a positive change of mood after spending time there (refreshed and more positive). Half said the garden increased their overall satisfaction with the hospital; three-quarters recommended that others visit the garden and said that it is important for hospitals to have healing gardens. A father with an infant in intensive care said, "This is a better place to wait than the waiting room. We couldn't stand being in there, wondering if she'd make it. This is quiet and peaceful. . . ." Another parent noted, "It makes me more happy. I think it is the playful colors, the feeling of being in a completely separate and unique place. . . ." A physician commented, "It makes me feel more positive, relaxed, serene, even though I can only be out here for a few minutes. It seems so removed from my work in the hospital."

Surprisingly, interviews inside the hospital revealed that 95 percent of respondents had never been to the garden (some didn't know they were "allowed"); and almost half did not know it was there. As a result of the study, plentiful signs in English and Spanish were added inside the hospital. An additional space for children was added on the roof of a new building. This was designed as more of a playground than a garden and fulfilled many of the wishes expressed in the 2001 study for a place where children would have more things to do.

A later study at the same hospital's hematology-oncology unit considered the use of three gardens (Sherman et al. 2006). The largest (6,279 sq. ft.) garden—the Garden of Dreams—was surrounded by patient rooms and received

7.1 A little girl caring for the plants in the children's garden at Randall Children's Hospital, Portland, Oregon. Designers: Johnson Design Studio; Gretchen Vadnais; Quatrefoil, Inc.
Courtesy of Legacy Health

the most use, with a child-height water feature—the River of Dreams—and a mosaic bird's nest sculpture being the most popular features (fig. 7.3). The Friendship Garden, intermediate in size (4,625 sq. ft.) and surrounded by a playroom and offices, had many child-friendly features, including a popular play house, fountain pool, and child-height bronze rabbit. The smallest of the gardens, the Buggy Garden (1,102 sq. ft.), was surrounded by patient rooms and a corridor. It included a mosaic fountain and caterpillar-shaped bench (fig. 7.4).

Significantly (but consistent with other studies of children's hospital gardens), many more adults used these gardens (88 percent), than children (9 percent) or teens (3 percent). Just over half the users of all three gardens spent less than a minute there, using it to walk through. These were usually staff. Adult

visitors spent more time sitting, talking, relaxing, and walking around the gardens. The low incidence of child use may be due to the fact that many oncology patients receive outpatient care, and inpatients may have been too sick to go outside.

The 24 percent of staff who used the gardens on breaks for eating, socializing, and relaxing (rather than just walking through) overwhelmingly favored the Friendship Garden, where there was no direct access from patient rooms, presumably because they would be less likely to be interrupted by patients or their parents. This is further evidence for the importance of staff-only gardens.

All three gardens are fairly small and narrow, so it is not surprising that in all of them, the majority of patient room windows looking into the garden had their blinds drawn. This further supports the recommendation that there be adequate

7.2 While Leichtag Family Garden at Rady Children's Hospital, San Diego, California, was initially attractive to users, most did not stay long and some complained of the lack of places of privacy or refuge. Designer: Delaney Cochran & Castillo.

7.3 A crane sculpture—an attractive feature in the Garden of Dreams. Designer: Landscape architect, Michael Kato; Artist/sculptors, Kim Emerson and T.J. Dixon.
Photo by Clare Cooper Marcus

7.4 The Buggy Garden, Rady Children's Hospital, San Diego, California.
Photo by Clare Cooper Marcus

privacy between hospital gardens and adjacent rooms, for the benefit of people inside as well as for garden users. It also suggests that one-way glass or other privacy treatment be used in windows where a narrow space is inevitable.

A sample of twenty-two staff, visitors, and patients was asked about current levels of anxiety, sadness, anger, worry, fatigue, and pain using visual analogue scales—half within the gardens and half within the hospital. All scores were lower in the gardens, particularly those demonstrating pain, worry, and sadness (Sherman et al. 2006).

In a POE of the **Olson Family Garden** at St. Louis Children's Hospital, St. Louis, Missouri, a questionnaire survey of a random sample of seventy-two family members and caregivers revealed that only 21 percent did not know about the garden, a much lower percentage than at the Leichtag garden, probably because at the St. Louis hospital the garden is mentioned in orientation literature, is featured on a map, appears on commercials aired on hospital room televisions, and is often recommended to families by nurses and social workers (Sorensen 2002).

Family members of children with short-term stays were more likely to visit, and all of those who visited were more likely to visit when the patient was otherwise occupied (e.g., during surgery, sleeping, with another family member). Those who reported benefiting from garden visits gave one or more of the following reasons: peaceful and relaxing (36 percent), change of scenery/chance to get outside without leaving the hospital (22 percent), beautiful atmosphere (17 percent), fresh air and sunshine (15 percent). Nearly one-half reported having exceptionally positive experiences in the garden, including enjoying various garden elements (plants, fish, water features, and telescopes) (35 percent), social connections (conversations, picnics, seeing other people in similar predicaments) (27 percent), and relaxation (15 percent) (fig. 7.5).

According to family members/caregivers, their child/patient benefited from visiting the garden in one or more of the following ways: fresh air/sunshine/getting outside (33 percent), relaxing (24 percent), getting away from hospital room/distraction/hint of normalcy (20 percent), garden elements (plants, fish, water features) (14 percent). After the cafeteria, the garden was the most used space outside the patient's room, compared with other semipublic spaces in the hospital (family lounge, children's playroom, teen lounge, Child Life playroom, family resource center, and the chapel). (A case study of this garden appears below).

Five gardens were studied at three Texas children's hospitals—Texas Children's Hospital in Houston, Legacy Campus Children's Medical Center of Dallas in Plano, and Dell

7.5 Parents bring their children to the roof top garden at St. Louis Children's Hospital, St. Louis, Missouri, to enjoy a break from the hospital interior. Particularly popular are telescopes that afford views over Forest Park and downtown St. Louis. Designer: EDAW.
Copyright AECOM; photo by Dixi Carrillo

7.6 A study of three Texas children's hospitals found a correlation between the frequency of garden visits and amenities that interested children. Comfortable, movable, and diverse seating was a high priority for staff. This garden fulfilled none of these requirements.
Photo by Samira Pasha

Children's Medical Center in Austin. This study researched the hypothesis that the presence of seats and shade, coupled with nature-dominated design, would encourage the use of outdoor spaces located in high-traffic zones (Pasha forthcoming; Pasha and Shepley 2013). Surveys found that in the three gardens that had water features, this was the item that both staff and visitors liked best. The predominant complaint from both groups was the lack of shade, a significant problem in the hot climate of Texas. Insufficient or uncomfortable seating was the next most frequently mentioned barrier to use, especially by staff, many of whom are on their feet all day and look to a garden as place to sit comfortably during a break. As in the Whitehouse et al. study (2001), pediatric inpatients comprised only a small percentage of garden users (fig. 7.6).

7.7 An intriguing child-sized entry door entices children to enter the Huntington Library Children's Garden, Pasadena, California.
Photo by Naomi Sachs

A positive correlation was found between the frequency of garden visits and the availability of amenities that interested children (presumably well siblings or outpatients). While adults often focus on what a place looks like, children are more likely to judge a setting by "What can I do here?" Using a children's garden audit tool developed by Clare Cooper Marcus, Pasha (forthcoming) found that gardens with higher scores in shade, seats, and planting had higher levels of use. In addition, higher scores for walking paths and amenities for children encouraged more active, more frequent, and longer garden visits by family groups. This study concluded with the following observations:

1. Providing comfortable, movable, and diverse seating in a garden can increase the duration and frequency of stay, especially for staff.

2. Appropriate positioning of the garden in relation to the building, plus suitable structures, is essential in creating shade, especially during the middle of the day—the hottest time of the day and the time that gardens are most frequently used by staff.

3. Design features that support play will produce higher levels of garden use by families with children (fig. 7.7).

4. Proximity to patient rooms and wheelchair-friendly paths are essential to support garden use by hospitalized patients.

5. Garden use is increased when outdoor space is integrated with spaces that people use in their daily routine, since a busy schedule was cited as the main barrier to garden visits for both visitors and staff.

The Challenge of Multiple User Groups

Meeting the needs of users in a children's hospital garden is a particular challenge for the design team. Assuming that there is only one garden (which is usually the case), a variety of users may be seeking quite different things in an outdoor space, and somehow all their needs must be fulfilled. The following are among those who might come to a garden:

1. Parents of sick children seeking solace and privacy while their child is undergoing surgery or treatment

2. Parents accompanying a sick inpatient or outpatient, looking for ways to distract them from pain or discomfort

3. Parents with one or more well siblings of a sick child, with the sibling(s) seeking active play and possibly "acting out" to gain attention from a parent focused on the sick child

4. Teenage patients (who are treated in children's hospitals until the age of eighteen) who may want to distance themselves from children, hang out in small groups, or find unconventional things to do

5. Child or teen cancer patients who have lost their hair, feel self-conscious, and want to find semiprivate spaces where they can "hide"

6. Staff looking to get away from their work environment, converse with a colleague, or even hold an informal staff meeting outdoors

7. Physical, occupational, and horticultural therapists (as well as other allied professionals) working with patients in the garden

8. The parents of a child who has died or who is being taken off life-support seeking a place of privacy while confronting their grief

It is rare to find a garden that can provide for all of these needs. The outdoor space at some children's hospitals is focused primarily of children's play. A rooftop with colorful play items at Children's Hospital in Albuquerque, New Mexico, serves ambulatory children and Child Life staff, but provides nothing for parents or staff seeking a quiet, restorative setting. Gardens at children's hospitals in Boston, Atlanta, and Sydney, Australia, are green, restorative settings appealing to parents and staff, but with little to engage children. A few hospitals, such as those in Houston and Seattle, have created separate outdoor areas for quiet restoration and for children's play; a very few, such as those at St. Louis Children's Hospital, St. Louis, Missouri, and Randall Children's Hospital, Portland, Oregon (see case studies below), have gardens that provide equally successfully for sick children, well siblings, parents, staff working with children, and staff taking a break. It is also very rare to find a garden sensitively designed for the specific, therapeutic needs of children with brain injuries and mobility problems, such as that at Rusk Institute of Rehabilitative Medicine, New York, New York (see case study below).

Design Guidelines

In addition to all of the general healthcare guidelines covered in chapter 6, the following are elements that are essential to consider for an outdoor space serving a children's hospital (fig. 7.8).

7.8 The sign at the entry to the Children's Garden at Randall Children's Hospital, Portland, Oregon. Designers: Johnson Design Studio, Gretchen Vadnais, and Quatrefoil, Inc
Courtesy of Legacy Health.

General guidelines

Required

1. The client and designer need to consider the possibility of **several gardens for different uses:** an active play area for well children; a quiet garden with some intriguing features could serve worried parents and those seeking to distract sick children; a separate bereavement garden that might be attached to a chapel or meditation space; and several small gardens for staff—best located close to break rooms. Where there is room for only two kinds of outdoor spaces, create one that has the characteristics of a **"passive" healing garden** designed for quiet reflection and conversation (for worried or grieving parents, very sick children, staff on a break), and one that is clearly a **playground** (for well siblings and out patient children). A successful example of the latter at Seattle Children's Hospital, Seattle, Washington, includes a "village" of play elements set on a rubberized surface (barber shop with mirror, gas station with pumps and prices, telephone with numbers to push, and so on); and many kid-sized vehicles.

2. In designing for active play, employ the notion of **"affordances," or play opportunities**. A small fixed rock may be seen by a child as something to climb or sit on, lean against, touch, or run around. Sand may be seen as something to lie down in, dig in, load into a play truck, or sift through one's fingers (fig. 7.9).

7.9 Slide, shaded sandbox, and rainbow-prism sculpture are among many features in the PlayGarden at Rusk Institute of Rehabilitation Medicine, New York, New York, that attract children while also fulfilling rehabilitation goals. Designer: Johansson Design Collaborative.
Photo courtesy of Johansson Design Collaborative

3. If there are **play features**, these should be spread out so that children who are cautious, shy, or have a disability can find some element that engages them. A central, integrated play feature that is actively used can be frightening to such children. The category "children" of course encompasses a wide developmental range.

4. Provide **elements that would be intriguing and distracting for a sick child**, such as elements of whimsy or surprise, a gazing ball, a sundial, or sculpted animal figures half-hidden in the planting. Keep in mind that some children will be brought to the garden in a wheelchair or wagon, or with an IV pole, or perhaps even on a gurney.

5. **Create strong boundaries** that, more than just giving the appearance of boundedness, entirely surround the garden physically. A parent with a sick child needs to feel assured that a well sibling who wants to run around and explore will not inadvertently wander away.

6. **Educate staff** about the location and purpose of the garden(s) and how to incorporate its use into patient and family care. Periodic feedback, via a visitor's book, about how families benefit from the garden is essential.

7. **Include details acknowledging that adults—both family members and staff—are usually the most frequent visitors** to gardens in children's hospitals (fig. 7.10). Adequate shade and comfortable seating are essential. In addition, adults in a California garden mentioned the following as most helpful: the sound of running water, being outside/fresh air/sunshine/ breezes, bright colors, greenery, artwork, a sense of enclosure,

7.10 Staff and adult family members often outnumber children in children's hospital gardens. Staff at the Randall Children's Hospital, Portland, Oregon, have found a comfortable place to eat their lunch and socialize in the garden.
Photo by Clare Cooper Marcus

and the opportunity for multisensory stimulation (Whitehouse et al. 2001).

8. **Consult early in the design process with therapists** regarding elements that would facilitate their work with child-patients in the garden. These might include planter edges of different heights, handrails, differing path surfaces, types of plants, and the like.

Recommended

1. Provide features that a well or sick child could **directly interact with**, such as touching water, looking through a kaleidoscope, rearranging rocks, putting messages in a mailbox.

2. Consider elements that are **activated by the sun or weather**, such as wind chimes, hanging crystals, features that cast recognizable colors or shadows on the ground, or rain chains.

3. Provide some **elements in the garden that are familiar to children**, such as **images of animals, insects,** or birds (fig. 7.11). Avoid art elements that are likely to have no meaning to children.

4. Introduce as much **topography as possible**—most of the world a child encounters on the streets and in a hospital is flat and linear. Children can enjoy running up and down a slope or using a slide set into hill.

5. Where **sand** is included (in a sandbox or under equipment) use gold construction sand with some texture, not reflective white "Caribbean" sand.

6. Include **"loose parts"** that a child can manipulate and use in creative ways—wagons, trucks, play tools, watering cans, small logs, and the like.

7. **Avoid any features** in the garden that are labeled **"In Memory of. . ."**; These could be upsetting or depressing to a sick child, parents, or siblings.

Pathways

Recommended

1. Design pathways and include **elements that may entice a child recovering from surgery or a temporary disability to ambulate in the garden**, giving them a sense of autonomy (fig. 7.12). These might include a path leading to a secret hiding place or to a special feature; crawl spaces, bridges, diverse terrain; a play space that requires climbing into; a grassy hill to climb up and roll down.

7.11 A mosaic turtle is a favorite play feature at the Randall Children's Hospital garden, Portland, Oregon.
Photo by Melissa Bierman

Seating

Required

1. Position some seating so that the **whole garden can be surveilled by** parents and caregivers and they can easily keep an eye on the children.

2. Provide plenty of seating in private **places of refuge** and quiet for worried or bereaved parents, sick children, stressed staff, and adolescent patients who may feel self-conscious about hair loss due from cancer treatment or about being in a wheelchair (fig. 7.13).

7.12 Stepping-stones between richly planted raised beds encourages a child to explore in the Olson Family Garden at St. Louis Children's Hospital, St. Louis, Missouri. Designer: EDAW.
Copyright AECOM; photo by Herb Schall

7.13 Two visitors to the Children's Garden, Randall Children's Hospital, Portland, Oregon, have found a comfortable place to sit and read under the shade of an ornamental plum tree. Designers: Johnson Design Studio, Gretchen Vadnais, and Quatrefoil, Inc.
Courtesy of Legacy Health

3. Provide some moveable **child-sized chairs and tables**.

4. Provide at least one table at the proper height for a **child in a wheelchair** to sit at and work on a project or look at a book.

5. Provide a **glider swing that accommodates a stroller or wheelchair**.

6. Provide a **glider seat where parents with a small baby could swing**, bringing kinesthetic pleasure to parents and the child.

Planting

Required

1. **Do not include any poisonous or otherwise harmful plants.** For example, the red berries of the yew may be tempting to pick and eat, but the seeds are highly toxic. While hydrangeas might be specified as a background shrub in a children's garden, they should never be used where children might have direct contact, since the cyanogenic glycoside hydrangin is found in its leaves and ingestion can cause vomiting and other serious symptoms. Many children, and in particular those who are brain injured, like to experiment with touch and taste.

2. Ensure that **every plant has a purpose**. Use the "rule of three." (For more detail, see chapter 17).

Recommended

1. Create a **mix of "clipped" and "wild" nature**, to encourage the presence of wildlife in the garden and to instruct parents about the importance of nature contact for children. Children live through their senses and learn through interactions with the physical environment (fig. 7.14).

2. Include plants that **engage children's attention** and multiple senses—very unusual plants, such as *Gunnera* leaves, for example, that are labeled as "dinosaur food"; plants labeled "Touch me—I am soft" or "Smell me—I am lavender"; or plants with unusual seed pods that could be used in play.

3. Include plants that have **plentiful flowers**, with a sign inviting children to pick a flower and give it to someone or place it in a fountain or on special stone.

Utilities

Required

1. As in any healing garden, a **storage shed** for maintenance equipment must be provided. But in a children's garden, the

7.14 Do not be overzealous in maintaining a children's garden. Fallen leaves, acorns, or twigs can be intriguing treasures, collected, used in games, or given to parents as "presents."
Photo from www.henrydomke.com

shed should be much larger so it can store wagons, watering cans, and other objects children play with.

Recommended

1. Include elements permitting a child to contribute to the **upkeep of the garden**, such as a faucet that can easily be turned on; child-sized watering cans, rakes, and brooms; small compost containers into which children could be encouraged to deposit spent flowers and fallen leaves (fig. 7.15).

2. Provide **electrical outlets** for battery-powered wheelchairs and clearly post their location.

3. Provide a section of the garden with a **potting area** where children can work with an HT gardening and planting.

7.15 Brooms and rakes encourage children (and adults) to help take care of the garden at Randall Children's Hospital, Portland, Oregon.
Photo by Clare Cooper Marcus

Case Studies

The three case studies that follow are all of successful gardens at children's hospitals, their success hinging on many of the following critical factors:

1. Sufficient funding to construct the garden

2. Funding and arrangements for maintenance

3. Top-down support for the garden (at least initially)

4. An interdisciplinary design team, including staff who work with children, to ensure appropriate design of the outdoor space

5. Continuing stewardship by staff who use the garden to work with children and encourage families to use it

6. Hospital administration, foundation, or other body that encourages use of the garden for concerts, art shows, and other events

7. A visitors book that allows people to record their appreciation for the garden

CASE STUDY

The Children's Garden, Randall Children's Hospital, Legacy Emanuel Medical Center, Portland, Oregon

Designers: Johnson Design Studio and Gretchen Vadnais

Description of the Facility and Its History

In 1996, Legacy Health System hired Portland architects Johnson Design Studio to remodel and coordinate the pediatric facilities at what is now known as Randall Children's Hospital at Legacy Emanuel Medical Center, and to create a new corridor linking the main hospital foyer to elevators accessing the pediatric check-in on an upper floor. Visible through the windows of the new corridor was an unkempt courtyard with a soggy patch of lawn. The CEO of Legacy Health, John G. King, was moving the hospital toward more patient-centered care; creating a new garden in the courtyard fit in with this goal.

Johnson Design Studio created a conceptual design and then brought in Portland landscape architect Gretchen Vadnais to work on grading and planting. Therapists who would be working with children in the garden (physical, occupational, horticultural, speech, and recreational) were involved in the design process. (See chapter 5 for more on this process used in Legacy Health System.) Since money was scarce, the garden was created in phases, the first being a small wildlife habitat installed in 1996.

The new design was endorsed enthusiastically by the hospital administration, but the design team was told that the money for the initial component—construction of a wildlife habitat—had to be found. Staff began to see the potential for the garden; the head of pediatrics organized a committee to provide artwork for the garden and the adjacent corridor. The designers produced a workbook for potential donors that listed each element needed for the garden and its cost. The initial construction phase cost of the 9,000-square-foot garden was $17 per square foot.

Design Philosophy

The garden is available to adult patients at the medical center, but it is especially geared towards pediatric patients and their families. A pamphlet given to parents of children entering the hospital explains the philosophy of the garden:

> Hospitalized children experience change and loss in both their physical capabilities and in the normal context of their social-emotional interactions. . . . As a vehicle for healing children, gardens have special significance because of the way in which children relate to the world through play and their attraction to nature. . . . Creating space for siblings to interact and parents to experience usual everyday interactions with their child outside of the medical environment are also very significant goals in a pediatric facility where patients are often hospitalized for long stays and repeat visits are frequent.

In the garden, children can replicate play and leisure activities they enjoy at home. . . . Rehabilitation goals are promoted when therapists use the garden as a treatment setting. Therapeutic horticulture activities promote restorative as well as therapeutic goals. Family members participate in these positive experiences, which enhance the well-being of the child and the family.

Description of the Outdoor Space

The 9,000-square-foot garden fills a triangular courtyard bounded by glass-sided corridors on two sides and is highly visible to people inside the hospital. A figure-eight path winds through a richly planted landscape. A large, central, red-leafed ornamental plum scales down the surrounding five-story buildings. Five subareas partially screened by planting enable groups to find a private spot in the garden and to visit and chat while not being overheard by others (fig. 7.16).

A courtyard garden in a hospital must ensure that those in the garden do not feel stared at by those inside the building. While people passing by in the corridors that skirt the garden on its west and south sides can certainly see the garden—some plant labels are even turned toward the corridors to provide information for those passing by—Vadnais developed a planting design of low-growing trees (Japanese maple),

Legacy Emanuel Children's Garden

Gretchen Vadnais
landscape architects, l. l. c.

7.16 Site plan of the garden at Randall Children's Hospital, Portland, Oregon.
Courtesy of Legacy Health

shrubs (Ribes), and tall perennials (Cosmos, Acanthus) close to the building edge in order to create a filtered green screen protecting the privacy of those within the garden space.

The northeast side of the garden consists of patient rooms and offices. Here, a low wall backed by shrubs and maples creates a green barrier between the hospital interior and the garden. One portion of this wall has slats on top for casual seating. People sitting here have their backs to the windows of hospital rooms and thus do not intrude on patients' privacy.

One floor above the garden on its west side is a garden deck that provides maternity and adult cardiac patients with views into the courtyard.

How the Garden Is Used

The garden was designed for the widest range of abilities, including the needs of outpatients, ambulatory patients and their families, siblings who need to "run off steam," inpatient children pulled in a wagon provided by the hospital, and adult patients who use the garden during unstructured time. Through the careful selection of plants, garden users are able enjoy a year-round multisensory experience including hearing, touch, taste, and smell.

Under the ornamental plum are two comfortable wooden benches close enough for a group conversation. Late on a sunny afternoon, three adult family members were observed seated there with a teenage patient who was wearing a head restraint. Over the course of the next hour, three teen friends or siblings arrived with an outsize get-well card, talking and laughing, the foliage above and on three sides subtly defining a comfortable private space. One can imagine that such a gathering would not have been so relaxed had they met in the patient's room, which might have been shared with another patient.

Many use the garden for gentle, therapeutic exercise: staff members wander through, stopping to read plant labels or examine a flower; family members push a child in a wheelchair, stopping to look at the sculpture of the Tin Man encountered on the painted Yellow Brick Road; well children run around the looped pathways playing at "Now you see me, now you don't." The planting design and curving pathways provide surprising views and changing vistas, even in this relatively small garden (fig. 7.17).

The designers, and, later, the horticultural therapy staff, added elements to the garden that engage the interest of adults and children alike as they move around the garden:

- plant labels with Latin and common names, as well as brief information on growing habits

- bird feeders and nesting boxes

- small, sculpted figures, half hidden in the planting

- planters with edible plants (pole beans, lettuce, tomatoes)

- a wall decorated with tiles made by children

- a mailbox beside a bench ("Here's a letter for you, Daddy," a little girl calls out as she takes an invisible letter out of the brightly painted box and runs to give it to her father.)

- a large mosaic-covered cow, and two climbable mosaic turtles

- a statue of the Tin Man

A number of spigots and brightly colored watering cans, as well as child-sized brooms and rakes, encourage children to become engaged in maintaining the garden. After these were added, adults said they also wanted to be involved, so full-sized brooms were added. Although many hospitals discourage attracting birds into their gardens, this has not been a problem at the Children's Garden. Immune-suppressed patients follow their doctor's instructions; other patients will, in any case, be discharged to environments at home where birds are likely to be present.

The garden is used extensively for a variety of therapeutic and educational activities (fig. 7.18):

- Occupational therapists conduct treatments in the garden by having children pick, hold, grasp/release, and describe different plants.

- Physical therapists work with children on balance activities and walking on a variety of surfaces and grades. Walking rails of two heights meet the needs of a wide age range of children who are relearning balance and ambulation skills.

- Speech and language therapists use the garden for cognitive activities with patients. A therapist may have a child scan the garden to find sunflowers, describe them, and compare them with other plants.

- Classroom teachers in the hospital-based public school program use the garden and nature materials for art, math, reading, science, and other activities.

- Child Life specialists use the garden for play and activity with children.

- Horticultural therapists create pediatric nature stations and organize the entire treatment team for year-round, garden-related events. In cold or rainy weather, activities take place in the wide hallway overlooking the garden so that the children are at eye level with nature. In 2007 a large pavilion structure was erected (at a cost of $56,000)

7.17 Winding paths, such as "the yellow brick road," and rich planting encourage children and adults alike to explore the garden.
Courtesy of Legacy Health

7.18 Staff work with children using nature materials in the garden as part of a summer program for neighborhood children.
Courtesy of Legacy Health

7.19 A pavilion is used for garden-related outdoor activities organized by horticultural therapy staff and provides shade and shelter.
Courtesy of Legacy Health

to replace a temporary activity tent. Tables and benches are used for various outdoor activities that require shade or shelter from summer showers (fig. 7.19).

- The garden is maintained as follows: nine hours per week by a paid horticultural therapy (HT) gardener (grooming, planting, pruning, soil amendment); fifteen hours per week by HT volunteers (weeding, watering, sweeping, grooming); irrigation repairs, tree grooming, fountain maintenance, and power washing are done by the hospital facilities department.

In July 2000, the garden received an award from the American Horticultural Therapy Association. The garden has also received recognition as a National Wildlife Federation Schoolyard Habitat.

Key Garden Merits

- Visible from well-used corridors.
- Open around the clock.

- Includes a number of semiprivate niches in a relatively small garden.
- Paths and planting provide a supportive milieu for staff-led therapies.
- Planting along paths accessible for children in wheelchairs.
- Many details attract children's attention.
- Planting provides privacy for adjacent rooms.
- Attractive views onto garden from deck one floor above.

Some Possible Concerns

- A water feature with rocks proved to be a hazard, as some children tried to get into it, slipped, and were hurt. A low fence now prevents access.
- Donor bricks set into pathways proved to be a maintenance problem; they were moved to a seating wall.

Olson Family Garden, St. Louis Children's Hospital, St. Louis, Missouri

Designer: Herb Schaal, FASLA, EDAW, Fort Collins, Colorado

Description of the Facility and Its History

The Olson Family Garden, which is located on the eighth-floor roof of the St. Louis Children's Hospital, was donated by a local philanthropic family and opened in 1999. The garden cost $1.9 million to build and is blessed with a $30,000 per year endowment to cover its upkeep. It is maintained by a team of gardeners overseen by horticultural therapist Gary Wangler, who organizes forty-plus programs a year in the garden for hospitalized children and their siblings.

Design Philosophy

While recognizing the importance of objective criteria, the landscape architect felt that the beauty of a coherent, well-designed garden comprising a tapestry of well-proportioned complementary spaces and sequences of experience contributes the most to healing (fig. 7.20).

In the Olson Family Garden the covered entry was provided as a calming transition from interior to exterior (fig. 7.21). Shade was considered critical for comfort and a variety of small water features were integrated to engage users and make the garden seem larger and more mysterious.

The flowing lines of the paths were intended to soothe and create a sequence of changing views of nature and diverse plant compositions.

7.21 View into the garden from the entry patio.
Photo by Gary Wangler

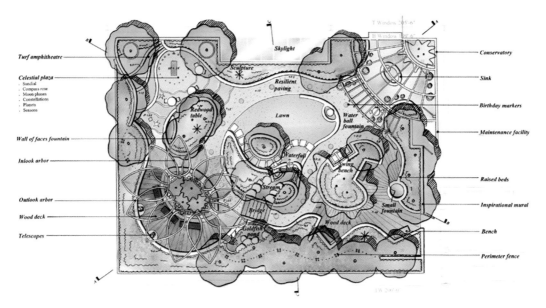

7.20 Site plan of the Olson Family Garden, St Louis Children's Hospital, St Louis, Missouri.
© *AECOM*

7.22 Children and adults alike are attracted to the round cubby windows with views over Forest Park.
Photo by Gary Wangler

Description of the Outdoor Space

The garden is accessed at the end of a short corridor. A covered entry patio provides a place to sit for those who do not want to venture further. The garden boundaries comprise the wall of the hospital on one long side to the north, stucco walls on the east and west, and tall steel mesh fences on the south and a portion of the west. A tall border of arbor vitae outside the mesh fence on the south screens the view of a nearby building and emphasizes the view toward Forest Park. A stucco wall with round cubby windows looking west is an unusual feature attracting attention to the far end of the garden (fig. 7.22).

In a relatively small space—8,000 square feet—a great variety of elements engage people's attention.

Pathways form a rough figure-eight with a rubberized walking surface that makes it easy for those using wheelchairs and IV poles to move around in the garden and provides a pleasant spongy feel for those who are used to hard corridors and sidewalks (fig. 7.23).

Great care has been taken in offering a variety of seating options, locations, and design. Types of seating include a swing seat, chaise longues, and seats for one, two, or three people. Stone retaining walls provide supplemental seating for memorial services and summer evening concerts. There

7.23 A rubberized walking surface facilitates use of the garden by those using wheelchairs or pulling an IV pole.
Photo by Clare Cooper Marcus

are a great variety of seating locations, including those in sun and shade at different times of the day. All of the seating is made of wood, with backs and arms, and all of the seats are placed with the comforting experience of a wall and planting behind them. Planting and retaining walls create eleven semi-private seating niches for smaller or larger groups.

The garden has the feel of a lush, green oasis, with a small lawn and seventeen sizable multitrunked trees, including crab apple, redbud, river birch, and Amur maple that provide shade and visual and seasonal interest. Seven tall hornbeam trees located inside a columnar structure provide little shade but create a good "block" of green in the garden.

There are many raised beds planted with perennials, shrubs, and groundcover, plus individual planters and hanging baskets potted up with annuals.

Five water features include a fish pond, stepping-stones through shallow water, a child-height millstone dripping fountain, a granite globe rotating in water with country outlines etched into it, and a shallow dish-pool where children can spot a sculpted snake on the bottom when the sun shines on it at a particular angle. All of the water features are checked daily for chlorine readings.

Although the garden doesn't have the feel or look of a playground, there are many enticing elements for children:

- Stepping-stones that cross over a shallow pond, disappear behind a planter, and appear again. Each stone is etched with an animal symbol (fish, turtle, frog, and the like). The other water features are intriguing to look at or touch.

- Two telescopes look over Forest Park and distant buildings from the far end of the garden.

- Round cubby windows allow one or two children, or a child and adult, to curl up and talk or look at the view.

- A kaleidoscope-sculpture has one viewing eyepiece at adult height, as well as one for a child, oriented to a flower planter that can be rotated. Physical therapists bring children out to the garden and have them hold the eyepiece with one hand and rotate the planter with the other.

Sensitive provision of utilities includes lighting fixtures set into retaining walls at a height of about 8 inches, and uplighting under many of the trees. Fifteen electrical outlets with small copper lids enable patients to plug in battery-powered wheelchairs or battery-powered medical equipment, enabling them to stay in the garden longer. These outlets are also used for amplification equipment and speakers at summer concerts.

How the Garden Is Used

"This is a really, really pretty garden!" exclaims a girl aged about ten who runs around with two siblings while their mother carries a baby and slowly wheels an IV pole. The father walks behind. "Come here, Daddy!" the girl calls out to her father. The children all look through telescopes, then get into the cubby windows or balance on stepping-stones—several times—looking carefully at images on the stones. The family sits and lets the baby touch some water. A girl finds a redwood-burl table and spins it. "The table moves! I wish we had a garden like this," she says. Her father sits on a swing seat looking worried—or perhaps bored. The girls follow the stepping-stones again, then return to the telescopes. The mother bends to look into the kaleidoscope, while her son holds the baby. She calls her girls over.

One girl returns to follow the stepping-stones again. All three children spend time at the kaleidoscope. Mother and father sit with the baby on the swing seat and talk. Their boy follows the stepping-stones. One of the girls puts her hands into the earth of an empty planter; the boy dips his hands into a fountain. The girls follow the stepping-stones again. The boy returns to the telescope. One girl balances, calling out, "Mummy—look at me!" The whole family leaves as the boy follows the stepping-stones one more time. They have been in the garden for twenty minutes, from 11:35 to 11:55 a.m. on a sunny Sunday in early May.

This is a typical scene on warm days, when many visitors come to the garden. What makes the garden so successful is that it has intriguing elements that are engaging for children and aesthetic qualities that are appealing to adults.

The more senses that can be engaged in a garden, the more children and adults will experience it as restorative. The design of the Olson Family Garden provides an admirable array of sensory experiences. Children can *run* along paths looping around raised beds, evoking a strong sense of exploration; *balance* on stepping-stones and retaining walls; *touch* water, stone walls, soil, leaves; *look* at flowers and fish; *look* through telescopes and into a kaleidoscope; *listen* to birds, wind chimes, the sound of water; *smell* flowers; *rock* on a swing seat.

In addition to these more obvious features are some that Gary Wangler utilizes in garden programs for hospitalized children and their well siblings:

- Small bronze sculptures of lizards, frogs, turtles, and the like are on planter edges and on rocks in the water. Some are movable. Gary may move one and the next time he brings children outside, he says: "Oh—where is the lizard?" and they have to go look for it.

- A child with impaired vision might be directed to feel a rock or a sculpted salamander.

7.24 A swing seat with a view over the garden is the favorite among a variety of seating options that includes fixed benches, movable seats, planter edges, and chaise longues.
Photo by Clare Cooper Marcus

- On top of planter walls are the names of the months and numbers for dates. On their birthday, a child may be told: "There's a present for you in the garden." They have to find their present on the right date.

- A large sundial symbol is set into soft paving in the northwest corner of garden, where—when people stand on the symbol for the month and raise their arms—it shows the time and phase of the moon.

- A small sign near the entry explains that children have come here from all fifty states and fifty-six countries. Six circular planters have been inscribed with words for "Welcome" in six languages (Bosnian, Russian, Arabic, Chinese, English, and Spanish). With a plaque near the entry depicting the six pots, children brought to the garden are encouraged to look for them.

- Gary Wangler runs horticulture therapy programs in the garden three times a week and organizes many special events throughout the year, such as a butterfly release and a Kid's Garden with plants that have animal names (lamb's ear, snapdragon).

While the garden incorporates many elements that engage children's attention, it also provides an attractive and soothing setting for adults. Indeed, counts of those in the garden at peak times on a warm Sunday and Monday in early May 2010 revealed that almost three-fourths were adults. These included staff, visitors (perhaps waiting for a child undergoing treatment), and families accompanying a hospitalized child in the garden.

A number of sensitive design features make this garden particularly appealing to adults. Among these are the smooth walking surfaces, the variety of seating options, the variety of semiprivate niches where groups can claim temporary territory, the variety of green and water elements to engage people's attention, and a chance to take in distant views (fig. 7.24).

There is a pleasing sense of enclosure at the garden entry where some linger, particularly on a very hot or wet day, and look out over the greenery. In good weather, people are drawn into the garden, especially to the far end, where there are expansive views over Forest Park and beyond.

The hospital initially resisted the inclusion of a small area of lawn in the garden, but a chaplain insisted. Now the lawn is sometimes used by parents with a baby who has been taken off life support. They rest on the grass until the baby dies. The garden is closed to others at these times.

What makes the Olson Family Garden so successful is not only its excellent design but the commitment of a dedicated horticultural therapist—Gary Wangler—to provide engaging programs for hospitalized children and well siblings in the garden and the commitment of the hospital through patient information, staff recommendations, summer concerts, and the like to encourage families to use the garden (fig. 7.25).

Key Garden Merits

- Overall aesthetic quality of the design

- Many opportunities for sensory engagement

- Equally attractive and engaging for children and adults

- A colorful, lush environment

7.25 Horticultural therapist Gary Wangler working with Evan, a child patient, in the garden.
Courtesy Gary Wangler

- A wide variety of seating options—sun or shade, semiprivate or more public, different locations, views

- Comfortable covered entry for sitting in inclement weather

- Visitors book near entry allows users to record their appreciation for the garden (fig. 7.26).

Some Possible Concerns

- Emergency helicopters landing on a roof above and next to garden cause a huge amount of noise; however, some seem to enjoy watching the helicopters arrive and leave.

- Plastic butterflies, sunflowers, and "cute kid" sculptures stuck into planting beds seem a little jarring compared with the overall aesthetic of the garden.

- All of the stepping-stones have small inserts that read, "In memory of. . . ." These signs may be distressing to some visitors.

- Some retaining walls may have to be replaced, as trees are getting too big and roots moving laterally are pushing the blocks apart.

- Some walking surfaces only ⅛-inch thick and made of shredded tires have had to be replaced with thicker, more resilient surfaces.

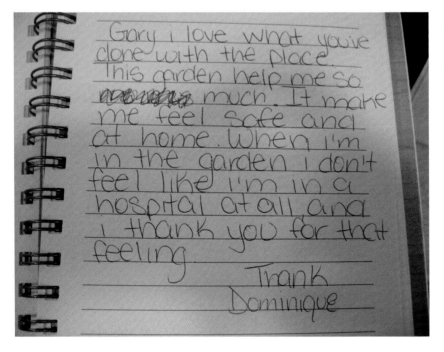

7.26 A visitors book near the entry to the Olson Family Garden allows people to record their appreciation of this rooftop oasis.
Photo by Clare Cooper Marcus

The Children's PlayGarden, Rusk Institute of Rehabilitation Medicine, New York, New York

Designers: Johansson and Walcavage

Note: Sadly, in November 2012, this garden was closed in the aftermath of Hurricane Sandy. It will remain closed to make way for hospital expansion and is scheduled to be replaced with a roof garden that will be accessible from the Hassenfeld Pediatric Center, the new children's hospital at New York University Langone Medical Center. We include it here as a case study because it was such a remarkable facility, one of very few specifically designed for the rehabilitation of children with brain injuries and mobility problems.

Description of the Facility and Its History

The Rusk Institute of Rehabilitation Medicine was located at 400 East 34th Street in Manhattan. A quarter of the Institute's 3,000 inpatients and more than 15,000 outpatients who receive services annually are children. They receive treatment for a variety of disabilities, including traumatic brain injury, cerebral palsy, amputation, spinal cord injuries, spina bifida, muscular dystrophy, and brain tumors.

A playground appropriate for children with disabilities was built in 1970, but twenty years later, as theories about disability and safety had evolved, it was deemed no longer adequate. In 1994, a project team was created to develop a new play garden, and the landscape architecture firm, Johansson and Walcavage, was hired to redesign the existing space. The project team consisted of every specialist who worked with children, including recreational, occupational, horticultural, and physical therapists, as well as teachers and physicians. The team also included a project manager representing the plant maintenance and construction department at the medical center (Johansson and Chambers 2005). The team approach of involving all stakeholders proved to be invaluable. The range of therapists made full and creative use of the garden because it was a more attractive setting for them than working indoors, because they saw how well it served the needs of the children, and because they (or former colleagues) had had a say in how it was designed.

For example, the horticultural therapists initially objected to swings in the play garden, preferring more plants. But the physical therapists insisted that swings were important for children's balance and kinesthetic experience. Small doors in a fanciful play house facade were required by the occupational therapists, who wanted children to develop their fine motor skills by manipulating locks and latches. The landscape architects responsible for pulling together all of the design ideas also had to make some adjustments. Referring to the faux house facades, Walcavage noted: "We rarely do things [in play areas] that are recognizable objects, but some of these kids have cognitive disorders, so it was really important to do things that actually looked like something they recognized" (Vanderbilt 1999).

Design Philosophy

Discussions between the therapists, headed by horticultural therapist Nancy Chambers, and the landscape architects determined that a standard play experience was not sufficient and that the new garden would be, according to Johansson and Chambers (2005),

> [a] nature-oriented environment to support and challenge disabled children in play and therapy. . . . The space would provide incentives for these children to explore and practice activities that would stimulate curiosity and promote independence, spontaneity, and creativity in the physical, cognitive, social, and sensory realms.
>
> The users were clearly defined. They included children up to 12 years of age, inpatients and outpatients; children's families, including siblings; therapists working with children; teachers; and families in the local community. . . . While the PlayGarden would be open to the public, children would be permitted only with a supervising adult and the PlayGarden would be open only when staff were present to provide oversight.

The budget for the Children's PlayGarden was capped at $400,000 because above that many state-level approvals were necessary. Nancy Chambers counsels others planning a therapeutic garden: "Never build a garden without an endowment for maintenance."

The garden had a staff of twelve, some of them part time. Rusk Institute paid for 3.6 salaries; the rest were covered by fundraising. The thorny issue of acknowledging donors by including plaques or "donor bricks" was subtly avoided by recording the names of donors on the leaves of a tree sculpture "growing" on a boundary fence (see fig. 19.1).

Description of the Outdoor Space

Within the relatively small area of 5,500 square feet, the garden was intricately designed so that every element fostered

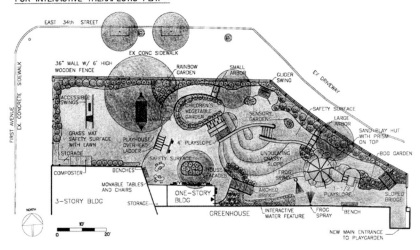

RUSK CHILDREN'S PLAYGARDEN
FOR INTERACTIVE THERAPEUTIC PLAY

challenges and sensory stimulation and was sculpted to meet the needs of disabled children. Its curvilinear appearance contrasted with the predominantly linear aesthetic of Manhattan's streets and buildings (fig. 7.27).

A grassy hill provided a focal point and physical challenge and made the space seem larger. There were several ways to get to the top of a slide tucked into the hill, and children decided which route to take, depending on their abilities and how much they wanted to challenge themselves.

A pathway looped around the garden, providing sensory interest along the way. It crossed a bridge over a plant-filled bog and went under an arbor. Mints and lavenders brushed against children as they wheeled or walked by; another bridge carried the path over a rock-lined brook. The path was originally designed without edges, but curbs were added to prevent wheelchairs from veering into the planting.

Specific play features provided challenges and promoted exercise. These included a playhouse with overhead rungs and hanging side bars to enhance upper body strength and balance, a swing to enhance balance and another to cradle a child with spinal injuries, and a sandbox, entered via large rock steps and edged with rocks, to provide challenges to coordination and motor skills. The philosophy behind the latter was that children, especially those with disabilities, are rarely allowed to take risks. The sandbox was surrounded by grass and rubberized surfaces, so if a child fell off a rock they landed on these.

A challenge to the designers was to provide as wide a range of sensory stimulation as possible and to ensure that all elements of the garden could be touched, experienced, and explored by young children in or out of wheelchairs. All children learn through their senses and through repetitive activities. This garden provided a rich range of experiences, from touching and hearing water in a stone channel; listening to birds attracted to the trees, breezes through grasses, and wind chimes; watching the play of rainbow colors from a prism over the sandbox; watching butterflies attracted to *Buddleia* and other plantings; examining the leaves and flowers beside the pathway; feeling grass, bark, sand, and rocks; and "driving a car" through a weeping willow and pretending it was a "car wash" (fig. 7.28, fig. 7.29).

Elements to enhance discovery and learning included fanciful playhouse facades where children learned to unfasten locks and clasps while developing fine motor skills, an iguana-shaped faucet that turned on frog misters and could be accessed by children in wheelchairs, and rocks to move around, which changed the flow in the brook. A vegetable garden and hands-on activities led by horticultural therapists aroused curiosity about the soil, water, and nurturing plants. Resident animals—a cat, a rabbit, and turtles—introduced children to other species and how to treat and care for them.

Children are not necessarily always on the move or physically active. Sometimes they want to withdraw or engage in social or imaginative play. The garden contained movable chairs, work tables, a hammock swing, a play house, and a wheelchair-accessible glider swing, offering opportunities for adults and children to be together. The profusion of plants, gently curving pathways, and pastel colors in a child-friendly

7.28 Children were intrigued with a stream of running water at the Children's PlayGarden.
Copyright Michael Rogol, courtesy of Johansson Design Collaborative

7.29 Children learn through their senses, and there were many ways to experience kinesthetic pleasure, touch, and hearing throughout the garden.
Photo by Gwenn Fried

environment provided a restorative contrast to the stress of the rather institutional hospital interior. There were no totally hidden places, just symbolic ones that allowed children to withdraw but ensured visibility for supervising adults.

How the Garden Was Used

Inpatient children visited the garden most days, depending on the weather. Many of them rode in a large, red wagon. Although various therapy staff were always present, children who were ambulatory or in wheelchairs often explored and experienced the garden on their own—rolling on the grassy hill, climbing into the sandbox, trailing fingers in the brook, swinging in the hammock or on the glider. At the time it was functioning, Johansson and Chambers (2005) wrote:

> [T]he range of topography, surfaces, and play equipment motivates the children to exercise all their muscles by running, crawling, sitting, bending, turning, swinging, and jumping. All the natural and man-made play elements foster challenges to motor-planning, eye-hand-foot coordination, balancing, spatial awareness, body positioning, and a multitude of challenging opportunities for a full range of gross motor and coordination skills.

Physical and occupational therapists who worked with adults at the Institute also regularly used the gentle slopes of the pathways for wheelchair and ambulation practice.

Unlike most gardens in healthcare facilities, the Rusk Institute garden was open to the local community, who often visited with their children, especially on weekends, and referred to it as "our park" (fig. 7.30).

The staff at the garden, headed by Nancy Chambers, developed a remarkable variety of outreach programs whereby outside groups came and used the garden. Children were brought from the pediatric unit of New York University (NYU) medical center. Students at an alternative high school ("city-as-school") worked at the garden for science credit. Residents from a nursing home were brought to the garden once a week by bus. Formerly homeless seniors living at the Woodstock Hotel, near Times Square, were brought to the

7.30 A festival day, with many families from the local community enjoying the garden.
Photo by Gwenn Fried

garden for horticulture classes. Developmentally disabled adults came to work in the garden along with their job coach. A very successful program involved children from another hospital who were HIV-positive. They learned how to be responsible for plants, and then for their own medications and nutrition.

In addition to these outreach programs, over three hundred U.S. and international professionals visited the garden each year to learn how the design, staffing, and running of this garden positively affected health outcomes for disabled children. These visitors were often encouraged to participate in a horticultural therapy activity while using a wheelchair, so as to experience—as much as is possible—how it is for a disabled individual.

The PlayGarden was recognized with many awards, including from the American Institute of Architects and the American Horticultural Therapy Association.

Key Garden Merits

- Designed for children of all abilities

- Range of outdoor experiences in a small space

- A team approach to design ensured use by a variety of staff working with children

- Open to the local community and many other groups

- Sensitive understanding of children's outdoor play needs

References

Johansson, S., and N. Chambers. 2005. "A Children's PlayGarden at the Rehabilitation Hospital: A Successful Collaboration Produces a Successful Outcome." *LATIS Forum on Therapeutic Garden Design*, 14–23, American Society of Landscape Architects, November. 2nd ed., 2011, 20–37.

Pasha, S. Forthcoming. "Barriers to Garden Visitation in Children's Hospitals." *Health Environments Research and Design Journal*.

Pasha, S. and M. Shepley. 2013. "Research Note: Physical Activity in Pediatric Hospital Gardens." *Landscape and Urban Planning* 118: 53–58.

Sherman, S. A., J. W. Varni, R.S. Ulrich, and V. L. Malcarne. 2006. "Post Occupancy Evaluation of Healing Gardens in a Pediatric Cancer Center." Pp. 330–42 in *The Architecture of Hospitals*, edited by Cor Wagenaar. Rotterdam: NAi Publishers.

Sorensen, K. T. 2002. "Effect of Time Spent in a Hospital Garden on Satisfaction with Hospital Care." Master of Landscape Architecture thesis, University of Illinois at Urbana-Champaign.

Vanderbilt, T. 1999. "Design for Child's Play." *Landscape Architecture Magazine*, March: 134–35.

Whitehouse, S., J. W. Varni, M. Seid, C. Cooper Marcus, M. J. Ensberg, J. R. Jacobs, and R. S. Mehlenbeck. 2001. "Evaluating a Children's Hospital Garden Environment: Utilization and Consumer Satisfaction." *Journal of Environmental Psychology* 21: 301–14.

CHAPTER 8

Gardens for Cancer Patients

A garden can be a wonderfully restorative setting, reminding us of the passage of the seasons and our place in the natural world. For people facing cancer, a garden can be especially important since it provides a comforting contrast to interior medical settings where they might be receiving treatment or listening to a frightening prognosis. Nature and gardens expect nothing of us. We can be alone with our thoughts and hopefully find comfort in the presence of beauty around us (fig. 8.1).

There appears to be little research on the restorative effects of nature as it specifically relates to cancer patients. This is surprising considering the prevalence of the disease and the fact that a diagnosis of cancer is one of the most feared medical pronouncements.

One study of 157 women with newly diagnosed breast cancer randomly assigned half of them to two hours of exposure to nature a week (gardening, walks in a park, and the like) and measured their capacity for directed attention (as opposed to attentional fatigue; see chapter 3 for more on attention restoration theory). Scores were compared seventeen days before and nineteen days after surgery. Controlling for education, age, and symptom distress, among other variables, this group displayed a significant improvement in directed attention compared with a control group (Cimprich and Ronis 2003).

A study involving semistructured interviews with fourteen women in Toronto, Ontario, at various stages of breast cancer recovery questioned them about landscapes for healing. While "landscapes" was interpreted widely and included a woman's own body, all of those interviewed identified the importance of seeing and connecting with nature on a daily basis. Among the responses were: "I can look in the garden downstairs. And then when I do that it doesn't feel like I'm living in this cement block." ". . . being able to be at home and look out at my backyard. . . . It's very treed, very calming. . . ." "I'm closer to nature than I was before, I embrace it. I want to go and hug a tree. . . . Thank you. . . . You're alive, I'm alive. . . that kind of closeness and proximity."

Half of the women spoke about the importance of nature in distant places (holiday cottages or vacation spots, for example), and there was an emphasis on water throughout the interviews. English, Wilson, and Keller-Olaman (2008) noted, "[T]he women interviewed perceived that nature possesses the ability to positively transform emotional and psychological health, and contributes to recovery from illness."

While no published research could be found relating directly to healthcare gardens and cancer, one unpublished survey found that cancer patients' preferences and desires regarding a garden differed little from those of any other kind of patient—they wanted greenery, soothing sounds (water, leaves, birdsong, chimes), comfortable seating, quiet, and places to be alone. When asked what should be avoided in such a garden, they mentioned man-made materials (steel, concrete, aluminum, plastic), piped-in music, too much formality/perfect grooming, public access, and overuse of flowers and fragrance (Cooper Marcus 2003) (fig. 8.2).

The general design guidelines discussed in chapter 6 apply equally to gardens serving cancer patients, but some are especially important, and a few need to be added for this particular patient group.

Shade is important in all healthcare gardens, but it is absolutely critical in gardens for cancer facilities since the chemotherapy drugs administered to many patients require that they stay out of direct sun light. Thus, if a cancer patient is to enjoy the restorative qualities of a green outdoor space, it is essential that there be an option of shaded places at all times of the day where a person might want to sit or walk.

Privacy is especially significant in spaces for cancer patients who are dealing with a frightening, possibly, terminal prognosis. There must be intimate, secluded niches where a person might meditate, pray, or cry alone or with a loved one. People undergoing chemotherapy and radiation are also often self-conscious about their appearance and may feel uncomfortable in a setting where they are highly visible (fig. 8.3).

Recent research reveals that physical exercise for cancer patients and survivors can improve physical function and decrease fatigue, nausea, and depression. **Places to walk**, even for short periods of time, encourage movement and exercise for patients undergoing treatment or rehabilitation (McNeeley et al. 2006; Galvão and Newton 2005). Because fatigue is a major symptom, especially during chemotherapy and radiation, **frequent benches along pathways** are essential.

8.1 Patients receiving chemotherapy treatment, as well as nursing and reception staff, have broad views over the natural landscape from the infusion area at Illinois Cancer Care. Interiors, Spellman Brady and Company; Architect, PSA Dewberry.
Photo by Debbie Franke

8.2 A garden on the roof of a residence for cancer patients and their families. The patients receive treatment at a nearby hospital but live too far away to easily travel there from their rural homes. This garden was designed and built by undergraduate students in landscape architecture at the University of Washington under the direction of Professor Daniel Winterbottom. Pete Gross House, Seattle, Washington.
Photo by Clare Cooper Marcus

8.3 A shady garden with walking paths and private seating in Norma's Garden at the Gathering Place, a cancer resource center in Cleveland, Ohio. Designer: Virginia Burt, Visionscapes.
Photo by Chris Garcia

In addition to these important qualities and all the general guidelines enumerated in chapter 6, there is one requirement for cancer gardens that does not apply to any other kind of healthcare outdoor space, and that is the need to **avoid highly fragrant flowers and plants**. People on chemotherapy are especially sensitive to smell, and any strong scent—of flowers, food, and the like—can trigger nausea. (For an exception, see the first case study, below.)

A few cancer clinic gardens in the United States have included plants, often labeled with descriptions, from which cancer drugs are refined. There is no evidence that cancer patients are comforted by seeing the plants from which

the chemotherapy drugs are derived. In fact, it seems possible that the opposite may be true—that patients visiting a healing garden want to be distracted from what is happening inside the hospital. Research on this question is needed.

In situations where a patient is severely immuno-compromised—such as after receiving a bone marrow transplant—exposure to soil (in planting beds, for example) or water (in a water feature or decorative fountain) is entirely precluded. In these cases a **view to an indoor or exterior garden** would be especially desirable. (See case study of the Stoneman Healing Garden, below).

CASE STUDY

Roof Gardens at Cancer Lifeline, the Dorothy S. O'Brien Center, Seattle, Washington

Description of the Facility and Its History

Cancer Lifeline is a private nonprofit, nonhospital resource for anyone touched by cancer. It is housed in an unassuming redesigned two-story building (originally a grocery store and apartment) in a quiet Seattle residential neighborhood. People come here for emotional support, to take part in groups and classes, to use the library, and to spend time in

one of three small rooftop gardens. All services are free. The center was funded by private donations and opened in 1999.

Design Philosophy

The gardens were designed and constructed during a ten-week program by fourth-year undergraduate landscape architecture students at the University of Washington under the direction of Professor Daniel Winterbottom. They worked in close collaboration with the staff and users of Cancer Lifeline to create simple, nurturing, affordable gardens that are appropriate for the users and for a rooftop location. Focus groups requested that the gardens be outside but protected and have contemplative aspects, elements of scent, and a sense of play. The gardens opened in 2001.

Description of the Outdoor Spaces

There are three second-floor gardens—two abutting the edge of the building, and one in a more central location. The Meditation Garden, with a wood-deck floor, is about 12 feet by 12 feet and is snugly enclosed on two and a half sides by the walls of the building. The other sides look out onto the neighborhood through a screen of bamboo. A right-angle corner bench and two movable chairs face a small revolving fountain set in pebbles. There is a small ceramic pot with a sign that reads: "This garden is your garden. Please feel free to remove any spent blossoms on the plants or fallen petals or debris you notice to the clay pot. The garden thanks you." The garden is intended for quiet contemplation and has a very restful feel, with the sight and sound of falling water, the soft feel of unpainted wood, quivering bamboo, varieties of green (but no actual flowers), and small art pieces (birdhouse, mosaic, Spirit House for the Ancestors). People's needs for physical comfort are subtly ensured by a glass roof partially covering the garden and a heater for chilly days (fig. 8.4).

The Celebration Garden, approximately 20 feet by 20 feet, is in a corner location, bordered on two sides by second-floor rooms in the building; on the other two sides, views over an open balustrade are of neighboring houses. There is seating set into wooden planters with trellises, and a variety of movable garden chairs and tables with umbrellas. The space has the feel of outdoor seating at a café and is intended for social groupings. Pots and planters contain lavender, rosemary, oregano, sage, thyme, and mint. Although some people on chemotherapy are sensitive to smell, this has apparently never been a problem here as the plants chosen can only be smelled by someone sitting very close or squeezing the leaves. A staff member remarked: "If we'd planted lilies, it might have been a different story."

The Earth and Sky Garden is visible from the main second-floor corridor and is entered via a handsome tree-shaped iron gate from the Celebration Garden and from a multipurpose/art room. Seating options include planter-edge benches, movable chairs, umbrella tables, and a chaise longue, with a wooden arbor feature overhead. The space is L-shaped, with a unique feature of two sliding panels of steel cut into tree

8.4 The sounds of falling water and quivering bamboo create a soothing atmosphere in the Meditation Garden.
Photo by Clare Cooper Marcus

motifs that can partially close off one half of the garden from the other (fig. 8.5). Hostas, penstemon, Solomon's seal, geranium, and dwarf pine provide a variety of textures and color. The planting on one side is relatively low, allowing glimpses into the space from the adjacent corridor. The planting on the opposite side is high, providing enclosure and privacy. Shade-cloth over part of the space offers some relief from bright sun in the summer.

How the Gardens Are Used

The Meditation Garden is used by people alone or by two people for quiet conversation and contemplation. Sometimes a person alone will use this garden for practicing Qigong. If someone is in the garden, it is unlikely another will enter, as it has the feel of a small, private space.

The Celebration Garden is sunny at midday and is often used by the staff or others for lunch or for small meetings. The growth of climbing plants over a copper plumbing arbor did not happen as planned, with the unintended consequence that the space is sunnier than it might have been. For most of the year that is an asset, given Seattle's rainy climate.

The aim of the Earth and Sky Garden is to allow people "to feel held," since so often with a cancer diagnosis, people feel their life and body are out of control. It is used for Qigong classes and nature appreciation, and, with the door open from the art studio, for creative expression classes in art and writing (fig. 8.6). Materials for Ikebana classes are gathered from plants in the garden. Some people come here to take a nap or to write.

8.5 The Earth and Sky Garden features a variety of planting and seating for small groups.
Photo by Clare Cooper Marcus

Key Garden Merits

- Plants, materials, and furnishings are low-key, domestic in scale, and appropriate to the region.

- Division of rooftop space into three separate gardens permits different groups or individuals to find privacy from each other.

- Different feel of these spaces offers settings for various moods or activities.

- Gardens offer green views from interior spaces on the second floor (corridor and multipurpose room).

- Plenty of opportunities exist for garden users to subtly reinforce a sense of control (choosing among the three spaces, moving garden furniture, picking up petals and plant debris) and to experience privacy.

Some Possible Concerns

- Celebration Garden feels a little too open to the street, neighboring houses, and traffic.

- Copper plumbing arbor (Celebration Garden) became too hot for jasmine and clematis vines that would have provided shade.

- Wood decking in all the gardens becomes slippery in the rainy season, even though it is pressure washed once a year.

8.6 Classes in creative expression for cancer patients are held in the Earth and Sky Garden.
Photo by Clare Cooper Marcus

The gardens are closed for use when the staff considers them too slippery. Decking will eventually be replaced with a combination material that inhibits slipping.

• Eventually the roof will have to be replaced, as leaks are occurring in the building, at which time the gardens will have to be removed and then replaced.

The Healing Garden, Mt. Zion—University of California San Francisco Medical Center

Designers: Ann Chamberlain, Professor, San Francisco Art Institute; and Katsy Swan, Garden Designer, Palo Alto, California

Description of the Facility

This large medical center is situated in the heart of San Francisco, at the intersection of two busy streets (Sutter and Divisadero). Across Sutter from the main high-rise building is a one-story Women's Health Center. This building and the courtyard garden "hidden" within it were once the home of the hospital's Clinical Cancer Center. The Center has since moved across the street to the main building, but the garden remains and is included here as a case study of an exemplary garden for cancer patients.

Description of the Garden and Its History

The courtyard garden, approximately 45 feet by 50 feet, is accessible from a corridor that skirts it on one side. The space is bounded by nine-story hospital buildings to the north and east, a suite of one-story offices to the south, and the backs of one-story commercial properties to the west screened by a decorative fence. At noon on a fall day, roughly half of the garden is in the sun—important in a climate such as San Francisco, where during most of the year people are seeking warmth.

The gardenesque style of this courtyard comprises curvilinear pathways of decomposed granite that border planting beds filled with a great variety of annuals and perennials, including white-blooming impatiens, hydrangeas, and Japanese anemone in the shady half of the garden and the colorful blooms of roses, begonia, penstemon, pansies, lavender, geranium, and *Osteospermum* in the sunnier half. The plants have been chosen to provide blooms throughout the year, as well as to offer a variety of shades of green—from the dark green of camellia and rhododendron to the variegated leaves of daphne and the soft gray-greens of artemesia. Attractive wooden garden benches with backs and arms, a number of round wooden tables with movable chairs, and a curvilinear

stone seating wall provide a variety of places to sit in the sun or shade. Low light fixtures directed at the pathways enable use of the garden after dark.

This simple, much-loved garden has a story behind it that is worth telling. The late Ann Chamberlain, artist and professor at the San Francisco Art Institute, was diagnosed with breast cancer in 1994. As she came for treatment at the cancer center, she was troubled by an unused concrete-paved courtyard (originally designed by iconic landscape architect Thomas Church). "Why isn't this a garden?" she asked her surgeon, Dr. Laura Esserman, who replied, "Why don't we make it into one?"

This was the start of a participatory process in which Esserman, who also holds an MBA, raised funds for a redesign, and Chamberlain brought seeds for chemotherapy patients to grow in paper cups and later plant in the sparse areas of the courtyard that were not paved. Some people brought plants from home to add to the environment. As people saw the potential for change, interest grew.

In 1995–96, Chamberlain was awarded a residency at the hospital as an artist through the Haas Family Fund. She continued to work with patients, organizing tile-making workshops and events in the garden to demonstrate that this was a place where things could happen.

Garden designer Katsy Swan was brought into the process. The three women made a powerful team: Chamberlain understood the dynamics of the hospital community and knew the site well; Swan had extensive knowledge of appropriate plants and drew schematic designs for a garden that could serve many different users; and Esserman knew how to draw in financial support.

As the design process progressed, a workshop was held with patients and staff. Participants asked for a variety of places to sit, a water element, lighting to extend use after dark, places to find privacy, baffles on a noisy air compressor,

8.7 Tile-making workshop with Dr. Laura Esserman (left) and Ann Chamberlain (right).
Photo by Clare Cooper Marcus

planting to shade a long interior corridor that felt like a furnace on summer afternoons, and some way to reduce the smell of fast food wafting into the garden from Divisadero Street. All but the last were achieved in the completed garden.

The energy generated around the creation of the garden instigated a series of changes that resulted in the transformation of the whole wing of the medical center, known as the Ida and Joseph Friend Cancer Resource Center. After spearheading the redesign of the garden, Chamberlain turned her attention to a long, glass-walled corridor that defined the eastern edge of the garden. She stated: "It was white and clinical and decorated with posters of lab technicians in white coats declaring, 'We are going to eradicate cancer!' I wanted something that spoke of the subjective experiences of patients. When Herb Caen, a much-loved local columnist, was being treated here for lung cancer, he termed it Dead Man Walking corridor!" (Cooper Marcus 2001, 41) (fig. 8.7).

Working with ceramists Kenyon Lewis, Martha Heavenston, and Cenri Nojima, Chamberlain started pressing leaves and flowers from the garden into 12 by 16 inch off-white tiles. This tile-making activity developed into a number of workshops where cancer patients, cancer survivors, and family members created a total of 525 tiles that now cover the interior wall of the corridor for a length of 85 feet. "People need to know that their story matters. We wanted to make it impossible for them ever to put up those dreadful posters again!" said Chamberlain. Each tile has a leaf or flower impressed into it, the Latin name beneath it, and a personal poem, story, or quotation inscribed by the tile-maker. The tiles not only provide a decorative and moving addition to an

otherwise bland corridor but also create a botanical element that brings the garden inside and an attractive "frieze" viewed from the garden through the glass wall of the corridor.

The constant change in the garden is balanced by the permanence of the tiles. The stories on the tiles are expressions of love, fear, grief, and faith that reflect the emotions aroused at a time of medical crisis. The inscription on Chamberlain's tile reads: "This year in the garden I learned to live with my eyes on the sky, to love the peachy pinkness of the pansy, to lie belly down on the warm cement as the wind picks up and watch the golden coreopsis dance and bob like exploding fireworks. This year, I learned to live like a plant."

How the Garden Is Used

(Note: The following account of how the garden is used draws on observations made in 2000, when this garden was still part of the Clinical Cancer Center. The garden is still used as part of the Women's Health Center, but the café mentioned below has closed.)

On a warm day around noon a woman sits at a small wooden table eating a brown-bag lunch and reading the newspaper. Three people stop in the corridor adjacent to the garden and point out various plants to each other. A man in a white coat sits at a table talking quietly on a cell phone, reads for a while, and then is joined by a woman bringing lunch from a café that opens onto the garden. Two young men sit on a bench facing the sun, close their eyes and talk, then start to write on notepads, move to a table, and talk intently for an hour. A man wheels a baby in a stroller up to a table, eats his lunch, then moves to a seating wall in the shade. A man and woman enter with take-out lunches from the cafe, move a bench a few feet into the sun, and sit down to eat. Three colleagues settle in the shade to eat; the man pulls a chair up to the bench so that one of the women can put her feet up, then he carefully erases the tracks the chair legs have made through the gravel (fig. 8.8).

This is a typical scenario between 11 a.m. and 3 p.m. on a summer day. People come into the garden to eat lunch, wait for an appointment, hold small staff meetings, sit or talk quietly with a family member, do paperwork, or relax in the sun. A small fountain-pool, made from tiles that fell off a hospital entryway during the 1989 Loma Prieta earthquake, forms a focal point at the west end of the garden and provides the soothing sound of falling water, though it cannot completely mask the constant background sound of traffic on nearby Divisadero Street. Smells from the kitchen of the fast-food outlet on the same street waft into the west end of the garden and can be troubling for chemotherapy patients, who avoid this part of the garden.

8.8 Lunchtime in the healing garden.
Photo by Clare Cooper Marcus

Some people visit a hospital garden to seek distraction, to forget for a moment the gloomy prognosis they may just have heard, or to gain some perspective before attending a difficult staff meeting. This garden offers plentiful, subtle, and soothing distractions: feathery shadows of leaves on a gravel pathway, the late afternoon sun illuminating the corridor tiles, a hummingbird hovering to drink at the fountain, tendrils of a climbing wisteria moving in the breeze, a

seagull circling high above. Many more people than those who actually enter the garden gain enjoyment from its presence: people passing along the tiled corridor often turn their eyes towards the garden as they go by, or stop briefly to look out at the greenery.

Esserman recalls, "One of my patients told me she always spent an hour in the garden before she came up to see me. She watched the garden change. Some flowers faded, others were just beginning, soon to be brilliant. It inspired her to believe that her illness may have its seasons, too. To her, the garden was hope" (Cooper Marcus 2001, 99).

Key Garden Merits

- A human-scale courtyard
- Green and colorful aesthetic
- Comfortable, movable seating
- Visible from main corridor
- Garden theme reflected in corridor tiles
- Sounds of water

A Concern

- Cooking smells apparent in part of garden

CASE STUDY

The Thea and James Stoneman Healing Garden, Dana-Farber Cancer Institute, Yawkey Center for Cancer Care, Boston, Massachusetts

Designers: Carol R. Johnson Associates, Landscape Architects, Zimmer Gunsul Frasca, Architects

Description of the Facility

The Yawkey Center for Cancer Care is an outpatient treatment and research facility connected to the existing Dana-Farber Cancer Institute (DFCI) in a highly urbanized area of Boston. The indoor garden occupies a corner location of the building bounded by Jimmy Fund Way and Brookline Avenue and highlights the new front door of DFCI (fig. 8.9).

Design Philosophy

The Healing Garden reflects Dana-Farber's commitment to support the well-being, health, and safety of its patients, families, and staff. The architects and landscape architects worked with a wide-ranging group of stakeholders, including representatives of Dana-Farber's Patient and Family Advisory

Council, pediatric and adult nursing staff, physicians, hospital administrators, safety and infection control, facilities management, and members of the Arts and Environment Committee. Key goals of the design were to accommodate users under stress by providing a relief from hard surfaces and a medical environment, while at the same time meeting the meticulous requirements of hospital infection control. The design, construction, and maintenance of the garden were made possible through a donation from Thea and James Stoneman.

Description of the Garden

The north-facing garden occupies 1,790 square feet in an 18-foot glass-walled corner that spans the third and fourth floors of the outpatient cancer center, which opened in 2011 (fig. 8.10). Easy

8.9 The exterior view of the garden serves as a beacon and a symbol of healing. The garden's third-floor location and lush plantings afford privacy for garden users.
Copyright Carol R. Johnson Associates, Inc.

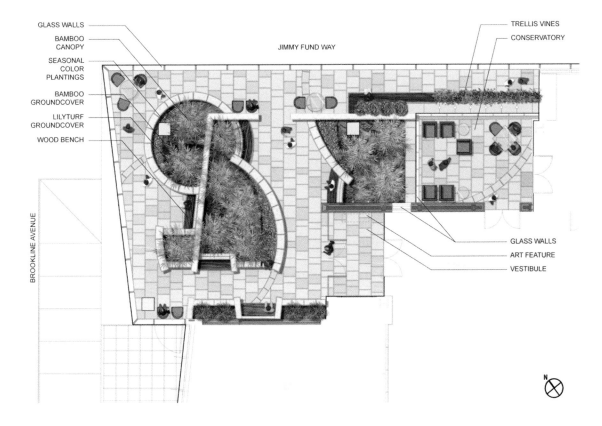

GLASS WALLS
BAMBOO CANOPY
SEASONAL COLOR PLANTINGS
BAMBOO GROUNDCOVER
LILYTURF GROUNDCOVER
WOOD BENCH

JIMMY FUND WAY

TRELLIS VINES
CONSERVATORY

BROOKLINE AVENUE

GLASS WALLS
ART FEATURE
VESTIBULE

N

8.10 Garden plan.
© *Carol R. Johnson Associates, Inc.*

8.11 Comfortable wooden benches of varying lengths are tucked into the raised planting beds throughout the garden. Movable chairs and stools augment the fixed seating. Colorful planting is rotated periodically, augmenting the evergreen bamboo.
Photo by Naomi Sachs

and safe access for patients, families, and staff is afforded by non-slip surfaces, and circulation space adequate for wheelchairs and maintenance equipment. Throughout the space, fixed wooden seating and movable wooden chairs invite use by individuals and small groups. Some seating areas are more public, some more private (fig. 8.11). Warm-colored natural stone defines raised planting beds; the wooden benches are tucked into niches in the retaining wall, facilitating a sense of prospect and refuge. Labels identify key plants, and decorative stones inscribed with the word "Hope" in several languages are placed in different locations throughout the garden (fig. 8.12, fig. 8.13).

Black bamboo, lady palms, dwarf white stripe bamboo, and lily turf form a simple plant palette that is augmented with frequent rotations of colorful flowers and foliage such as orchids, begonias, cyclamen, gloxinia bromeliads, and spring bulbs. The Stoneman's donation included an ongoing annual maintenance budget for planting, cleaning, and so on. Infection control was of paramount importance in the design. Only nontoxic

8.12 Stones set in planter beds throughout the garden are inscribed with the word with "Hope" in different languages.
Photo by Naomi Sachs

8.13 "Hope" in Russian.
Photo by Naomi Sachs

and pest-resistant plants were used, each in an individual self-watering pot that can easily be changed out. A sterile soil mix is covered with decorative Mexican beach stones. The black bamboo, which will eventually grow to sixteen feet, is cleaned weekly with an electrostatic cleaning system.

The garden entry is a 122-square-foot double-door vestibule with its own air-handling system to prevent garden air from mixing with the air-handling system that supplies other public and clinical areas. While the garden is located next to a new dining facility, no food, cell phones, or audible pagers are permitted in the space. Recordings of birdsong and rainfall help to mask the sounds of traffic on adjacent streets. Surrounded on two sides by the Healing Garden is the Richard P. and Claire W. Morse Conservatory, a separate 265-square-foot glass-walled space for severely immunocompromised patients who are not able to enter the healing garden itself; those patients can still benefit from views of and sounds from the garden.

Key Garden Merits

- Design responds to the needs of patients, families, and staff.

- Careful consideration of patient safety.

- Green, nurturing space in an urban setting.

- Warm, natural materials.

- Many choices of seating and views.

- Ample natural light to support plant health.

- Open around-the-clock and available in all seasons and weather conditions.

- Garden is well marked at its entrance and also on maps and signage throughout the facility.

- Funding ensures daily and specialized maintenance.

Maggie's Centre Gardens, United Kingdom

Named after landscape architect Maggie Keswick, who died of breast cancer in 1995, these centers offer information, support, and counseling to cancer patients and their families. Ten such centers have been built in the UK, and one in Hong Kong. Seven more are planned in the UK, and one in Barcelona, Spain.

Each of the Maggie's Centre buildings is focused around a welcoming homelike kitchen/sitting room, with adjacent offices and counseling rooms, and is located close to a hospital that offers cancer treatment. Each of the centers includes a garden. Observation of these in person and via the literature (Jencks and Heathcote 2010) suggests that they meet, with varying degrees of success, the recommendations for gardens serving cancer patients proposed in this book. For example, the garden proposed at Monklands General Hospital, Lanarkshire, Scotland, by Rankin Fraser, includes trees, shrubs, and perennials and echoes what most nondesigners (Maggie's clients) would recognize as a traditional garden. Others worthy of note are centers located on wooded sites, such as those at Nottingham, Gartnavel, Kirkcaldy, and in Swansea, southwest Wales, where views out to mature trees provide people inside the building with a chance to engage with the natural world and offer a sense of visual escape.

8.14 A lone, exposed bench in the garden at the Maggie's Centre in London does not provide a private, restorative setting. Designer: Dan Pearson.
Photo by Clare Cooper Marcus

The garden at the London Maggie's Centre, by Dan Pearson, is constrained by its narrow site between a parking lot and a busy street. It provides an attractive array of planting, but one lone, exposed bench does nothing to meet the needs that cancer patients may have for a place of withdrawal and privacy (fig. 8.14).

A number of the gardens (for example, those at Glasgow, Inverness, and Cheltenham) display metaphorical landscapes with mounded forms inspired by biological concepts such as cell division. Apart from the fact that the "green" provided by flat or mounded grass provides minimal engagement with nature, gardens incorporating intellectual concepts and metaphors may not succeed as restorative settings if the majority of users do not understand or appreciate their meaning, and if the gardens do not also provide the essentials of accessibility, comfort, privacy, and so on (fig. 8.15).

Charles Jencks (2006, 455) has written that among the goals of the Maggie's Centres is that they operate in "a peaceful and striking environment in which art and gardens play an important role." But perhaps the goals of an environment's being "peaceful" and "striking" are contradictory. To date, there have been no comprehensive postoccupancy evaluations of these gardens, which is unfortunate considering how much attention has been directed toward the iconic architecture of Centre buildings and how many centers have been built and are in the planning stages. A designer's insights, however well intentioned, are not enough. Feedback forms or a visitors book in which people record their appreciations, though a welcome touch, are not enough. It does not appear that the body of research on therapeutic gardens has been incorporated into the design brief (program) given to designers, which may partially explain why some of the gardens are not as suitable for their users as they might have been.

A professional landscape architect and cancer survivor had this to say in 2010 following her use of the resources at the Glasgow and Edinburgh Maggie's and her visits to look at those in Dundee, Fife, and Inverness: "What I felt I wanted above all else when I was really ill was: simplicity, peace and quiet, natural surroundings with natural materials. Birdsong and wildlife. Watching clouds and looking up through branches and leaves. Quiet places to sit with someone. The possibility of tea in the

8.15 View from the Highlands Maggie's Centre building in Inverness, Scotland, to the outdoor space is dominated by two mounds representing cells communicating and in dynamic balance. This artistic design does not provide a setting which most would recognize and use as a garden. Garden designer: Charles Jencks.
Photo by Clare Cooper Marcus

garden. Nice things to touch and smell, but not too much. . . . I don't think I was looking for inspiration in the way these architects present it. Sculpture on the whole did not do anything for me. . . . One thing I really liked was the rustle of the wind in bamboos. As I say, simple things" (pers. comm.).

In a comment on the thinkinGardens website, cancer patient Victoria Summerley (2009) noted, regarding the garden at the London Maggie's: "In a cancer care garden, in my view, you want movement, birdsong, water—any sort of indication that at least here life is continuing in a natural way and hopefully providing you with a distraction. On a practical note, I couldn't see much seating either. People who have had cancer treatment (especially chemo) don't usually feel up to standing around for any length of time. And neither do their loved ones: they're usually knackered!"

Maggie Keswick was passionate and knowledgeable about gardens. To honor her memory, it is important to ensure that in the future the gardens of Maggie's Centres are as supportive and nurturing as they can be for those affected by cancer who seek to use them.

References

Cimprich, B., and D. L. Ronis. 2003. "An Environmental Intervention to Restore Attention in Women with Newly Diagnosed Breast Cancer." *Cancer Nursing* 26 (4): 284–92.

Cooper Marcus, C. 2001. "Hospital Oasis: Through a Participatory Design Process, a Failed Tommy Church Garden in San Francisco Is Reconfigured as an Exemplary Therapeutic Landscape." *Landscape Architecture Magazine* 91 (12).

———. 2003. "Survey of Women with Cancer Attending the Healing Journeys Conference, Sacramento, CA." Unpublished paper.

English, J., K. Wilson, and S. Kelley-Olaman. 2008. "Health, Healing and Recovery: Therapeutic Landscapes and the Everyday Lives of Breast Cancer Survivors." *Social Science and Medicine* 67.

Galvão, D. A., and R. U. Newton. 2005. "Review of Exercise Intervention Studies in Cancer Patients." *Journal of Clinical Oncology* 23 (4): 899–909.

Jencks, C. 2006. "Maggie's Centres and the Architectural Placebo." Pp. 448-59 in *The Architecture of Hospitals*, edited by C. Wagenaar. Rotterdam: NAi Publishers.

Jencks, C., and E. Heathcote. 2010. *The Architecture of Hope.* London: Frances Lincoln.

McNeeley M. L., K. L. Campbell, B. H. Rowe, Terry P. Klassen, J. R. Mackey, and K. S. Courneya. 2006. "Effects of Exercise on Breast Cancer Patients and Survivors: A Systematic Review and Meta-analysis. *Canadian Medical Association Journal* 175 (1): 34–41.

Summerley, V. 2009. "Victoria Summerley on the Maggie Centre." *thinkinGardens*, February 25. thinkingardens.co.uk/uncategorized/victoria-summerley-on-the-maggie-centre/.

CHAPTER 9

Gardens for the Frail Elderly

THE NEXT FEW DECADES WILL SEE A BUR-GEONING need for facilities for seniors, many of whom will become increasingly frail. One estimate suggests that ten thousand baby boomers in the U.S. turn sixty-five every day. Although the great majority of them—perhaps as many as 95 percent—will remain living alone or with relatives, more and more purpose-built facilities are being developed to house seniors. Among such facilities are retirement communities, housing for independent living, assisted-living, skilled nursing (formerly known as nursing homes), and continuing-care retirement facilities (CCRCs), which usually incorporate independent living, assisted living, and skilled nursing on one large campus-like site.

It is critically important in terms of physical and psychosocial health that those who reside in any type of purpose-built facilities for seniors have access to outdoor space that is specifically designed for their needs. In terms of physical health, as people age they lose muscle mass and bone density, have problems with balance, are more prone to falls, often have difficulty sleeping; they are also more prone to depression. All of these issues can be ameliorated by exercise, notably walking, while bone density is enhanced by vitamin D production, which is stimulated by being outside in sunlight for as little as ten to fifteen minutes daily. The appropriate length of exposure will vary with latitude and must be balanced against the dangers of sunburn. In Australia, where natural UV radiation levels are higher than in much of the Northern Hemisphere and there is an increased risk of skin cancers, sun exposure is recommended only before 10 a.m. or after 2 p.m.

Daylight is just as effective as sunlight in helping to balance circadian rhythms, thus leading to better sleep patterns and up to a 70 percent reduction in the use of sleeping pills. Walking also helps people deal with stress and anxiety, lowers blood sugar, improves cognitive functioning, decreases the risk of a heart attack, cuts the risk of stroke in half, and reduces the risk of type-2 diabetes. But it is tempting, as people age, for them to become more and more sedentary. Hence the great importance of having outdoor space that is easily accessible, safe to negotiate, and attractive to spend time in (fig. 9.1).

In terms of psychosocial health, spending time outdoors improves mood, lessens agitation and aggression among those with dementia, and reduces depression among those with seasonal affective disorder (SAD). Psychosocial health also relates to people being able to meet and converse with others to the extent that they wish and also—when needed—to find places of privacy and solitude. The sensitive placement of seating, tables, movable furniture, and planting can enhance the use of the outdoors for programmed social events, informal meetings with other residents or visiting family members, and getting away from what, for some, may be the pressures of congregate living or sharing a room with a stranger. When people are living together in the same building, the importance of a restful, welcoming outdoor alternative cannot be overemphasized.

In a study of fourteen assisted-living facilities in Texas, residents noted that the primary barriers to going outside were doors that were hard to open, inadequate seating, lack of protection from the sun, and landscapes low in interest. Greenery, flowers, birds, water features, and fresh air were what people liked best about the outdoors. Preferred built features in the garden included overhead shelters, sitting areas, porches, and gazebos (Rodiek 2005). Other studies have noted the critical issue of an entry door that is hard to manipulate or a lip that impedes wheelchairs at the entry. A study of outdoor access in assisted-living facilities found that in those where residents could easily cross the door threshold, residents spent on average more than three hours a week outdoors, compared to facilities where this was not so (Rodiek 2009). This is a critical amount of time, considering the value to health of being outdoors, and it calls for serious design attention to the details of indoor/outdoor connection.

While it is important in designing for the elderly to think about removing barriers and preserving security, it is also important to support people's needs for independence and autonomy and allow for increased opportunities. For example,

9.1 It is critical for the physical and mental health of older people in residential facilities that they have access to an attractive outdoor space with a door that is easy to open, smooth walking paths, and a destination point to aim for.
Photo by Susan Rodiek

a person may not be able to bend or squat to garden as they did when they were younger, but by providing window boxes, raised beds, or waist-high tubs, they may maintain or even increase their ability to do so as they age.

It should be recognized that there will be a great range of abilities among those living in a facility for seniors. Those in their early sixties may have needs that are little different from those who are decades younger, whereas those in their nineties have likely experienced changes in strength, agility, gait, and posture (Stoneham and Thoday 1996, 19). Reduced mobility calls for careful attention to design details of garden egress, paths, handrails, steps, ramps, frequency of seating, choice of routes, and features of interest near the building. Visual impairment and sensitivity to glare call for care in selecting pathway surfaces and plant materials. The tendency

of elderly residents to shuffle and their fear of falling call for attention to pathway traction and maintenance. Sensitivity to extremes of weather calls for attention to shelter, shade, and the placement of seating. A good rule of thumb is that "outdoor design must provide for the more restricting disabilities yet offer a range of opportunities. Above all, designs should be flexible and allow for modifications over time" (ibid., 19). As the early cohorts of older baby boomers begin to reach their eighties and nineties, facilities that served them in their sixties will need to be adaptable to an increasingly frail or disabled population.

Interviews with residents of three long-term-care facilities in the Seattle, Washington, area found that their own physical limitations and the lack of staff assistance were the principal reasons why they did not go outside as much as they would wish. While staff time to accompany people outdoors may always be at a premium, thoughtful design can help to mitigate physical limitations. What people did in their favorite outdoor spaces were, in order of importance, observe plants, sit, watch/interact with other people, tend gardens, read, enjoy the fresh air and social functions, and sleep. Those who could not easily go outside enjoyed views from windows of plants, birds, people, scenery, wildlife, weather, and the sky (Kearney and Winterbottom 2005). One study of elderly women in a Canadian retirement residence who viewed a natural landscape through a window found that they exhibited lower systolic and diastolic blood pressure and lower heart rates than those measured in a control room with no windows (Tang and Brown 2005). This research emphasizes the importance of architects and landscape architects working closely together regarding site planning, window design and placement, views from the building, and so on. A study of sixty-eight US assisted-living facilities in a variety of climatic regions found that where usable outdoor areas were easily viewed from indoor common sitting areas, residents spent on average of four hours more a week outdoors than in facilities where this was not so (Rodiek 2009).

With many Western societies becoming increasingly multicultural, it is important to consider not only the general preferences of older adults but also subtle differences between cultural groups. While research is limited, one study of elderly US Hispanics found "furnished" garden settings such as plazas and courtyards more compatible with their preferred activities, such as group-oriented socializing. Anglo-American elderly, on the other hand, preferred "authentic" natural settings, such as a lawn and pond, more amenable to quiet reflection (Alves, Gulwadi, and Cohen 2005). Since many facilities may have a mix of cultural groups, it is advisable to provide a mix of built elements and natural features. When there is a preponderance of Chinese or Chinese-American residents, principles of feng shui should be considered in landscape design (fig. 9.2).

At Nikkei Manor, an assisted-living facility for Japanese-American seniors in Seattle, a courtyard garden designed and built by University of Washington landscape architecture students and their professors featured a traditional Japanese gate, cranes symbolizing longevity and good fortune, a lotus foundation, a small meditation space anchored by a stone Buddha, and a space for drum concerts. (See figure 19.6.)

As they age, many people experience increased boredom, helplessness, and loneliness (ibid.). A garden with ample green nature can buffer experiences of boredom by providing sensory stimulation and opportunities to engage in simple

9.2 At this California retirement facility, where most of the residents are Chinese-American, the garden design emphasizes rounded forms and red flowers, both of which indicate good luck in Chinese culture.
Photo by Clare Cooper Marcus

gardening tasks. A sense of helplessness can be ameliorated in a garden by providing a sense of choice and control as to where to go, what to do, and what to look at and by offering an escape from negative psychological states as people shift their attention from personal problems to the "soft fascination" of viewing nature.

Loss of physical abilities, friends, familiar surroundings, and employment can all contribute to feelings of loneliness. A well-designed garden can offer settings contributing to social support, such as places to meet with other residents or visiting family members, and for staff-programmed activities. A study of residents at a Swedish home for the very old found that time spent in the garden was most restorative—measured by lower blood pressure and heart rate—for those residents who had a low tolerance of others, were not helpful in group activities, and had a high frequency of hospital visits (Ottosson and Grahn 2005). Another study found that the positive effects of visits to the garden among elderly long-term-care residents were more pronounced among the depressed than among those who were not depressed (Rappe and Kivelä 2005). Assuming that these finding might be generalizable, here is another reason to promote gardens in senior living: access to green nature is particularly important for the most psychologically vulnerable in terms of restoring them to a state of balance.

Providing appropriate outdoor space in facilities for seniors is cost-effective in improving the quality of life for residents and caregivers, enhancing resident health and occupancy levels, promoting recommendations to future

9.3 An attractive garden, domestic in scale and design and with a variety of places to sit and walk and things to look at and touch, will encourage older residents to exercise and spend time outdoors, thus contributing to their overall health. Graham Garden, Saanich Community Hospital, Victoria, British Columbia. Designer: LeFrank & Associates.
Photo by Clare Cooper Marcus

residents, and ensuring staff satisfaction. But this space must be designed with very careful attention to the needs of residents. In addition to the General Design Guidelines (see chapter 6), the following guidelines emphasize the needs of the frail elderly, since this is the most vulnerable population group in facilities for seniors (fig. 9.3).

Design Guidelines

General considerations

Required

1. The outdoor space must have the **look of a domestic garden** in terms of scale, details, and planting. Designer of gardens for senior communities Jack Carman (2006) writes: "These areas should *look* home-like. Residents need to feel as though they are experiencing gardens familiar to them, and that they belong there." A not inconsequential issue is a landscape that impresses the adult children of an aging parent looking for a suitable "home away from home" to move the parent into—a move often accompanied by a mixture of sadness and guilt on the part of the adult children. A study of more than a thousand respondents in sixty-eight assisted-living facilities found that seniors themselves value nature very highly and that they "feel better outside" (Rodiek 2009).

2. Provide a simple, **clear garden layout** viewable from the garden entry, preferably with a simple looped, circular, or figure-eight pathway system.

3. Provide **appropriate destination points**, such as a gazebo, arbor, pavilion, or summer house that has ample seating and is large enough to be used for social events or programmed activities organized by the staff. Depending on the local climate, this space should ideally be supplied with lighting, heat lamps, and/or fans to extend outdoor use in cooler or hotter seasons. Screening against insects may also be necessary.

4. **Provide plenty of choice**—in seating, pathway routes, views, destinations, and the like. This is important for any healing garden, but especially for those catering to the elderly in a residential environment where there may not be many choices indoors and where they may not have many opportunities (or the energy) to seek choice in the wider community.

5. **Provide garden spaces both at the back of the building and in the front**. The latter are particularly popular as people like to watch for the person delivering mail or the car bringing a visitor. The front garden should be viewable from the main lobby so that people sitting there can feel secure, and just off to the side of the building entrance so those coming and going do not have to run the gauntlet of people sitting in the garden. Rodiek's (2009) study of US assisted-living facilities

9.4 Residents at a senior facility taking care of the planting beds, an activity that provides them with exercise and a sense of ownership and creates an attractive setting for others to enjoy.
Photo by Susan Rodiek

found that where residents could sit and view off-site vehicular activity from an outdoor area they spent on average almost three hours more per week outdoors than in facilities where this was not possible.

6. The philosophy of the institution and the training of the staff—often referred to as "organizational culture"—make a huge difference as to whether residents are allowed to go outside, or are encouraged to do so. Do staff members leave the doors unlocked? Do they promote activities outside? With staff encouragement, residents can be "tempted" outdoors with barbecues, ice cream socials, picnics, birthday parties, croquet, and so on. Designers need to **work closely with staff** or their representatives to assure them that safety, security, and accessibility have been fully addressed in the design of the outdoor space.

7. The **culture and attitudes of the residents toward nature** and the outdoors, as well their image of what a garden is, must be sensitively addressed. For example, low-income Londoners who may have left a garden at home with a small lawn, roses, and space for vegetables are not going to relate easily to an area of white gravel, blue urns, and a symmetrical Persian motif.

Recommended

1. Ensure that the garden is **attractive, well maintained, and rich with amenities,** to encourage family members to visit more often and take their relative outdoors.

2. **Allow for views** out to the wider landscape so that residents can feel a sense of belonging to a broader community.

3. Provide an **area specifically designed for gardening** (raised beds, tool shed, various large containers, access to water) that can allow older people to draw on past skills (fig. 9.4). A potting bench should ideally be designed with three different heights available: for a person standing, a person sitting, and a person using a wheelchair. If it is designed to be open on both sides, it can afford access from different directions for left- and right-handed people (Diaz Moore 2001).

4. If there is enough space, include a simple **recreational amenity** such as a putting green, shuffleboard court, or croquet lawn with nearby storage area for equipment. This will be used by the residents and also by visiting families, including older children.

5. Provide something that will be **attractive to younger visiting grandchildren**, such as a sandbox or a versatile piece of play equipment. Keeping children engaged may help a family extend their visits.

6. In regions with long winters and/or inclement weather, provide a **glass-enclosed atrium, solarium, or conservatory** with ample room for plants, seating, and perhaps a small water feature and/or aviary to allow residents to enjoy a semioutdoor experience year-round (fig. 9.5). Bright, natural light is beneficial to health, and the conservatory space can provide a setting for socializing and horticultural therapy.

9.5 At this retirement facility in Canada, where winters are long and cold, rocks that were extracted to construct the building were retained and used to create this indoor garden, well-lit with natural light from above and visible from the corridors that encircle this central space.
Photo by Clare Cooper Marcus

9.6 At this London residence for retired Anglican sisters, residents have a good view to the garden while seated in the main lounge.
Photo by Clare Cooper Marcus

(For examples from a number of facilities for older adults in northwestern Europe, see Regnier 1994.)

Visual access

Required

1. Locate the garden so that it is **clearly visible from inside the building**—particularly from frequently used areas such as the main lobby, day room, dining room, or main hallway—so that residents are aware it is there when going about their daily activities. Ensure that the arrangement of furniture and the presence of window coverings do not block the view out. Ensure that windows are large and low enough so that people seated inside have a good view out to the garden. These requirements dictate that there must be early collaboration among architect, interior designer, and landscape architect (fig. 9.6).

2. The major elements of planting should be arranged with a primary consideration for **views looking *out* of the building**, since for many residents this will be their principal daily experience of the garden. It is preferable to bias the display to those times when it may be too cold for people to go outside.

3. Where resident units look out onto the garden, ensure that the **windows are low enough** that there is a good view out from a seated position.

Recommended

1. Provide **attractive foreground and more distant views** from the entry patio to the back garden, since this space is likely to be used more than the garden itself.

2. The whole garden should be **viewable from inside the building by staff** going about their daily activities or from a nurses' station (if there is one) so that they can keep an eye on residents. If staff can view the outdoors from indoors, they are more likely to keep doors unlocked and allow or encourage residents to go outside (Rodiek 2009).

Physical access

Required

1. Ensure that at any garden entry there is a **patio/transition space to the outdoors**. Elderly people adjust to changes in temperature and light less easily than younger people, hence this space should be adequately sheltered, and it should provide sufficient shade so that people can adjust to brighter outdoor lighting. Skylights or higher-intensity lights just inside can balance the bright light outside for people reentering the building.

2. The **entry patio to a back garden should be large enough to accommodate several people** in wheelchairs, together with tables and chairs suitable for eating outside, and for programmed group activities such as barbecues, ice cream socials, and birthday parties (fig. 9.7). Whether or not a staff-led activity is taking place, this patio is likely to be the most

9.7 A shaded entry patio to the garden at a Canadian facility for the frail elderly. Graham Garden, Saanich Community Hospital, Victoria, British Columbia. Designer: LeFrank & Associates.
Photo by Clare Cooper Marcus

9.8 Frail residents with balance problems at Ferryfield House in Edinburgh, Scotland, can hold onto a handrail to reach a bench in the garden. Designer: Annie Pollock.
Photo by Annie Pollock

used space in the garden since many do not have the energy to venture further, or need to stay close to toilets in the building.

Recommended

1. Where resident units are on several floors, provide those at garden level with small, **semiprivate garden spaces** where residents can grow flowers or care for favorite plants they have brought from home. This space should have level access from the unit, a hard surface area large enough for two chairs, a small table, large tubs or raised planters for gardening, privacy screens separating the space from the one next door, and a symbolic boundary between this semiprivate space and the communal outdoor area.

Pathways

Required

1. **Level and glare-free paths with good traction** are especially important for the frail elderly since there are high incidences of osteoporosis and arthritis among them, and falls are often caused by glare reflected from light-colored paving and irregularities in a pathway surface. The fear of falling can drastically limit exercise, so the pathway system must not only be completely secure for those with limited mobility or the tendency to shuffle but must also be perceived to be secure. For example, avoid a shiny surface as this may be perceived as being slippery.

2. Provide **handrails** along all or part of pathway system to assist those with balance problems (fig. 9.8). In many cases, residents make use of handrails along corridors inside the facility. A continuation of that element may encourage use of the outdoors. If there are any steps on site, handrails must be provided on both sides to accommodate those with limited use of one arm.

3. Ensure that there is **consistent pathway color**, since an older person often reacts to contrasting ground plane colors as if there were a change in depth. Known as "visual cliffing," this is an example of agnosia, or the inability to understand and use sensory information.

4. In providing shade, **avoid any garden structure (arbor, trellis, or pergola) that might cast dark slatted shadows** on the pathway or patio. These can be misinterpreted as "troughs," or changes in depth.

Seating

Required

1. Since older people tend to lose muscle mass, they find it difficult to get up from a seated position. **Seat height** should be higher than usual (18–19"), with a maximum seat depth of 20", arm height of 25–26" and arms projecting forward from the seat to provide extra support when standing up. With a bench serving several people there should be armrests

9.9 This courtyard garden provides easy access from inside the building, a variety of seating, places to sit in the sun or shade, and hard surfaces that are easily negotiable by residents who use walkers or wheelchairs. Courtesy of the Plaza at Twin Rivers, Arkadelphia, Arkansas.
Photo by Wesley Kluck

between seating positions to assist people standing up. Some extra wide armrests provide space to put a drink or a book. Never specify the ubiquitous Adirondack chair, as it is particularly difficult for an older person to rise from the slumped back position in which it places the body, and this position is unhealthy for internal organs.

2. At transition places to the outdoors, provide **fixed and movable seating** with small tables beside or between seats as places to set down a drink, a book, or other personal belongings. Tables need to be sturdy since they are likely to be used as supports as people sit down or get up. Movable chairs need to be carefully selected as they need to be light enough for a person with limited strength to maneuver, but sturdy enough and with splayed legs so that they do not tip over when a person is leaning on them for support. Fabric or nylon mesh chairs and cane chairs are comfortable and easy to move (fig. 9.9).

3. Provide a **color contrast between seating and the ground plane** for ease of use by the sight-impaired.

4. Provide **seating**, alternating with a place to lean (planter edge or handrail, for example) **at relatively frequent intervals** along main pathways. A spacing of 15–20 feet is necessary for those who are quite frail and may encourage those who are unsure on their feet to take a short walk.

5. Since older people are particularly sensitive to the cold, some seating should be located to **catch the sun**, with adequate shelter and enclosure. Conversely, since older people have a hard time dealing with the glare of sunlight off light-colored surfaces, there should be some seating with adequate shade for use in the warmest season.

6. Provide seats for one or two people alone in **semiprivate spaces** for those who wish to talk with a visitor in private; for

A comfortable, tucked-away space to sit and enjoy a conversation.
Photo by Susan Rodiek

a resident who may want to retreat from the possible stress of living in a congregate setting or sharing a room; or for someone who seeks a place of solitude in nature. Seating for seniors often overemphasizes arrangements for socializing while overlooking the need for privacy. Never locate this or any other seating in exposed locations where people may feel on display, or on grass, which is an unstable surface for both pedestrians and those using wheeled mobility devices (fig. 9.10).

7. Provide some **seating at right angles or opposite each other a short distance apart** since seeing the person they are chatting with helps some older people who are hard of hearing.

8. Locate the most accessible/attractive **seating areas to catch the morning sun** since light at this time appears to suppress the production of sleep hormones (melatonin) and promotes the production of serotonin, which positively affects mood and appetite.

Recommended

1. Provide residents on upper floors with **balconies wide enough** for two chairs, a small table, and assorted containers for plants (fig. 9.11). If balconies cannot be provided, upper units need to have one window with sills wide enough to accommodate flowerpots.

2. Provide **padded cushions** for all or most of the outdoor seating since older people lose muscle mass and

9.11 The balconies at this California retirement facility are wide enough for chairs, a table, and potted plants while providing a green view of trees with predominantly vertical growth.
Photo by Clare Cooper Marcus

find hard surfaces uncomfortable to sit on for any length of time.

3. Provide one or two **glider chairs or seats**, with one of them designed to accommodate a wheelchair. Swinging is highly popular with children and is said to enhance vestibular and brain development. Might glider seats for the elderly also enhance brain capacity? They are certainly very popular when they are provided.

GARDENS FOR THE FRAIL ELDERLY **137**

Planting

Required

1. Ensure that **plant displays** and interest are spread **throughout the year**, since for many residents—because of age, disability, or inclement weather—their immediate outdoor environment is all that they will see and experience of the natural world. A study of sixty-eight US assisted-living facilities found that where the outdoor space had a broad range of plants, residents spent on average three and a half hours more per week outdoors than where this was not so (Rodiek 2009).

2. Emphasize plants with **flowers or foliage in saturated colors** such as red, yellow, or orange, since colors in the blue/lavender range tend to be perceived as grey when older people develop cataracts.

3. **Compress** as much **interest** as possible into small areas, especially near the garden entry, for those with limited mobility.

4. Emphasize **intricate planting** with varieties of color and texture at or below eye level, since some older people walk in a semistooped posture.

5. Create **small-scale design changes** along the major pathway so that a person moving slowly can have a variety of visual experiences (enclosed/open, sunny/shaded, varied planting, for example).

6. Provide some interesting **planting** to touch or smell **at the height** of someone using a **wheelchair**.

7. Include a range of **scented plants** that can be enjoyed throughout the year. Smell is one of the last senses to fade, and smelling certain plants, or pinching their leaves, can evoke powerful memories. The attractive experience of scents indoors suggests that some plants with evening fragrance should be planted close to entries or windows.

8. Create the potential to **observe wildlife** with, for example, plants that attract birds or butterflies; bird feeder, birdbath, or nesting box; or a fish pond (fig. 9.12). Feeders and birdbaths placed within view of people seated in a communal area (lounge, day room, or dining room) are especially appreciated. A variety of birds will find the garden an attractive habitat if it is planted with a diverse mixture of evergreen and deciduous trees, groundcover, vines on walls and trellises, herbaceous perennials, and shrubs that provide fruit, nuts, and seeds. Be sensitive to possible cultural differences and ascertain if the culture of the majority resident group actually like birds.

9.12 At this Chicago retirement facility, family members visiting residents enjoy sitting with them at the entry to the garden and watching birds attracted to feeders and a family of ducks that has taken up residence in a small pond.
Photo by Clare Cooper Marcus

Recommended

1. Plant selection should take into account the **interests and hobbies** of the residents and the recommendations of any staff who may work with them—horticultural therapists, for example.

2. Include herbaceous flowering plants that are particularly popular with older residents and may have **nostalgic value** and be reminiscent of the garden left behind.

3. Research which species of plants have special **sacred or cultural significance** for the group that makes up the majority of the residents.

4. **Mature trees** (or those that will mature in a relatively short time) can provide a symbolic sense of longevity. Indeed, research has shown that people live longer when in environments populated with trees (Takano, Nakamura, and Watanabe 2002).

Utilities

Recommended

1. In regions with significant **insect problems**, the entry patio should be screened and lit at night.

2. Provide a few brooms, rakes, and watering cans so that residents who wish to can experience a sense of ownership by **helping to maintain the garden**.

Roger Smith Memorial Garden, Friendship Village, Schaumburg, Illinois

Designer: Hitchcock Design Group, Naperville, Illinois

Description of the Facility and Its History

Friendship Village is a large retirement community in suburban Chicago with three kinds of accommodation: small houses and apartments for independent residents, assisted-living units, and a memory-support wing for those with early to middle stages of dementia. Two building wings of independent-living apartments intersect in a large three-story atrium/entry lounge. The garden is entered through a door located in one corner of this space.

Design Philosophy

The garden was developed as a living tribute to Roger Smith, a former resident and long-time board member of Friendship Village. The goals of the designers were to provide outdoor seating, seasonal planting interest, an intergenerational activity (a putting green), and a flexible multiuse space for shuffleboard and temporary seating for outdoor gatherings.

Description of the Outdoor Space

The garden is almost completely enclosed by two-story residential wings and has a pleasing, human-scale, and welcoming feel. It is full of varied and well-maintained planting and has a clear layout with seating, as well as pathways forming shorter and longer loops for exercise (fig. 9.13).

Pathways

At the garden entry there is a brick-paved patio with seating and a choice of tinted concrete pathways that form a loop around the garden, with a cut off through a central multiuse area forming a shorter loop.

Seating

Almost all of the seating consists of attractive wooden garden furniture with backs and arms appropriate for an elderly population. There are plenty of opportunities to sit in the sun or shade. There is a pleasing cluster of movable chairs and tables on the west side of the garden (fig. 9.14).

Planting

There is diverse visual interest in terms of color, texture, and seasonal change. There are many different species of trees, shrubs, and flowering perennials, as well as mounded areas of lawn. The choice of flowering plants in the white/silver/yellow/orange/red range is particularly appropriate for aging

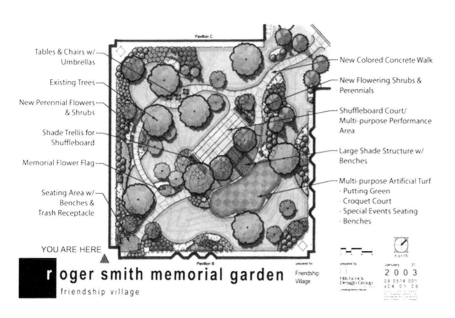

9.13 Site plan of Roger Smith Memorial Garden by Hitchcock Design Group, Naperville, Illinois.
Courtesy: Hitchcock Design Group

eyes (day lilies, hostas, impatiens, white hydrangea, petunias, and bee balm).

Design details

An artificially surfaced putting green provides an activity space for younger visitors. A central shuffleboard area with plenty of adjacent seating doubles as a performance space.

How the Garden Is Used

A postoccupancy study of this garden (Cooper Marcus and Barnes 2008) recorded that by far the most frequent activity was sitting and talking. A few who were observed in the garden alone sat reading or dozing. Relatively few were walking or strolling, and almost all of these were able-bodied or accompanied by an able-bodied companion. On a warm Sunday in July, more than half of those outdoors were residents, and just over one-third were family members visiting relatives. The garden provides a very attractive setting for family visits, as it feels less institutional than the indoors and offers triggers for conversation (birds, plants, the weather, other people) (fig. 9.14). Family members often spoke loudly to those they were visiting, suggesting a garden may be an attractive location for conversations with the hard of hearing.

The patio/porch just outside the entry was the most used space. All of those who came to the garden alone and used a cane or walker stayed in this space. Second in

popularity was the putting green, both in terms of absolute numbers and in duration. This space, together with equipment in a storage container near the entry, provided an attractive destination for visiting families, especially those with children.

Very few staff were seen using this garden, especially compared with hospital gardens, where staff are often the principal users. This may reflect a more amenable break room than at some hospitals, or the fact that residents are less likely to respect social boundaries when a staff person is taking a break outdoors.

Key Garden Merits

- Mature, well-maintained planting.

- Human-scale and a pleasing sense of enclosure.

- Comfortable, sturdy garden-style seating.

- Activity space for young visitors.

- Lighting enhances garden use.

- Clear, simple layout; welcoming feel.

- Visible from many windows.

- Tinted concrete prevents glare.

9.14 The garden is an attractive resource for residents and visitors, with choice of seating in sun and shade, looped pathways, and mature, well-maintained planting.
Photo by Clare Cooper Marcus

- Most paths wide enough for two to walk abreast.

- High ratio of green to hard surfaces.

Possible Concerns

- Little protection from sun or rain at entry patio.

- No tables for a book or a cup of coffee at entry patio.

- Uninteresting planting near garden entry is unlikely to engage interest of those moving slowly or in a stooped position.

- No edges along paths to prevent soil wash out or to provide a sense of security for wheelchair and walker users.

- Slatted shadows caused by shade arbors may provoke visual cliffing.

- Lack of seating at frequent intervals along pathway loops.

- Lack of seating in semiprivate locations.

- Cluster of movable garden furniture located such that those using walkers or wheelchairs have a hard time passing by it.

- Lip at entry door is an impediment for wheelchairs.

- Automatic door opener inside entry is awkward to use.

- Slumping between bricks and pavers, wide gaps between pavers form hazards for those using wheelchairs, walkers, or canes.

CASE STUDY

The Gardens at The Pavilion, Jupiter Medical Center, Jupiter, Florida

Designer: Connie Roy-Fisher/Studio Sprout, Jupiter, Florida
By Chris Garcia

Description of the Facility and Its History

The Pavilion is a 120-bed nonprofit nursing home and rehabilitation center in Jupiter, Florida, that offers palliative care for long-term residents and rehabilitative therapy for patients transferred from Jupiter Medical Center.

The Pavilion's residents face a range of physical challenges, including severe dementia and stroke. Most are not ambulatory, use wheelchairs, and need the assistance of family, staff, or volunteers to go outside.

Roy-Fisher Associates/Studio Sprout developed the master plan for The Pavilion grounds in 2001. The design team consulted with the administrator, rehabilitation staff, and patients to determine how the outdoor spaces could be programmed for therapeutic use. The outdoor spaces were built over a period of eight years through facility support, private donations, municipal grants, and volunteer work. Roy-Fisher Associates supported fundraising efforts by finding grants, creating a donor brochure, and educating staff on the benefits of therapeutic gardens.

Design Philosophy

A series of connected gardens spanning most of the campus emphasize four therapeutic outcomes based on the theory of supportive gardens by Roger Ulrich (1999):

1. Sense of control: Choices to sit in sun or shade and in groups or alone. A continuous pathway unifies the outdoor areas, allowing access from multiple locations. Residents and patients can choose where and how far into the gardens they wish to explore.

2. Exposure to nature: Lush plantings predominate. A bird garden, raised water garden, and native plantings along a retention pond provide wildlife habitat. Primary social spaces are oriented to offer predominant southeast breezes.

3. Exercise: Winding paths encourage patients and staff to stroll or explore in wheelchairs. Benches and features such as water fountains provide landmark "goals" to reach.

4. Social support: Places for people to gather with spatial considerations for wheelchairs. Focal points facilitate conversation (fig. 9.15).

Description of the Outdoor Spaces

Two planted courtyards next to the entrance immediately capture a visitor's attention. In one, a trellis with dense vines frames a large tiered fountain and creates a view from the adjacent dining room. Opposite, a small garden courtyard is surrounded by resident rooms and staff offices. A large specimen palm, perimeter shrubs, and vibrant foliage provide privacy, shade, and visual interest. Two seating alcoves face a blue bowl of gently spilling water, which distracts from the

9.15 Sitting by the retention pond, a favorite place for residents and visitors to feel a breeze and enjoy casual conversation.
Photo by Chris Garcia

9.16 Residents rest in the deep shade on a hot Florida day while enjoying a view of the garden.
Photo by Chris Garcia

hum of an air-conditioning unit and has a calming effect that one resident said "will knock you out, it's so soothing."

A strolling path connects six outdoor spaces along the east and north sides of the building. These include:

- Fountain courtyard: An entry patio overhang provides shelter from inclement weather and allows eyes to adjust to daylight. Movable chairs create a social space where visitors can enjoy the view of a tiered fountain at the center of a circular lawn and looping path. Umbrella tables provide seating for those who are too weak, uncomfortable, or visually impaired to travel far outside. A well-defined perimeter of two stories of resident rooms on three sides provides shade and creates a sense of privacy and security, especially important for dementia patients who may feel insecure or even frightened about straying beyond the building (fig. 9.16).

- Pond viewing area: A 12 × 40-foot brick seating area overlooks a large retention pond and fountain with a green chain link fence that safely separates users from the pond embankment. Two wheelchair-accessible picnic tables and several movable chairs and tables form an adaptable social setting for different group sizes. The ducks, fountain, breeze, and large shade trees promote conversation, comfort, and long visits.

- Gazebo: A pathway node acts as a traffic circle for those in wheelchairs to travel back to the fountain courtyard or to continue further to a series of semiprivate spaces. Along a 5-foot-wide brick path, the first of three destinations is a gazebo, a favorite spot used by families and staff for resting and socializing. The structure is oriented to the prevailing

winds, and two large cassia shade trees hide the two-story building and create an attractive setting. A short 5 percent ramp and 31-inch parallel handrails accommodate ambulation and balance exercises for rehabilitation patients.

- Donor bird garden: The path wraps around the facility to an alcove featuring a central birdbath embedded in a mass planting of flowers. This is the most private sitting area on the grounds. A landscaped setback buffers the adjacent emergency room parking lot. A southern live oak provides shade in an area that lacks a consistent breeze.

- Water trough loop: The brick path loops around a lawn with three mature trees, and seating focuses on a central water trough with a bubbling urn. Staff members use a shaded picnic table on the lawn for lunch breaks.

- Dining patio: The final (or first) space along the loop is a covered patio that is directly accessible from the dining room. Ceiling fans, barbecue grills, and movable tables and chairs make it an ideal place to eat, socialize, or host outdoor events. A regional mural depicting the Jupiter Inlet connects the space with its greater South Florida context.

How the Garden Is Used

In the outdoor spaces, residents engage in activities with restorative benefits—viewing, strolling, resting, and socializing. By far the most popular outdoor activity is socializing. Seventy-five percent of outdoor visits involve sitting and talking with one or more peers. Rooms are shared, so many family visitors take residents outside for privacy. Social interaction is an important factor in stimulating residents and facilitating a positive mood. The variety of outdoor spaces, sensory cues, and interaction with wildlife play vital roles in promoting conversation. One visitor asserted that the pond viewing area was the only place at the facility where one could have an "old-fashioned" conversation with residents and other visitors, indicating the level of comfort and normalcy felt outside.

Second in popularity is sitting or resting quietly, mostly by independent residents and short-term rehabilitation patients. Residents who sit at the pond often watch the fountain or ducks and fall into a nap while enjoying the breeze and shade.

The most frequent repetitive users throughout the day are those who walk or wheel along the strolling path, indicating the importance of having a series of connected spaces to promote exercise. Both independent wheelchair users and visitors aiding family members utilize the walking path. Therapists also use the outdoor spaces by bringing weights out or for calming a resident who is being incompliant.

Key Garden Merits

- A series of connected outdoor spaces and landmarks encourage strolling and social interaction.

- Plentiful shade and breezes in seating areas promote thermal comfort and long outdoor stays.

- The fountain retention pond and native plantings attract ducks, various birds, squirrels, and lizards that animate the garden and trigger conversation.

- Two-thirds of residents have window views to a designed outdoor space.

- A variety of movable seating and wheelchair-accessible tables accommodate groups of all sizes and seating arrangements.

Possible Concerns

- Many residents on the second floor have severe dementia and are completely reliant on staff and family for safe outdoor visits.

- The fountain courtyard must be accessed through a stairwell space, necessitating entry through two separate automatic doors.

- Wheelchairs often stray off a tapering, 4-foot concrete path that leads to the pond and get stuck.

- The brick path creates tripping hazards.

- There is no active program for outdoor therapy.

- The is a lack of a variety of vibrant flowers (the number-one request in a resident survey).

Banfield Pavilion Roof top Patio Garden, Vancouver General Hospital, Vancouver, British Columbia

Designers: Ann Clement and Shelagh Smith, with contributions from residents and visitors
By Shelagh Smith

Description and History

Banfield Pavilion is a four-story facility that opened in 1972 and is home to 192 residents with complex care needs. While most of the residents use wheelchairs, some of the more recently admitted residents can walk independently. The residents and staff reflect Vancouver's multicultural demographics, with the majority of residents being of European and Chinese descent.

The garden areas of Banfield Pavilion include (1) a shady front entrance walkway on the east side of the building, with hanging baskets, planting areas, benches, and trees; (2) a small eight-sided glass greenhouse with adjacent work area and planters on the north side of the building; (3) large north-facing balconies outside the common rooms on each of three floors, which provide a colorful view (except in winter) for residents who spend all their time indoors; and (4) a south-facing 3,000-square-foot rooftop patio garden on the second floor.

Design Philosophy

In 1990, Ann Clement, a volunteer who visited the residents with her dog, was asked by a resident to provide him with soil to grow a few beans. At the time, the rooftop patio garden was bleak, consisting of a row of empty planter boxes and three arbor structures. Thus began an incremental garden-design process, which followed three guiding principles: (1) to imbue life into an unused outdoor space; (2) to provide a home garden that welcomed more residents to garden and putter around; and (3) to be responsive to resident desires (and staff needs), allowing for individual creativity rather than an ordered design. Additions to the garden included many plants, "rooms" created by vertical lattice panels, and a shed. The arbor color was changed from beige to forest green.

In 1994 Shelagh Smith joined Ann's efforts, and in 1997 she accepted the newly created part-time position of horticultural activity worker to engage more Banfield residents in gardening. The garden plantings continue to be resident-directed. Accessible gardening and sensory engagement experiences for residents with various abilities became increasingly important.

The Eden Philosophy guides the care of Banfield Pavilion residents and encourages regular contact with plants. Most of the window views include trees and other greenery, and some views include the distant mountains. Indoor plants, fresh flowers, murals, and other nature-based artwork contribute to the residents' daily engagement with plants and nature.

Description of Outdoor Space

The 3,000-square-foot patio garden is on the second floor rooftop, above a mechanical room, storage, and workshop spaces. The garden faces south to an alley and a medical building and west to a grassy park with mature trees. About a quarter of the resident rooms look out on the garden, with screens for privacy if desired.

From spring to fall the patio garden is a lush oasis that contrasts with the institutional interior of the building. Some sixty-five planter boxes and containers of various accessible shapes and heights hold plants that grow in layers, from small annuals to mature trees and overhead vines (fig. 9.17). The plantings

9.17 A variety of layered planting growing in boxes and containers creates a lush oasis in this urban rooftop garden for seniors.
Photo by Clare Cooper Marcus

are always a work in progress according to the participatory decisions of the resident gardeners, plant health, and the condition of the planting containers.

The garden is loosely sectioned into several areas, including edible plants, climbing roses and companion plants, a leafy nook with a bench and whisky barrel water feature, an Asian "island" planting with smiling Buddha, a wall of shrubs next to the alley, and a shady and private rhododendron and native-plant area that merges with the overarching park trees.

Several plants provide winter interest, such as early spring bulbs, a witch hazel, and a corkscrew hazel, and others are gradually being added throughout the garden.

The patio furniture consists of three wheelchair-accessible tables and a dozen or more chairs, all sturdy yet lightweight, with armrests and flat seats for ease of use. The chairs have slatted seats, so the rain keeps them clean and they dry rapidly.

9.18 A resident enjoys summer gardening in the rooftop garden of Banfield Pavilion.
Photo by Shelagh Smith

How the Garden Is Used

Several residents go out to the patio garden independently on a regular basis, weather permitting. Staff and family members bring out residents who require assistance. The patio garden is used for visiting with family and friends; for enjoying fresh air, sunshine, plants and wildlife; and for gardening.

At least two weekly group gardening activities take place on the patio. When weather keeps residents indoors, movable pots from the various gardens are brought inside to work on. These activities are facilitated by the horticulture activity worker with the assistance of volunteers.

Every year several residents who garden independently (or with a family member) grow plants in a container labeled with their name. Other residents independently contribute to the general maintenance of the garden by sweeping leaves, weeding, and watering or trimming plants (fig. 9.18). Herbs and produce are harvested by residents for their own use as well as for a weekly cooking and eating group facilitated by recreation staff and volunteers. In the summer, weekly ice cream socials, occasional picnics, and at least one evening music concert take place in the garden. Some of the staff take breaks or regularly eat their lunch in the garden.

Key Garden Merits

- Wayfinding signs in elevators and at the garden entrance are in both English and Chinese.

- Automatic doors that open when approached, and a covered entryway, promote easy access.

- There is a choice of routes through the garden.

- Human scale is provided by the "ceiling" of tree canopies and arbor structures covered with mature vines; a sense of enclosure is provided by building and plantings.

- There is a view to a neighboring park.

- Vertical trellis panels create three leafy private nooks that include movable seating; a central area provides room for larger group functions.

- There are familiar and natural materials, mostly wood, and a variety of planter heights for accessibility.

- There is a diversity of mature plants, as well as annuals that change each year.

- Many plants are chosen for their sensory appeal and are placed strategically for accessibility; plants are also chosen for use in activities and meals.

- Some containers have labels with their gardener's name, and a small cedar shed at the garden entrance makes tools accessible to residents when they wish to garden independently; two lever taps above small watering can platforms provide accessible water for resident gardeners (fig. 9.19).

- An automatic watering system keeps the plants alive in sunny dry weather.

- Chickadees nest in two boxes made by residents, and a squirrel- and rat-proof bird feeder attracts a variety of birds.

- A smiling Buddha and St. Francis statues provide spiritual/religious focal points.

9.19 Residents become very protective of the plants that they grow.
Photo Clare Cooper Marcus

- Two days per week throughout the year, the horticulture activity worker engages residents in garden and nature-related activities.

- The hospital maintenance department is available upon request for structural, plumbing, and electrical work.

Possible Concerns

- The patio garden can be viewed from several resident rooms, but not from a staff area.

- Movable seating is sometimes left in the middle of pathways, blocking access for residents using wheelchairs.

- When the roofing membrane leaked in 2003, all of the planting containers were moved off the patio to an empty first-floor deck. Some planters and the large plants did not survive the move. After repairs to the rooftop membrane were complete, the garden was restored with the addition of many new planters and plants.

- The rubber tiles used for pathways are too soft, providing challenging passage for residents propelling their wheelchairs. These tiles were chosen by residents who tried them out on a neighboring rooftop, but the "recipe" for the tiles was changed in the interim to make them spongier for children's playgrounds, resulting in their being too soft for wheelchair use. The tiles also become slippery next to planting containers that leak water and soil, requiring more frequent power washing than desirable.

- London plane trees in the adjacent park drop leaves year-round onto one end of the garden, causing allergic reactions such as discomfort in the throat and coughing for some people.

- There is noise from truck engines at a loading dock in an adjacent alley.

- The care needs of the residents are more complex than they used to be, and their overall ability to care for the garden has declined over the years. Much of the larger garden maintenance and improvement work relies on volunteers and is supervised by the part-time horticultural activity worker, whose job is primarily to engage residents in garden activities.

- Toxicity and other safety concerns place limits on plant choices.

- The garden needs planting with more winter interest.

- Staff members do not have their own garden separate from the residents'.

References

Alves, S. M., G. B. Gulwadi, and U. Cohen. 2005. "Accommodating Culturally Meaningful Activities in Outdoor Settings for Older Adults." Pp. 109–40 in *The Role of the Outdoors in Residential Environments for Aging,* edited by S. Rodiek and B. Schwarz. Binghamton, NY: Haworth Press.

Carman, J. P. 2006. "Re-creating 'The Backyard' in Senior Communities." *The Journal of Active Aging* January/February: 74–75.

Cooper Marcus, C., and M. Barnes. 2008. *Evaluations of Six Chicago Area Healing Gardens.* Unpublished manuscript. Naperville, IL: Consultant Report for Hitchcock Design Group.

Diaz Moore, K. 2001. *Designing a Better Day: Adult Day Centers, Comparative Case Studies.* Milwaukee: Center for Architecture and Urban Planning Research, University of Wisconsin–Milwaukee.

Kearney, A. R., and D. Winterbottom. 2005. "Nearby Nature and Long-Term Care Facility Residents: Benefits and Design Recommendations." Pp. 7–28 in *The Role of the Outdoors in Residential Environments for Aging,* edited by S. Rodiek and B. Schwarz. Binghamton, NY: Haworth Press.

Ottosson, J., and P. Grahn. 2005. "Measurements of Restoration in Geriatric Care Residences: The Influence of Nature on Elderly

People's Power of Concentration, Blood Pressure and Pulse Rate." Pp. 227–56 in *The Role of the Outdoors in Residential Environments for Aging*, edited by S. Rodiek and B. Schwarz. Binghamton, NY: Haworth Press.

Rappe, E., and S.-L. Kivelä. 2005. "Effects of Garden Visits on Long-Term Care Residents as Related to Depression." *Horticultural Technology* 15: 98–303.

Regnier, V. 1994. *Assisted Living for the Elderly: Design Innovations from the United States and Europe*. New York: John Wiley and Sons.

Rodiek, S. 2005. "Perceptions of Physical Environment Features that Influence Outdoor Usage at Assisted Living Facilities." Pp. 95–107 in *The Role of the Outdoors in Residential Environments for Aging*, edited by S. Rodiek and B. Schwarz. Binghamton, NY: Haworth Press.

———. 2009. "Environmental Influence on Outdoor Usage in Facilities for the Elderly." Paper presented at the 6th World Congress on Design and Health, Singapore, June 27.

Stoneham, J., and P. Thoday. 1996. *Landscape Design for Elderly and Disabled People*. London: Garden Art Press.

Takano, T., K. Nakamura, and M. Watanabe. 2002. "Urban Residential Environments and Senior Citizens' Longevity in Megacity Areas: The Importance of Walkable Green Spaces." *Journal of Epidemiology and Community Health* 56 (12): 913–18.

Tang, J. W., and R. D. Brown. 2005. "The Effect of Viewing a Landscape on Physiological Health of Elderly Women." Pp. 187–202 in *The Role of the Outdoors in Residential Environments for Aging*, edited by S. Rodiek and B. Schwarz. Binghamton, NY: Haworth Press.

Ulrich, R. S. 1999. "Effects of Gardens on Health Outcomes: Theory and Research." Pp. 27–86 in *Healing Gardens: Therapeutic Benefits and Design Recommendations*, edited by C. Cooper Marcus and M. Barnes. New York: John Wiley and Sons.

CHAPTER 10

Gardens for People with Alzheimer's and Other Dementias

Introduction

People with Alzheimer's disease make up the majority of residents in facilities for dementia or memory care. While Alzheimer's disease has no known cure, other forms of dementia have different, often treatable, causes. These include dementia associated with vitamin B-12 deficiency, AIDS, depression, thyroid disorder, hypoglycemia, drug and alcohol dependence, stroke, and traumatic brain injury. The terms *Alzheimer's* and *dementia* will be used interchangeably in this chapter.

Alzheimer's disease is characterized by the degeneration and loss of nerve cells in the brain that are associated with memory, learning, and judgment. It is estimated that one in eight people age 65 and older have this disease and nearly one in two over age 85 have it (Rodiek and Schwarz 2007, 4) In 2012, 5.4 million Americans were living with Alzheimer's and other forms of dementia. Unless a cure is found, it is estimated that by 2050 between 13 and 16 million will be living with the disease in the United States, and the economic cost will have risen to $1 trillion. Clearly, providing care for people with Alzheimer's disease is going to be a major challenge for society in the coming decades.

Patients with Alzheimer's disease experience high rates of noncognitive, behavioral, and psychiatric symptoms that may include hallucinations, delusions, depression, physical aggression, pacing, wandering, and sleep disorders (Zeisel 2007). While there is still no cure, considerable advances have been made in the provision of nonpharmacological treatments in the form of specialized care settings focusing on security, stimulation, companionship, and making the most of a person's strengths that remain (Calkins, Szmerekovsky, and Biddle 2007; Zeisel 2010).

Although some people with dementia continue to live at home—in the UK approximately two-thirds of people with this condition do so—guidelines in this chapter relate to outdoor space in residential and day facilities for this patient group (fig. 10.1). Relatively small, homelike facilities, as opposed to nursing homes or hospital wards, are becoming the norm, since people with mild to moderate forms of dementia function at a higher level in such settings. In an experimental Swedish study where patients were moved from a geriatric hospital to two collective housing units decorated in traditional styles, "The change in spirit and behavior occurred in all the patients, without exception. It was so dramatic that it astonished everybody involved in the project" (Küller 1991, 265).

Contact with nature is an important component of Alzheimer's care with beneficial effects on people's sense of well-being and quality of life. Thanks to research, postoccupancy evaluations, and best-practice observations, there is probably more known about designing outdoor space for this patient group than any other. (See Rodiek and Schwarz 2007; Marshall and Pollock 2012). People with dementia, like those with other physical or psychological disabilities, are strongly affected by the design of the environment since they are less able to alter it themselves (Day, Carreon, and Stump 2000).

Outdoor environments in special care settings offer both residents and staff healthy exposure to fresh air and sunlight, opportunities for exercise and socialization, and the ability to engage in familiar activities such as gardening, filling bird feeders, sweeping pathways, and so on. Such spaces can make the most of people's strengths that are still present—in other words, act as a prosthetic support. Benefits to persons with Alzheimer's from spending time outdoors include decreased agitation and aggressive behavior, better sleep patterns, improved hormone balance, and increased production of vitamin D (Calkins and Connell 2003; Cohen-Mansfield and Werner 1998; McMinn and Hinton 2000; Mooney and Nicell 1992; Pollock and McMair 2012; Rodiek 2002).

At the Martin Luther Alzheimer Garden in Holt, Michigan, nursing records were examined for eight variables (aggressive and nonaggressive behavior, physician-ordered

10.1 Garden at a residential memory care facility. The Serenades by Sonata, Longwood, Florida. Designer: Baker Barrios.
Photo by Clare Cooper Marcus

and as-needed medications, pulse rate, diastolic and systolic blood pressure, and weight change) during spring and summer 2000. When these variables were compared to the amount of time people spent outside, residents showed significant improvements on virtually every parameter with as little as ten to fifteen minutes of unprogrammed activity in the garden each day during the summer months (Galbraith and Westphall 2004).

In a survey of the nursing staff at ten facilities for people with dementia in Finland, researchers concluded that plants, both indoors and outdoors, contributed significantly to the psychological and social well-being of residents (Rappe and Lindén 2004). In particular, staff observed that familiar plants helped evoke residents' memories; caring for plants helped residents maintain their functional abilities; and plants

helped residents orient in space, stimulated their senses, created positive emotions, and were a good topic of conversation between staff and patients. They recommended plants that could tolerate harsh treatment and excessive watering.

A one-year study of the effects of outdoor activity on the sleep patterns of people with dementia found that those residents who engaged in outdoor activities experienced better sleep duration and reduced verbal agitation, as compared to a control group engaged in indoor activities (Connell, Sanford, and Lewis 2007). The difference was assumed to be caused by the effect of daylight and sunlight on circadian rhythms, a crucial determinant of sleep, and on structured activities, including gardening, which are found to be effective in reducing behavior disturbance. Better sleep patterns mean fewer demands on the staff at night and less money spent on

10.2 Exposure to sunlight, opportunities for exercise, and access to nature are all critically important for the health of people living with dementia. Two sets of gates in this garden allow it to be divided into three separate areas for different activities. The Serenades by Sonata, Longwood, Florida. Designer: Baker Barrios.
Photo by Clare Cooper Marcus

10.3 A nonglare pathway, seating, and gazebo destination point encourage use of this garden at a residential facility for people with dementia in the small Scottish town of Blairgowrie. Designer: Annie Pollock.
Photo by Annie Pollock

medications, both of which translate into lower costs in running the facility (fig. 10.2).

Another study found that escorting residents who pace frequently to an outdoor area had a positive effect on mood, pacing behavior, and attempts at elopement (Cohen-Mansfield and Werner 1998). When denied access to the outdoors, incidents of verbal and physical aggression increased among highly disturbed residents. Researchers concluded that patients derived benefits from contact with daylight, with weather changes, and with the earth and plants, although these were not the sole factors affecting behavior (McMinn and Henton 2000).

Researchers Mooney and Nicell (1992) examined the number of violent incidents and falls at five nursing homes for patients with Alzheimer's disease. At the facilities without gardens, the rate of violent incidents increased by 681 percent (1989–90), while the total rate of incidents increased 319 percent. By contrast, in those facilities with gardens, the rate of violent incidents declined by 19 percent during the same period, while the total rate of incidents fell by 3.5 percent.

A study of a garden at a day-use facility for Alzheimer's patients in Canada revealed that staff used the garden to facilitate calming and help manage behavioral problems. "Sometimes this was by providing a venue to remove the client from a source of agitation, other times the focal points in the garden were a distraction, and sometimes just being outside was seen to be calming" (Lovering et al. 2002, 22).

Sadly, even when outdoor space is available, it is not always designed with the special needs of dementia patients in mind, nor are they always encouraged (or allowed) to go outside. A review of wards for people with dementia in Scottish hospitals found only 7 out of 16 hospitals visited had enclosed, dementia-friendly gardens. Looking at care plans for 29 patients across those 16 wards revealed that only 12 patients had been outdoors in the past 3 months (Lyons 2012) (fig. 10.3).

A survey of 320 US facilities for Alzheimers' patients with outdoor areas found that 69 percent of them relied on staff members accompanying residents outside (Cohen-Mansfield 2007). This can pose an inordinate cost to the facility in terms of staff time and may lead to complete nonuse of the garden. Hence the critical importance of designing the garden so that it is completely safe for residents to use on their own, which can translate into substantial savings in staff stress, the cost of medications, and so on. Several studies have concluded that involving the administration and staff and convincing them of the importance of access to nature can be more critical to the success of the garden than its actual design (Grant and Wineman 2007). An organizational policy, or "organizational culture," that promotes residents' independence and incorporates a positive attitude toward the outdoors can translate into staff training and regular programmed activities in the garden (ibid.).

While the guidelines that follow are offered as suggestions for the design of outdoor space for an Alzheimer's facility, even the most thoughtful design will not guarantee that residents will use it. People with dementia often have problems planning and carrying out such seemingly simple tasks as deciding to go outdoors, putting on the appropriate clothes, or finding the door. One study observed that "outdoor space use by residents with dementia is far more likely to occur if structured activities programming is provided and staff are available to assist residents in going outdoors, offer activities that are meaningful to them, and provided them with the appropriate level of assistance to keep them engaged" (Connell, Sanford, and Lewis 2007, 199).

Design Guidelines

All of the guidelines in the list of general design guidelines (chapter 6), plus all of those pertaining to the frail elderly (chapter 9), also apply to gardens for people with dementia and are not repeated here. The guidelines below are specifically and critically important for this group.

General considerations

Required

1. **Involve management and staff in the design of the garden**. Management and staff need to be involved in the design of the garden from the very beginning. A comprehensive study of five Alzheimer's gardens found that organizational policy and staff attitudes were just as important as design in encouraging use of the outdoors (Grant and Wineman 2007). In some facilities, the door to the garden was kept permanently locked to prevent use, either because staff members were afraid to let residents outside alone and they didn't have time to accompany them or because they had no understanding of how time outdoors could benefit the residents. This suggests the importance of a user's manual or something equivalent, so that management and staff understand the purpose and value of outdoor space provided. Since there may be a lot of staff turnover, reviewing the user's manual should be included in the training of new staff.

2. Locate the garden so that it is **clearly visible from inside the building** by residents going about their daily activities. Changes in the brain of dementia patients may result in difficulty knowing the time—hours, days, seasons—without

external clues (Zeisel 2007). Unobstructed views to the garden from well-used interior spaces can provide information about time of day and season, as well as help with wayfinding (fig. 10.4). With short-term memory loss, residents may forget that a garden is available even if they spent time in it the day before; or when encouraged to go outside, they may have a mental picture of another garden experienced negatively (always cold, uncomfortable seats) and resist the invitation (Chalfont 2008). In a survey of 320 US facilities serving Alzheimer's patients, 25 percent reported that the outdoor area was not used as much as it could be because the building and the exterior space were too far from each other or because heavy doors limited access from one to the other (Cohen-Mansfield 2007). To ensure that this critical requirement is met, an acknowledged expert in this field recommends that garden designers "always include both inside and outside spaces linked in a single environment throughout the entire

10.4 The garden must be visible from a well-used interior space. View to garden-courtyard from a day room.
Photo by Alberto Salvatore

design process. . .from the first conceptual sketch until construction documents" (Zeisel 2007).

3. **Visual contact from a staff area**, TV monitors, alarms, and other features can ensure that residents are allowed go outside alone, thus enhancing autonomy and sense of control. In some situations where this is not the case, staff keep the exterior door locked (Grant and Wineman 2007).

4. **All parts of the garden should be visible at all times by the user in the garden**. Best practice indicates that Alzheimer's patients feel most comfortable in a garden where the whole layout is visible and there are no disorienting hidden areas where they may lose sight of the route back to the building (Furness and Moriarty 2006). This is in contrast to traditional garden design, including healing gardens in, for example, an acute-care hospital, a cancer facility, or a hospice, where planting and winding paths encourage exploration and facilitate a sense of getting away.

5. The culture where the facility is based, and in particular, **attitudes of its residents to nature and the outdoors must be sensitively addressed**. For example, most Americans raised with the ideal of a house with a well-maintained yard would be most comfortable in a setting where they can recognize something like this, even if it is of a different scale. In contrast, the designers of a care home for older Anangu Aboriginal people in South Australia recognized that the residents had spent most of their lives outdoors, which they regarded as a place to live, not a place to visit. The landscape, nature, seeing the horizon, sitting around a fire, watching the path of the sun and the moon, are integral to their life and identity. For them it was quite acceptable that the building was simple, with small windows and limited natural light, since it was perceived as a place of safety where residents would go only to retreat from the outdoors in bad weather or in ill health (Bennett 2012).

6. **Locate the garden so that its use is optimized during morning hours**. Research suggests that Alzheimer's patients with mild to moderate forms of the disease exhibit a delay in the onset of agitated behavior after exposure to bright morning light (Ancoli-Israel et al. 2003). As well as supplying vitamin D, natural light is particularly important for people with dementia, as they often suffer from dislocation of diurnal rhythms that may result in sleep disorders and depression.

7. **Where possible, locate the garden to ensure only a monolithic building shadow is cast into the garden by the afternoon sun**. Alzheimer's patients often display increased agitation in the late afternoon, a phenomenon known as sundowning. The cause is uncertain, but it is thought that the position of the sun and the casting of long—perhaps frightening—shadows by trees or shrubs may contribute to the problem. One study suggests that positioning the building so that only simple, straight-line shadows are cast into the garden by late afternoon sun is one way to alleviate this problem (Randall et al. 1990). Alternatively, a seating area could be located to **receive late afternoon sun**, thus avoiding long shadows at that time of day.

8. While **shade** is important in any healthcare garden, it is critical for individuals with Alzheimer's dementia since they have difficulty recognizing when they are too hot and would not think to put on a hat or sun block.

9. Provide some **features that might evoke memories** for residents and allow them to engage in meaningful activities outdoors (fig. 10.5). Depending on location and cultural background, these might include a garden shed, washing line, mail box, vegetable garden, barbecue, cultural or religious icon, flagpole, or small piece of farm equipment (fixed to ground). For example, a dementia facility in rural Norway includes two structures familiar to residents: a "milk house," where farmers would store the day's milk, and a "stabur" or raised house used for chopping and stacking wood, an important activity for male residents (Grefsfjord and Gerlach-Spriggs 2012). The outdoor space at a facility in rural Australia for people with advanced memory loss includes a farm shed with a tractor and workbench, as well as farm animals (sheep, alpacas, chickens), which residents can visit, talk to, feed, and check on their water (Birkett 2012). Electronic cameras enable staff to monitor residents and allow them to wander on their own. In a number of US, Canadian, and UK facilities, antique cars have been bolted down in the garden; male residents wash and polish them as part of a programmed activity.

Clients at a Canadian day-use facility particularly enjoyed those activities they had engaged in throughout their lives, including barbecuing, sitting in lawn chairs or around a campfire, weeding, planting, watering, harvesting, cutting the grass, filling bird feeders, and hanging out laundry (Lovering 2002). While washing lines continue to be provided in many gardens, one wonders how many actually hung out washing in their lives, and the question remains: What will be the familiar daily routines remembered by today's baby boomers when they enter dementia facilities in the coming years? Just as designers must be aware of the culture of the place, they must also **be aware of the generation they are designing for**—hence again, the importance of talking and listening to staff, patients, and family members.

10.5 Many of the residents in this Canadian facility grew up on the prairies. To prompt early memories, the courtyard includes a garden shed and unmown grasses familiar from that region. Chemainus Health Care Centre, Chemainus, British Columbia. Designer: Edward Stillinger. *Photo by Clare Cooper Marcus.*

10. Ensure that the garden is **attractive and well maintained** so that family members might be encouraged to visit more often and take their relative outdoors. Gardens are often the preferred locales for visits between residents and their families, offering "props" to spark conversation (Chapman and Carder 2003). An increase in visits by relatives was recorded at a Swedish facility after a garden was created (Rappe 2003).

11. Ensure that the **building edge encloses the garden** as much as possible, so that the degree to which the garden has to be fenced is minimized. However, care should be taken that this does not result in too much of the garden being shaded at times of the day (usually morning) when most residents might choose to be outside. There is a tendency for Alzheimer's patients to want to "go home." They may become agitated and insist that they must be there when their children come home from school or their spouse returns from work. A view out from the garden to an adjacent street or parking lot can exacerbate this feeling. It has been suggested that views out to serene landscapes or to distant cars and traffic seem to provide a quiet yet interesting stimulus that does not exacerbate the desire to elope (Randall et al. 1990). An article on best practice recommends an open fence when the garden overlooks a natural scenic area, but a solid fence when it looks onto an active parking lot or roadway (Carman 2002).

The problem of "elopement" must be carefully addressed in the design, or staff members will have to be constantly on the alert. They may even decide to keep the door to the garden permanently locked.

12. Where a garden is not enclosed by the building, the **boundaries of the garden** should provide complete enclosure, with trees and tall shrubs screening the view of fences or walls. The goal is to create a secure space without creating a sense of being fenced in. Attention should be focused on a variety of spaces and activities within the garden rather than what is outside it.

13. Where any **boundary wall or fence** is not screened by planting, ensure that it is at least 8 feet high, and avoid any potential foothold on the garden side, so that it is not climbable even if a chair or bench is moved close to it (fig. 10.6).

14. Be aware of the **cultural implications of fencing**. In some cultures—for example, in Australia—a fence around a backyard to keep animals out is normal, so visible fencing is viewed by those with dementia as keeping them safe rather than keeping them in (Pollock and Marshall 2012).

15. A **gate** to enable maintenance staff to enter, or residents to leave in an emergency, needs to be subtly located or designed to look like **part of an opaque fence**.

10.6 This small side garden is enclosed by a building and an opaque fence. It provides fixed and movable seating, a choice of sun or shade at most times of the day, a setting for barbecues, and a smooth walking surface. Aegis Living, Napa, California.
Photo by Clare Cooper Marcus

Recommended

1. Provide **separate gardens for patients in the mild, moderate, and severe stages** of Alzheimer's disease where different wards or units serve each stage. A facility in Ohio (Beckwith and Gilster 1997) and one in Maine (Hoover 1999) provide differently designed gardens for those with mild, moderate, and severe stages of Alzheimer's disease. While no formal postoccupancy evaluations of these three-stage gardens have been conducted to date, it seems reasonable to assume that subtly different gardens should be provided where a facility is large enough and has sufficient residents in each of the three stages of the disease.

2. Provide elements that **encourage residents to assist in the care of the garden**—a small working garden, a garden shed, raised beds, a greenhouse, a potting table accessible to a person in a wheelchair, and outdoor water taps can support gardening, whether in a formal horticultural therapy program or as an informal activity with family members or staff. Rakes, brooms, and small, lightweight watering cans left in the garden may prompt people to engage in satisfying outdoor activities. It is reported that 40 percent of Americans identify themselves as gardeners, thus horticultural activities will allow many people with dementia to draw on past experience and skills (Butterfield 2006). Providing individual raised flower boxes or large pots allows people to tend their own small garden, bringing satisfaction and helping to maintain cognitive abilities. If the

environment provides adequate cues as to what behavior is permitted, this will encourage people to engage in activities that help them to maintain competence and enhance self-esteem (Moore 2002).

3. Provide space and facilities for **culturally appropriate activities**. Maintaining a sense of cultural identity is important for all older adults, but particularly so for those with dementia, since they experience so many losses, including memory and functional ability. It is estimated that by 2020, more than 20 percent of Americans older than 65 will be Hispanic, African American, Asian American/Pacific Islander, Indian American, and Native American (Yeo 1996).

As cognitive regression associated with dementia occurs, people often lose second languages they acquired later in life, and those who previously had assimilated into the dominant culture revert to the traditional values and behavior of their culture of origin (Day and Cohen 2000). Incorporating elements in garden design to support cultural identity is a complex process, and needs a more considered approach than merely adding artworks or religious icons. In a study of how this might be approached for a population of Russian Jewish immigrant elderly in Milwaukee, Wisconsin, and West Hollywood, California, Cohen and Day (2000) noted that regardless of age or weather, people in Russia like to spend a great deal of time outdoors and that there is a cultural tradition of elders caring for grandchildren. This suggests that outdoor space is crucial for this cultural group and that it might contain a play area with adjacent seating so that elders (with discreet supervision by a volunteer or staff) might care for grandchildren, even on a limited basis.

Other features of Russian social life include playing board games (especially chess) and engaging in small-group debates on political and social issues. Cohen and Day suggest that these might be accommodated by tables to seat two to eight persons located outdoors as well as in an indoor activity room. In creating outdoor spaces for a particular cultural group, designers need to interview family members, elders, and caregivers to discern what would be culturally enhancing activities and values and how these might be provided. Where there is a mix of cultures, appropriate activities or features need to be even more carefully chosen.

4. **Provide elements, such as water, that may evoke genetic memories**. However, care should be taken in *how* water is incorporated (fig. 10.7). At a facility in Victoria, British Columbia, a simulated stream proved to be an attractive hazard as people tried to get into it. The problem was solved by

10.7 At a Canadian facility for residents with Alzheimer's disease, a water feature with rocks provides a pleasing visual and aural feature on a roof deck outdoor space. For security, the rocks are all fixed in place with epoxy. Oak Bay-Kiwanis residential facility, Victoria, British Columbia. Designer: LeFrank & Associates.
Photo by Deborah LeFrank

placing a leaning-height barrier of glass and wood between a path and the stream so that people could stop and look at it (Tyson and Zeisel 1999). In a day facility in Grand Rapids, Michigan, a large waterfall and pond can be viewed and heard from a much-used gazebo, but cannot be accessed (Cooper Marcus 2005). Another solution is to incorporate a waist-high bubbling fountain where the water can be heard and perhaps touched but is impossible for anyone to climb into. There are differing views as to whether the sound of water triggers a need to urinate, so the staff should be consulted regarding the inclusion of a water feature.

5. Include a small play area or basketball hoop to **engage visiting grandchildren**, who may be puzzled or concerned about changes of behavior in a grandparent or who might get bored during a visit.

6. Avoid plant **shapes, structures, shadows, statues**, and the like that **might trigger delusions**: Alzheimer's patients may perceive things differently and become agitated.

Physical access

Required

1. Provide a **single entry door** to the garden, designed as a landmark, perhaps through the use of color or a distinctive overhang, so that those using the garden can easily see it from everywhere in the garden and understand where they have to return to in order to get back indoors.

2. **Provide easy access from the building to the garden**. Critically important in facilitating garden access is that the door have an automatic opener or an easily usable handle and that the entry should not have a lip that might impede wheelchair access. A postoccupancy study of a Canadian care facility with eight well-designed courtyards found that use by residents was low in part because the facility lacked automatic doors and signs. These were added as a result of the study (Heath 2004). Interviews with the staff of a day-use facility revealed that a heavy door—often kept closed on hot days because of the need for air conditioning—was a significant barrier to garden use. Lack of a window in the door, or next to it, further exacerbated this problem, as clients did not want to go out when they couldn't actually see the garden (Lovering et al. 2002).

3. The **door to the garden should be kept unlocked** as often as possible for free (unprogrammed) access to the outdoors (fig. 10.8). In a study investigating the degree of use of outdoor spaces at five long-term-care facilities for the cognitively impaired elderly, researchers found that at one facility, a section of the mission statement promoting "freedom of movement through the large, friendly open areas and outdoor gardens" was completely at odds with a policy of keeping the door to an attractive outdoor area locked at all times (Grant and Wineman 2007). When staff members were asked why residents might not use the outdoor space, most responded that "the area is exposed to sun, wind, etc." Only one mentioned the locked door as a likely reason. At another facility, the door was unlocked all day, and residents could go in and out independently. When the door was propped open, residents went out twice as much as when the door was closed but not locked.

In another study, researchers observed the effects of unlocking previously locked doors in a facility for people with dementia and found that wandering and agitation were greatly reduced in the unlocked condition (Namazi and DeNatale-Johnson 1992). Often subjects did not actually go out. Simply knowing that they could do so was enough to calm them. The more that the staff comfort level is maximized regarding residents being outside alone, the more the staff will encourage garden use and leave doors unlocked. Studies have shown that violent behavior decreased when residents with dementia have access to a secure outdoor environment (Mooney and Nicell 1992), and behaviors such as verbal abuse and talking to oneself significantly declined when a door to the outside was unlocked (Namazi and Johnson 1992).

10.8 A door that is easily opened, a pleasant place to sit just outside, and a return to the building that is easily visible throughout the garden facilitate residents' use of this courtyard on their own. The Serenades by Sonata, a memory-care residential facility, Longwood, Florida. Designer: Baker Barrios. *Photo by Clare Cooper Marcus*

Recommended

1. Locate **restrooms very close to the garden entry**. Patients with dementia, as well as older people in general, may have problems with incontinence. In a survey of 320 US facilities for Alzheimer's patients, only 11 percent reported that there was easy access to a bathroom from the garden (Cohen-Mansfield 2007). In a study of a Canadian day-use facility, staff reported that lack of convenient access to restrooms was a major deterrent to use of the garden by both staff and clients (Lovering 2002). Sometimes staff members had to interrupt an activity in the garden and leave clients alone as they helped someone to go indoors to the restroom. One staff member remarked: "If only you could just cut a hole

in the wall and put in another bathroom." The study concluded that if this problem is not addressed in the initial design of the building, many outdoor spaces will simply not be used.

Seating

Required

1. Provide seating at relatively **frequent intervals** along pathways since dementia patients are often restless. They sometimes pace, rest briefly, and then pace again.

2. Provide plenty of **different types of seating** (for example, a variety of fixed and movable seats) in different locations and with a choice of sun or shade.

Pathways

Required

1. Provide a **simple looped or figure-eight pathway circuit** to minimize spatial confusion (Zeisel and Tyson 1999; Cooper Marcus 2005; Furness and Moriarty 2006; Randall et al. 1990). Exercise is associated with a delay in the onset of dementia and Alzheimer's disease (Larson et al. 2006), and there is a correlation between exercise and improvement in cognitive performance and emotional well-being (Bastone and Filho 2004). A garden with at least one walking path encourages exercise (fig. 10.9). Wandering away from home is one of the more common behaviors exhibited by those with Alzheimer's and other dementias and is often what prompts a family to decide on institutionalized care, since wandering can occur at any time, day or night, and may result in life-threatening situations. There are thought to be several underlying motivations (Calkins 1991, 243). These include ingrained rituals such as going home or leaving for work, lack of sensory stimulation, or continuation of a long-held habit of taking walks.

A goal in addressing this issue is to provide "secure freedom," or "opportunities for the person to wander within an environment that has controlled perimeters and limits access to potentially hazardous situations" (Calkins 1991, 243). People with dementia often experience disorientation, since their ability to make a mental map of a space and to remember pathways from past experience is severely limited. Thus a pathway that simply loops around a garden in a circular, figure-eight or bisected loop, with no dead ends or intriguing forks in the road, and beginning and ending at the same door, will minimize confusion and provide a suitable locale for wandering (fig. 10.10). In a dead-end path system, a user may stop and become agitated. Any minor pathway, such as a shortcut, should intersect the main path at 90 degrees (and possibly be of a different material) so that there is a clear choice between main and side path, not a confusing fork. While garden circulation design may have minimal impact on a person without cognitive impairment—in fact they may enjoy exploring hidden corners—it has a major impact on a person with limited competency.

2. Provide **markers, landmarks, and interesting elements along the pathway**—such as bird feeders, a weather vane, garden ornaments, a wheelbarrow full of flowers, a flagpole—to assist with spatial orientation and to allow staff or family members to measure how far a resident can walk. In Alzheimer's and other dementias, the part of the brain used

10.9 A smooth pathway with defined edges provides a comfortable route through the garden for a resident who uses a wheelchair. The Graham Garden, Saanich Community Hospital, Victoria, British Columbia. Designer: LeFrank & Associates.
Photo by Clare Cooper Marcus

10.10 A simple figure-eight pathway with tinted concrete and handrail facilitate use of this courtyard garden. The Lodge at Broadmead, Victoria, British Columbia. Designer: LeFrank & Associates.
Photo by Clare Cooper Marcus

to remember places and sequences of places is compromised (Zeisel 2007). The simpler the garden organization is, and the more that familiar landmarks punctuate walking paths, the easier it will be for people to navigate and use the outdoor space (fig. 10.11).

As a person's mental and physical abilities decline, the importance of the physical environment increases. Although circulation routes need to be simple, they must not be monotonous. A study of wayfinding among dementia patients in a Montreal nursing home found that people moved from one decision point to the next in a sequential and linear order

10.11 A sculptural piece that invites touch provides a wayfinding cue in this garden for the frail elderly and those with dementia. Graham Garden, Saanich Peninsula Hospital, Victoria, British Columbia. Designer: LeFrank & Associates.

Photo by Clare Cooper Marcus

(Passini et al. 2000). Thus, residents became more disoriented in uniform corridors than in those punctuated by reference points such as a clock, entrance hall, nursing station, water fountain, and the like. The study provides clear implications for garden design. The authors recommended wayfinding reference points that differ from other elements by form, by function, and, if possible, by meaning. Another expert recommends that multiple cues, such as focal points and handrails, are better than one, and that robust cueing involving sound, smell, and touch as well as sight should be considered: "A person may not remember to take the second left but may instead be prompted to turn at the yellow wheelbarrow full of lavender" (Chalfont 2008, 105). Interviews with staff at a Michigan day-use facility indicated that, among other elements, a gazebo, an arbor, a flagpole, and a statue of the Virgin Mary (the site was formerly a convent) were important wayfinding devices along the looped garden path (Cooper Marcus 2005).

3. A **level pathway system** is especially important for those with Alzheimer's disease, since they suffer from apraxia—forgetting how to perform simple motor acts such as walking. This begins with shuffling and clumsiness and proceeds to a profound lack of coordination and balance (Randall et al. 1990).

Recommended

1. **Provide challenges for residents who are more physically able**. While safety should be the prime concern, it is also important to offer some physical challenges. Although dementia patients display a decline in cognitive ability, some remain quite physically active. For these individuals, it is important to offer some challenges outdoors, such as steps beside a ramp or an area of the garden that requires some exertion to reach (Chalfont 2008).

Planting

Required

1. **Avoid toxic plants** in gardens for late-stage Alzheimer's patients, since people tend to revert to infancy and put everything in their mouth at this stage of the disease. Commonly used plants that have poisonous elements include azaleas, bleeding hearts, chrysanthemums, hydrangeas, daffodils, wisteria, ivy, and foxglove. Plants that are harmful to touch, such as roses with many thorns, should also be excluded. (For additional information on toxic plants, see chapter 17.)

2. As appropriate to the region and culture of the facility, include plants that the staff may use in "reminiscence therapy"; that is, **include plants that were popular during the youth or residents**, such as roses and lilacs in New England, **or that have cultural significance**, such as flowering quince, associated with Chinese New Year. Plants that stimulate the senses should also be emphasized, such as lavender (smell and touch), roses (color and smell), lamb's ears and artemesia (touch) (fig. 10.12).

Lighting

Recommended

1. Ensure that the garden is **usable and attractive at night** by installing lighting that does not leave dark pools of shadow, spotlighting special features, and placing seating areas that people might use at a distance from bedrooms windows. People with dementia often have trouble sleeping at night, and they should be allowed to wander outside to alleviate restlessness and frustration. Staff, too, will appreciate being able to take a break outdoors on a balmy evening (Macintosh 2012). It is generally recommended that tall standards be used rather than low-level fixtures which may attract people with Alzheimer's to investigate or manipulate and can also be tripping hazards.

Maintenance

Required

1. **The garden should be designed for ease of maintenance**. A study of a Canadian day-use facility reported that maintenance was a major barrier to use of the garden

10.12 In the Garden of the Senses, residents in two adjacent Alzheimer's facilities in Stockholm, Sweden, enjoy a range of familiar wild and cultivated flowers.
Photo by Clare Cooper Marcus

(Lovering 2002). Settling of stone-dust pathways created tripping hazards and puddles; weeds in planting beds and a general deterioration of the garden since its opening three years before caused some staff to avoid taking clients outdoors. This study recommended that maintenance staff be involved at the planning stage, that an operational budget and garden-care plan be in place, and that the designer conduct ongoing postoccupancy evaluations to assess the needs for upgrading and/or additions to the garden: "The garden should be viewed as a tool that needs to be appropriately maintained just like any other piece of equipment" (Lovering 2002, 426).

CASE STUDY

The Living Garden at the Family Life Center, Grand Rapids, Michigan[1]

Designer: Martha Tyson of Douglas Hills Associates, Evanston, Illinois

Founded in 1991, the Family Life Center is a healthcare facility housed in a former convent. The facility serves as a day center for people with Alzheimer's disease, other forms of dementia, schizophrenia, multiple sclerosis, Parkinson's, and Huntington's disease who live at home with their families. Patient ages range from 36 to 90.

Design Philosophy

Martha Tyson was very familiar with the research literature on the environmental needs of those with dementia. She had previously designed a number of successful gardens for nursing homes and Alzheimer's facilities. Her design philosophy embraced the need to include all the potential stakeholders in the design process, which she did at the Family Life Center by soliciting input from representatives of patients' families, the center's staff, and horticultural therapists from a nearby botanical garden.

Description of the Outdoor Space

A dining/activity room and a large, glass-roofed atrium have views and access to the garden. Also overlooking the garden is a large conservatory, which is heavily used in colder weather for indoor horticultural activities. The doors remain unlocked during the day. There are two main components to the half-acre site: the main strolling and viewing garden, and the working garden. The working garden is a rectangular area

---

1. A longer version of this case study appeared as "No Ordinary Garden: Alzheimer's and Other Patients Find Refuge in a Michigan Dementia-Care Facility," *Landscape Architecture Magazine* 95 (3) (March 2005): 26–39.

east of the building with raised beds and trellises for horticultural therapy, a potting area with shade and a sink, a garden shed, a small orchard, a butterfly garden, and an umbrella-shaded area for seating near the atrium entry door. The larger component, the main garden, is entered through an arbor from the working garden and consists of lawns, paths, perennial beds, gazebos, a waterfall and pond, and various places to sit (fig. 10.13).

The garden provides a great deal of variety: flowers to look at and talk about, vegetables to touch and perhaps eat, and spaces where people alone or in a group can find places to sit. This garden allows users to see the layout at a glance and offers a simple circular or figure-eight circulation system. The main garden has a clear perimeter path of tinted concrete bisected by a curving brick pathway, thus allowing those who are restless a number of alternatives for moving around the garden. One trip around the 6-foot-wide loop path provides a 300-foot route with changing details but no anxiety-provoking choices in wayfinding that can lead to confusion, agitation, and even aggression. The entry arbor, a flagpole, a grotto with a statue of the Virgin Mary (50 percent of the center's users are Roman Catholic), and bird feeders hanging from trees provide landmarks to aid in orientation. Areas such as the working garden and the lawn provide gathering places encouraging physical and social activity. Two wooden gazebos (the Garden House and the Tea House) provide destination points and comfortable settings for scheduled activities. The building, walls, fence, and peripheral plantings provide edges defining the space.

The garden has plenty of seating in the two gazebos and elsewhere. There are three comfortable gliders (swinging seats), patio seating with tables and umbrellas outside the conservatory, a curved stone seating wall, and numerous movable chairs scattered throughout the garden. Since one of characteristics of Alzheimer's patients is that they frequently try to "find their way home," an outdoor space serving this group needs to be visually enclosed so that people are not exposed to tempting views of "the outside world." Tyson's design fulfills this need in a functional and aesthetically pleasing manner. The garden is bounded on the north side by the building and conservatory, on the west and south sides by high walls of mellow, buff-colored brick, and on the east side (facing the parking area) by a steel fence. The walls and fences are almost invisible, screened by a variety of trees—mostly evergreen—so that even in winter, the boundaries of the garden are blurred. One exception is a steel gate allowing entry from the parking lot for service personnel and people arriving for an event in the garden.

While the boundaries of the garden are marked by moderately tall trees stepping down in height to shrubs (lilac, roses, rhododendrons, and dogwood) and perennial borders, the center of the garden is an open lawn that is, in turn, bounded by the circular concrete path. The slightly mounded western lawn is partially bounded by a stone seating wall (permitting transfer from a wheelchair onto the grass) and punctuated by a beech tree and a playhouse with steps and a slide for visiting grandchildren.

In one corner, a fenced staff patio with an expansive view of the garden provides an essential respite from the stress of work and the demands of patients (fig. 10.14).

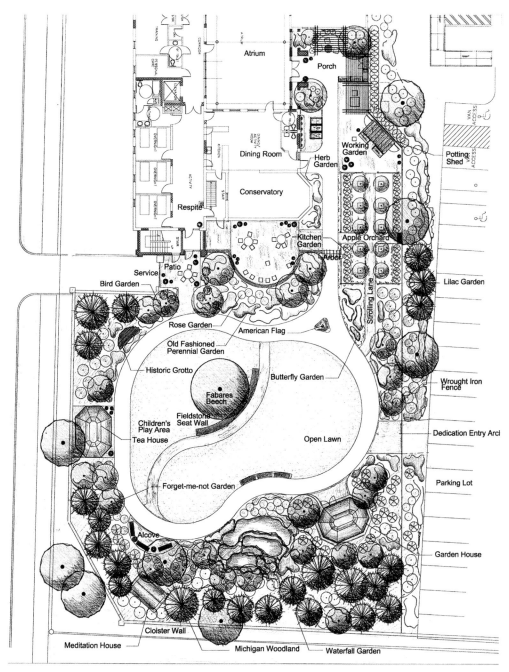

Atrium

Porch

Working
Garden

Potting
Shed

Herb
Garden

Dining Room

Conservatory

Apple Orchard

Lilac Garden

Respite

Kitchen
Garden

Arbor

Patio

Service

Bird Garden

Rose Garden

American Flag

Strolling Lane

Wrought Iron
Fence

Old Fashioned
Perennial Garden

Historic Grotto

Butterfly Garden

Fabares
Beech

Fieldstone
Seat Wall

Children's
Play Area

Tea House

Open Lawn

Dedication Entry Arch

Parking Lot

Forget-me-not Garden

Alcove

Garden House

Cloister Wall

Meditation House

Michigan Woodland

Waterfall Garden

10.14 Site plan of the Living Center garden by Martha Tyson.
Courtesy of Douglas Hills Associates

How the Garden Is Used

A garden is an important component of daily therapy; for some, it may be just as important as a dose of medication. In the Living Garden, some patients who do not need to be monitored go freely back and forth from the building to the garden. Those who need constant care are accompanied on garden visits twice a day.

The design works extraordinarily well for scheduled activities: chairs in a semicircle on the lawn for conversation, a garden house for listening to music and singing, a flat lawn for croquet, a concrete path for wheelchair races, access to water for tending the flower beds, and raised beds, tables, and a potting shed for gardening. "The garden also works very, very well for physical therapy staff working with people who have had a stroke or need help walking," says Sherry Gaines, the program and activity manager. "It has a wonderfully calming effect on people who are agitated. The facility has a ratio of staff to customers of 1 to 5, and when volunteers and interns are factored in, it is 2 to 1."

On a visit in early October 2004, over twenty-five varieties of flowers were in bloom. Staff members use these flowers to stimulate conversations about the seasons, next year's garden, and memories from childhood. Star jasmine and tobacco flowers smell good, and the feathery blooms of Amaranthus and the seed-heads of coneflower tempt garden visitors to reach out and touch, while the staff collects their seeds for arts and crafts activities in the winter. Color and smell stimulate parts of the brain not reached by intellectual activities, and even those with little cognitive ability seem able to sense the tranquility and beauty of a garden on a precognitive, affective basis. A garden, in contrast to an unchanging building's interior, is also a metaphor for growth, blossoming, maturity, decay, and renewal. All toxic plants have been avoided in the design.

To understand the importance of gardens, more postoccupancy evaluation studies are needed, such as that conducted at the Living Garden by Charlotte Grant as part of her PhD dissertation. She mapped activities for 10-minute periods at 20-minute intervals from 9 a.m. to 4 p.m. during five days of observation in mid-September 2001. Of those using the garden, 45 percent were day clients, 38 percent were staff (paid and volunteer) working with clients, and 17 percent were maintenance staff. Of the day clients in the garden, 41 percent were walking, sitting, or talking on the loop path, 27 percent were in the Garden House participating in organized activities, 20 percent were in the working garden, and 11 percent were sitting in the Tea House (a gazebo on the west side of the garden). A large number of staff members were observed on the patio reserved for their use.

Key Garden Merits

- One entry door to the garden to avoid confusion

- A looped path for "wandering behavior" (fig. 10.15)

- A sense of entry (an arbor) into the main garden and a destination point (a gazebo) visible from that entry

- A variety of fixed and movable seating

- A variety of nontoxic flowering plants, many popular when current residents were younger

- A central lawn for gathering and to evoke a memory of "home"

- Secure garden boundaries, subtly screened with planting

- Space for gardening activities (garden shed, potting table, vegetable beds, and fruit trees)

Some Possible Concerns

- Among the seating are three marble slabs inscribed with "In Loving Memory." Family members sometimes want to dedicate a tree, an arbor, or a bench in memory of someone who has died. In addition to these slabs not being comfortable, the inscriptions beg the question—how is this for the living, who are reminded of death each time they walk in the garden?

- The sound of falling water adds a soothing touch, but to keep some individuals from getting into the water, the pond and waterfall at the southern end of the garden had to be screened from view by shrubs.

10.15 The looped walking path in the garden is highly used by many who come daily to the Family Life Center.
Photo by Clare Cooper Marcus

References

Ancoli-Israel, S., J. L. Martin, P. Gehrman, T. Shochat, J. Cory-Bloom, M. Marler, S. Nolan, and L. Levi. 2003. "Effect of Light on Agitation in Institutionalized Patients with Severe Alzheimer Disease." *American Journal of Geriatric Psychiatry* 11 (April): 194–203.

Bastone, A. C., and W. J. Filho. 2004. "Effect of an Exercise Program on Functional Performance of Institutionalized Elderly." *Journal of Rehabilitation Research and Development* 41 (5) 659–64.

Beckwith, M. E., and S. D. Gilster. 1997. "The Paradise Garden: A Model Garden Design for Those with Alzheimer's Disease." *Activities, Adaptation and Aging* 22 (1/2): 3–16.

Brawley, E. 1997. *Designing for Alzheimer's Disease: Strategies for Creating Better Care Environments.* New York: John Wiley and Sons.

Calkins, M. P. 1991. "Design for Dementia." Pp. 239–53 in *Design Intervention: Toward a More Humane Architecture*, edited by W. F. E. Preiser, J. C. Vischer, and E. T. White. New York: Van Nostrand Reinhold.

Calkins, M., and B. R. Connell. 2003. "Mary, Mary, Quite Contrary: How Do You Get People to Use Your Garden?" Paper presented at the Joint Conference of the National Council on Aging and the American Society on Aging, March 16, Chicago.

Carman, J. 2002. "Special Needs Gardens for Alzheimer's Residents." *Nursing Homes: Long Term Care Management* 51 (6): 22–26.

Carstens, D. 1985. *Site Planning and Design for the Elderly: Issues, Guidelines and Alternatives.* New York: Van Nostrand Reinhold.

Chalfont, G. 2006. *Connection to Nature at the Building Edge: Towards a Therapeutic Architecture for Dementia Care Environments.* PhD dissertation, University of Sheffield, Sheffield, UK.

———. 2008. *Design for Nature in Dementia Care.* London: Jessica Kingsley Publishers.

Chalfont, G. E., and S. Rodiek. 2005. "Building Edge: An Ecological Approach to Research and Design of Environments for People with Dementia." *Alzheimer's Care Quarterly*, 6 (4): 341–48.

Cohen, U., and K. Day. 2000. "The Role of Culture in Designing Environments for People with Dementia: A Study of Russian Jewish Immigrants." *Environment and Behavior* 32 (3): 361–99.

Cohen, U., and G. D. Weisman. 1988. *Environments for People with Dementia: Case Studies.* Washington, DC: Health Facilities Research Program, AIA/ACSA Council on Architectural Research.

Cohen-Mansfield, J. 2007. "Outdoor Wandering Parks for Persons with Dementia." *Journal of Housing for the Elderly* 21 (1/2): 35–53.

Cohen-Mansfield, J., and P. Werner. 1998. "Visits to an Outdoor Garden: Impact on Behavior and Mood of Nursing Home Residents Who Pace." Pp. 419–36 in *Research and Practice in Alzheimer's Disease*, edited by B. Vellas and L. J. Fitten. New York: Springer Publishing.

Connell, B. R., J. A. Sanford, and D. Lewis. 2007. "Therapeutic Effects of an Outdoor Activity Program on Nursing Home Residents with Dementia." Pp. 195–209 in *Outdoor Environments for People with Dementia*, edited by S. Rodiek and B. Schwarz. Binghamton, NY: The Haworth Press.

Cooper Marcus, C. 2005. "No Ordinary Garden: Alzheimer's and Other Patients Find Refuge in a Michigan Dementia-Care Facility." *Landscape Architecture Magazine* 95 (3) (March): 26–39.

———. 2007. "Alzheimer's Garden Audit Tool." *Journal of Housing for the Elderly* 21 (1/2): 179–91.

Furness, S., and J. Moriarty. 2006. "Designing a Garden for People with Dementia in a Public Space." *Dementia* 5 (1): 139–43.

Galbraith, J., and J. M. Westphal. 2004. "Therapeutic Garden Design: Martin Luther Alzheimer Garden." *Proceedings of the Annual Meeting of American Society of Landscape Architects*, Salt Lake City.

Grant, C. 2003. "Factors Influencing the Use of Outdoor Space by Residents with Dementia in Long-Term Care Facilities." PhD dissertation, Department of Architecture, Georgia Institute of Technology.

Grant, C. F., and J. D. Wineman. 2007. "The Garden-Use Model—An Environmental Tool for Increasing the Use of Outdoor Space by Residents with Dementia in Long-Term Care Facilities." *Journal of Housing for the Elderly* 21 (1/2): 89–115.

Heath, Y. 2004. "Evaluating the Effect of Therapeutic Gardens." *American Journal of Alzheimer's Disease and Other Dementias* 19: 239–42.

Hoover, R. 1999. "Sedgewood Common, Falmouth Maine, Case Study." Pp. 480–88 in *Healing Gardens: Therapeutic Benefits and Design Recommendations*, edited by C. Cooper Marcus and M. Barnes. New York: John Wiley and Sons.

Küller, R. 1991. "Familiar Design Helps Dementia Patients Cope." Pp. 255–67 in *Design Intervention: Toward a More Humane Architecture*, edited by W. F. E. Preiser, J. C. Vischer, and E. T. White. New York: Van Nostrand Reinhold.

Larson, E. B., L. Wang, J. D. Bowen, W. C. McCormick. 2006. "Exercise Is Associated with Reduced Risk for Incident Dementia among Persons 65 Years of Age and Older." *Annals of Internal Medicine* 144 (2): 73–81.

Lovering, M. J., C. A. Cott, D. L. Wells, J. Schleifer Taylor, L. M. Wells. 2002. "A Study of a Secure Garden in the Care of People with Alzheimer's Disease," *Canadian Journal on Aging* 21 (3), 417–27.

Lyons, Donald. 2012. "Going Out—Rights and Responsibilities." Pp. 53–57 in *Designing Outdoor Spaces for People with Dementia*, edited by A. Pollock and M. Marshall. Sydney, Australia: HammondCare.

Mather, J. A., D. Nemecek, and K. Oliver. 1997. "The Effect of a Walled Garden on Behavior of Individuals with Alzheimer's." *American Journal of Alzheimer's Disease* 12 (6): 252–57.

McMinn, B. G., and L. Hinton. 2000. "Confined to Barracks: The Effects of Indoor Confinement on Aggressive Behavior among Inpatients of an Acute Psychogeriatric Unit." *American Journal of Alzheimer's Disease* 15 (1) (January/February): 36–41.

Mitchell, L., E. Burton, and S. Raman. 2004. "Dementia-Friendly Cities: Designing Intelligible Neighborhoods for Life." *Journal of Urban Design*, 9 (1) (Feb.): 89–101.

Mooney, P., and P. L. Nicell. 1992. "The Importance of Exterior Environment for Alzheimer's Residents: Effective Care and Risk Management." *Health Care Management Forum* 5 (2): 23–29.

Moore, K. D. 2001a. *Dementia Day Care Design: Solutions from an Interprofessional Student Practicum.* Center for Architecture and Urban Planning Research, University of Wisconsin–Milwaukee.

———. 2001b. *Designing A Better Day: Adult Day Centers, Comparative Case Studies.* Center for Architecture and Urban Planning Research, University of Wisconsin–Milwaukee.

———. 2002. *Dementia Day Care Facility: Development Workbook.* Milwaukee, WI: Center for Architecture and Urban Planning Research, University of Wisconsin–Milwaukee.

———. 2007. "Restorative Dementia Gardens: Exploring How Design May Ameliorate Attention Fatigue." *Journal of Housing for the Elderly* 21 (1/2): 73–88.

Namazi, K. H., and B. D. Johnson. 1992. "Pertinent Autonomy for Residents with Dementias: Modifications of the Physical Environment to Enhance Independence." *American Journal of Alzheimer's Disease and Other Dementias*, 71 (1): 16–21.

Passini, R., H. Pigot, C. Rainville, and M.-H. Tétreault. 2000. "Wayfinding in a Nursing Home for Advanced Dementia of the Alzheimer's Type." *Environment and Behavior* 32 (5) (September): 684–710.

Pollock, A., and M. Marshall, eds. 2012. *Designing Outdoor Spaces for People with Dementia.* Sydney, Australia: HammondCare.

Pollock, A., and D. McMair. 2012. "Going Outside Is Essential for Health and Wellbeing." In A. Pollock and M. Marshall, eds. *Designing Outdoor Spaces for People with Dementia.* Sydney, Australia: HammondCare.

Randall, P., S. S. J. Burkhardt, and J. Kutcher. 1990. "Exterior Space for Alzheimer's Disease and Related Disorders." *The American Journal of Alzheimer's Care and Related Disorders and Research* 5 (July/August): 31–37.

Rappe, E., and L. Lindén. 1992. "Plants in Health Care Environments: Experiences of the Nursing Personnel in Homes of People with Dementia." Pp. 75–81 in D. Relf, ed., *The Role of Horticulture in Human Well-Being and Social Development.* Portland, Oregon: Timber Press.

Regnier, V. 1985. *Behavioral and Environmental Aspects of Outdoor Space Use in Housing for the Elderly.* Los Angeles: School of Architecture, University of Southern California.

———. 1995. *Assisted Living for the Aged and Frail: Innovations in Design, Management and Financing.* New York: Columbia University Press.

Rodiek, S. D. 2002. "Influence of an Outdoor Garden on Mood and Stress in Older Persons." *Journal of Therapeutic Horticulture* 13: 13–21.

Ulrich, R. S., R. F. Simons, B. D. Losito, E. Fiorito, M. A. Miles, and M. Zelson. 1991. "Stress Recovery During Exposure to Natural and Urban Environments." *Journal of Environmental Psychology* 2: 201–30.

Wilkins, C. H., Y. L. Sheline, C. M. Roe, S. J. Birge, and J. C. Morris. 2006. "Vitamin D Deficiency Is Associated with Low Mood and Worse Cognitive Performance in Older Adults." *American Journal of Geriatric Psychiatry* 14 (Dec.): 1032–40.

Yeo, G. 1996. "Background." Pp. 3–8 in *Ethnicity and the Dementias*, edited by G. Yeo and D. Gallagher-Thompson. Washington, DC: Taylor and Francis. As quoted in Cohen and Day 2000.

Zeisel, J. 2007. "Creating a Therapeutic Garden that Works for People Living with Alzheimer's." *Journal of Housing for the Elderly* 21 (1/2): 13–33.

———. 2010. *I'm Still Here: A New Philosophy of Alzheimer's Care.* New York: Avery/Penguin Group.

Zeisel, J., and M. Tyson. 1999. "Alzheimer's Treatment Gardens." Pp. 437–504 in *Healing Gardens: Therapeutic Benefits and Design Recommendations*, edited by C. Cooper Marcus and M. Barnes. New York: John Wiley and Sons.

CHAPTER 11

Hospice Gardens

While medieval monasteries and, later, civic hospitals frequently served the sick and dying, the hospice as a place whose sole function was the care of the dying emerged in the English-speaking world in the late nineteenth and early twentieth centuries in Dublin, Sydney, New York City, and London.

It was the work of Dr. Cicely Saunders and the establishment of St. Christopher's Hospice in London in 1967 that marked the beginning of the modern hospice movement, with its emphasis on pain control and consoling dying patients and their families. The 1975 publication of Elizabeth Kübler-Ross's groundbreaking book *On Death and Dying* called for a radical new approach. The first US home-care hospice program was initiated in New Haven, Connecticut, in 1974, soon after to become a fifty-two-bed inpatient facility. The British hospice movement inspired developments in Scandinavia, Canada, and Australia, as well as in Japan, China, and Latin America in the 1990s.

In the United States, hospice care is usually confined to individuals facing a life-threatening illness and who, according to their physicians, have probably entered the last six months of their life. Counseling and bereavement support are provided to families. The emphasis is on comfort and care rather than cure. In certain areas of the United States, hospice care consists entirely of home care; in other areas there are purpose-built inpatient facilities. Some of these are associated with a hospital, some are not. Finally, some hospitals have special wards or segments for palliative-care.

Hospice care for children is a relatively new concept. Helen House in Oxford, the first pediatric-only hospice in the UK, opened in 1982 (fig. 11.1). By 2012 more than sixty purpose-built hospices or hospice-care programs were in operation in that country. The first Canadian children's hospice—Canuck House—opened in Vancouver in 1995. The first US inpatient children's hospice facility—the George Mark Children's House Hospice—was opened in San Leandro, California (near San Francisco), in 2003.

While the provision of a garden in a hospital sometimes has to be vigorously promoted, the inclusion of a garden in a hospice facility is almost never questioned. Outdoor spaces of hospices range from extensive landscaped grounds to walled gardens, courtyards, roof gardens, and walking routes around the building (fig. 11.2). With modern hospice care came "a newer sensibility created around the belief that we are also a part of nature and that in surrendering to the natural world. . .we may become strengthened and healed. . . . Many people find comfort in the idea that in dying we return to the earth, like other species. Nature in this view is our ally and our ultimate home" (Worpole 2009, 80). In the UK, where there is growing support for "natural" or "woodland" burials, hospice gardens increasingly incorporate woodland and uncultivated elements "evocative of a more primal world" (ibid.). St. Nicholas Hospice in Suffolk and Princess Alice Hospice in Esher have paths that lead from formal patios and flower gardens into an adjacent woodland. Joseph Weld Hospice in Dorchester and St. Richard's Hospice in Worcester have paths that lead though naturalistic wildflower meadows. The gardens at St. Richard's were developed around a badger sett in order to preserve it (ibid., 84).

In urban settings where extensive sites are less available, hospice gardens often include design elements that facilitate a sense of getting away. Meandering pathways through a series of outdoor rooms at Trinity Hospice in London enable garden users to completely lose sight of the building. The same is true at the Texas Medical Center Hospice in Houston, where as well as open lawns, hidden pathways and benches secreted in dense stands of azaleas provide a sense of escape and privacy.

Design Guidelines for Hospice Gardens

All the general design guidelines in chapter 6 apply equally to hospice gardens, but, in addition, the recommendations below are of particular importance.

General considerations

Required

1. **A familiar landscape**. People at the end of life are not looking for anything that is strange or challenging. In times of stress people are comforted by what is familiar, hence most people's preference—if there is a choice—is to die at home. Modern hospice buildings often reflect the familiar,

11.1 Helen House children's hospice, Oxford, England.
Photo by Clare Cooper Marcus

residential image of the culture in which they are located. The Seirei-Mikatagahara Hospital Hospice in Shizuoka Prefecture, Japan, for example, is designed as a rural village streetscape with cascading roofs and staggered rooms that sharply contrast with the architecture of an adjacent medical center (Verderber and Refuerzo 2006, 112). Canuck House in Vancouver—the first freestanding children's hospice in North America—is housed in an adapted historic mansion with a residential feel to all aspects of its design (ibid., 163–64). A familiar aesthetic should extend to the garden, and its design should echo the essential feel of a residential garden in the region and culture in which the hospice is located.

2. **Transcendent image**. No matter what a person's beliefs may be about the possibility of life after death, there is almost universal apprehension about the passage from life into some unknown beyond. Authors of a book on hospice design recommended that the environment transcend the common realities of everyday life while embracing all that is associated with home and the familiar; that it should be a meaningful synthesis of the ordinary and the unique (ibid.). How this can be translated into physical form cannot easily be worded as a guideline. Aspiring to this goal must permeate every aspect of design for a hospice garden—a more challenging assignment than the creation of any other type of healthcare garden. Above all, the designer needs to understand the cultural attitudes towards death and dying of those being served. For example, the designers of the San Juan Medical Center in Farmington, New Mexico, recognizing that many patients in the locality are Navajo and their tradition is to die outside, provided a balcony for every room.

3. **Maximize the number of sun-facing rooms**. Nature does not only comprise green, growing things; it also incorporates

11.2 A streamside path through the forest in the garden at Bonner Hospice, Sandpoint, Idaho. Designers: John Siegmund and Tom Runa.

Photo by Chris Garcia

a connection to the sky, the sun, the clouds. Orientation and window design that permits access to these elements links a person to the world beyond their room: "A terminally ill businessman . . . looked forward to the time each day when the sun came into his room. The sun traveled on a path beginning at the foot of his bed, gradually reaching his chest, warming him from toe to chest each afternoon. . . . His comment revealed a side of him his children had never before been permitted to see" (Sovich 1995).

4. **Soothing natural sounds**. While soothing sounds are appreciated in any kind of healthcare garden, they are especially pertinent in the garden for a hospice, as hearing is the last of the senses to remain before death. The sounds of birds and crickets, the gentle fall of water, leaves or grasses rustling, wind chimes magnifying the sound of a breeze—all are immensely important (Healy 1986) (fig. 11.3). As a patient's disease progresses, loud sounds can be painful, while soft sounds may be inaudible (ibid.). There should be opportunities to be close

11.3 An echo chamber behind the falling water in this feature at the Bonner Hospice garden in Sandpoint, Idaho, projects the sounds throughout the garden. Designers: John Siegmund and Tom Runa.
Photo by Chris Garcia

to water, with seating and space for a patient gurney. Where possible, the sounds of water should be audible in most patient rooms, although some rooms should be available for those who do not want water sounds. The noise of air-conditioning equipment, recycling pumps, delivery vehicles, and the like should be kept completely away from the garden or be adequately muffled. At the Joseph Weld Hospice in Dorchester, for example, the sounds of a nearby motorway and railroad are successfully muffled by a fountain and rushing waterfall that can be heard in the garden and from patient rooms.

5. **Getting away**. The design of the whole garden—its pathways, planting, seating, distracting views, and other elements—should respond to the need for visitors, staff, and patients, including those being pushed in a wheelchair or on a gurney, to experience a real sense of getting away from the hospice. However sensitively the latter is designed, it will always be a reminder of its function—a place to facilitate the dying process. Families who have been sitting at a loved one's bedside and seek a place for confidential conversation, thought, and prayer, and staff who have been ministering to patients, need to escape at times to secluded seating clusters, a gazebo, or a garden shelter that offers some privacy.

6. **Private garden**. If the hospice has a chapel, meditation room, or viewing room, an adjacent small private garden with comfortable seating and a water feature will be appreciated by grieving family members. At Farleigh Hospice in Chelmsford, UK, a walled garden with a glass sphere at its center and

cutout windows revealing glimpses of the surrounding natural landscape creates a peaceful setting for grief and reflection (Worpole 2009).

7. **First impressions**. Perhaps more than any other kind of healthcare facility, the impression created for first-time visitors at a hospice is critical (fig. 11.4). For an anxious family member or patient, the whole notion of a hospice can arouse extreme emotions. For this reason, the drive onto the site, the ease of parking close to the entrance, a building softened with appropriate landscaping should all be thought of as providing as much reassurance as possible (ibid., 34).

8. **A memorial garden—or not?** There are differing cultural views as to whether commemorative trees, plaques, or tiles should be allowed or discouraged in a hospice garden. In many hospice gardens in the United States, plaques, inscribed bricks or paving stones, or even photos of deceased loved ones are permitted as a way of allowing families to leave a mark in the garden and for the hospice to raise money. In the UK, however, this practice is strongly resisted. After visiting many British hospices, a commentator on hospice design wrote: "Nearly all hospice managers resist the request to plant commemorative trees or shrubs following the deaths of patients, or allow plaques or benches with inscriptions to be donated and installed in the gardens. What the hospice garden cannot be, I was told time and time again, is a memorial garden. It has to be imbued with a sense of life, change, and hope for the future, and for 'the journey ahead'" (ibid., 88). The designer of a hospice garden needs to be clear on what the policy is in the country or region where he or she is working.

9. **Outdoor play for children**. A child's visit to a family member or friend in hospice can be a bewildering and perhaps frightening experience. A play area visible from indoors and incorporating some familiar and some unusual movable elements can provide a stimulating environment (fig. 11.5, fig. 11.6). This is even more important for children in a pediatric hospice, where play elements need to be appealing to a range of ages and physical abilities.

Recommended

1. **Bird feeders**. As life and good health fade, the desire to observe that life in the natural world goes on becomes especially poignant. Reports from many hospices document how positively patients respond to seeing birds and other wildlife through the window or when they are outdoors in the garden. At Hospice House in Portland, Oregon, there is at least one bird feeder outside every patient's window. A volunteer

11.4 Vine-covered arbors provide an attractive, shaded path from the parking area to the main entrance of San Diego Hospice, San Diego, California. Designer: Wimmer Yamada and Caughey.
Photo by Naomi Sachs

11.5 A play area and space for running around can be a welcome amenity for children, for whom a hospice visit may be a bewildering experience. San Diego Hospice, San Diego, California. Designer: Wimmer Yamada and Caughey.
Photo by Clare Cooper Marcus

11.6 A play fort constructed from local driftwood in the garden of the Bonner Hospice, Sandpoint, Idaho. Designers: John Siegmund and Tom Runa.
Photo by Chris Garcia

remarked: "Patients and their families really appreciate having that kind of life outside their rooms. Squirrels and chipmunks and birds eat out of the feeders, and most people have a sensitivity to those things at that point in their life. Family members reported that the bird feeders were a pleasing diversion to take their minds off their grief." Until it was moved to a third-floor location in the rebuilt hospital, the hospice at Laguna Honda Hospital and Rehabilitation

Center, San Francisco, California, had bird feeders in its garden for more that twenty years, as well as a water feature where birds drank and bathed daily. This never proved to be a problem in terms of potential diseases passed from bird droppings to immunocompromised patients. Nothing can prevent birds from flying into a garden, but in certain health care situations—such as an acute-care hospital where there may be acutely immunocompromised patients, those with open wounds, or those undergoing bone marrow transplants—birds should not be encouraged by locating bird feeders in the garden. But in residential facilities for the elderly where people are not necessarily sick, and in hospices for the dying, the remote possibility of bird-borne diseases being transmitted to humans is vastly outweighed by the joy brought by the presence of birds.

2. **Water and wildlife**. The presence of water will often attract wildlife, especially in regions where there is a long dry season. Wildlife reminds people that whatever their medical condition, life goes on (fig. 11.7). At the AHI Hospice in Aichi Prefecture, Japan, a stream runs parallel to the main entry path. In Japanese culture, "water is life giving and life sustaining and is an important aspect of zen spirituality. . . . The fish in the stream symbolize the never-ending flow of life" (Verderber and Refuerzo 2006, 34, 35).

3. **Facilities for pets**. In some US hospices, quarters for family pets are provided at the hospice or pets are allowed to visit, as interaction with an animal is found to have therapeutic value. The George Mark Children's Hospice in San Leandro, California, provides a dog kennel and a horse stable and has space outdoors for children and teens to interact with their pets (ibid., 68).

11.7 The presence of birds and other wildlife, as a symbol of life, can bring joy to those who are sick or dying. A snowy egret reflected in a pond.
Photo from www.henrydomke.com

Visual access

Required

1. Hospice facilities often provide patient rooms **with access to a semiprivate patio or balcony** (fig. 11.8). It is essential that there be clear views to the ground plane, layers of natural vegetation, and views to the sky for the patient (in a bed or chair) and a visitor (sitting or standing) without either having to twist sideways. Orientation to weather, the seasons, and the time of day facilitates a connection to the natural world. Where the building design allows for a bed to be rolled outside, natural views from a horizontal position should also be carefully considered.

Recommended

1. **Panoramic view**. Where the topography of the site permits, a panoramic view across lawns to mature trees or to landscapes beyond may enable some people to "get things into perspective," to "see the big picture." Such a view should be considered in both the orientation of windows from patient rooms and the siting of garden seating.

Physical access

Required

1. A **door outside to a patio or balcony** provides access to fresh air, wider views, and a chance for patient or family member to take a break from the room. It is not uncommon for a patient, when close to death, to ask to be taken outside. Perhaps it is a sense of returning to the natural

11.8 Private balconies for each room allow views out to the hospice landscape and beyond. San Diego Hospice, San Diego, California. Designer: Wimmer Yamada and Caughey.
Photo by Naomi Sachs

world that prompts some to want—in their last moments of consciousness—to feel the sun on their face, to hear birdsong, to watch the clouds. There must be some exit point from the building to the garden that is smooth and wide enough for a gurney to be wheeled outside and from there to a semiprivate space in the garden.

Planting

Recommended

1. Swaths of **ornamental grasses and long-lasting perennials** are the preferred plant palette for hospice gardens. Since smell is one of the last senses to leave before death, it is appropriate to include fragrant plants such as lavender and rosemary, and

fragrant climbers such as jasmine, clematis, and wisteria—especially near the windows of patient rooms. The inclusion of aromatic herbs such as sage, thyme, and lemon balm along pathways invites those in the garden to pick and smell them. It is not appropriate to include beds of annuals that have to be torn out when dying or dead, as these hardly make the right impression in a hospice garden (Worpole 2009, 87). Plants, shrubs, and trees that move in the wind, or even in a slight breeze, add energy to a garden (fig. 11.9). Familiar plants that people might have grown at home may trigger conversation in the garden, as might the inclusion of a few quite unfamiliar but intriguing plants. Continuity and certainty can be conveyed through seasonal changes. Care should be taken in

11.9 Looking closely at the details of plants and leaves can evoke a calm, meditative state. Redbud leaves in the sun.
Photo from www.henrydomke.com

providing a nearby view of varying colors and textures from the patient's room, as well as a more distant view of bold groupings and pleasing contrasts.

Maintenance

1. Any healthcare garden needs a **clear maintenance manual** describing its initial conceptual framework and recommendations for upkeep. This is particularly true for a hospice garden where additions of inappropriate decorations or changes in planting design can easily compromise the original goal of a peaceful and calming environment. Where maintenance is primarily by volunteers or an outside contractor, this is especially important. (See chapter 17 for more on maintenance of therapeutic gardens).

CASE STUDY

Bonner Healing Garden, Bonner Community Hospice, Sandpoint, Idaho

Designers: John Siegmund and Tom Runa
By Chris Garcia

Description of the Facility and Its History

Next to Bonner General Hospital in Sandpoint, Idaho, Bonner Community Hospice occupies a building formerly known as the Brown House. This incorporates offices for hospice workers and home health employees who provide in-home support and palliative care for patients and family members during the last phases of an incurable illness. The hospice does not have inpatient beds.

In 2002, Gene Tomt, the CEO of Bonner General Hospital, proposed a plan for developing a garden on the hospice grounds. The hospital board quickly approved the project with the agreement that funding would come from donations. Tomt appointed Debra Kellerman, director of Bonner Hospice, to lead a task force to secure in-kind donations and plan the 11,000-square-foot site. The hospital provided a loan to maintain momentum on the project. The garden opened less than two years later, in October 2004, and the task force repaid the loan by 2007. A successful community fundraising campaign and in-kind donations funded 81 percent and 19 percent, respectively, of the garden's total cost of $207,000. The cost of the garden amounted to $18.80 per square foot.

The idea for a garden began with a visit to Sacred Heart Medical Center in Spokane, Washington, where a combination of chapels, meditation rooms, and gardens greatly influenced Tomt and Kellerman. The planning process was informed by this visit and by a study of four hospital gardens in the San Francisco area (Cooper Marcus and Barnes 1995). A task force including a landscape architect, a master gardener, an interior designer, therapists, patients, and community volunteers met every few weeks from the summer of 2003 to the fall of 2004 to plan and promote the garden. The preliminary design was later modified by garden contractor John Siegmund.

Design Philosophy

The proposal outlined by Gene Tomt was "to create a garden sanctuary of healing, remembrance, and contemplation for people of all faiths and backgrounds within the healthcare environment." The task force envisioned a place of solace and comfort in contrast to the clinical nature of healthcare and the chaos of illness, stress, and grief. They also recognized that the garden could provide a welcoming park for everyone in Sandpoint (fig. 11.10).

A local family exemplified the sense of community that the task force hoped the garden would inspire. The Allens, from the nearby town of Hope, planned their family reunion as an all-day work party to clear the garden site for construction. Equipped with tools and forty pairs of hands, the entire extended family came together in memory of their late father and in gratitude for hospice care.

11.10 Visitors enjoying the flowers outside the chapel at Bonner Hospice, Sandpoint, Idaho.
Photo by Chris Garcia

John Siegmund, contractor for the garden, used feng shui design principles to lay out the paths and structures. He used his artistic expertise in concrete and salvaged materials to create a series of naturalistic structures that blend with the site, conveying a sense of permanence.

Description of the Outdoor Spaces

The garden can be accessed from several key locations. A crosswalk from the hospital parking lot leads directly to an entry trellis. Other access points include a small stairway from an outpatient parking lot and through a porch and deck from the Brown House.

Despite adjacent parking, the garden site is completely natural in character. The primary garden space is located on the banks of Sand Creek, a broad stream that feeds Lake Pend Oreille. The cabin-like Brown House and old-growth forest,

which define the boundaries of the site, frame the entire garden in a homelike, natural setting.

The garden layout facilitates a journey of choice through a series of sensory gardens and distinct structural features. The main ADA-compliant path is 6 feet wide, with heating tubes beneath that permit year-round access. The textured and colored concrete paving resembles native stone and is comfortable to the eye (fig. 11.11).

These are the main features of the garden, in their approximate order along the path circuit:

- A clematis-covered entry trellis and a dense row of pine trees welcoming garden visitors.

- A memorial wall of three slate boulders with small metal plaques recognizing donors and loved ones.

11.11 Entry to the Healing Garden at Bonner Hospice in Sandpoint, Idaho. The pathway of textured and colored concrete has heating tubes beneath it to ensure year-round access.
Photo by Chris Garcia

- A rose garden with three arbors and an arching stone wall perforated with a symbolic circular void.

- A cantilevered water wall, raised pond, and stream bed: water pours onto native boulders in front of an echo chamber, which projects the sounds far into the garden. A raised pond with seat walls pools the water and releases it into a stream bed with a series of small cascades that end at a circular reflection pool, from where it is recirculated. In winter, the water wall becomes a free-form ice sculpture.

- A teahouse intended for quiet conversation and meditation.

- A gable-roofed chapel constructed with seventy-year-old larch beams salvaged from the old Brown House dock. The chapel is nondenominational and does not contain any religious imagery. Heating tubes embedded in the concrete floor provide winter warmth. Personal possessions are often left on the windowsill as expressions of grief or gratitude.

- A children's garden defined by a "stump" fort that is crafted with drift wood and a bench constructed by local Eagle Scouts (see fig. 11.6).

- A walkway with a 5 percent grade, with two seating alcoves along the forested banks of Sand Creek (see fig. 11.2).

How the Garden Is Used

Bonner Healing Garden accommodates two distinct sets of users: It is a healing environment for patients, families, and staff from the hospice and hospital, and it acts as a public park for the community. Clinical staff, patients, and family members use the garden for physical, emotional, and spiritual support (fig. 11.12). Bereavement counselors and spiritual-support staff use the chapel and teahouse to meet with families and dying loved ones who visit from their homes (fig. 11.13). Families and friends use the garden to stroll and meditate. Youth counselors in an adolescent wellness program facilitate activities in the garden to express emotions and as a metaphor for life. Physical therapists from the hospital use two short stairways and the 5 percent creek path to conduct ambulation exercises with clients. Outpatients from the adjacent medical building visit the garden to relax before or after a doctor's appointment. Patients and staff from the three adjacent medical facilities ensure that the garden is well used throughout the day.

The Sandpoint community embraces the healing garden as a place of celebration and spiritual connection. Small weddings have taken place there, as well as family and school reunions. High school students take their prom photos in the garden. Couples and friends often walk though the garden at dusk. Art exhibitions and barbecues on behalf of the hospital and hospice take place there annually.

Key Garden Merits

- Built structures facilitate a sequence of contemplative experiences that often take on personal meaning.

- The natural site and quaint construction details give the garden a sense of permanence.

- The garden's proximity to a residential neighborhood and downtown Sandpoint make it a public park accessible to a diverse set of visitors.

- The chapel and teahouse provide private sanctuaries for spiritual support.

- Universal symbols of the cycle of life, such as sculptural tree trunks that have survived forest fires, leaf fossils imprinted in the concrete paths, and a totem pole of a bald eagle head

11.12 The forested site of the Bonner Hospice garden lends an air of permanence and tranquility for patients, staff, visitors, and the community.

Photo by Chris Garcia

salvaged from the Brown House dock are placed throughout the site.

- Profusely planted sensory gardens engage people and attract wildlife.

- Ample night lighting allows for around-the-clock use. Heating tubes under the main path allow for year-round access.

Possible Concerns

- Site erosion has exposed segments of path edges, creating 2- to 3-inch ledges that may be hazardous to wheelchair users.

- Several small warning signs along the path are used to discourage vandalism and trespassing. The chapel, originally planned for twenty-four-hour use, must now be locked at night. Due to safety concerns, the eternal flame has not burned since a first vandalism incident.

- Despite the best efforts of the designer and original staff to argue against them, new administrators and staff have added artificial features, such as plastic ornaments and children's play features, that clash with the garden's natural appearance and ambience.

11.13 Grief counselors and family members meet in the tranquil setting of the Teahouse in the Bonner Hospice Garden, Sandpoint, Idaho.
Photo by Chris Garcia

San Diego Hospice, San Diego, California

Designers: Wimmer Yamada and Caughey

History of the Faciity

The San Diego Hospice and the Institute for Palliative Medicine were established in 1977, offering volunteer in-home respite care. The inpatient hospice-hospital—designed to meet short-term acute-care needs of patients—was opened in 1990, and the first patient was admitted in 1991.

Description of the Garden

The most notable feature of the San Diego Hospice and the surrounding Tribute Garden is its location on a high, steep-sided bluff overlooking a large valley that once was the bed of the San Diego River and is now covered with built-up areas of the city. Leading from the parking area to the main

entrance are attractive wooden trellis structures that provide shade from the hot Southern California sun (see fig. 11.4) Inspiring quotes are affixed to the support columns. To the right of the main entrance, on one of the site's few sizable flat spaces, is an area of lawn and swings for young visitors (see fig. 11.5). From this point a long, smooth path circles the hospice through a linear garden accessed from nine building exits. The steep sides of the site necessitate that the garden is relatively narrow for much of its extent, with a winding path, dense plantings of trees, shrubs, and perennials—mostly native and drought-tolerant—and panoramic views over the distant cityscape (fig. 11.14). Benches are located along the path, and at some places the path widens

11.14 A wandering path at the edge of a steep-sided bluff encircles the San Diego Hospice.
Photo by Clare Cooper Marcus

to incorporate a patio space with wooden tables and cushioned movable garden seats. Memorial Point, at the far end of the promontory path, has a paved area with a flagpole, arbor overlook, seating, a sculpture of a woman and child, and "columns" that feature photographs of deceased family members. Twenty-four semiprivate patio spaces lead off patient rooms into the garden at grade; above-grade rooms have balconies with views (see fig. 11.8). The garden is maintained by weekly contract gardeners in addition to the in-house maintenance staff, who help with routine care.

How the Garden Is Used

The garden is used by everyone in or visiting the hospice: staff on breaks, patients being wheeled through the garden or sitting outside, family members taking a break from sitting by a loved one's bedside, and volunteers. The location and design of the garden allow people to take a stroll with changing views, stop and sit at various locations, eat meals outdoors, or sit to take in panoramic views of the city (fig. 11.15). A staff nurse commented: "I think this setting sometimes prompts families to remember the things they did with their loved ones." Remembrance gatherings are held occasionally at Memorial Point. Families of the deceased can make donations to the hospice by sponsoring a Tribute Stone, an inscribed paving

11.15 Seating areas provide places where visitors and staff can take a break outdoors and look out over a panoramic view.
Photo by Clare Cooper Marcus

block placed at Memorial Point and in the Tribute Garden. For a donation of $1,000, the name of a loved one or colleague is inscribed on a leaf in the mosaic Wall of Tribute (fig. 11.16). Sometimes families return to spend time in the garden on the anniversary of a loved one's death.

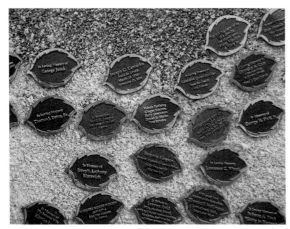

11.16 The Wall of Tribute, an unobtrusive leaf mosaic, provides a way for family members to memorialize the names of their loved ones and to make a donation to the hospice.
Photo by Naomi Sachs

- Panoramic views

- Small play space and lawn area for visiting children

- Dark, nonreflective surface along part of pathway circuit

- Unobtrusive leaf mosaic donor wall

Possible Problems

- Large paved area at Memorial Point with a semicircle of backless concrete benches is in sharp contrast to the garden atmosphere of the rest of the outdoor space.

- Some segments of light, highly reflective concrete paving.

- "In memory of. . ." paving stones may be depressing for patients and visitors.

Key Garden Merits

- Overall calming feel of the garden

- A peaceful place of rest and renewal

- Nothing too bold or overpowering

- Seating places in many different locations

References

Cooper Marcus, C., and M. Barnes. 1995. *Gardens in Healthcare Facilities: Uses, Therapeutic Benefits and Design Recommendations.* Concord, CA: Center for Health Design.

Healy, V. 1986. "The Hospice Garden: Addressing the Patients' Needs through Landscape," in *American Journal of Hospice Care* 3 (5): 18–23; 3 (6): 32–36.

Kübler-Ross, E. 1975. *On Death and Dying.* Macmillan: New York.

Sovich, R. M. 1995. "A Place for Hospice Care." R. M. Sovich Archtecture. Online. http://rmsovich.home.mindspring.com/papers.html (accessed 23 July 2004). As quoted in Verderber and Refuerzo 2006, 33.

Verderber, S., and B. J. Refuerzo. 2006. *Innovations in Hospice Architecture.* Taylor and Francis: New York.

Worpole, K. 2009. *Modern Hospice Design.* Routledge: Abingdon, UK.

CHAPTER 12

Gardens for Mental and Behavioral Health Facilities

Vincent van Gogh painted his famous "Iris" series at the Asylum of Saint Paul de Mausole in Saint-Rémy, France, in 1889. Allowed to roam the asylum's grounds, van Gogh wrote in a letter to his brother, Theo, "When I send you the four canvases of the garden. . .you'll see that considering that life happens above all in the garden, it isn't so sad." In a letter to his mother and sister he wrote, "But precisely for one's health, as you say—it's very necessary to work in the garden and to see the flowers growing" (Van Gogh 2009; fig. 12.1).

The mental health benefits of interacting with nature, either passively or actively, are numerous and have been well documented (see chapter 3). The benefits may be all the more important for people who are struggling with mental illness. Mental illness touches almost every individual, either directly or through someone they know. One in every four people who seeks health services is troubled with mental or behavioral health disorders, which are often misdiagnosed and/or mistreated (WHO 2001). Based on the World Health Organization's estimates of mortality and burden of disease for 2002, Mathers and Locar (2006) projected global and regional mortality and burden of disease for the years 2000, 2010, and 2030, predicting that the three leading causes of burden of disease in 2030 will be HIV/AIDS, ischemic heart disease, and unipolar depressive disorders. Only a small percentage of people suffering from mental illness will receive treatment, and an even smaller percentage will be hospitalized. However, for those healthcare facilities that provide in- or outpatient care, the provision of nature and safe, nurturing therapeutic gardens is paramount.

Curtis et al. (2007) conducted a postoccupancy evaluation of a new mental health inpatient unit in East London, England. The participants—former patients and staff—discussed their views on aspects of the hospital's environment of care (including but not limited to the physical environment) that were beneficial or detrimental to their health and well-being. Among the themes that emerged were surveillance versus freedom and openness; territoriality, privacy, refuge, and social interactions; and *homeliness and contact with nature* (emphasis added). Gross et al. (1998) found that psychiatric facilities that had natural settings and elements of nature incorporated into the design could potentially assist in mental health treatment. In a study on the redesign of multiple psychiatric units, Devlin (1992) identified the addition of plants as the most positively rated feature overall.

Aggression against patients and staff in mental healthcare facilities, especially acute-care psychiatric hospitals, is a global problem. Some researchers are looking at ways in which the physical environment can promote the reduction of violence and the need for patient restraint. In a recent study, Ulrich, Bogren, and Lundin (2012) identified ten evidence-based environmental features that can potentially reduce stress and aggression in psychiatric facilities. Window views of nature, access to gardens, and daylight exposure were specified as three of the features (fig. 12.2).

Research specifically on gardens for mental and behavioral health facilities is scant. This may in part be due to the difficulty of gaining access, including Internal Review Board (IRB) approval, to places that care for people who are mentally or emotionally vulnerable or cognitively impaired. The population served by inpatient and outpatient facilities is also incredibly broad and varied. Mental health disorders affect people of all ages and abilities and include depression; psychosis and bipolar disorders; child and adolescent mental disorders, such as attention-hyperactivity disorder (ADHD) and autism spectrum disorder; self-harm and suicide; eating disorders; substance abuse; anxiety disorders; and other

12.1 Siberian iris.
Photo from www.henrydomke.com

12.2 At the Östra Psychiatric Hospital in Gothenburg, Sweden, patient units were designed as "neighborhoods," with one garden for every fourteen patients. Each garden is a separate courtyard surrounded by walls/wings of Östra, providing security. Though each garden is different, all offer a variety of seating choices, access to shade, and prominent vegetation—including flower color during spring through early fall.
Photo by Roger Ulrich

significant medical and unexplained somatic complaints. (For a discussion of posttraumatic stress disorder [PTSD], see chapter 13.) Many of these disorders, such as depression and suicide, are interrelated. Healthcare facilities may treat one specific disorder, such as substance abuse (see the case study of Rosecrance Healing Garden in this chapter) or many disorders. The length of stay for inpatient facilities ranges from one night to life-long care, including forensic care (facilities for those determined by the court as "criminally insane"). Countries and states have different policies about treatment, including allowing people outside. For example, in 2011, over thirty inpatient psychiatric hospitals and group residences in Massachusetts denied patients/residents all access to the outdoors (Jonathan Dosick, pers. comm., 2011).

Barnhart, Perkins, and Fitzsimonds (1998) studied behavior and outdoor setting preferences among staff and patients at a 312-bed Canadian psychiatric hospital situated on forty-eight acres in Guelph, Ontario. Staff and patients both indicated as their first choice natural, open settings for passive behaviors like sitting and looking at scenery and natural, enclosed settings for active behaviors such as walking and talking with others. Larsen (1992) found that schizophrenic patients had a preference for enclosed, visually complex outdoor spaces. Research on outdoor spaces for children with autism reveals the importance of designing for this specific population. Despite the oft-quoted statement, "If you've met one child with autism, you've met one child with autism," certain characteristics of outdoor spaces have been found to be universally important. For example, a garden or landscape that is clearly legible to the user; spaces within the garden for children to "cocoon" when they are experiencing sensory overload; a garden sited away from loud, sporadic noises such as sirens, trucks backing up, and the like; and elements of continuity throughout the garden such as colors, shapes, and textures (Etherington 2012; Vincenta et al. 2012; Sachs and Vincenta 2011). Lundgren (2004) and Millet (2009), among others, have documented the potential for horticultural therapy to assist in the rehabilitation process for communication disorders and fatigue and stress disorders.

In an article on best practices for psychiatric hospital design, Karlin and Zeiss (2006) listed the following biophilic design features as important:

- Natural daylight.
- Good air quality, fresh air, good ventilation, and neutral odors.

- Vegetation, and visual and physical connection to the outdoors. They state that "large, low windows may improve sensory abilities and reduce delirium and paranoia" (p. 1377), but they do not cite their source specifically.

Karlin and Zeiss also identified the following features that translate to the design of outdoor as well as indoor spaces:

- Features that enhance privacy and autonomy.
- Incorporation of spatial flexibility.
- Separate staff areas.
- Places for family.
- A homelike, noninstitutional environment.
- Movable furniture—heavy enough not to be used as a weapon but light enough to be movable.
- Design that reinforces treatment goals by providing a "latent message" of care. In a study that looked at the effects of remodeling of two psychiatric wards, researchers found that remodeling improved patient satisfaction, self-image, and behavior. The remodel also improved staff mood and punctuality.

Design Guidelines

As with every chapter addressing the needs of specific patient populations, all of the general design guidelines from chapter 6 should be applied in addition to those listed below, which are especially significant for people with mental and behavioral illness. Due to the breadth of issues associated with mental illness, each and every design decision must be specific to the population being served. This cannot be emphasized enough. The designer/design team must work closely with the healthcare facility throughout the design and construction process. The facility will likely already have policies and design parameters in place that will guide decisions.

Required

1. **Safety first**. The safety of all garden users—patients, visitors, and staff—is the primary concern for the design of any space in mental and behavioral healthcare facilities. The specific concerns will vary according to the population. A garden for drug and alcohol rehabilitation patients will not need the kinds of high-security measures required for a facility serving those at high risk of suicide. A garden where patients are attended by staff 100 percent of the time may not need such tight design restrictions.

12.3 This tree-staking technique was seen, surprisingly, at a healthcare facility for psychiatric patients. The rubber used for tree staking could be used to harm oneself or others.
Photo by Naomi Sachs

2. **Avoid objects that can be used to harm others or oneself.** Decorative stones, plants in small pots, lighting fixtures that can be broken off, screws and bolts, thorns, bricks, wire, landscape fabric pins, tree staking material (fig. 12.3); these are just a few of the objects that can potentially be used as weapons. Fixtures—whether attached to or separate from the building—must be impossible to use for self-harm. Tree branches may need to be limbed up. Avoid poisonous vegetation. Though most patients will not ingest harmful plants on purpose, they may put things—flowers or berries, for example—in their mouths without thinking of possible consequences. Some patients, even when they do not mean to harm themselves, may not be aware of how high their pain threshold is.

3. **Avoid elopement opportunities** provided by trees, benches, retaining walls, trellises, or other fixed or movable structures that could be put against a fence or wall to be climbed over.

4. **Balance security and privacy.** In facilities where patients are allowed outside on their own, an ability for staff to monitor patients may still be necessary. Spaces within the garden should *feel* relatively private and secure but still be visible to staff.

5. Create a **homelike, noninstitutional environment**. A garden provides an excellent opportunity for patients and family members to enjoy a feeling of normalcy and a sense of getting away—perhaps all the more important for those who are prohibited from leaving.

6. Provide **visual as well as physical access to nature**. Enable visual access to the outdoors from as many spaces within the building as possible—communal gathering areas such as dining rooms and lounges, patient rooms, even some therapy rooms. While visual access is important for everyone, especially in inclement weather, it is essential for people whose outdoor access may be severely, if not completely, limited.

7. Design for **social support**. Provide seating for one-on-one conversations as well as for large groups, such as group-therapy sessions. This must be carefully thought through since, unlike other patient groups, those in behavioral health settings are generally not allowed access to movable garden seating because of security concerns.

8. **Provide shade and avoid glare**. Patients with certain cognitive and mental disorders are often sensitive to glare. Additionally, many antidepressant and antipsychotic medications make people more sensitive to UV rays. Avoid paving and other surfaces, including building materials such as glass or metal, that create glare. Provide plenty of places for patients to sit and walk in the shade.

9. Provide **areas and outlets for exercise** such as paths for strolling, tracks for walking or jogging, exercise equipment, and so on. Physical activity, including walking, can ease symptoms of depression (Carek, Laibstain, and Carek 2011), and research indicates that "green exercise"—physical activity in nature—may offer even greater benefits (see chapter 3 for more on green exercise). Research by Roe and Aspinall (2011) underscores the importance of creating naturalistic spaces, whenever possible, where people can walk and exercise. The researchers compared adults with good and poor mental health (referred by specialist mental health service providers) walking in rural and urban environments. Both groups showed higher affective and cognitive restoration after the rural walks, but the benefits were greater with the poor mental health group. Faber Taylor and Kuo have found that when children with ADHD spend time (playing, walking, and so on) in nature settings such as parks, their symptoms diminish significantly (Faber Taylor, Kuo, and Sullivan 2001; Kuo and Faber Taylor 2004; Faber Taylor and Kuo 2009).

10. **Avoid potentially threatening material**. People with mental illness sometimes experience visual and auditory delusions. For example, knots and patterns in wood may be seen as ghoulish faces. Plant material and other objects should be chosen with this in mind.

11. The garden should be **easily "legible"** by someone who is about to venture into it. The unknown is especially unnerving for people with mental illness. In addition, wayfinding cues will help people who are confused or disoriented to find their way back to the garden entrance (fig. 12.4).

Recommended

1. Provide **human scale**. In small spaces dominated by tall buildings, or in large spaces without a sense of enclosure, vegetation and other features (arbors, seating, and the like) can bring the garden to a comfortable scale.

2. Provide **opportunities for indoor nature connection**. Potted plants and indoor atria can allow people easy and safe access to nature. At Butler Hospital in Providence, Rhode Island, a small indoor atrium with a seating area is located next to the stairway from the central building area to the inpatient ward floors. Patients and staff walk by the atrium at least twice a day and sometimes stop to sit by themselves or visit with each other.

3. Provide at least one **water feature** (fig. 12.5). The sound, sight, and even the smell of water can be especially soothing to people who are agitated or unstable. Mental health clients are, for the most part, one of the few patient populations that do not have

12.5 This courtyard provides a shady, calm place with an attractive fountain as centerpiece and wayfinding marker. Movable chairs allow people to sit alone or with two or more people.
Photo by Brian Bainnson

compromised immune systems. Thus the threat of harmful bacteria such as *Legionella* being spread by water aerosolization is much less of a concern. Water features should still be designed so that they are easy to maintain and do not pose any other health threat (such as drowning) to garden users.

12.6 Dogwood trees provide four-season interest with spring blossoms, green foliage for summer shade, brilliant fall color, and red berries in winter. *Photo from www.henrydomke.com*

4. Provide **separate spaces for staff**. Whenever possible, separate outdoor spaces for staff should be available, preferably near the break room or somewhere else easily accessible and not visible to patients or visitors.

5. Provide **temporal cues**. Plant material, clocks, sundials, and other design features can be an aid and a comfort to people with a distorted sense of time. Vegetation can offer daily cues—sunflowers that move to face the sun, or flowers that open in the day and close at night—and seasonal cues—trees or shrubs that flower in spring and turn color in the fall (fig. 12.6).

CASE STUDY

A Garden at a Crisis Shelter for Women and Children Survivors of Domestic Violence: Danner's Garden, Copenhagen, Denmark

Designer: Schonherr, Copenhagen, Denmark

By Victoria L. Lygum and Ulrika K. Stigsdotter

The United Nations (UN) defines domestic violence as any form of physical, sexual, psychological, or economic violence involving individuals who are or have been in an intimate relationship, individuals with family relationships to one another, and members of the same household (UN 2010). Both sexes can be victims of the violence regardless of sexual orientation. In most cases, domestic violence is perpetrated by men against women (UNICEF 2000). Studies estimate that from country to country, between 20 and 50 percent of women have experienced violence perpetrated by their partners or ex-partners (WHO 1996). In the United States, one woman in four experiences this kind of violence at some point in her life (Tjaden and Thoennes 2000).

Such violence may result in women suffering numerous health consequences, including mental health effects such as depression and posttraumatic stress disorder (Campbell 2002; Coid et al. 2003) as well as physical health effects, including injury (Plichta 2004; Guth and Pachter 2000) and chronic pain (Plichta 2004; Campbell 2002; Diaz-Olavarrieta et al. 1999). Domestic violence may also damage the health and well-being of children in the family, as the mother's capacity for parenting may be reduced (WHO 2010). A wide range of developmental outcomes may be compromised (Wolfe et al. 2003) and the children may have emotional and behavioral problems as well

as physical symptoms such as headaches and disturbed sleep (Fantuzzo and Mohr 1999; Campbell 1997). Moreover, studies reveal that children who are exposed to domestic violence have an increased risk of becoming either victims or perpetrators of violence as adults (The Body Shop/UNICEF 2006).

The numerous health consequences and the fact that domestic violence happens in a private setting and is often considered taboo make it hard for victims to seek help. When a woman make the decision to flee, a crisis shelter (CS) can play an important role by providing safe accommodation, counseling and therapy, and by helping the woman and her children start a new life without violence.[1]

A CS garden that is carefully designed to match the needs of its users has the potential to be a salutogenic (health-promoting) resource supporting CS functions. First, the garden can offer an optimized setting for everyday activities. Second, the benefits of contact with nature can be used actively in therapy, expanding the set of tools available to staff. By offering soothing as well as challenging experiences that are meaningful on both a concrete and a more symbolic level, the garden can help residents cope better with stress, achieve

---

1. There are several terms to describe a place that offers support and safe accommodation for women and children who have been exposed to domestic violence, including "shelter" and "women's shelter." Here the term "crisis shelter" is used.

heightened body awareness, strengthen feelings of self worth, and improve social competence.

The purpose of this case study is to support practitioners working with evidence-based design of CS gardens from a salutogenic perspective. The guidelines, design, and associated therapy program of Danner's Garden were developed as a part of a research project funded by Nordea-fonden at the Danish Center for Forest and Landscape, University of Copenhagen.

Guidelines for Crisis Shelter Gardens

While the general design guidelines in chapter 6 apply to all healthcare gardens, the additional guidelines apply to gardens at crisis shelters.

Security and feeling safe

Security against intrusion is a fundamental aspect of a CS garden because of the risk that the perpetrators will seek out residents. For the women and children, feeling safe is a fundamental part of the support they need.

1. The parts of the garden that are visible to the public should follow the strategy of the CS building—for example, an anonymous CS that blends in with its surroundings.

2. In the immediate CS environs, security may be optimized by providing sightlines and lighting and by avoiding potential hiding places for perpetrators.

3. The garden should be enclosed. All entrances to the garden from public areas should be locked, and video surveillance may be necessary. Views from public spaces into the garden should be minimized.

4. Easy visual access to the garden from the building is important to ensure physical and emotional safety. This allows for staff surveillance and visual contact between mothers and children. Good upkeep (e.g., by having a shed for maintenance items and storage) and lighting can support this goal.

5. Enhancing a pleasant, homelike image, as opposed to an institutional one, can also support the residents' sense of safety. Landscaping can soften and beautify the appearance of security measures such as fences, gates, and cameras and can function as a visual buffer covering stark surroundings.

Garden access

While at the CS, residents' activities such as going to work or school can be disrupted, and danger from a perpetrator can force some residents to stay on CS property. This makes the garden an important place (sometimes the only place) where residents can gain respite from the indoor environment and benefit from contact with nature. However, the numerous health consequences that the women may experience can hinder their own and, thereby, their children's use of the garden. It is therefore important that the garden be as accessible as possible, both through its physical design and the activities it offers.

1. A transition area between the building and the garden, such as a covered porch or a terrace, can be a safe place from which to start using the garden.

2. Designs that support activities that correspond to the capacities of the residents can enhance their feeling of safety and their use of the garden. The garden could, for instance, include elements familiar to residents from kindergarten, after-school activities, or their own gardens.

3. Residents' use of the garden depends to a high degree on staff initiative. Plans for how the garden is to be used for CS functions ranging from everyday activities to therapy programs may vary from CS to CS. It is important to allow for these plans in the design process. Elements such as watering cans, bird feeders, and barbecues can be starting points for outdoor activities and might help the staff in taking the initiative.

Different levels of social involvement

One of the consequences of violence is that both women and children may suffer from social dysfunction. Establishing social relationships with the staff and other residents is critical. A garden that accommodates different levels of social involvement can take varying needs for social and private activities into account and thereby support social competence.

1. The garden can constitute an informal environment where it is easier to initiate contact and establish relationships. Seating along pathways can allow intermittent interaction. Seating areas for smaller and larger groups can accommodate social CS activities such as communal eating, meetings, and group counseling.

2. Semienclosed spaces, from where it is possible to watch social activities from a distance, can help residents not to feel entirely cut off from social life without having to participate actively themselves.

3. Spaces that are more secluded can provide a calm refuge and facilitate private activities such as conversational therapy.

4. Visual contact between different types of seating areas and the play area makes activities such as counseling and

meetings possible while adults keep an eye on children playing nearby.

Safe play

Women and children at a CS are in a state of crisis. At the same time, they are living in temporary housing, in close proximity to strangers. This can result in a tense and distressing indoor atmosphere. The garden may afford children greater scope for play and self-expression than indoors. Furthermore, having the children outside can help to create a calmer indoor environment.

1. The emotional distress, depression, and anxiety that mothers may experience can cause them to be less attentive towards their children. This accentuates the importance of child safety in all aspects of the garden.

2. The garden should include a versatile play area that offers challenges for children of various ages with play equipment that can be used in different ways according to the children's abilities and preferences. For teenagers, semienclosed areas can constitute places to "hang out."

3. Designing for good visual contact between adults and children in the placement and layout of the play area is essential for staff in charge of child care and mother/child contact. Seating near the play area can facilitate surveillance.

4. The play area should encourage children to use their bodies in different ways and should support physical exercise. Spaces for quiet play, where children can occasionally withdraw from active play, are also important.

5. Some children may be unclear about the boundaries between what they can and cannot do. Conflicts can occur when children's aggression is directed toward elements in the garden or toward one another. This can be addressed by having robust play elements that yet discourage excessive speed or dangerous activities such as jumping from high places, as from a merry-go-round. Furthermore, objects that might be used as weapons should be avoided.

6. Contact with domestic animals may benefit the children on many levels but should be subject to staff supervision.

Description of the Facility and Its History

Danner is a private humanitarian organization that runs a CS for women and children survivors of domestic violence. The building in which Danner is situated is a landmark in the center of Copenhagen and is one of Denmark's finest examples of Neo-Renaissance architecture. Danner is also a research center on issues of violence; it houses 35 employees and 250 volunteers and has room for 17 women and their children. Between 2010 and 2012, Danner underwent renovation, and its outdoor space was redesigned as Danner's Garden.

Design Philosophy

Danner's Garden was developed using evidence-based design, in a collaboration involving staff from Danner, the landscape architecture firm Schonherr, and the interdisciplinary health design research team at the University of Copenhagen. The garden is designed to be a safe and secure environment supporting positive distractions, physical exercise, and opportunities for both social activities and inner reflection. It is a multifunctional space that accommodates everyday activities such as relaxation, play, and eating outdoors, as well as activities led by staff, including meetings, counseling sessions, and therapy programs. The therapy programs consist of conversational therapy and physical exercise, each of which take advantage of the garden setting, as well as horticultural activities. The therapy program is intended to support the expected healing process, which operates at various levels, fostering feelings of safety, recollection, grief, and reconnection to everyday life (Danner 2011). The garden aims to contribute to improved methods in helping women and children at all CSs. Eventually, the design and the therapy programs will be systematically evaluated.

Description of the Garden

Access to the 11,300-square-foot garden is only possible through the CS building or through locked gates from a semiprivate entrance area. The garden, which is first and foremost for the residents, is enclosed by a high fence covered by climbing plants. Situated in an urban location, the garden is not protected from views from neighboring apartment buildings. It does, however, offer several spaces that are shielded by elements of the built environment or vegetation. The relatively simple design ensures the flexibility necessary to accommodate a variety of uses. It provides opportunities to participate in social activities, observe activities from a distance, or find a private space to be in small groups or alone (fig. 12.7).

In order for the garden to be used as much as possible throughout the seasons, visual and physical accessibility is incorporated into the design. There are attractive views from inside the building, and dispersed ground-level lighting makes the garden accessible after dark. Illumination is of great importance in Denmark, where nights are long in winter months. A children's program house and a glass pavilion

Danner's Garden

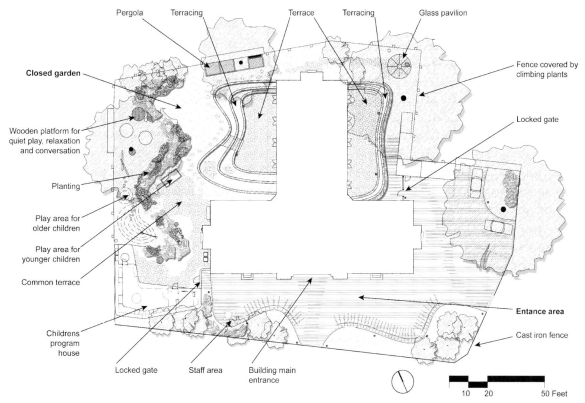

Pergola   Terracing   Terrace   Terracing   Glass pavilion

Closed garden

Fence covered by
climbing plants

Wooden platform for
quiet play, relaxation
and conversation

Locked gate

Planting

Play area for
older children

Play area for
younger children

Common terrace

Entance area

Childrens
program
house

Cast iron fence

Locked gate   Staff area   Building main
entrance

10   20   50 Feet

12.7 Plan of Danner's Garden
Courtesy of Schonherr

mean that activities can take place in the garden even in bad weather. All the exits from the building to the garden lead directly to paths or large areas paved with slate, of which one is an area situated 3.5 feet below the garden level. From there, access to the garden is via steps and three terraces that can be used as informal seating.

The garden is designed to offer positive distractions through both hardscape and planting. Natural sounds of whispering grasses, leaves, and trickling water from a strategically located fountain offer a pleasant alternative to the traffic noise from the roads nearby. The structure of the planting, slate paths, and a number of low wooden platforms enable close contact with the plants. The planting has something to offer year-round, provides habitat for birds and insects, and adds color, scent, texture, and edibles that can be used in the outdoor kitchen. The garden also features raised planters used in horticultural activities and a lawn with space for physical exercise such as yoga (fig. 12.8).

The play area is next to a slate-paved terrace at garden level, providing the main seating area for adults. Closest to the terrace is a sandbox and a water fountain for the younger children. A little farther away, there are opportunities for older children to play in a low hilly area with balancing logs and poles, a climbing rope, and small, semitransparent willow huts. To promote physical exercise, the different elements have been arranged as parts of an obstacle course. The play area also provides access to shrubbery, allowing children to use plants in their games. Platforms to sit or lie on close to plantings constitute semienclosed spaces for quiet play for children and relaxation for teenagers. Although the play area accounts for a large part of the garden, natural materials ensure that it is well integrated. Colorful wooden figures demonstrate that this is the main area for children. Play elements are chosen with the aim of avoiding dangerous activities.

12.8 Sketch of Danner's Garden.
Courtesy of Schonherr

The 720-square-foot children's program house adjoining the play area is designed to be flexible and facilitate a variety of uses, such as conversational therapy, learning activities, and play. The house creates a solid barrier to the surrounding neighborhood, while large windows and several doors assure good visual and physical access to the garden. The intention is that the children can put a certain distance between themselves and the sometimes tense and distressing atmosphere in the main building. It also gives the mothers a break from looking after their children and contributes to a calmer indoor environment.

For the adults, counseling is possible in various partly shielded areas, such as under a pergola or on the platforms in the play area, from which the mothers may keep an eye on their children. A glass pavilion, situated away from the common areas, offers a shielded space designed to facilitate some of the more private activities, such as conversational therapy. The 140-square-foot pavilion is hexagonal, made of glass with a matte finish, and offers comfortable chairs, scented plants, and the sound of trickling water from a fountain.

General Bibliography

Campbell, J. C. 2002. "Health Consequences of Intimate Partner Violence." *The Lancet* 359:1331–36.

Campbell, J. C., and L. A. Lewandowski. 1997. "Mental and Physical Health Effects of Intimate Partner Violence on Women and Children." *Psychiatric Clinics of North America* 20 (2): 353–74.

Coid, J., A. Petruckevitch, W. S. Chung, J. Richardson, S. Moorey, and G. Feder 2003. "Abusive Experiences and Psychiatric Morbidity in Women Primary Care Attenders." *British Journal of Psychiatry* 183: 332–39.

Danner 2011. *Sådan Arbejder Vi: Metoder og Praksis i Danners Krisecenter*. København: Danner.

Diaz-Olavarrieta, C., J. Campbell, C. Garcia de la Cadena, F. Paz, and A. R. Villa. 1999. "Domestic Violence against Patients with Chronic Neurologic Disorders." *Archives of Neurology* 56: 681–85.

Fantuzzo, J. W., and W. K. Mohr. 1999. "Prevalence and Effects of Child Exposure to Domestic Violence." *The Future of Children: Domestic Violence and Children* 9 (3): 21–32.

Guth, A. A., and H. L. Pachter. 2000. "Domestic Violence and the Trauma Surgeon." *American Journal of Surgery* 179: 134–40.

Holt, S., H. Buckley, and S. Whelan. 2008. "The Impact of Exposure to Domestic Violence on Children and Young People." *Child Abuse and Neglect* 32: 797–810.

Kitzmann, K. M., N. K. Gaylord, A. R. Holt, and E. D. Kenny. 2003. "Child Witnesses to Domestic Violence: A Meta-analytic Review." *Journal of Consultative Clinical Psychology* 71 (2): 339–52.

Lindqvist, B. M., K. H. Partapuoli, and L.H. Spenceley. 2004. *Kvinderummet. Dannerhuset som Kvindepolitisk Forum og Krisecenter.* København: Informations Forlag.

McGuigan, W. M. and C. C. Pratt. 2001. "The Predictive Impact of Domestic Violence on Three Types of Child Maltreatment." *Child Abuse and Neglect* 25: 869–883.

Plichta, S. B. 2004. "Intimate Partner Violence and Physical Health Consequences: Policy and Practice Implications." *Journal of Interpersonal Violence* 19 (11): 1296–1323.

The Body Shop/UNICEF. 2006. *Behind Closed Doors. The Impact of Domestic Violence on Children.* London: The Body Shop International Plc. Retrieved from www.unicef.org/protection/files/BehindClosedDoors.pdf.

Tjaden, P., and N. Thoennes. 2000. *Extent, Nature, and Consequences of Intimate Partner Violence.* National Institute of Justice and the Centers for Disease Control and Prevention. Retrieved from https://www.ncjrs.gov/pdffiles1/nij/181867.pdf.

UN (United Nations). 2010. *Handbook for Legislation on Violence against Women.* New York: United Nations.

UNICEF. 2000. "Domestic Violence against Women and Girls." *Innocenti Digest* 6. Florence: United Nations Children's Fund–Innocenti Research Centre. Retrieved from http://www.unicef-irc.org/publications/pdf/digest6e.pdf.

Wolfe, D. A., C. V. Crooks, V. Lee, A. McIntyre-Smith, and P. G. Jaffe. 2003. "The Effects of Children's Exposure to Domestic Violence: A Meta-analysis and Critique." *Clinical Child and Family Psychology Review* 6 (3): 171–87.

WHO (World Health Organization). 1996. *Violence against Women.* WHO Consultation, Geneva: World Health Organization. Retrieved from whqlibdoc.who.int/hq/1996/FRH_WHD_96.27.pdf.

———. 2010. *Preventing Intimate Partner and Sexual Violence against Women—Taking Action and Generating Evidence.* Geneva: World Health Organization. Retrieved from www.who.int/violence_injury_prevention/publications/violence/9789241564007_eng.pdf.

Studies that Informed the Design Guidelines

Keeley, J., A. S. Leigh. 1999. "Design and Implementation of Horticultural Therapy with Children Affected by Homelessness and Domestic Violence." *Journal of Therapeutic Horticulture* 10:34–39.

Lee, S., M. S. Kim, and J. K. Suh. 2008. "Effects of Horticultural Therapy of Self-Esteem and Depression of Battered Women at a Shelter in Korea." Pp. 139–42 in *VIIIth International People-plant Symposium Proceedings. Acta Horticulturae (ISHS),* edited by E. Matsuo, P. D. Relf, and M. Burchett. Retrieved from www.actahort.org/books/790/790_19.htm.

Lygum, V. L. 2012. *Healing Gardens at Crisis Shelters for Women and Children Survivors of Domestic Violence.* Forest and Landscape Research. No. 55–2012. Frederiksberg, Denmark.

Pierce, C. A., and L. M. Seals. 2006. "The Importance of Community Gardening for Homeless Women: A Pilot Study." *Journal of Therapeutic Horticulture* 17: 20–26.

Refuerzo, B. J., and S. Verderber. 1988. "Creating a Safe Refuge: The Functions of Nature in the Design of Shelters for Battered Women and Their Children." Pp. 63–69 in *Paths for Co-Existence (EDRA 19 Proceedings),* edited by D. Lawrence, R. Habe, A. Hacker, and D. Sherrod. Washington, DC: Environmental Design Research Association.

Robinson, J., W. Shippee, J. Schlimgen, and R. Solow. 1982. *Women's Advocates Shelter: An Evaluation.* University of Minnesota, Minneapolis: Center for Urban and Regional Affairs and School of Architecture and Landscape Architecture.

Seals, L. M., and A. P. Pierce. 2007. "Extension Master Gardeners: Helping the Homeless to Heal." *Journal of Extension* 45 (3): 1–8.

Stuart, S. M. 2005. "Lifting Spirits: Creating Gardens in California Domestic Violence Shelters." Pp. 61–88 in *Urban Place: Reconnecting with the Natural World,* edited by P. F. Barlett. Cambridge, MA: MIT Press.

CASE STUDY

Rosecrance Healing Garden, Griffin Williamson Adolescent Treatment Center, Rockford, Illinois

Designer: Hoichi Kurisu, Kurisu International, Portland, Oregon

By Jessy Bergeman

Description and History

Rosecrance is a private, nonprofit organization offering behavioral health services for families, adults, adolescents, and children. Rosecrance assists more than 13,000 families per year and offers outpatient mental health assistance, as well as addiction treatment services. These comprehensive

12.9 The garden provides a variety of ways for patients, visitors, and families to interact with nature. The "serenity bridge" over the pond serves as a focal point. It is pitched symbolically "like a mountain, because one must work to get to a better place."
Photo by Jessy Bergeman

services include prevention, intervention, detoxification, experiential therapies, dual-diagnosis care, inpatient and out-patient treatment, and family education.

Rosecrance is comprised of a number of substance abuse and mental health treatment facilities and includes clinics, offices, residential houses, and campuses. Of these campuses, two are focused on addiction: the Harrison campus for adults and the Griffin Williamson campus for adolescents.

The Rosecrance healing garden is located on the grounds of the 40-acre Griffin Williamson adolescent treatment center—a $14-million, 67,000-square-foot, 78-bed residential facility. The facility treats adolescents twelve to eighteen years old, a majority of whom have dual-diagnoses such as a mental or behavioral health condition in addition to addiction. The facility includes an on-site school, chapel, gymnasium, fitness center, dining hall, and patio. Underscoring the idea that patients have choices, the facility is secure but is not locked. There are six separate patient wings, each of which includes a large living space from which the healing garden can be viewed (fig. 12.9, fig. 12.10).

The healing garden was constructed in two phases. Phase I was completed in the fall of 2004, and Phase II was completed in the spring of 2006.

Design Philosophy

The six-acre healing garden was designed by Hoichi Kurisu of Kurisu International of Portland, Oregon. The mission of the firm states:

12.10 Perspective sketch of garden.
Courtesy of Kurisu International

Whether designing a simple water garden pond or cascading garden waterfall, landscaping with rock to create a Zen stone garden, or working out the landscape architecture to design acres of public park, each garden design draws on the integrity of nature's forces. Kurisu garden designs bring balance to hearts and minds by providing exceptional public and private spaces in which to engage with nature. (Kurisu International 2013)

As is the case with the majority of landscapes designed by Kurisu International, the Rosecrance healing garden "harmonizes Japanese garden design principles with contemporary sensibilities" (Rosecrance n.d.). The garden was designed without any straight lines, with the intent that curved lines and pathways encourage visitors to explore and discover. Boulders and stones provide a balance of both vertical and horizontal movement

12.11 The Grateful Overlook is the garden's highest point. The waterfall cascades down twelve levels, symbolizing the twelve steps of a traditional recovery program. The "guardian stone" emerging from the water at the base of the falls functions, according to traditional belief, as protector of the garden. The water makes distinctly different sounds as it strikes stones in three different locations.
Photo by Jessy Bergeman

and are generally grouped in odd numbers, as is customary in Japanese design. Planting design is based upon subtle variations rather than an abundance of colors and textures (fig. 12.11).

The garden includes redbud, burning bush, serviceberries, oak leaf hydrangea, azalea, witch hazel, pachysandra, and boxwood. It also features Scotch pines, Katsura trees, red maples, Japanese maples, weeping Alaskan cedars, and Kentucky coffee trees. Thus, the majority of the foliage within the healing garden is most brilliant in the spring and fall—symbolically, beginnings and endings.

The Outdoor Space

The garden was designed to bring "balance to hearts and minds" by providing an "exceptional" space in which to engage with nature (Kurisu International 2013). Kurisu incorporated a number of specific design features with this intention, and its unique users, in mind.

A pond, fed from rain and city water, is the centerpiece of the garden. It features a deck that juts out over the water, providing a space for reflection as well as a place from which to observe the numerous koi in the pond. The tranquil water helps orient visitors and stands in dramatic contrast to the woods, which serve as a backdrop for the garden (fig. 12.12).

The healing garden contains bridges of varying sizes and materials, the most significant being the cedar "serenity bridge," which for many serves as the garden's focal point. The bridge is pitched symbolically "like a mountain, because one must work to get to a better place," and was designed to give

12.12 The viewing platform is a popular spot from which to observe wildlife in the water below.
Photo by Jessy Bergeman

"the appearance of being fragile, but holding great strength." Additional bridges such as the "open stone bridge"—featuring large stepping stones—are designed to allow visitors a greater sense of interaction with the water (Rosecrance, n.d.).

The garden also includes a waterfall that cascades down twelve levels, symbolizing the twelve steps of traditional recovery programs. It is anchored by a 40-ton boulder with a "guardian stone" emerging from the water at its base, which in the traditional Japanese style serves to protect the garden. Water flows over the fall at more than 1,200 gallons per

12.13 The waterfall provides visual and auditory stimuli. Planting was selected for seasonal interest, including fall foliage.
Photo by Jessy Bergeman

minute and makes distinctly different sounds as it strikes stones in three different locations (fig. 12.13).

Six separate "serenity circles," comprised of large stones, create spaces for sitting. The smallest of these circles can comfortably seat two and is used for private conversation. The largest can accommodate approximately twenty people and is used for group activities.

A variety of winding pathways within the garden, both primary and secondary, total approximately 1.5 miles, with a range of surfaces—pavement, gravel, crusher fines, and dirt. Pathways encircle the pond and extend into woods adjacent to the healing garden.

The bell tower, markedly set apart from other spaces within the garden, is a unique feature in that it is both symbolic and highly interactive. Ringing a bell has signified purification as well as the desire for a balanced life since ancient times. At Rosecrance, upon successful completion of his or her treatment program, adolescents strike the bell during a special ceremony (fig. 12.14).

How the Garden Is Used

The healing garden is used primarily by three groups: patients, staff, and families of patients, although—perhaps surprisingly—it is also open to the public.

For patients, the garden is a key component of the experiential therapies program that emphasizes body and soul, enjoying life, and staying in the moment. It is used for one-on-one talks and group "processing." In addition, the garden provides a valuable space for practicing critical coping skills such as meditation, walking, journaling, and breathing exercises. Patients may not go into the garden alone; they are always accompanied by a staff member.

To protect the garden and take full advantage of its potential, an extensive formal curriculum was developed in collaboration with the education curator at the Denver Botanic Gardens. Patients are taught what the garden is intended for and know that they must respect the space or they will receive garden restriction.

12.14 The bell tower is used for special ceremonies and is considered sacred space.
Photo by Jessy Bergeman

The garden is used by staff members as a place to walk or sit during (relatively infrequent) breaks. The garden is also used by visiting family members, particularly during family orientation weekend. Up to forty public tours of the garden are given throughout the year, scheduled to avoid times when patients are in the garden.

Key Garden Merits

The Rosecrance Healing Garden provides benefits common to all user groups as well as benefits particular to each of the three groups.

For all users:

- Many elements, especially the waterfall, birds, and fish, provide visual and auditory natural distractions.

- The garden provides stress reduction, which can last from several hours to days.

- Because the garden can be viewed from residential and staff spaces, it provides benefits for individuals who may not be in the space.

For patients:

- The garden gives patients an increased sense of control by allowing them a choice of where to sit or walk and opportunities for unstructured conversation in a less confined space.

- Pathways provide the opportunity for mild outdoor exercise (sometimes the only exercise possible for individuals whose bodies have been weakened by drug use).

- The garden is a valuable space for beginning to reestablish stability and routine through activities such as walking a lap around the pond after each meal.

- Elements such as the "serenity circles" and benches provide areas for social support, both active ("walk and talks") and passive (simply sharing space with others).

- Several elements in the garden aid in developing useful coping skills, such as learning to journal and raking gravel pathways.

- The garden allows patients to recognize and connect with a higher power or guiding force in their lives, whether it be a particular diety or nature itself.

- The space provides an opportunity for patients who frequently used substances outdoors to experience being "triggered" while in a safe and supportive environment.

For staff:

- The healing garden provides a place to escape the stress of their job and indoor activities.

- The space provides an opportunity for time alone.

For families:

- Several garden elements provide spaces for interaction with loved ones.

- Pathways and seating areas provide opportunities for social support.

- Elements in the garden, such as fish and interesting plants, provide neutral subjects for conversation, a valuable first step in repairing oft-strained relationships.

Possible Concerns

- Staff members frequently visit the garden to escape work stress. Because there is no separate area for staff, this time can be disrupted by patient activities.

- The garden is not used as frequently as it could be for family visits because until a patient has reached a specific level of treatment, these visits generally must be overseen by staff.

- Although patients must always be supervised, opportunities could exist for them to be given a greater sense of choice within the garden, such as being being able to decide where to walk after meals or where to sit for various activities.

References

Kurisu International. 2013. "About." www.kurisu.com/kurisu-about.shtml.

Rosecrance. n.d. *Rosecrance Healing Garden: A Self-Guided Walking Tour Map*. Rockford, IL: Rosecrance Healing Garden.

Alnarp Rehabilitation Garden, Alnarp, Sweden

Designers: Patrik Grahn, Ulrika A. Stigsdotter, Sarah Lundström, Frederik Stauchnitz

Description of the Facility and Its History

This 2-hectare (5-acre) garden is located on the grounds of the Alnarp campus of the Swedish University of Agricultural Sciences in southwest Sweden. It was created in 2001 as a unique environment for the treatment of people suffering from a variety of stress-related diseases and as a setting for research on how a garden functions for such people. By the year 2000, stress-related illness in Sweden was said to have "reached the level of a national disease" (Ivarsson and Grahn 2010, 1).

Design Philosophy

The design of the Alnarp garden was influenced by three theories regarding the healing benefits of gardens. The healing garden theory proposes that health effects are derived from just being in the garden. The horticultural therapy theory asserts that health effects derive from gardening activities. The cognitive school proposes that health effects derive from a combination of experiences in the garden, activities in the garden, and the visitor's personality and background.

Description of the Garden

The garden is located on a verdant agricultural campus that incorporates many mature trees, and is sited in an area where fruits and berries were cultivated for more than seventy years. Pruned beech hedges that bordered the berry plots were adopted as the basic structure of the garden, providing shelter and privacy screens between different outdoor rooms. The garden is divided into a variety of spaces, from the less demanding, focusing on wild and designed nature, to the more demanding, focusing on cultivation and horticultural therapy. The aim was to create garden rooms that are not too abstract or challenging, that are somewhat familiar, and that yet promote interest and exploration: "Each participant must first make contact with their surrounding world . . . Thus, the garden . . . must have several kinds of spaces so people have possibilities to start this process" (Grahn et al. 2010, 132) (fig. 12.15).

On arriving at the garden, the visitor has a choice of entering a low-key, welcoming building or the hedge-bordered Welcoming Garden with blue and white flowers, a pool, mounded lawn, meandering path, and a variety of places to sit. The space is familiar and replete with sensory experience, but it makes few demands on the visitor.

For those seeking restoration in a wilder environment, the nature area of the garden comprises two rooms: the Grove and the Meadow. The Grove is characteristic of the southern Swedish countryside and suggestive of a savannah. The Meadow contrasts with the more geometric cultivated areas and is another landscape type with strong associations for Swedish people, evoking memories of poems and folk songs learned in childhood.

For participants who want to engage more actively in the garden, four areas focus on horticultural therapy, ranging from the most demanding to the least demanding: A hardscape room comprising planting beds varying in height; familiar Swedish allotment (community) gardens with geometric beds; a large traditional greenhouse for horticultural therapy activities of seed sowing, watering, and propagation; and the Wildlife Garden Room, where participants can make their own creative contributions in a more organic setting. Other nature-oriented activities include making and putting up nesting boxes, tending animals (chickens and rabbits),

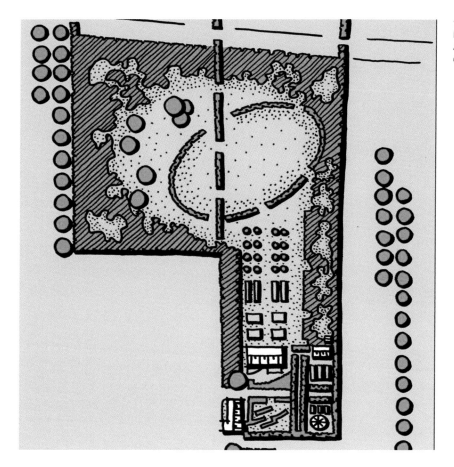

12.15 Site plan of Alnarp Rehabilitation Garden, Alnarp, Sweden.
Courtesy of Ulrika Stigsdotter

and harvesting produce for use in cooking and handicrafts (fig. 12.16). The aim here is a focus on activities—gardening and horticultural therapy—and, eventually, to be able to assess the relative benefits of these versus more introspective experiences in the nature areas.

How the Garden Is Used

People are referred to the garden by their doctor, insurance company, or employer (the cost is covered by Swedish national health insurance). They relax or work in the garden under the care of professional staff comprising an occupational therapist, horticultural therapist, landscape architect, physiotherapist, and psychotherapist, on a schedule that varies from one half day to four half days per week over a period of twelve weeks. Participants can engage in art therapy using the garden as a metaphor and source of materials; a physiotherapist offers massage and group relaxation sessions; a psychotherapist holds forty-minute sessions in the geodesic greenhouse; and a landscape architect/gardener works with

participants on garden maintenance and cultivation. The progress of the participants is being compared with that of a group of individuals with the same stress-related symptoms who are receiving more standard treatment—a long period of at-home rest, the use of antidepressants such as Prozac or Zoloft, and five or six sessions of psychotherapy.

The participants who have come to the garden range in age from twenty-two to sixty-one. They have included students, teachers, doctors, nurses, and people from the business world. All have been highly ambitious, creative, and competent in their careers but have suffered some kind of psychological or physical collapse due to stress that has rendered them unable to work—sometimes for as long as three to four years.

Since the experience in the garden is often very different from their day-to-day life, participants initially come for just one morning a week, which is gradually increased to four mornings a week. In winter, those who want to engage in physical work shovel snow, rake leaves, dig in the garden, or saw wood. Others may work in the greenhouse or engage in ceramics

12.16 A light-filled conservatory provides space for small group meetings and craft activities.
Photo by Lena Welen Andersson

and nature-based handicrafts in the main building. The psychotherapist who comes to the garden once a week says, "The work is more intense, and changes happen much faster than when I work in my regular office." Frederick Stauchnitz, who works with people outside on garden maintenance, remarks, "As much as possible, we work with recycled materials: wood to build planters, old apple crates in the greenhouse. The subtle metaphor is that discarded things can have a new use."

After the completion of a twelve-week treatment program, all report that their quality of life has improved. Sixty percent return to work, but to a different type of employment so they are not faced with the same stressful conditions. The staff at the garden observes that many participants have not just learned to handle stress better, but that a deeper healing process has occurred, leading to permanent change. For some, the twelve weeks are not enough to break a lifetime of workaholic patterns or the fear of not being able to deal with stress. They can return to the garden when they wish. For many, being in the garden and seeing how it functions is an eye-opening, soul-touching experience. A man with a desk job moved rocks for three weeks to help form a pond in the garden and reported he'd never slept so well in his life. "People in crisis seem to be more dependent on the nonhuman environment. . . Ordinary environments that perhaps people have never noticed before may mean a great deal, in both positive and negative senses. . .The individual seems to have a need to revert to simpler relations, to simple objects in nature. . . Stones and plants

are not associated with confusing demands or guilt" (Grahn et al. 2010, 154) (fig. 12.17).

To study how people experience and use this therapeutic setting, qualitative, semistructured interviews were conducted with ten people who had participated in the garden program for at least six weeks (Ivarsson and Grahn 2010). The interviews were analyzed using a form of content analysis. The authors noted, "This study focuses on the behavior of the participants. Do they seek support from different garden rooms during their rehabilitation program? If so, can we find a certain pattern in that process?"

The analysis gave rise to several themes in visitor behavior. One theme was "to escape, observe, and get sensory stimulation." Many participants spoke about "just being," wandering randomly, or actively seeking a refuge, such as lying in the grass or sitting on a bench in a bower overgrown with artichokes (ibid).

Walking was another way of escaping. Some said that they took endless walks along the loop around the pond. Another woman noted: "Many times I have walked to the rabbit cages and then I have just walked up and down these paths for a while, and then sat down on the bench behind the willow fence. I cannot really tell what I have been doing" (ibid.). The fence and the gate surrounding the garden were mentioned as being very important. The safety they provided helped patients achieve the psychological peace they needed to be able to relax in the setting.

Many indicated that as they walked around or spent time in a "refuge" they became more aware of sights, sounds, and

12.17 Individuals who come to the garden find elements of nature more easy to relate to than the environments that contributed to their stress.
Photo Lena Welen Andersson

12.18 As people spent more time in the garden, they started to relate to it in creative ways, such as painting and collecting leaves to make herb tea or pesto. (Note: The "model" is a student at SLU, Alnarp, Sweden)
Photo Lena Welen Andersson

smells in the garden. Sounds of water falling into a small pond were mentioned positively, while sounds from a motorway half a mile (one kilometer) away were a negative experience. People particularly appreciated aspects of the environment that demanded nothing of them—watching the chickens and rabbits, walking among trees, sitting in the garden. Aspects mentioned as disliked included the "too straight" lines and shapes of the cultivation garden, a big open gravel area around a geodesic greenhouse ("I hate passing that area"), and the "too open" expanse of the Meadow that people experienced as "cold, naked, and barren." What most wanted changed were large open areas transformed into "smaller rooms in three dimensions. . . more grown up and lush vegetation, cozy rounded rooms, more woodland and more trees" (ibid).

A second main theme that emerged was one of growing fascination with the environment, experiencing satisfaction, and welcoming social interaction. People were stimulated not only by quietly observing but by participating in an activity. "Many have not been giving themselves time to be creative. . . Other things in life have taken over. The garden provides many opportunities for regenerating, the taking of one thing and making something new out of it. . . making herbal tea, which many participants liked a lot. An important aspect is also the ability to take things . . . not only the things themselves, but also the phenomena experienced. . . ." (ibid) (fig. 12.18).

People also appreciated meeting others who had progressed further in the rehabilitation process, and started to open up. Many also began to see parallels between what was happening in the garden and their own life—that there is constant change.

This study concludes with a consideration of how the results relate to "the pyramid of strength of mind" (Stigsdotter and Grahn 2002). At Level 1 people seek support from nature and avoid others—hence those who sought escape in wandering, refuges, and the desire for more "cozy rooms." Level 2, emotional participation, is represented by those who begin to take an interest in their social surroundings, sometimes starting by observing at a distance. Level 3, active participation, is illustrated by those who enjoy working in the greenhouses or making tea or pesto. Patients in this program rarely reach Level 4, having the strength to lead a group of people.

Changes in the garden that are planned include: more white and blue flowers and fewer red, yellow, and orange, since participants found these intense colors difficult; the addition of more water elements; more small garden rooms; and strengthening of nature elements close to the entrance. "Symbols have become far more important than we could ever have expected. The participants have asked for poisonous and thorny plants, for nettles, thistles, and dead trees. So, we will develop a more unpleasant room, perhaps with a Refuge dimension" (Grahn et al., 2010, 156). Future studies include measuring participants' levels of cortisol (stress hormones) and oxytocin (pleasure hormone).

References

Grahn, P., C. T. Ivarsson, U. A. Stigsdotter, and I. Bengtsson. 2010. "Using Affordances as a Health-Promoting Tool in a Therapeutic Garden." Pp. 120–59 in *Innovative Approaches to Researching Landscape and Health,* edited by C. Ward Thompson, S. Bell, and P. Aspinall. London: Taylor and Francis.

Ivarsson, C. T., and P. Grahn. 2010. "Patients' Experiences and Use of a Therapeutic Garden: From a Designer's Perspective." *Schweizerische Zeitschrift fur Forstwesen* 161 (3): 104–13.

Stigsdotter, U. A., and P. Grahn. 2002. "What Makes a Garden a Healing Garden?" *Journal of Therapeutic Horticulture* 13: 60–69.

———. 2003. "Experiencing a Garden: A Healing Garden for People Suffering from Burnout Diseases." *Journal of Therapeutic Horticulture* 14: 38–48.

Nacadia Healing Forest Garden, Hoersholm Arboretum, Copenhagen, Denmark

Designer: Ulrika K. Stigsdotter

By Ulrika K. Stigsdotter

Description and History

Nacadia is the first therapy garden to be connected to research and education at a Danish university. It is located in the Hoersholm Arboretum, which covers almost 98 acres (40 hectares) and is some 40 miles north of Copenhagen (fig. 12.19). The arboretum is a unit of the Department of Geosciences and Natural Resource Management at the University of Copenhagen and is open to the public every day until sunset. Nacadia is a self-sufficient research and development project within the department. Landscape architect Ulrika K. Stigsdotter designed the garden with input from two groups of experts: researchers within landscape architecture, architecture, and environmental psychology; and medical clinicians, including doctors, psychologists, and therapists, with expertise in nature-based therapy. The garden covers 2 acres (1.1 hectares) and incorporates two existing buildings: a gardener's building designed by the famous Danish architect Steen Eiler Rasmussen and a large greenhouse.[2]

2. Rasmussen is the author of the classic architecture books *Towns and Building* (1949) and *Experiencing Architecture* (1959).

12.19 The garden has a water theme, with a spring feeding a stream flowing into a small lake with stepping stones to an island.
Photo Ulrika Karlsson Stigsdotter

The buildings have been redesigned, and the gardener's building now includes therapists' and researchers' offices, restrooms, dressing rooms, and showers. Although the goal is to conduct as much of the therapy as possible outdoors, the greenhouse offers both horticultural activities and rest opportunities when the weather is too harsh.

Nacadia has four main objectives:

1. Provide nature-based treatment for patients with stress-related illnesses, such as war veterans suffering from posttraumatic stress disorder (PTSD). The treatment is an umbrella term referring to therapy that is based on experiences and activities in natural settings and is specifically designed to support the treatment process.

2. Obtain evidence-based knowledge about the effect of supportive garden design and nature-based therapy for this client group.

3. Offer education within the field of health design and nature-based therapy.

4. Serve as a knowledge and demonstration center.

Nacadia had its official opening in November 2011. In September of the following year, the first group of patients, eight male war veterans suffering from PTSD, started their nature-based therapy. The patients were on sick leave due to stress-related illnesses, and their treatment cost was covered by the department's research grants or by the patient's private health insurance, pension fund, or employer. (For more on veterans with PTSD, see chapter 13).

Design Philosophy

Nacadia's design is based on an exploratory model of an evidence-based health design process (E-BHD) that has three components:

1. Aesthetic and practical landscape architectural skills and experiences.

2. Research evidence and valid practical experience.

3. The specific patient group's special needs, wishes, and preferences, the treatment program, and the patients' expected rehabilitation process.

One important aspect of this model is that the process does not stop when the design has been implemented. The space must be continuously evaluated so that newly documented experiences and research results can be incorporated into its design.

To conduct research in a therapy garden is not easy. When investigating the influence of the garden on the patients' process of getting better, many environmental and social factors can influence the patients' experiences, behavior, and healing processes. It was, therefore, a prerequisite to design five outdoor rooms in Nacadia with some constant conditions: same shape, size, and orientation, but each with different content (fig. 12.20). Behavior mapping will record where people spend time, and interviews regarding their experiences will be conducted at the start, middle, and end of treatment.

Against this background, Nacadia was designed according to ten overall criteria, based on research results as well as documented experience in several supportive garden projects:

1. Spatial structure
The garden must be experienced as a whole so that it is demarcated from its surroundings. It consists of a large "outdoor room" with several smaller rooms, where the walls are created by shrubs or green fences, the floors are made of grass, stone, or wood, and the roofs are formed by treetops, pergolas with flowering climbers, and the open sky.

2. Living building material
Vibrant and constantly changing plant material is a cornerstone of the garden. The amount of greenery is important in relation to its healing qualities.

3. Easy to interpret
The patients must be able to understand what the garden can offer them, and what they can and may do.

4. Security
Nacadia provides a sense of total security. The garden's green walls help to achieve this by obstructing outsiders' visual or physical access. This demarcation must not make the patients feel like they are trapped but rather that their problems and worries have been shut out.

5. Levels of safety
During the healing process, the patients must be exposed to less safe areas at a slow pace. Nacadia's location within the arboretum offers an extra semisafe zone, which the patients can visit as they get stronger

6. Strength of mind
Nacadia is designed to accommodate patients at all levels of emotional and cognitive strength (referred to as "strength of mind," or "mental strength"). The patients' experience of nature and the level of demands they are able to handle depend on their mental strength. This can be illustrated as a pyramid, where the need for natural environments that place few demands on the individual is large at the bottom and smaller at the top.

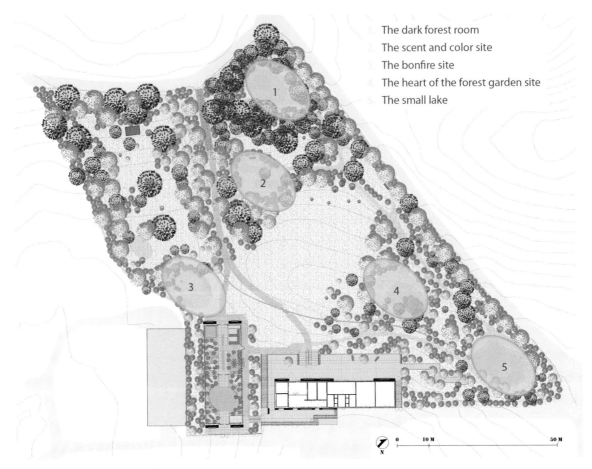

1. The dark forest room
2. The scent and color site
3. The bonfire site
4. The heart of the forest garden site
5. The small lake

12.20 Site plan of Nacadia, showing five outdoor rooms.
Courtesy of Ulrika K. Stigsdotter

At the bottom of the pyramid is inner-directed involvement, where emotional strength is very weak and the need for undemanding nature experiences is significant. On the next level, *emotional participation*, the patient's mental strength is somewhat greater and the patient is beginning to take an interest in his or her social surroundings. On the *active participation* level, the patient possesses enough mental strength to give and share. At the top, the *outgoing involvement* level, the patient's mental strength is very strong and he or she is able to lead a group of people.

7. Mental and physical accessibility

If a patient has been ill for a long time, spending time in a garden is not always an obvious choice. To help attract the patients into the garden after they have changed into work clothes in the gardener's building, the barrier between inside and outside has been minimized with glass doors

and a large tree terrace. At the same time, the attractions that can be viewed from the inside are also physically accessible. Stepping stones in a small lake that lead out to an island are one example. Acute stress can undermine bodily awareness; the use of different natural paving materials and varied terrain is meant to bolster patients' body awareness and fitness. Large parts of the garden are made accessible to patients with disabilities without ruining the forest-like experience.

8. Flexibility and participation

As a result of an E-BHD process, Nacadia will be regularly evaluated and redesigned over the years. Another example of the flexibility of the design is an area called "the free forest," where patients can be creative—building, planting, and putting their own stamp on the garden's design.

12.21 A platform under a larch tree provides a secluded place to sit in the forest garden.
Photo Maja Steen Moller

9. Perceived sensory dimensions of nature

In previous research, people were found to classify natural environments in terms of eight specific characteristics, called perceived sensory dimensions (PSDs) (Grahn and Stigsdotter 2010; Stigsdotter and Grahn 2011). People in general prefer "serene" (silent and calm), followed by "space" (spacious and free), "nature" (wild and untouched), "rich in species" (animals and plants), "refuge" (safe, benches), "culture" (fountains and ornamental plants), "prospect" (flat surfaces and vistas), and finally "social" (entertainment and services). A combination of "refuge," "nature," and "rich in species," and a low presence or absence of "social," could be interpreted as the most restorative environment for stressed individuals. All eight PSDs are included in Nacadia. In order to gain new knowledge, different combinations of the PSDs will be tested (fig. 12.21).

10. Opportunities for nature-based activities

A fundamental goal has been to design the garden so that it offers opportunities for meaningful activities year-round. Some are practical, such as picking fruit and chopping wood.

Others are symbolic, such as stepping stones over a stream that might be used in conversations with a therapist as a metaphor for starting something new and leaving worries behind. Edible plants can be found almost everywhere in the garden, and a kitchen garden area provides a forest-like experience, where blackberries grow on an old pine tree and blueberries, lingonberries, and bog myrtle provide the structure under which carrots, lettuce, and other vegetables grow. Symbolically, it shows how larger and more robust plants can support the living conditions for smaller and weaker plants.

Description of Outdoor Space

Nacadia is characterized as a forest garden, with plant material creating rooms with floors, walls, and ceilings that enhance the feeling of being immersed in nature and thereby support the healing process.

To reach the entrance to Nacadia, patients walk about 600 yards (600 meters) through the forested arboretum. The garden's entrance is shaped like a welcoming embrace. A pergola with several kinds of flowering vines growing on it supports and guides patients into the garden. Where the pergola ends, nature takes over. High tree canopies meet over people's heads, encouraging patients to walk down the gently sloping terrain toward the light in the meadow ahead (fig. 12.22).

Where the tree canopies end, the gardener's building and the greenhouse come into view, the sound of a bubbling spring takes over, and the stream leads patients to the garden's heart, the bonfire site.

There are several seating choices in the garden. Some are more exposed to other people, such as the staircase leading up to the gardener's building, while others are hidden, such as one under the dense branches of some cypresses and one that is approached via a ladder to a platform in a larch tree. The benches in the garden are smaller than usual so that patients can choose whether to invite others to sit down next to them. If a patient sits down in the middle of the bench, there is not enough space for others.

The garden has a recurring water theme. A small spring leads to a stream that ends in a small lake with an island. The dark forest room has a reflecting pond, where the silhouettes of trees and the sky stand out and the clouds and the sun are reflected. Inside the greenhouse is a stylized stream in the form of an oblong basin.

A large wooden terrace entered from the gardener's building offers space for social gatherings and views of the garden. Part of the terrace continues as a raised causeway 12 feet (4 meters) up in the air, which leads out onto a platform overlooking the lake.

12.22 Paths leading to the gardener's building and the greenhouse
Photo Ulrika Karlsson Stigsdotter

In the greenhouse (formerly used for tree research), a profusion of plants and climbing vines enclose several semi-private places for relaxation furnished with chaises longues and hammocks. A small octagonal greenhouse inside the large greenhouse offers a place for private conversation. A small wood-walled room offers a place of limited sensory input. There is a central linear pool with goldfish, an area for indoor horticultural therapy, a social area around a table for small meetings, a large wood-decked area where chairs can be arranged for presentations, and two wood-burning stoves providing a cozy atmosphere on rainy days (fig. 12.23).

How the Garden Is Used

The treatment at Nacadia has a salutogenic (health-creating) perspective. The focus is on developing and strengthening patients' capacities as a means to overcoming illness and enhancing their overall quality of life. The emphasis is on what is strong and healthy within each patient, no matter what his or her diagnosis, to enable them to restore their physical, psychological, and mental balance. It is also important that patients develop and establish healthy stress preparedness so that they can prevent new negative stress from occurring in the future. At Nacadia, horticultural therapists use mindfulness-inspired, nature-based therapy as a therapeutic tool. The patients' experiences, perceptions, activities, and the surrounding garden are essential parts of the therapeutic process. The mindfulness activities are used to bring the patients' attention to and acceptance of the present moment by paying nonjudgmental attention to their thoughts and feelings.

Nacadia provides a ten-week program during which patients receive three hours of therapy in the morning for three days a week. The therapy is carried out in a group of eight patients led by two horticultural therapists and an assistant gardener. At the beginning of the treatment, the patients need both peace and rest from outside social demands and physical exertion. At Nacadia, no demands are placed on them; the treatment process is implemented at a pace that suits each individual. Here, the rooms of the garden play an important role. When the patient is ready, the garden presents opportunities for stimulation and challenge through contact with the more demanding rooms and activities.

Treatment is offered year-round, and the framework for the treatment is the same every day: The patients arrive, change into work clothes, and gather in silence around the bonfire, where the horticultural therapists guide a relaxation or meditative exercise and present the day's theme (fig. 12.24). Then the patients spread out to different rooms in the garden and engage in activities that are meaningfully and individually customized. The horticultural therapists walk around and assist the patients. Individual sessions, such as therapeutic conversations, also take place in some of the more secluded rooms of the garden. Toward the end of the day, the group gathers around the bonfire to round off the day, and the horticultural therapists present exercises for the patients to conduct at home, such as mindfulness exercises.

Former patients are invited to Nacadia one month, three months, six months, and one year after finishing treatment for gatherings and a few hours of nature-based therapy, as well as to meet the research team. Practitioners, students,

12.23 A place to relax in the warmth of the greenhouse on a rainy day.
Photo by Clare Cooper Marcus

12.24 For participants in the programs at Nacadia, the day begins and ends with a gathering around the bonfire.
Photo by Clare Cooper Marcus

and researchers are invited every fall for an annual seminar to share experiences and to network. Each spring the public is invited to an open house at Nacadia.

Key Garden Merits

- Even though the garden is new, the old trees and shrubs give it a mature and natural expression.

- Some garden functions are flexible. For example, the working tables within the greenhouse can be easily moved outdoors to be close to an outdoor kitchen and herb plants.

Some Possible Concerns

- Many trees, shrubs, and climbers were planted along the garden's border and fence in order to prevent people outside from being able to watch the patients in the garden. Unfortunately, many of these plants are still quite small.

- Keeping the main path system accessible for all requires a lot of maintenance, such as removing leaves and small tree branches that have fallen to the ground.

- Although the greenhouse has a pellet-burning stove and two wood stoves, on winter days it is still rather cold inside. Conversely, on sunny summer days it gets very warm. Large doors and curtains help with cooling.

References

Grahn, P. and U. K. Stigsdotter. 2010. "The Relation between Perceived Sensory Dimensions of Urban Green Space and Stress Restoration." *Landscape and Urban Planning* 94 (3–4): 264–75.

Stigsdotter, U. K. and P. Grahn. 2011. "Stressed Individual's Preferences for Activities and Environmental Characteristics in Green Spaces." *Urban Forestry and Urban Greening*. 10: 295–304.

References

Barnhart, S. K., N. H. Perkins, and J. Fitzsimonds. 1998. "Behaviour and Outdoor Setting Preferences at a Psychiatric Hospital." *Landscape and Urban Planning* 42 (2): 147–56.

Carek, P. J., S. E. Laibstain, and S. M. Carek. 2011. "Exercise for the Treatment of Depression and Anxiety." *International Journal of Psychiatry in Medicine* 41 (1): 15–28.

Curtis, S., W. Gesler, K. Fabian, S. Francis, and S. Priebe. 2007. "Therapeutic Landscapes in Hospital Design: A Qualitative Assessment by Staff and Service Users of the Design of a New Mental Health Inpatient Unit." *Environment and Planning C: Government and Policy* 25 (4): 591–610.

Devlin, A. S. 1992. "Psychiatric Ward Renovation: Staff Perception, and Patient Behavior." *Environment and Behavior* 24 (1): 66–84.

Etherington, N. 2012. *Gardening for Children with Autism Spectrum Disorders and Special Educational Needs.* London: Jessica Kingsley Publishers.

Faber Taylor, A., and F. E. Kuo. 2009. "Children with Attention Deficits Concentrate Better after Walk in the Park." *Journal of Attention Disorders* 12 (5): 402–9.

Faber Taylor, A., F. E. Kuo, and W. C. Sullivan. 2001. "Coping with ADD: The Surprising Connection to Green Play Settings." *Environment and Behavior* 33 (1): 54–77.

Gross, R., Y. Sasson, M. Zarhy, and J. Zohar. 1998. "Healing Environment in Psychiatric Hospital Design." *General Hospital Psychiatry* 20 (2): 108–14.

Karlin, B. E., and R. A. Zeiss. 2006. "Environmental and Therapeutic Issues in Psychiatric Hospital Design: Toward Best Practices." *Psychiatric Services* 57 (10): 1376–78.

Kuo, F. E., and A. Faber Taylor. 2004. "A Potential Natural Treatment for Attention-Deficit/Hyperactivity Disorder: Evidence from a National Study." *American Journal of Public Health* 94 (9): 1580–86.

Larsen, L. 1992. "Nature as Therapy: An Assessment of Schizophrenic Patients' Visual Preferences for Institutional Outdoor Environments." Master in landscape architecture thesis, University of Guelph, Ontario.

Lundgren, K. 2004. "Nature-Based Therapy: It's Potential as a Complementary Approach to Treating Communication Disorders." *Seminars in Speech and Language* 25 (2): 121–31.

Mathers, C. D., and D. Loncar. 2006. "Projections of Global Mortality and Burden of Disease from 2002 to 2030." *PLOS Medicine* 3(11).www.plosmedicine.org/article/info:doi/10.1371/journal.pmed.0030442.

Millet, P. 2009. "Integrating Horticulture into the Vocational Rehabilitation Process of Individuals with Fatigue, Chronic Fatigue, and Burnout: A Theoretical Model." *Journal of Therapeutic Horticulture* 19: 11–22.

Roe, J., and P. Aspinall. 2011. "The Restorative Benefits of Walking in Urban and Rural Settings in Adults with Good and Poor Mental Health." *Health and Place* 17 (1): 103–13.

Sachs, N. A., and T. Vincenta. 2011. "Outdoor Environments for Children with Autism and Special Needs." *Implications* 9 (1): 1–8. www.informedesign.org/_news/april_v09-p.pdf.

Ulrich, R. S., L. Bogren, and S. Lundin. 2012. "Toward a Design Theory for Reducing Aggression in Psychiatric Facilities." Paper presented at ARCH12: Architecture/Research/Care/

Health conference, Chalmers, Gothenburg, Sweden, November 13–14.

Van Gogh, Vincent. 2009. *Vincent van Gogh–The Letters: The Complete Illustrated and Annotated Edition.* Edited by Leo Jansen, Hans Luijten, and Nienke Bakker of the Van Gogh Museum in association with the Huygens Institute. London: Thames and Hudson Ltd. Letters 776 and 889 retrieved from http://www.vangoghletters.org/vg/letters.html on May 8, 2013.

Vincenta, T., J. Sando, B. Johnston, and V. Lattanzio. 2012. "Bridging the Landscape of Autism." Paper presented at the ASLA 2012 National Meeting, Phoenix, Arizona, September 28.

WHO (World Health Organization). 2001. *Ministerial Round Tables 2001, 54th World Health Assembly: Mental Health: A Call for Action by World Health Ministers.* Geneva: World Health Organization.

CHAPTER 13

Gardens for Veterans and Active Service Personnel

> I have found it comforting to know that the earth recycles. She accepts all things and uses them as elements of creation. I found it healing to give my anger, rage, shame, despair, etc. to the earth. I have yelled it, cried it . . . It is a great exercise of release (fig. 13.1).
>
> —Veterans survey participant (Parkins 2011, 82)

The Wounds of War

With every war, a percentage of veterans sustain injuries that sometimes last for decades after discharge. In addition to physical problems, they may face a range of other issues, such as mental illness, substance abuse, and homelessness. With Operation Iraqi Freedom (OIF) and Operation Enduring Freedom (OEF) in Afghanistan, improvements in body armor and advanced medical treatments have enabled an unprecedented number of military personnel to survive incidents that in previous wars would have killed them. As a result, many are returning with severe, often multiple injuries, referred to as polytrauma. These include visually apparent damage such as limb loss, burns, and spinal cord injuries and also "invisible wounds of war"—traumatic brain injuries (TBIs), severe depression, and emotional disturbance from combat-related stress, including posttraumatic stress disorder (PTSD) (Tanielian and Jaycox 2008). About one-third of soldiers previously deployed to Iraq and Afghanistan have reported symptoms of TBI, PTSD, and/or major depression. War touches loved ones as well as those directly affected. A survey by the American Psychiatric Association found that more than one-third of military members and spouses under age fifty-five reported frequent feelings of anxiety (military member 38 percent, military spouse 39 percent) and depression (military member 40 percent, military spouse 33 percent). Though many veterans struggle to cope with physical disfigurement when they return home, the stigma of mental health disorders continues to keep many individuals from seeking treatment. The same survey found that more than 60 percent of military members think that seeking help for mental health concerns would have some negative impact on their career (APA 2012a).

Traumatic brain injury

Traumatic brain injury—often referred to as the "signature wound" of the wars in Iraq and Afghanistan—occurs when the head is hit with significant force, causing injury ranging from a mild, momentary concussion to permanent brain damage. Individuals who sustain a TBI may experience a range of short- and long-term effects, including headaches; weakness in extremities; sleep disturbance; memory loss; inability to concentrate; an alteration of some or all of the senses; difficulty with reasoning and language; and emotional and behavioral shifts such as changes in personality, social inappropriateness, anger and violent behavior, poor impulse control, depression, and suicidal thoughts. TBIs can also cause epilepsy and lead to an increased risk for conditions such as Alzheimer's disease, Parkinson's disease, and other brain disorders that become more prevalent with age (NCIPC 2003).

Posttraumatic stress disorder

Stress-related symptoms linked to military trauma have had many names, including battle fatigue, Da Costa's syndrome, soldier's heart, and shell shock (Andreasen 2004; Lipton 1994; Parkins 2011). The term *posttraumatic stress disorder* was first coined in the 1970s to replace *post-Vietnam syndrome*. The condition was formally recognized in 1980 in the DSM-IV (Shalev, Yehuda, and Alexander 2000).

PTSD generally appears within three months after a traumatic experience such as sexual or psychological abuse or assault, a serious accident, natural disaster, or war-related event(s). It often occurs with—and may be exacerbated by or contribute to—related disorders, including depression, substance abuse, memory loss, and other physical and mental health problems. Symptoms fall into three categories:

13.1 A veteran at Gardening Leave, a facility for returning soldiers in Scotland, proudly shows off his potato harvest.
Photo courtesy of Gardening Leave Limited

1. Intrusion: Flashbacks in the form of strong memories and nightmares that intrude, often unexpectedly, into current life.

2. Avoidance: Avoidance of close emotional relationships with family, friends, and colleagues, as well as situations that could be reminders of the trauma. Common experiences include numbness, diminished emotions, and a sense of disassociation from everyday life. Feelings are difficult to discuss.

3. Hyperarousal: An acute sense of alertness from a perception of being in constant danger. People experiencing hyperarousal can become irritable or explosive, even when not provoked. They may also have difficulty with concentration, memory, and impulse control, leading to a higher risk for violence against others and self (self-harm or suicide) (APA 2012b).

A Dearth of Research

Design of inpatient and outpatient healthcare facilities for veterans and wounded warriors is a new field. To date, little research has been conducted on the effects (positive and negative) of the physical environment on this population, making evidence-based design a challenge. In particular, little is known about what *types* of outdoor spaces, and what *elements and activities* in those outdoor spaces, will be of greatest benefit. The complex combination of physical and neurological injuries interwoven with long-lasting emotional challenges may call for unique design concepts. To add to the challenge, the affected population comprises a wide range of ages and experience, from senior citizens through active duty personnel in their teens and early twenties. This extreme variation in time, type, and location of combat makes any kind of universal "best practice" difficult, if not impossible, to define. Finally, a confluence of "stiff upper lip" military culture and symptoms of avoidance for people with TBIs and PTSD makes it difficult to elicit thoughts, feelings, and experiences that would help designers and researchers.

The Veterans Administration (VA) serves veterans of all US wars. Additionally, the Department of Defense (DOD) serves some veterans and all active duty military personnel, often referred to as "wounded warriors." The Wounded Warrior Program was established in 2005 and serves veterans and active duty personnel who have been wounded physically and/or emotionally during operations in Iraq or Afghanistan (U.S. Army Posture Statement 2008). Due in part to a strong commitment to evidence-based design and family-centered care from the VA and the DOD, the coming decade will likely see progress in research, design, and policy.

Existing Research to Inform Design

Research that has informed the guidelines below includes two master of landscape architecture (MLA) theses, both from 2011, that focused specifically on therapeutic gardens for veterans; additional research studies, including unpublished theses and postoccupancy evaluations; research from other fields, such as social science and medicine; anecdotal evidence; and examples of built works.

For her MLA thesis, Michelle Parkins (2011) conducted surveys of US veterans about their views on nature and hypothetical (rather than existing) therapeutic gardens. Of the thirty-eight survey respondents, fifteen had fought in the Vietnam War and seventeen had fought in Iraq or Afghanistan. Thirty-three percent of respondents reported having an official diagnosis of PTSD. Regarding potential intended benefits one might receive in a healing garden, of greatest importance were "getting away by yourself," "being in nature," and "meditation."

In response to the open-ended question, "Are there any elements/items that would draw you to a healing garden environment? Why? Examples: Water, birds, colors, certain plants, sky, air quality," 68 percent named water as an important element. In three answers, water was the only element noted. Other important elements included "wildlife" and "other nature sounds." Parkins also asked, "Are there certain elements that might distract you from enjoying the healing garden environment? Examples: Too open of an area, feeling of enclosure, certain colors, desert sand, plant types, palm trees, insects (flying or crawling), heat and/or humidity, foliage too

dense/tropical." Of the nineteen responses, 47 percent cited enclosure as a potential cause of discomfort; 26 percent cited exposed spaces as problematic. Five of the nineteen responses indicated that a healing garden should be neither too open nor too enclosed. Thirty-seven percent cited noise—specifically helicopters, traffic, barking dogs, and "kids yelling and screaming." Excessive heat and humidity and insects were also noted as potentially detracting from a healing experience. In response to a question about sound, "Which of the following statements below most closely describes how you feel about sound in general as it relates to *easing* stress levels or symptoms of PTSD in a garden setting?" Seventy-seven percent noted "nature sounds (water/wind)"; 13 percent noted "artificial sounds" (personal music device); 3 percent said "no sound," and 7 percent said "other sounds."

Though some preferences—such as the presence of water, the absence of unpleasant noises, and the importance of a balance between open and enclosed spaces—were found, perhaps just as important was the breadth of experiences, even among a small population. Parkins's research highlights the importance of design that can be flexible and accommodate specific users. For example, one respondent said,

Myself, I prefer a space that is cool rather than hot. Heat makes me sleepy, and that is how I escape by sleeping as, I don't have nightmares, but many other vets do. I am not claustrophobic, but again I know friends with PTSD that can't face a wall and must have their backs to it at all times, so a clear path for departure is a must. High humidity and dense foliage may remind people of the jungles of Vietnam, expanses of sand could trigger the same for Iraq and Afganistan vets, so I guess you might want to have a variety if possible so could pick your spot [sic]. (Parkins 2011, 80)

Parkins's thesis is an important contribution to a field that needs further exploration. For example, there are contrasting views regarding one design element in her research—water. The Parkins survey participants expressed a strong desire for some sort of water feature. While risk of infection from *Legionella* and other waterborne bacteria is minimal in this group, since most veterans are not immunocompromised, water's role in the landscape for veterans and wounded warriors raises complicated issues.

Dorinda Wolfe Murray, of the UK organization Independent Gardening, states:

Veterans who are from the naval services have a completely different way of looking at water than those who are from the infantry or air force. The sound of rushing water can, for Falkland veterans, say, be the sound of a breach in their ship's hull. The worst type of sound they could ever hear; a harbinger of death by drowning. For veterans who have been out on the ground on "ops," the sudden sound of a water jet can have them hitting the ground. (I have seen this at a show in London where, as part of a "therapeutic garden," the designer had small fountains coming off and on in her show garden. The combination of sudden noise and movement had both the veterans I was with so stressed we had to move away within a few seconds).

Most people consider the white noise that water make useful, especially when it masks other, undesirable sounds such as traffic, air conditioners, other people's conversations, and the like. However, it can be disturbing to people with heightened sensory awareness. Murray comments:

It is almost undetectable until turned off. At that point you realize how noisy it has been. It adds a subtle layer of stress. And imagine what that must be like when you are already depressed, or your nerves are stretched to breaking point.

Water can also represent a very real threat to veterans. Bridges over water can be used for booby-trapping the road, and the struts can provide hidden locations for mines or IEDs [improvised explosive devices]. A very effective way to prevent such fear is to have white lines painted on either side of a bridge. This could be done with white-coloured stone or inserts dependent on what surface you are covering the bridge with. Quite simply, the white lines represent the white tape that is used by NATO and other forces to indicate that the path has been checked and cleared of mines. It represents safe passage.

Murray believes that the most effective use of water in a garden for veterans is a

calm, still pool, preferably with some form of vegetation, such as water lilies. This provides a contemplative focus and has little perceived threat. In addition, calm water reflects the sky bringing light into a confined space and "lifting" the atmosphere. It also attracts wildlife, becoming a focal point. Veterans have an almost obsessive interest in wildlife, be they bugs, butterflies, birds, or mammals—even vermin. It is as if the fundamental fact that they have been taught how to kill has to be balanced by an overwhelming desire to preserve life, no matter how small or insignificant. In fact, one of the most requested aspects of any garden that I have designed has been that it be wildlife friendly—and water plays a vital role in that. (Dorinda Wolfe Murray, pers. comm., 2012)

Built Works

The nature of polytrauma for veterans and wounded warriors necessitates design that can address multiple physical injuries and cognitive and emotional impairment. Even facilities serving a specific user group, such as the the Center for the Intrepid in San Antonio, Texas, which provides physical rehabilitation for the most severely wounded military service personnel, also incorporate individual and group counseling for personnel with TBI and emotional disorders. Likewise, at the National Intrepid Center of Excellence (NICoE) in Bethesda, Maryland—the first facility designed specifically to treat service personnel with TBI and PTSD—spaces must also accommodate those with physical injuries beyond those to the nervous system.

The NICoE is an example of the military's commitment to a different, more holistic approach to healthcare. A driving goal of the design team, headed by SmithGroupJJR, was to provide for the physical treatment needs of patients and the emotional and spiritual needs of families and caregivers—an embodiment of the family-centered care model. Another overarching principle was to treat patients and their families with dignity and imbue them with control throughout the treatment experience.

Evidence-based design practices were used, and research continues now that the facility is open. Extensive interviews with veterans, wounded warriors, family members, and healthcare professionals guided the design of all spaces. Every effort—with building layout, surfaces, colors, artwork, wayfinding—was made to ensure that the physical design would support the program and the building occupants' specific needs, including sensory challenges such as altered spatial awareness and higher visual and auditory sensitivity. High-contrast colors and bright lighting were avoided; even the building's orientation was designed to reduce harsh exposure. To reduce loud and reverberating sound, carpeting was installed in all public areas and the building was equipped with a white noise system. Another key concern was a heightened need for privacy but at the same time a strong desire to not feel trapped in an enclosed space. A balance of small and large public and private spaces was essential (SmithGroupJJR 2011).

One design feature that brings nature into the facility is an intimate interior skylit atrium called Central Park (fig. 13.2). Often referred to as the symbolic heart of the NICoE, the circular room is a quiet, contemplative space. It has received much positive feedback from patients and staff. The floor contains a labyrinth pattern of two different types and colors of wood, with benches and potted plants along the perimeter. While the space is mostly used for walking the labyrinth, it is also used for meditation, yoga, and other group activities. Within the room, but surrounded by vine-covered walls that separate the space, a rehabilitation terrain path allows people to participate in

13.2 The interior atrium, "Central Park," is considered to be the symbolic heart of the National Intrepid Center of Excellence in Bethesda, Maryland. Designer: SmithGroupJJR

Copyright, Maxwell MacKenzie

physical therapy, alone or with a therapist, while immersed in the serene environment. Glass doors to the room allow patients and family members to discretely watch someone walking the labyrinth, which for many is a somewhat unknown tool. Upon seeing how it is done, observers are then more likely to enter and participate (SmithGroupJJR 2012b).

The Combat Stress Garden in Leatherhead, UK, was designed for ex-service personnel undergoing rehabilitation for TBI and PTSD at the nearby Tyrwhitt House (headquarters of the charity Combat Stress). The garden was first installed at the Royal Horticultural Society's Hampton Court Palace Flower Show in 2010, where it won a silver medal. It was then dismantled and reinstalled in Leatherhead. Dorinda Wolfe Murray, of Independent Gardening, collaborated with Fi Boyle on the design. Murray's experience with service personnel informed many of the decisions. For example, red and orange flowers were avoided because they reminded users of blood and explosions; pathways are a warm brown color to prevent glare; a raised bed around an oak tree serves as a place to rest for those with an unsteady gait; sightlines in the garden are clear; and spaces—including the custom benches—are designed to reduce fear that bombs might be hidden there: "The benches are high-backed, set against walls, and cantilevered so there are no legs behind which IEDs . . . could be lurking" (Jardine 2010) (fig. 13.3).

For his MLA thesis, Brock Anderson (2011) completed a case study of the Salem VA Medical Center (SVAMC) in Salem, Virginia. The facility has a long history of connecting veterans with the land. In 1934, President Franklin D. Roosevelt dedicated a 445-acre, 472-bed veteran hospital complex, part of a countrywide focus on horticultural and occupational therapy for veterans (Detweiler et al. 2010). Work with plants and gardens became an official therapeutic modality (horticultural therapy) after World War II.

13.3 The Combat Stress Garden for veterans undergoing rehabilitation, Leatherhead, UK. Custom benches are designed to reduce fear that bombs might be hidden underneath. A still water feature allows for reflection while also reflecting plants and the sky. Designers: Fi Boyle and Dorinda Wolfe Murray.

Photo by Dorinda Wolfe Murray,
Independent Gardening Ltd.

The grounds included a farm with crops and animals that patients cared for as part of their psychiatric rehabilitation. SVAMC treatment no longer incorporates farm labor, but the Compensated Work Therapy program provides an opportunity for veterans to work with a variety of plants in greenhouses and gardens (ibid.). A 2012 television news program featured James Lugumira, an army veteran who lives with high blood pressure and PTSD. In 2006, he began working in the greenhouse as part of SVAMC's work therapy program. "Every time I'm around plants my blood pressure goes down. I relax," he explained. "Instead of using so much medication for it now I just come down and grow my plants. I look at my plants (and it's) almost (as though) they are talking to me and then I become calmer and calmer every day" (Jadhon 2012).

The Family Garden, adjacent to the greenhouse, was constructed by senior Girl Scouts as a place of respite for the families of veterans who might be spending the bulk of a day at the hospital. The greenhouse provided the plants, and the Girl Scouts paid for all of the other materials through fundraisers. The Family Garden includes vertical gardens, a human-scale checkerboard, a butterfly garden, and a Zen garden complete with rakes.

As a continuing effort to connect veterans with nature, SVAMC approached landscape architect Jack Carman, principal at Design for Generations, to create a therapeutic courtyard garden. Carman worked closely with staff psychiatrist Mark Detweiler, MD, and horticultural therapist Sandy Lane, HTR. The garden is currently in the construction planning phase, with all funding secured for Phase I. Key design goals were to keep the garden as natural as possible, incorporate both passive and active areas for the wide range of veterans being served, and include a Memory Support Garden for veterans with Alzheimer's disease and other forms of dementia.

Passive areas were designed to be tranquil and meditative. They include meandering paths, plantings, a mixture of private and more public benches and seating areas; water features such as a meandering stream and a waterfall; and a woodland garden. Active areas were designed to offer specific programming for therapy and rehabilitation, including physcial, occupational, horticultural, and music therapy, and neurocognitive rehabilitation. The active areas include raised planters for vegetables and herbs; fruiting trees and shrubs; a conservatory for year-round use, including therapy sessions; an exercise station; and a variety of walking surfaces (fig. 13.4).

The garden also includes a labyrinth. While labyrinths in healthcare gardens often take up a lot of space and are minimally used, Anderson (2011, 46) makes some points that bear consideration:

One of the basic reasons for walking a labyrinth is to restore a connection with the body as a means of eliminating. . . stress. . . One psychotherapist has her clients walk a labyrinth before therapy sessions as a way to encourage them to turn inward. The clients then walk the labyrinth again after the session to help settle any issues that were raised. Another SVAMC staff member foresees the labyrinth as an integral part of therapy for her PTSD patients. The labyrinth will be a place where. . .staff can take ten to thirteen veterans at a time to go out and explore. The labyrinth could also be used as a meditative tool to teach the veterans about mindfulness and awareness. Some issues that were worked on successfully are trust, surrender, grief and loss, communication, values, and commitment.

The East Orange Campus of the Department of Veterans Affairs New Jersey Health Care System (VA NJHCS) organized a master gardener and landscaping technologist certification course. Clients use 20-by-50-foot plots to grow vegetables and herbs, which they provide to the Foxhole Café restaurant at one campus. Over a thousand pounds were produced in 2010. The first group of eight veterans received their landscaping technologist certification in October 2010. Another course in stormwater management was added and implemented on campus through the building of rain gardens and installation of permeable pavement. Most recently, the VA NJHCS received $100,000 from a VHA Innovation Funding for the Advancement of Patient-Centered Care grant to construct a greenhouse so that gardening could take place year-round (Brown 2011).

At the VA Greater Los Angeles Healthcare System in California, veterans operate a 15-acre garden as part of the horticulture therapy program. Established in 1986 as a work therapy program, the garden runs as a self-sufficient business selling organic produce to individual customers and local restaurants. Income from the garden provides vocational training and therapy stipends for veterans transitioning back into the community. The garden also collaborates with local schools and offers a work setting for developmentally disabled adults.

Groups outside of the military healthcare system, such as community gardens and farms, are also doing important work. The Farmer Veteran Coalition's (FVC) mission is

to mobilize veterans to feed America. We cultivate a new generation of farmers and food leaders, and develop viable employment and meaningful careers through the collaboration of the farming and military communities. We believe that veterans possess the unique skills and character needed to strengthen rural communities and create sustainable food systems for all.

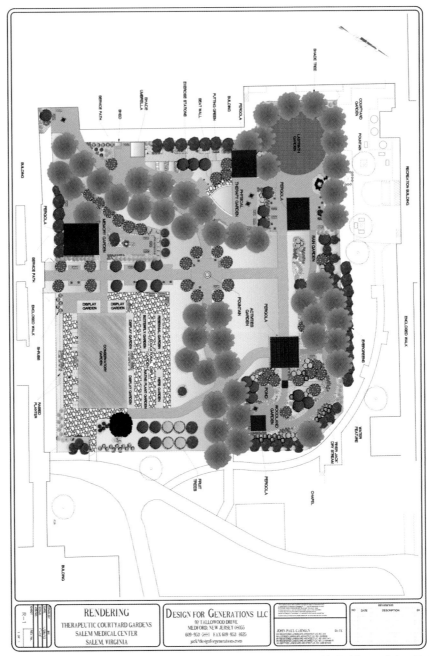

13.4 Rendering of the Therapeutic Courtyard Gardens within the Salem Veterans Affairs Medical Center, Salem, Virginia.

Courtesy of Design for Generations, LLC, by Jack Carman, FASLA

We believe that food production offers purpose, opportunity, as well as physical and psychological benefits. (FVC 2013)

The FVC supports other organizations, such as Veterans to Farmers (2013), whose mission is "to provide American veterans of the Iraq and Afghanistan conflicts with pride, education and fulfillment through a permanent source of sustainable income, community and contribution: the family farm." Whether or not these organizations are familiar with the term "healing gardens," they recognize the importance of connecting people with the land in a way that supports health.

There are horticultural therapy programs that work with active and retired service members in other parts of the world. The first eight patients at Nacadia, in Denmark, are veterans being treated for PTSD (see the case study on Nacadia in chapter 12). The Scottish charity Gardening Leave oversees horticultural therapy projects—growing fruit and vegetables in walled gardens—for military and ex-military men and women throughout the UK (fig. 13.5). Gardening Leave, founded by Anna Baker Cresswell and Col. Clive Fairweather, recently commissioned the Mental Health Foundation to externally evaluate well-being, mental health symptoms, and cost-effectiveness at two of their projects. Walled gardens may be another example of how cultural differences affect design decisions. In the UK, walled gardens are traditional in the culture and are perceived as safe, protected spaces and thus are ideal for those grappling with PTSD. In other countries, however, combat survivors may feel too claustrophobic inside such an enclosed space.

It may be that with military service personnel, active engagement with nature plays an especially important role.

13.5 The walled garden facility for veterans, operated by Gardening Leave in Auchincruive, Ayrshire, Scotland.
Photo courtesy of Gardening Leave Limited

They are trained for peak performance and to act as part of a unit or team. Activities that provide opportunities to develop an increasing sense of mastery, combined with opportunities to inspire and assist one another, can support the "warrior ethos." Through growing and nurturing plants, participants regain control of and a sense of agency in their lives physically, emotionally, socially, and perhaps even spiritually. Many participants are able to apply their horticultural knowledge elsewhere, in new jobs or at home with their families. The role of therapeutic horticulture for veterans and active-duty service personnel—perhaps even during, rather than just after, service—warrants further research (fig. 13.6).

Guidelines

The guidelines listed below apply specifically to military service personnel. The general design guidelines (chapter 6), which address the needs of all users, must also be applied. Because of the combination of physical and psychological challenges for this population, guidelines from chapter 12, on mental and behavioral health, and chapter 14, on rehabilitation, may be useful.

"On the ground" research and sharing information

While interdisciplinary collaboration is always important, it is even more critical with military service personnel due to the breadth of age, type of combat, and range of symptoms. With so little published research to inform design decisions on the ground, collaboration with all of the stakeholders, especially those who will be using the garden, may be the best tool for guiding successful design. Commenting on the inclusion of service personnel in the NICoE design process, one family member remarked: "Another thing that I love is that they consider him a part of the team, not just the patient. He is considered an intricate and valuable part of the team with a voice!! Why isn't all medical care this way?" (SmithGroupJJR 2011). Additionally, because so little information is available, sharing any research findings through observation, anecdotal information, postoccupancy evaluation, or other means is critical.

The need for flexibility

Perhaps more than with other populations, gardens for military personnel must be flexible. Formal postoccupancy evaluations, comments from users, and observations from staff may reveal problems to be addressed. For example, more or less screening—with walls, fences, or plantings—may be necessary, or the sound of a water feature may need adjustment.

13.6 A veteran sowing seeds in the walled garden operated by Gardening Leave in Auchincruive, Ayrshire, Scotland.
Photo courtesy of Gardening Leave Ltd.

As veterans' age and combat locations change, specific design features may no longer apply to the intended user group.

Logistical challenges

As with any design involving a government entity, projects for the Veterans Administration and the Department of Defense pose challenges of bureaucracy, budget, and policy, which are all subject to the shifting sands of the political landscape. One landscape architect with experience in therapeutic garden design for veterans offers these recommendations: (1) research the local administration hierarchy and personalities; (2) organize local volunteer effort and funding for a garden with specific goals; (3) with strong local backing, approach the local VA with a project concept; and (4) be politically palatable at all levels (Rick Spalenka, pers. corr., 2011).

Physical design guidelines

1. **Control:** As with any illness, and especially with combat-related polytrauma, one's sense of control is stripped away. The body is uncooperative. The mind is unreliable. Friends and loved ones may not relate. Many feel as if the rug has been pulled out from under them. Providing opportunities to regain control is essential: choices of where to sit, ambulate, and look; who and what to interact with; what to manipulate, including seating that can be moved around, plants and water that can be touched, birds that can be fed.

2. **Accessibility:** Any outdoor space for veterans/wounded warriors should be fully accessible (with the exception of intentionally designed physical challenges, which are discussed below). Depending on the type of facility and population, the environment may need to go above and beyond ADA regulations. Among the very few changes implemented following a postoccupancy evaluation (POE) at the Center for the Intrepid were automatic sensor doors at both building entrances. Those learning to navigate with crutches, wheeled mobility devices, and new prosthetics simply could not manage the doors (SmithGroupJJR 2012a).

3. **Intentionally designed physical challenges:** Especially for gardens designed for rehabilitation, the landscape architect should work closely with physical, occupational, horticultural, and other allied professional therapists and staff to design opportunities for a range of outdoor physical challenges.

4. **Physical and emotional safety and security:** Risks of accidents are higher when patients have severe injuries and cognitive and emotional disturbance. In some facilities, individuals may be learning to navigate their environment under

very different and difficult circumstances. The outdoor environment should be a safe place to both get away to and to learn and heal within. Precautions against physical harm of others or self should be considered. At one military medical center, a rooftop garden included raised planters abutting the garden's perimeter fencing. The combination of the built-in "step" and scalable fencing created a suicide risk, and the garden has now been retrofitted.

5. **Balance of prospect/refuge:** People who have engaged in combat, especially those with PTSD, need to feel safe. Almost all of the research and examples of built works reveal the need for a space—or perhaps a choice of spaces—that provides privacy and some degree of enclosure but does not provoke feelings of claustrophobia. Perspective sketches, models, 3D renderings, or even scale mock-ups may be helpful tools in achieving the right balance.

6. **Preventing UV exposure, glare, and visual distress:** Many antidepressants and antianxiety medications make people more susceptible to the sun's ultraviolet rays and to glare. A variety of shaded areas throughout the garden—some adjacent to the building, some that allow for groups, some that allow for only one or two people, for example—are an absolute necessity. The color of paving and other surfaces (chairs, benches, tables, sculpture) should minimize glare. TBI and related injuries make people more susceptible to "cliffing," which occurs with contrasting dark and light patterns on the ground plane. The change in tone is perceived as a change in grade and can at best make people uneasy about where to walk, and at worst can cause people to fall as they try to navigate what they perceive as a step or a hole. A POE of the NICoE found that even the relatively subtle two-toned wood labyrinth pattern proved disconcerting for some users (SmithGroupJJR 2012a). Contrast on the ground—shadows from an overhead trellis, varying colors on the ground plane, for example—should be avoided.

7. **Attention to positive and negative sensory stimuli:** Due to heightened sensory experience, sounds that may not be noticed by others can prove irritating to those suffering from TBI or PTSD. Without forcing visitors to interact, the garden should provide opportunities for sensory engagement, such as through plants that are pleasant or interesting to touch, smell, and taste.

8. **Items of familiarity/homelike environment:** People who have undergone serious trauma need comfort and reassurance in a safe space. They should not be challenged with cutting-edge design gestures or features. A familiar, homelike environment will help them transition from the healthcare setting back to the community.

9. **Places for gathering, places to be alone:** People with PTSD and related disorders have a tendency to isolate, so while a garden should allow for moments of solitude and contemplation, it should also provide plenty of opportunities for one-on-one and group connection. Consider large areas for gatherings, such as a covered pavilion that can be used for group therapy, social events, and ceremonies.

10. **Places for ritual and reflection:** Parkins (2011) found that areas for ritual were important in gardens for veterans. Examples included fireside and memorial areas; places for reflection—sometimes literally, such as a reflecting pool; symbolic water features, and the like. "The fireside area is a gathering space where the element of fire is used as a spiritual release for those who wish to 'burn' away negative thoughts, images, pain, burdens, feelings, or anything the user wishes to let go of," said Parkins (59) (fig. 13.7). Unless the population being served has extensive involvement in the design from the beginning, places for ritual may be best incorporated after a garden is built. An obvious example would be to avoid a fireside area for a garden many of the users of which are burn survivors. Other decisions may be less clear and must be guided by members of the design team.

11. **Places for children:** If families will be accompanying service personnel in the garden, space should be set aside

13.7 Fire pit and sweat lodge at the Salt Lake City VA Medical Center GEM Court Garden and Purtkwahgahm (Healing Ground), Salt Lake City, Utah. Designer: George E. Wahlen.
Photo by Chris Garcia

for children to play. These areas can be important places for patients to reconnect with their children in a nonclinical setting much like the playgrounds they will return to at home. However, the loud, staccato sounds of children (who sometimes shriek with excitement during play) can be irritating—and sometimes even distressing—so careful attention must be paid to the siting of play areas. At some facilities, such as VA outpatient clinics, families rarely attend; in this case, the space will be better used for something other than a play area.

12. **Areas for service dogs:** A relatively high percentage of veterans are accompanied by dogs for physical and/or emotional support. A garden should provide space for people to exercise and interact with their animals.

13. **Smoking areas:** If the garden is large enough, provide areas for smoking (fig. 13.8). Regarding this somewhat controversial topic, landscape architect Rick Spalenka—who was a registered nurse in a psychiatric facility before changing careers—says:

> My experience with Vet patients in psych and med/surgical care is the importance of smoking! Smoking activity and smoking privileges have therapeutic qualities despite seeming so contrary to health. You remove smoking privileges from psych patients, you will face hostility and anger. You prohibit smoking activity from med/surgical patients and you face increased anxiety. The most popular meeting place for Vet patients is the smoke shack. They socialize and get physical activity. I used to tell my patients, "The only one who

13.8 "Designated Smoking & Tobacco Usage Area Only." Warrior and Family Support Center, San Antonio, Texas.
Photo by Naomi Sachs

ever got better in bed was Casanova. Get out of bed." (pers. comm., 2010)

Warrior and Family Support Center Therapeutic Garden, Returning Heroes Home, San Antonio, Texas

Designer: Quatrefoil, Inc., Portland, Oregon. Principal in charge: Brian E. Bainnson, PLA, ASLA
By Brian Bainnson

Description of the Facility and Its History

The Warrior and Family Support Center (WFSC) provides a "living room" environment for wounded warriors and their families who are at Fort Sam Houston receiving medical treatment. Fort Sam Houston includes San Antonio Military Medical Center (SAMC), Brooke Army Medical Center (BAMC), the Center for the Intrepid, Fort Sam Houston Primary Care Clinic, McWethy Troop Medical Clinic, Schertz

Medical Home, and the Taylor Burk Health Clinic. The WFSC provides computer training, private counseling, job skills, social and recreational activities for wounded warriors and their families, and a much needed break from hospital and barracks (fig. 13.9).

The 20,000-square-foot garden was planned as a place for wounded warriors—active duty military personnel and veterans returning from combat in Iraq and Afghanistan—to use for physical and psychological recovery from their injuries and to complement the services provided within the Support Center. The design process took place during the summer of 2008 and the garden was constructed in the fall and winter of that year. The garden was planned for both passive and active therapeutic activities for small and large groups and as a place where wounded warriors could feel safe, be with their families, and regain the elements of a normal life. Many will spend years receiving treatment for their injuries with short and long stays at Fort Sam Houston. The gardens have been designed as a place to be outside of the stressful environments found at the medical center and base housing where the warriors (many with their families) live while they are receiving outpatient treatment (fig. 13.10). The average warrior receiving treatment is in his or her early twenties. Eighty percent will be medically retired from the military and will transition back into civilian life.

Design Philosophy

It was fundamental that the design of the garden be collaborative and grow out of the clinical needs and culture of the military personnel, their families, and the caregivers. The design team included a landscape architect, occupational therapists, behavioral therapists, members of the nursing staff at BAMC, and therapists with the Center for the Intrepid, as well as wounded warriors and their families receiving treatment at the medical center. It was important that the team came to the initial meeting without any preconceived notions of what the garden might look like and what materials, forms, and design elements it would contain. This allowed the team to listen to and find inspiration from the people who would use the garden. The landscape architect felt that working collaboratively is as much a design skill as knowing how to mix colors and textures of plants to achieve a pleasing end.

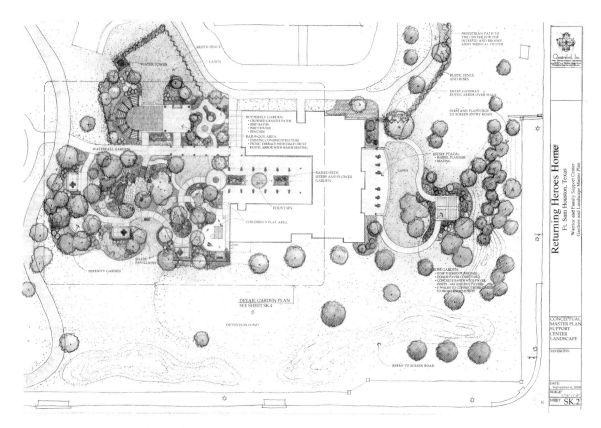

13.9 Plan of Warrior and Family Support Center garden.
Courtesy of Quatrefoil Inc.

13.10 Several covered areas, varying in size and location, are provided throughout the garden. Because many patients at SAMC are being treated for burns, TBI, and other injuries that cause sensitivity to sun and light, shade—both for cooling and for minimizing glare—is essential.
Photo Courtesy of Quatrefoil Inc.

As with many therapeutic gardens, the WFSC garden was designed for the very specific clinical needs of its users. Many share a complex combination of physical injuries (including severe burns, amputations, and traumatic brain injury) and emotional challenges (such as posttraumatic stress disorder) that are specific to this population. Additionally, they share other specific characteristics, such as age, military training and culture, and the experience of war.

Description of the Outdoor Space

Entering the garden from the Support Center, one first comes into a small courtyard defined by the U-shaped building with a wide porch on three sides (fig. 13.11). The courtyard, which features raised planters and a fountain in the middle, was designed for patients who would be unable to go further than this point. The main garden beyond the courtyard is divided into two primary areas: a more active space and a more passive space. The active space contains a covered grill area, a large plaza for gatherings and events, a children's playground, and a putting green. The passive area of the garden contains a curving walk connecting a series of more intimate gathering spaces. Two of these spaces have shelters to provide sun and weather protection. A limestone waterfall is located in the center of this area and provides a focal point with the sound

13.11 Porches extend beyond the building as a shaded colonnade to connect people with the gardens.
Photo by Naomi Sachs.

and movement of water. A small interactive children's garden provides a place to explore. Adjacent to the Therapeutic Garden is Freedom Park, an area with an amphitheater for large events and a trail system that connects several fitness courses designed for the clinical needs of the wounded warriors (fig. 13.12).

13.12 The fitness trail in Freedom Park, the outermost part of the garden, provides opportunities for individual or PT-guided movement and exercise. Covered seating areas along the pathway allow people to stop and rest or socialize away from the main garden area.
Photo by Naomi Sachs

Well-defined perimeters

The garden is defined by buildings, fencing, low berms, and plant material. Care was taken to screen out the busy traffic of adjacent roads and parking areas while at the same time dealing with the reality that many of these wounded warriors have a fear of enclosed spaces and, in particular, earthen berms that remind them of the landscapes of Iraq and Afghanistan.

Features modified to improve accessibility

The garden was designed to meet the needs of all types of physical challenges. All spaces are fully accessible for those using wheelchairs, with numerous raised beds of different heights and sizes throughout the garden. A variety of pavement types provides safe access while also offering physical challenge to those who are ready.

A profusion of plants and people/plant interactions

The garden, being located in San Antonio, enjoys an excellent climate for growing plants. The design team decided early in the planning process to honor the garden's Texas home and focus areas of the space on various native landscapes in the state. The planting areas are themed by region and showcase plants from the hot desert landscapes to the lush tropical landscapes that are found in Texas. One area, designated as a butterfly garden, brims with a profusion of color all year long. A challenge in the planting design was to avoid the use of palm trees or other planting combinations that could remind warriors of the landscapes where they lived and fought while on active duty.

Benign and supportive conditions

Because many patients at SAMC are being treated for severe burns, TBI, and other injuries that cause extreme sensitivity to light, shade—both for cooling and for minimizing glare—in the hot Texas landscape was paramount. The courtyard garden's wrap-around porch extends out from the building as a covered connection to the covered outdoor kitchen/barbeque area. Within the WFSC Therapeutic Garden, several large covered pavilions provide year-round shade. Additionally, many large trees, including existing manzinitas, were incorporated into the design.

The play area is an important feature that gives wounded warriors a place to spend time with their children and begin the process of healing their families while learning to deal with the new physical and psychological realities of their condition.

Recognizable place making

Although the facility treats wounded warriors from all fifty states as well as from the territories of the United States, the team decided early in the design process that garden elements should reflect the vernacular of the warriors' temporary home in Texas. Many features give the garden a sense of place and make it memorable, including a large Texas limestone waterfall in the center of the garden and covered pavilions in a Texas Hill Country design style with dark wood timbers. Wagon wheels and whiskey barrels are used throughout the garden, and a traditional Texas windmill and water tower provide focal points. A large Texas star is also featured in the paving in one of the many gathering spaces.

How the Garden Is Used

The most important use of the garden is as a setting for warriors and their families to find a place of peace and sanctuary. The garden provides a place for people to experience nature as they walk, relax, and spend time alone or with friends and family. It is a place where warriors and their families can work on strengthening their relationship during the arduous process of healing their physical wounds.

The garden accommodates a wide range of activities, from individual counseling sessions with a variety of therapists and social workers, to group activities and regularly scheduled social events, including Purple Heart ceremonies and weddings. Occupational, physical, and other therapists from SAMC can schedule sessions with their patients away from the hospital if they feel that a garden environment will aid in their recovery (fig. 13.13). Wounded warriors face physical, psychological, and social issues that are unprecedented in our time. The gardens, in conjunction with the activities available in the Wounded Warrior and Family Support Center, are a true model of family-centered care, where the entire individual, along with the families who will be their primary support network, is included in the healing process.

13.13 Lush native plantings create the feeling of an oasis despite the San Antonio desert heat.
Photo by Naomi Sachs

Key Garden Merits

- Collaborative design process

- Recognition of clinical as well as social needs

- Fully accessible

- Use of existing mature trees, lush plantings, and water features create a feeling of being in nature

- Passive and active, public and semiprivate spaces

- Recognition of Texas vernacular

Future Plans and Concerns

- Additional programming of activities in the garden

- Sustainable garden maintenance plan

- Horticultural therapist, who could oversee garden maintenance and programming

References

Anderson, B. 2011. "An Exploration of the Potential Benefits of Healing Gardens on Veterans with PTSD." Master of landscape architecture thesis, Utah State University. digitalcommons.usu.edu/gradreports/50.

Andreasen, N. C. 2004. *Brave New Brain: Conquering Mental Illness in the Era of the Genome*. New York: Oxford University Press.

APA (American Psychiatric Association). 2012a. "Military." American Psychiatric Association. Accessed December 30. www.psychiatry.org/mental-health/people/military.

APA (American Psychiatric Association). 2012b. "PTSD." American Psychiatric Association. Accessed December 30. www.psychiatry.org/ptsd.

Brown, J. 2011. "VA Campus Takes on Healing Gardens." *Healthcare Design*, July 27. www.healthcaredesignmagazine.com/article/va-campus-takes-healing-gardens.

Detweiler, M. B., T. Sharma, S. Lane, M. Kim, B. C. Johnson, and K. Y. Kim. 2010. "Practitioner Forum: The Case for Using Restorative Natural Environments in Veterans' Rehabilitation Programs." *Federal Practitioner* 1: 26–28.

FVC (Farmer Veteran Coalition). 2013. "Our Mission." Farmer Veteran Coalition. www.farmvetco.org/.

Jadhon, J. 2012. "Poinsettias Aren't Just Pretty: How They're Therapeutic in Salem." *WDBJ7.com*, December 03. articles.wdbj7.com/2012-12-03/greenhouse_35577229.

Jardine, C. 2010. "RHS Hampton Court Palace Flower Show 2010: Building a Sanctuary for Stress Sufferers." *The Telegraph*, July 8. www.telegraph.co.uk/gardening/hampton-court-flower-show/7872397/RHS-Hampton-Court-Palace-Flower-Show-2010-Building-a-sanctuary-for-stress-sufferers.html.

Lipton, M. I. 1994. *Post-Traumatic Stress Disorder—Additional Perspectives*. Springfield, MO: Charles C. Thomas.

NCIPC (National Center for Injury Prevention and Control). 2003. *Report to Congress on Mild Traumatic Brain Injury in the United States: Steps to Prevent a Serious Public Health Problem*. Atlanta, GA: Centers for Disease Control and Prevention.

Parkins, M. 2011. "Soft Touch for a Silent Voice: Creating Outdoor Healing Environments for Veterans with Post Traumatic Stress Disorder." Master of landscape architecture thesis, University of Oregon.

Shalev, A. Y., R. Yehuda, and A. C. McFarlane. 2000. *International Handbook of Human Response to Trauma*. New York: Kluwer Academic/Plenum Press.

SmithGroupJJR. 2011. *Building Design + Construction Award Text, National Intrepid Center of Excellence, May—Award Recipient*. Washington, DC: American Institute of Architects.

———. 2012a. *Post-Occupancy Evaluations of the National Intrepid Center of Excellence, Baltimore, Maryland, and the Center for the Intrepid, San Antonio, Texas*. Unpublished manuscript.

———. 2012b. *National AIA Healthcare Design Award Submission: Innovation and Design, National Intrepid Center of Excellence, January—Award Recipient*. Washington, DC: American Institute of Architects.

Tanielian, T. L., and L. Jaycox. 2008. *Invisible Wounds of War: Psychological and Cognitive Injuries, Their Consequences, and Services to Assist Recovery*. Santa Monica, CA: RAND Corporation.

U.S. Army Posture Statement. 2008. "Information Papers: U.S. Army Wounded Warrior Program." Department of the Army, United States of America. www.army.mil/aps/08/information_papers/sustain/US_Wounded_Warrior_Program.html.

Veterans to Farmers. 2013. "What Is Veterans to Farmers?" Veterans to Farmers. www.veterantofarmer.org/.

CHAPTER 14

Rehabilitation Gardens

TRADITIONALLY, REHABILITATION FOR PATIENTS recovering from stroke, brain injuries, or other mobility problems is carried out by clinical staff in a gymlike interior space in a hospital or outpatient clinic. But increasingly, rehabilitation hospitals, or those with a rehabilitation ward, are looking to a specially designed outdoor space as an alternative—contact with nature, sunlight, and a more normalized environment being seen as a setting where patients are more relaxed and where they may be distracted from the pain and stresses of their recovery (fig. 14.1).

Almost all the guidelines enumerated in chapter 6 apply to these gardens and should be consulted prior to the start of site planning, conceptual design, and other elements of the process. One guideline in that chapter should be especially emphasized, and one should not be followed. The latter is the suggestion that a healing garden should be open to the wider community. In the case of rehabilitation patients undergoing therapy outdoors, it is preferable that they have privacy, as they may be self-conscious about their condition. Whether the garden should be open for use by other patients, staff, and visitors in the hospital is a question that must be carefully addressed at the initial planning stage. Decisions on this issue may rest on the views of the rehabilitation staff, the location of the garden, and the presence of other gardens on the site, among other considerations.

The recommendation that the interdisciplinary design team incorporate members of the clinical staff who will work with patients in the garden cannot be emphasized enough. In fact, it is impossible here to articulate all the design details that a rehabilitation garden might need, since these will vary depending on whether the patients are recovering from strokes, brain injuries, spinal cord injuries, amputations, or burns, for example; on whether they have cognitive problems; and on other factors. For this reason it is essential that the designer work with all levels of the clinical staff, as well as current and former patients and their families, to develop the best possible design solution (fig. 14.2).

There is little empirical research on the design of rehabilitation gardens, or postoccupancy evaluations (POEs) of those that exist. One useful study (Davis 2011) elaborating some pitfalls that can occur is of a rooftop garden at Fort Sanders Regional Medical Center in Knoxville, Tennessee, that was created in 1993. A rehabilitation center at the hospital provides physical, occupational, and speech therapy for patients recovering from strokes, accidents, and major surgery. It is located two floors above a garden that can be accessed only by a small elevator. The garden is barely visible from the center, and there are no signs there or elsewhere in the hospital that signal its existence. The garden was created as an outdoor option for physical therapy and includes a rubberized and concrete "therapy walk" with steps of varying height, a small basketball court, a putting green, and a play area. Metal benches in sun and shade and a metal gazebo provide seating. The design team included every type of therapist who might work with patients. An annual $8,500 budget is dedicated to maintenance.

The study revealed barren areas and unhealthy vegetation, which left people feeling exposed; backless benches that were uncomfortable; lack of movable seating which precluded families from creating social clusters; and a lack of subareas for greater privacy. As a result of poor planning at the design stage, other problems arose. Two lawn areas and an outdoor grill had to be removed because staff in the surgery suite beneath the garden complained of fumes from cooking and gas-powered lawn mowers entering air intakes on the roof.

Staff responded positively to the idea of the garden, but few ever used it personally, because it was too inconvenient for a quick break or to do paperwork. When asked if the garden helped patients regain life skills, such as mobility and self-confidence, in a way different from indoor areas, the response was overwhelmingly affirmative, in that the garden presented real-life situations, in contrast to the simulated situations of an indoor gym or recreation room. To improve garden use, staff members asked for easier access, better maintenance, more comfortable seating, more greenery, and a greenhouse for year-round use. Patients in need of constant care cannot easily use the garden because lack of visibility makes it impossible for staff to monitor them from indoors.

All of the thirteen patients interviewed rated the garden important—as an option different from indoors, as a place to spend time with family, to find some privacy, and to do

14.1 A speech therapist encourages a patient to smell and talk about the blooms of crape myrtle in the Stenzel Healing Garden, Good Samaritan Medical Center, Portland, Oregon. Designer: Ron Mah, David Evans Associates.
Courtesy of Legacy Health

physical therapy outdoors. They reported staying in the garden from thirty to sixty minutes, and half said they went there daily or several times a week. All but one said they preferred the garden over an indoor gym because of the monotony of hospital walls, and that being outside helped them maintain a sense of self and a more positive outlook.

This study pointed to the lack of easy access as a major impediment to the success of this garden: "Early plans for the garden called for floor-level access, which would have eliminated the need for the costly elevator and opened the garden for use by more of the hospital. . .Floor-level access was eliminated based on the rehabilitation center's desire to be in control of the garden. . . . Visitors and. . . staff working in other parts of the hospital receive an explicit "Keep out" message. . . . A shared garden. . .might have resulted in greater use

and subsequent increased investment by the hospital" (Davis 2011, 34).

As a result of the Center's wish to be in control of the garden, it was solely responsible for maintenance, which deteriorated over time. In 2001 half of the trees were dead or declining in health. By 2009 all of the weeping willows, which offered a soft character, were replaced with stiff, upright evergreens. Therapists, not gardeners, were in charge of maintenance, resulting in severe pruning and the removal of plants that offered privacy to adjacent patient rooms. The original concepts for the garden were not understood or were ignored. This highlights the critical importance of appropriate maintenance and the need for a manual that explains the design and therapeutic intent of the original planting, as discussed in chapter 17.

14.2 At Jupiter Medical Center, Jupiter, Florida, a physical therapist initiated the Jacqueline Fiske Healing Garden so that cardio-rehabilitation patients could look out at the garden while exercising. Designer: Studio Sprout.

Courtesy of Studio Sprout; photo by Michiko Kurisu

14.3 Pet therapy in the Stenzel Healing Garden, Good Samaritan Medical Center, Portland, Oregon, can take place outside but not inside the hospital. Interacting with pets releases the hormone oxytocin, which lowers blood pressure and brings an experience of well-being. Inpatients are sometimes allowed to be with pets from home that are brought to a hospital garden by family members. Designer: Ron Mah, David Evans Associates.

Courtesy of Legacy Health

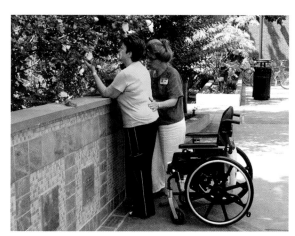

14.4 Horticultural therapist Teresia Hazen assists a patient who stands and examines a flower in the Stenzel Healing Garden, Good Samaritan Medical Center, Portland, Oregon.

Courtesy of Legacy Health

In contrast, the two case studies that follow represent gardens for rehabilitation patients where the original design included input from clinical staff, current and former patients, family members, and maintenance staff, and where ongoing maintenance supports the original design and therapeutic intent of the garden (fig. 14.3, fig. 14.4).

The Stenzel Healing Garden, Good Samaritan Medical Center, Portland, Oregon

Designer: Ron Mah, David Evans Associates, Portland, Oregon

Description of the Facility and Its History

In 1996, as local architects Mic and Connie Johnson were designing a new entry foyer for Good Samaritan Hospital, administrators set aside $14,000 to remove an asphalt parking lot adjacent to the entry and put in low-maintenance shrubs and concrete paths to facilitate movement between buildings. The group that helped create the Healing Garden—the Johnsons, landscape architect Ron Mah, and in-house horticultural therapist Teresia Hazen—discussed the proposal and concluded that much more could be done with this space than what the clients were asking for (Cooper Marcus 2003).

Mah's role on the design team was especially poignant. "My love of gardens began with my father," he recalls. "When I visited him during his last illness from a degenerative brain disease, he always wanted to go outside, but there was no garden, no shade—just some lawn where it was impossible to push a wheelchair. That memory has never left me. When the chance came to design a garden at Good Samaritan, I thought, here's my chance to create a usable hospital garden!" (ibid.).

After the first team meeting, Mah produced a concept plan for a healing garden that was soon refined. The Good Samaritan Foundation funded the needed $300,000, which was later supplemented by a gift from Frank R. Stenzel, MD, and Kathryn Stenzel, for whom the garden is named.

For a two-year period, a local specialty nursery in Portland was invited to provide a demonstration garden in a raised bed near the entry. This is a good model for other cash-strapped hospital gardens to consider: showcase a local nursery and get free plants in return. Many hospital gardens—and this one is no exception—not only must devise ways to fund planting but also must pay for maintenance. Hazen supervises maintenance of the Healing Garden, coordinating the work of contract gardeners trained in horticultural therapy and volunteers, including past patients—even those with brain injuries who can only perform simple watering tasks.

Design Philosophy

Hazen formed an interdisciplinary team of staff, patients, former patients, and community members to begin planning. As the original concept was refined, staff members who would use the garden in their work with patients provided input during three interdisciplinary design team meetings. (See chapter 5 for more details.) The clinical program drove the design. Staff members who worked with mobility-impaired patients asked for a variety of walking surfaces—gravel, a rubberized surface, and concrete scored in different patterns. Horticultural therapists needed places where patients could plant and water, so the edges of the raised planters were originally left unplanted.

In 1998, the Healing Garden at Good Samaritan received the Therapeutic Garden Design Award from the American Horticultural Therapy Association. After a July 2001 accreditation visit by the Joint Commission on Accreditation of Healthcare Organizations (JCAHO), the Healing Garden at Good Samaritan (and the Children's Garden at Legacy Emanuel) received special commendation "for achievements in demonstrating commitment to the psychosocial well-being of patients through such aspects of care as the patient gardens." This was the first such commendation for gardens in a hospital facility awarded by JCAHO.

Description of the Outdoor Space

The configuration of the garden includes two large and one smaller raised concrete planters, both richly planted; pathways, designed to slow people down, that curve around and between the planters; ground-level planting along the garden's southern edge; and a small plaza with seven garden benches at its western end. The height of the raised planters varies from 1 to 3 feet, while the planting design creates an appealing layered effect. Some planting segments are at eye level for a person in a wheelchair; others are low enough for a child to look down onto the details of color and texture (fig. 14.5).

With plants building up in tiers from the edges to the centers of the beds, two people looking at plants and labels on one side of the bed do not intrude on the personal space of other garden visitors who may be only a few feet away across the bed. This is a subtle but very significant element of planting design in a hospital garden, and the smaller the garden, the more important it is. In a public park, where people may be strolling through, the planting is rarely a topic of

14.5 The Stenzel Healing Garden. Entry from main hospital foyer, top right. A walking route (on the left) connects two city blocks and brings members of the public to the garden. The blue circle of rubberized material has been replaced with tinted concrete.
Courtesy of Legacy Health

14.6 Views to the garden can be enjoyed by those taking a break in the cafeteria.
Courtesy of Legacy Health

conversation, and for most it may merely be a green backdrop. In a hospital garden, however, many users are seeking distraction or looking for something to talk about. Plant selection, therefore, should be meticulous and labeling clear and informative. Varied heights, textures, colors, and seasonal growth habits should be carefully coordinated. The designers of the Stenzel Garden deserve high grades in this respect.

Within this relatively small site, a number of different theme sections were created: a perennial garden, a butterfly garden, a fragrant garden, a miniature rose garden, and two native plant gardens with Northwest species such as Pacific crabapple, Alaska weeping cedar, deer fern, and Oregon grape, all carefully labeled with common and Latin names and a few sentences on growth habits.

The designers avoided the cliché of planting medicinal herbs labeled with their therapeutic qualities (of dubious interest to those already swamped with medical information) and have taken the approach of using familiar garden favorites as well as Oregon natives—stimulating comments from visitors such as, "Do you remember seeing those on our hike last summer?"

How the Garden Is Used

The Stenzel Garden, widely recognized by the hospital community as an important therapeutic environment, is visible from the ground-floor cafeteria and is accessible via glass doors from the main foyer (fig. 14.6).

The garden is used for everything from physical and horticultural therapy to much-needed respite from the hospital environment—which, with its frightening diagnoses, painful treatments, and clinical sterility, can be extremely stressful. The director of pastoral care advises family members and ambulatory patients to go into the garden. "It gives people who are deeply anxious permission to relax, to feel a sense of life around them. They often go inside again with a renewed sense of hope." A physical therapist may encourage patients who have had strokes or brain injuries to walk up a gentle incline, to bend down to read plant labels, to recall the names of flowers they grow at home, and to negotiate a set of steps. "The garden can be a centering experience," agrees Vi Hansen, a clinical social worker who runs support groups and encourages patients and their families to use the garden.

The garden's simple design enables it to be enjoyed in a variety of ways. Close to the main hospital entrance, greenery and colorful banners draw people's attention to an attractive shrub-lined passageway that forms a midblock path from one street to another, and that passes by the garden. People who may have nothing to do with the hospital wander through, glancing at the plants, sometimes stopping to read the labels, and then walk on. This is a benefit also for patients who see people going about their daily business and thus feel less isolated from the world.

Staff and visitors carry their lunch out from the hospital cafeteria and settle at one of a row of picnic tables shaded by blue umbrellas in the northwest segment of the garden. Benches are well distributed and are of an attractive, traditional design: wooden slatted seats and backs, with metal arms.

Another value of a hospital garden is to provide a space where visiting children can run off steam. Something about the design of the garden at Good Samaritan fosters this behavior. Rarely do children enter this garden without setting off at a run as soon as they come into the space. Maybe it is the relief of being outside the hospital building, but probably it is also the skewed figure-eight pattern formed by the paths so that children can play hide-and-seek without parental concerns that they will run into the street.

Among the conversations most frequently overheard in the garden are those about the vegetation: people pointing out plants to each other, reading out labels, or expressing surprise at a plant they'd never seen before. When hospital staff or visitors take patients through the garden, discussing the plants and their names can be a stimulating and therapeutic topic of conversation, as well as a distraction from the latest treatment or test results. Physical therapists use the garden to encourage exercise and make use of the plant labels by asking patients to read them or to test their ability for recall—"Do you remember the name of the plant with bright yellow flowers?" (fig. 14.7)

A postoccupancy evaluation (Garcia 2009) found that visitors and staff were the two largest groups using the garden,

with much lower use by patients (alone or with family members staff). The limited use by patients is not an unusual finding, since many are either too sick to be brought outdoors or are in the hospital for a very limited stay. Half of all users spent up to fifteen minutes in the garden; approximately one-third were just passing through; and a small number spent more than fifteen minutes. The peak time of use was 11:30 a.m. to 12:30 p.m., when a large proportion of users were staff on their lunch break, with a lower peak between 4:30 p.m. and 5:30 p.m., when staff and visitors were still the predominant users, but patients and people passing through made up larger proportions than at any other time. The primary activities throughout the day were (in order of importance): socializing, looking at/interacting with plants, eating, sitting, reading, and using a wheelchair (individually or being pushed).

Key Garden Merits

- Planned and designed with input from therapy staff who use the garden to work with patients.

- Different planter heights allow for transfer from wheelchair, perching, leaning.

- Plant labels stimulate interest and conversation.

- Members of the public can pass by the garden, providing patients and the hospital with a link to the community.

- Different ground surfaces provide experience for those learning to walk again or use a wheelchair, scooter, or walker.

- Wide variety of plants provide seasonal interest and opportunities for horticultural therapy.

Possible Concerns

- A water feature would have been a restorative addition, but a proposed pool was eliminated for budgetary reasons.

- A longer path surfaced with gravel or dirt would be a good addition, since many patients come from rural areas and need to learn to walk again on familiar surfaces.

- A blue circle of rubberized material that had no particular functional purpose started to grow algae in the wet winter months, had to be treated with chemicals, and eventually was removed and replaced with tinted concrete.

- Gaps between bricks in the red brick paving near the garden entry are just wide enough to present a hazard for those using walkers or pulling IV poles.

14.7 A patient practices using her left hand while planting pansies in a raised bed at the Stenzel Healing Garden.
Courtesy Legacy Health

Oregon Burn Center Garden, Legacy Emanuel Medical Center, Portland, Oregon

Designer: Brian Bainnson, Quatrefoil, Inc., Portland, Oregon

Description of the Facility and Its History

The Oregon Burn Center provides care for people with burns and skin-destroying diseases. It is the only facility of its kind between Seattle, Washington, and Sacramento, California. The Center moved into its newly renovated facility in 2002, and a 9,000-square-foot therapeutic garden created in an existing courtyard was opened in 2004 at a cost of $25 per square foot. Legacy Emanuel was the first hospital in the United States to offer a therapeutic garden specifically for burn survivors.

Design Philosophy

Landscape Architect Brian Bainnson worked with a team of medical staff, current and former patients, and their families in a three-meeting process (programming, conceptual design, final master plan) facilitated by Legacy's horticultural therapist, Teresia Hazen, during the fall of 2003. This process, comprising one meeting a month for three months, was fine-tuned by Hazen when she was orchestrating the design of two earlier therapeutic gardens—the Healing Garden at Good Samaritan Hospital (Portland) and the Children's Garden at Legacy Emanuel (now know as Randall Children's Hospital). "Medical staff are busy people," Hazen has noted. "We don't want to impinge too much on their time, but it's essential we have their input. They are the people who know how a garden can help their patients, and who will eventually encourage patients and families to use it. Meetings are organized during paid time, and we need to schedule patient-care coverage to allow staff to come to these design meetings so we keep them organized and relatively short." (For more information on the three-meeting process, see chapter 4.)

In the first meeting, the team was introduced, the site was reviewed, and after brainstorming, preliminary goals were set. Bainnson then visited the unit and met with staff to educate himself further about clinical needs. At the second meeting, he solicited feedback on three possible designs and gave team members copies to discuss with their colleagues.

At the final meeting, the completed plan was presented and the team had food and drink to celebrate (always important in a participatory process). At this point, the design was ready to go out for fund-raising, which took six months. Among the chief donors were Portland General Electric Employee Giving Campaign, the International Brotherhood of Electrical Workers Local 125, and Emanuel Medical Center Volunteer Guild. In 2006, the Burn Center Garden received a Therapeutic Garden Design Award from the American Horticultural Therapy Association.

When Bainnson was asked at a presentation "Aren't all gardens therapeutic?" he responded,

> Not necessarily. A therapeutic garden functions as part of care, it supports the goals of the caregivers, it has a therapeutic role. . . . If horticulture therapists are going to work in and with the garden, they need to be consulted as to what plants they want to use. The design needs to be a strong enough structure to encompass changes over time, such as temporary additions. I've seen a Japanese garden at a hospital that was hardly used. It had gravel paths, steps without handrails, steep inclines. The staff worried about the safety of patients and did not encourage them to go. . . . It worked to look out at, but not to be in. The main problem with gardens which are supposed to be therapeutic but are not is that the staff [members] weren't involved in the initial design. They end up with a garden that they don't know how to use, that doesn't support their care-giving. They were not included as stakeholders.

The Burn Center Garden is an exemplary case of a healthcare outdoor space created with the needs of a particular patient group uppermost in mind and the views of clinical staff and patients incorporated into the design process. Even if designers themselves have experienced a particular illness, they cannot assume that their experiences and needs are universal (nor are they trained in clinical protocols). A participatory process involving clinical staff is essential, not least because once involved in decision making they are more likely to feel a sense of ownership of the garden, to cherish and care for it, and to encourage patients and visitors to experience it as a healing oasis (fig. 14.8).

Description of the Outdoor Space

The garden at the Oregon Burn Center is enclosed on two sides by a two-story building, with patient rooms on the first floor looking out on the garden. The other two sides are bounded by a ten-foot wall, its brick echoing the facade of the building. The garden has restricted access since burn patients are highly susceptible to infection and also benefit

14.8 Staff enjoying lunch in the garden under a shade structure.
Courtesy of Quatrefoil Inc.

from privacy and a secure setting to enhance their recovery and transition back to the community.

Shade is essential for those recovering from burns and skin graft healing. The garden incorporates two $5,000 shade structures with steel roofs (fire codes preclude the use of wood). Movable garden furniture creates attractive settings for physical therapists to work outside with patients and for visiting family groups to gather. The shade structures are open on three sides, and on the fourth side a mesh "wall" supports clematis and other climbing vines. A third shade structure—the Shadow Pergola, a sculptural piece designed by local artist Ean Eldred—forms a pleasing sculptural accent in the southeast corner of the garden, where Akebia grapes and other vines growing over the structure provide shade. To enhance evening use, lighting was added to the two shade structures and the pergola (fig. 14.9).

As well as shade, a garden for burn patients must provide a variety of walking surfaces and slopes since those recovering are often weak and need to rebuild strength and endurance. Walking surfaces provided in the garden include concrete pavers (with brick edging) around most of the garden; a gravel path through a rose arbor and halfway around a circular lawn; and the surface of the lawn itself, slightly mounded in the middle. Handrails assist patients along the path at the entry from the burn unit, and again along a central path. The entry sequence into the garden at its northwest corner has been sensitively designed. The concrete path slopes at a shallow incline so that a person with limited mobility can at least get to the end of the incline while holding onto the handrail. The ramp is wide enough to bring a patient outside on a bed or gurney with several staff in attendance. A canopy at the entry tempers the sometimes jarring contrast from interior to outdoor light levels and allows the garden to be entered even on rainy days.

For its relatively small size, the garden has a rich variety of plants. Midheight trees and tall shrubs—including Japanese stewartia, western dogwood, weeping sequoia, Full Moon Japanese maple, golden raindrop crabapple, Katsura trees, incense cedar, star magnolia, Italian cypress, butterfly bush, flowering currant, and pink-flowering styrax—provide a variety of shape, texture, height, spring blossoms, and fall color. A variety of perennials, including roses, penstemon, coral bells, lavender, rosemary, daylilies, New Zealand flax, peonies, hosta, Japanese anemone, sedum, and ornamental grasses create a rich palette of heights, massing, textures, and color. Excess storm water drains into three small bio-swales planted with Northwest native plants. A sprinkling of annuals—pansies, African marigolds, sweet peas—are planted at different seasons.

In the fall and winter, cool temperatures preclude much use of the garden, but a variety of color can still be viewed through the windows: maples, red-twig dogwood, oak-leaf hydrangea, small conifers, and splashes of yellow and white from variegated leaves in a predominantly green expanse. The large planter pots, handrails, and steel members of the shade structures add accents of blue.

A variety of seating options includes wooden benches with backs and arms at intervals along the pathways and clusters of easily movable molded plastic chairs for adults and children. Attractive wooden seats and a table are positioned under each of the two shade structures.

The pathway system, forming a rough figure-eight, along with the great variety of plant materials, provides a constantly changing vista for someone walking or seated in a wheelchair. Great care has been taken in providing garden users with a rich sensory experience, especially important for distracting patients from their pain and visitors from anxiety about their loved ones. Sounds include birds, chimes, and a small, bubbling fountain that it is not easy to touch, since the staff was concerned about infection control and patient safety.

There are many fragrant plants, which are often used by the staff to initiate conversation with patients, especially children, who comprise one-third of those in the facility. Taste has not been forgotten, and at the right season, people can "graze" in the garden. Large round blue planters filled with peas, blueberries, strawberries, and tomatoes are placed at the edge of the path, easy to access by a person using a wheelchair.

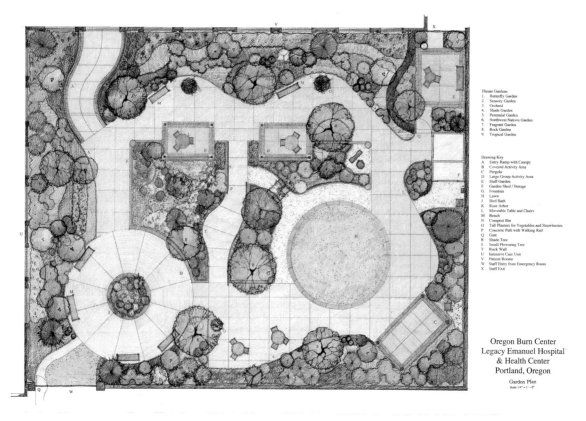

Theme Gardens
1. Butterfly Garden
2. Sensory Garden
3. Orchard
4. Shade Garden
5. Perennial Garden
6. Northwest Natives Garden
7. Fragrant Garden
8. Rock Garden
9. Tropical Garden

Drawing Key
A Entry Ramp with Canopy
B Covered Activity Area
C Pergola
D Large Group Activity Area
E Staff Garden
F Garden Shed / Storage
G Fountain
H Lawn
J Bird Bath
K Rose Arbor
L Moveable Table and Chairs
M Bench
N Compost Bin
O Tall Planters for Vegetables and Strawberries
P Concrete Path with Walking Rail
Q Gate
R Shade Tree
S Small Flowering Tree
T Rock Wall
U Intensive Care Unit
V Patient Rooms
W Staff Entry from Emergency Room
X Staff Exit

Oregon Burn Center
Legacy Emanuel Hospital
& Health Center
Portland, Oregon

Garden Plan
Scale 1/4" = 1' - 0"

14.9 Site plan of the Oregon Burn Center garden. Designer: Brian Bainnson, Quatrefoil, Inc.
Courtesy of Legacy Health

Plants such as lambs' ears and ornamental grasses are tempting to touch, as are the small bowls of succulents on top of each litter container, just the right height for someone in a wheelchair to examine. Thoughtful details such as these set this garden apart from the average hospital outdoor space.

The garden is maintained by a paid horticultural therapist for five hours of work a week and by HT volunteers for six hours a week. Irrigation repairs and power washing are managed by the Emanuel Facilities Department.

How the Garden Is Used

Bainnson initially had tall shrubs and perennials planted outside patient room windows to provide for privacy. But patients asked, "Why can't we see more of the garden?" and staff and visitors found that identifying plants and birds through the window was both calming and a great tool for conversation. The tall plants were removed or kept trimmed. Privacy in patient rooms turned out to be a nonissue. Sometimes patients in rooms that do not face the garden (half of the total) ask if they can move. The move is made if a room is available. A solarium or day room with views to the garden would have been a nice amenity for these patients. Some enjoy sitting in the hall entry looking out to the garden.

Observation of the garden in 2007 revealed that the shade structures were used by family groups visiting with patients in wheelchairs; by staff members conducting short meetings; and sometimes by a social worker discussing insurance forms with a patient or by an occupational therapist doing exercises with a patient (fig. 14.10).

A conversation with occupational therapist (OT) Don Reiner highlighted many of the benefits of this small but thoughtfully designed garden. He commented:

One of the best experiences I have with patients is bringing them out after many days or weeks in bed, maybe on a ventilator. It's very important to connect them with the real world again after the trauma of an accident and being bed-bound. In the scarring phase, patients' temperature regulation is disturbed, oil glands

14.10 Shade is essential in a garden serving patients who are recovering from burns and skin grafts.
Courtesy of Legacy Health

and collagen fibers are injured, and they are at risk for sunburn, so shade is essential. The garden is great in that respect. Also, the terrain challenges—the level paths, the gravel, the grass mound. I can take patients out for a turn around the garden when they're beginning to walk again. The aim here is to stabilize patients and then release them to their home, or to rehab or a nursing home. When they're able to walk around the garden unaided, they're ready to be released. (Cooper Marcus 2008)

Linda, a patient, had been in the unit two weeks when she observed, "Even though there are buildings all around, it feels like being in the woods out here, it's so peaceful and quiet. It's neat to walk around and look at the plants and find things in the big blue planters that you can eat, like peas, blueberries, and strawberries. I'll bring my family out here when they come to visit later today."

"For those who are unconscious (and some are kept in a medically induced coma for days or weeks), the garden may be the first view they wake up to," says Kathleen Johnson, an OT. "It is very calming for them to look out of the window and perhaps identify birds or plants they can see.... When the patient is stable enough, the doctor will write a prescription: 'Take them out in the garden.' They are often foggy from medication and trauma, and may have been on a ventilator. It helps them to be able to breathe fresh air again. I give them rosemary to smell, ask them to read some of the plant labels, give them choices" (fig. 14.11).

A visitors book on a table under a shade structure records user feedback on the garden. One visitor commented, "This garden gives me something to look forward to while staying here and being in such pain.... I can forget the pain for just a small while. Very therapeutic."

14.11 A patient accompanied by a physical therapist and a nurse pulling an IV pole enjoys the sights, sounds, and aromas of the garden after many weeks in a hospital bed.
Photo by Clare Cooper Marcus

Another visitor had this to say: "I love this garden. It is nice to sit and enjoy the fountain and all the different plants. At first I could only come out and sit. Then I started to walk a little, and each day I walked a little more. The garden made me want to walk more and more. It helped me to build up my endurance so I could go back home. I really like doing my horticultural and occupational therapy sessions watering plants with the hose."

When James, a registered nurse on the unit, was asked if he used the garden, he responded enthusiastically, "Absolutely! It's awesome out here, a place of release. I try to get the patients out of their rooms. They're so troubled by the pain, the medication, and worries over health insurance. Looking at everything and reading the plant labels stimulates conversation. Families too—I bring them out to talk to them. They're worried too, about the patient and how they're going to pay

14.12 An ambulatory patient enjoys eating her lunch in the garden and reading in the shade.
Courtesy of Legacy Health

14.13 A play firehouse helps child patients and their siblings deal with the trauma of being burned.
Courtesy of Legacy Health

for treatment. Before a patient is well enough to come outside, they're often flat on their back, and visitors have to stand to talk to them. They get tired."

In postoccupancy evaluation studies of hospital gardens, staff members are often found to be the prime users. The Burn Center Garden is no exception. The staff makes full use of the garden, both in working with patients and for their own relaxation. A private staff garden is located in the northeast corner of the garden, screened by a hedge and with its own private entry from the building (see fig. 6.6). James, the nurse, remarked: "I must have been out to this garden more than a hundred times, and every time I see something new. I stop to read the label and think—maybe I could grow that at home. My three little kids come for lunch sometimes, then we eat in the staff area. The whole garden is used in lots of ways. We've had receptions here, and sometimes musicians come to perform."

A patient recalled his first stay at the Oregon Burn Center after a serious accident. "To be inside, strapped down for twenty-three hours a day, is extremely stressful. Now I'm back for skin grafts. It took four days before I could even put my feet on the ground. It was a major accomplishment to get outside to the garden, even for a few minutes. But it was a great help. . . . Now I come out every day, even when the pain medication makes me feel nauseous. I'm a gardener at home. Every day I find another favorite spot here, another unusual plant to smell. I was out six times yesterday!" (fig. 14.12).

One-third of the patients in the burn unit are children, and their needs have not been forgotten in the garden. A

bright red fire hydrant is a distraction for children, who delight in turning on and off the three taps at different heights to fill watering cans that are left around the garden for them to play with. Because of infection concerns, visiting children under twelve are not allowed inside the Burn Center, so having something in the garden to engage them is important.

In 2012, a play firehouse a was added to the garden, donated and constructed by local Portland firefighters. Though it may seem a strange addition to remind children of the experience of being burned, playing at being firemen apparently helps them deal with the trauma of that event (especially when guided by clinical staff). They can put on firefighting clothing, and rolling out a hose provides education on fire safety and is used by PT and OT staff to gets arms stretching and muscles strengthened. The firehouse is also used with children or siblings of burn patients to understand what has happened and to deal with the experience of fire and the people who help the victims (fig. 14.13).

Key Garden Merits

- Garden design fully meets the needs of burn patients and the staff who work with them outdoors.

- A rich variety of plant materials and changing views in a relatively small site.

- Ample opportunities for families, staff, and patients to find places of privacy and shade in the garden.

- Attractive views from patient rooms adjacent to garden.

- Elements that engage children.

- Variety of seating options.

- Secluded staff-only area.

Some Possible Concerns

- Black steel gates, though necessary to limit access from the rest of the Legacy Emanuel campus, lend a somewhat jarring, prisonlike feel to the southeast corner of the garden.

- While the plant labels are engaging, in some places there may be almost too many labels, including those with donors' names or names of different segments of the garden. For some, too much "verbiage" can interfere with their enjoyment of a seminatural place.

- A cluster of birdhouses made of cast-off tools has been added since the original design. While three or four such birdhouses would have been charming, thirteen may be just too many.

References

Cooper Marcus, C. 2003. "Healing Havens: Two Hospital Gardens in Portland Win Awards for Therapeutic Values. *Landscape Architecture Magazine* 93 (8) August.

———. 2008. "For Burn Patients, a Place to Heal." *Landscape Architecture Magazine* 8 (4) April.

Davis, B. E. 2011. "Rooftop Hospital Gardens for Physical Therapy: A Post-Occupancy Evaluation." *Health Environments Research and Design* 4 (2): 14–43.

Garcia, Chris. 2009. "Post-occupancy Evaluation of Stenzel Healing Garden: Good Samaritan Hospital, Portland, OR." Unpublished manuscript.

CHAPTER 15

Restorative Gardens in Public Spaces

THE RECOGNITION OF NATURE'S RESTOR-ATIVE effects has prompted the creation of healing gardens in parks, botanical gardens, and other public and semipublic places in many parts of the world. This is a welcome development. People who are stressed or recovering from a period of physical or mental illness are not necessarily in a healthcare facility. For everyone seeking a place for quiet contemplation and contact with nature, restorative spaces in the public realm provide settings that can have significant health benefits.

For example, in Cottage Grove Park, West Seattle, Washington, a small meditation garden is dedicated to people recovering from substance abuse. At the Roman Catholic Cathedral of Oakland, California, a small garden has been created to honor those who have suffered sexual abuse. At Willard Middle School in Berkeley, California, a garden and labyrinth are used by students and the surrounding neighborhood. In two Seattle, Washington, parks, acupressure paths made of rounded rocks and pebbles of different sizes appeal to local immigrants from Southeast Asia, where such paths are often found in public places. The Singapore Botanical Garden includes a 6-acre (2.5 hectare) healing garden designed as a tranquil retreat that showcases more than five hundred plants used medicinally in Southeast Asia. The plants are laid out thematically as relating to component parts of the human body.

Within the Cleveland Botanical Garden in Cleveland, Ohio, the aim of the Elizabeth and Nona Evans Restorative Garden, designed by Dirtworks, PC, is to provide a setting where people of all abilities can learn and benefit from the positive role that plants play in our lives (Cleveland Botanical Garden 2013). Groups from nursing homes and veterans facilities and children with special needs such as autism and ADHD visit the garden, where the focus is on touching and smelling the plant material. The Contemplative Garden is a favorite place for visitors to linger. Flowers and fragrances are minimized and shades of green predominate. Yoga and tai chi classes take place on the lawn. Plants and water cascading down a high stone wall in the Demonstration/

Exploration Garden create a variety of opportunities for sensory engagement (fig. 15.1). Signs in the Horticultural Therapy Garden encourage visitors to touch and smell plants. A dozen varieties of basil growing at different heights allow visitors standing, or sitting in a wheelchair, to have the same experience of the fragrant plant at eye and nose level (see fig. 1.6).

The TKF Foundation has created over 150 "Open Spaces Sacred Spaces" in the New York-Philadelphia-Baltimore-Washington, DC, area. The foundation believes that when people are "beset with ever increasing stress and overwhelmed with technology, the need for open, sacred places in nature is more important than ever." Each space includes an iconic bench built from recycled wood by prison inmates. Beneath the bench a waterproof blank book and pen invite visitors to share their thoughts and reflections with each other (www.opensacred.org).

The Quiet Garden movement, started in the UK, has now spread to many parts of the world. The original impetus was a Christian minister who in 1992 saw the need for simple places of contemplation. People offered their private gardens as occasional places of retreat; unused churchyards—with the addition of benches and a welcoming sign—became places of quiet reflection for those who did not seek the busyness of a public park. The idea spread to schools, hospitals, and prisons. There are now more than three hundred such gardens in Europe, North America, India, Australia, and Africa—and the number is growing (Quiet Garden Trust 2010).

In rare cases, a hospital has spearheaded the development of a public park next to its facilities for the use of its patients and staff as well as the residents of the surrounding neighborhood. This is the case with Lake Beauty Park in Orlando, Florida, where a 3.5-acre park was opened in 2013 next to the auto- and building- dominated campus of Orlando Health. The park features an existing 2-acre lake, mature stands of bald cypress and live oak trees, a quarter mile of accessible waterside paths (including a boardwalk over open water), sun and shade seating for large and small groups, an open lawn, fountains, artistic shade structures, innovative stormwater

15.1 A visitor reaches out to touch the water in the Restorative Garden at the Cleveland Botanical Garden, Cleveland, Ohio.
Courtesy of Dirtworks, PC. Photo by Bruce Buck

planters, native plantings, and signage (fig. 15.2). There are views to the park's greenery from some patient rooms, public spaces, and offices on the medical campus, as well as for those driving by on an adjacent street. While users have to cross a street to access the park, there are crosswalks and a four-way stop at a major intersection.

These developments are an encouraging sign that restorative settings in nature are not only being embraced by

15.2 Lake Beauty Park, adjacent to Orlando Health Medical Center in Orlando, Florida, is a rare example of a healthcare facility promoting the development of a park for the use of its staff, visitors, and patients, as well as for the general public. Designer: AECOM Design + Planning. *Rendering by Alex Ottich.*

healthcare facilities but are also being recognized by society at large as places of preventive care. Featured below are case studies of garden plots in a public space for victims of torture; an enabling garden for people with disabilities sited in a botanical garden; a garden for people with Alzheimer's disease in a public park; a restorative landscape in a public park created by and for survivors of the AIDS epidemic; and a public healing garden as part of a healthcare campus. Elsewhere in this book are other case studies of spaces within healthcare settings where the public is welcome: a children's garden in New York City (chapter 7), a hospice garden in Sandpoint, Idaho (chapter 11), gardens at an alcohol and drug rehabilitation center in Rockford, Illinois (chapter 12), and a healing garden at a hospital in Portland, Oregon (chapter 14).

The Natural Growth Project, London, England

The Natural Growth Project is a component of the Medical Foundation for the Care of Victims of Torture, a charity in London, England, that provides free medical treatment, practical assistance, counseling, and psychotherapy to survivors of torture and organized violence (Freedom from Torture 2011). Most of the Natural Growth Project's clients come from the Middle East and Africa, the remainder from Europe, South America, and the Far East. Created in 1992, the Project set out to provide refugee-clients with a unique program of horticultural work and psychotherapy to help them adjust to a different culture, language, landscape, and climate.

The program sites consist of thirty community garden plots (allotments) at two locations in North London and a Remembrance Garden attached to the Foundation's main building. The team running the Project consists of two psychotherapists and one organic gardener.

The Remembrance Garden is a "working space for clients who are too physically disabled to cope with the work demanded by the allotments. Here clients work in a supportive and enclosed environment, meeting for a fixed session weekly to do light gardening work. They are asked to create things in the garden that will remind them of their past and help them to come to terms with it" (Linden and Grut 2002, 12).

The project focusing on gardening plots was initiated in response to the difficulties some clients had in expressing themselves in formal consulting rooms. However, many were "reminiscing about their past in their gardens or farms or fields back home with affection and even some joy. This was seen as one of the few 'good' memories they could hold among the many horrific and frightening memories that still plagued them daily" (ibid., 18).

Each of the thirty clients is given a 90-by-30-foot (30-by-10 meter) plot and a basic set of equipment—spade, fork, trowel, gloves, and boots. A small shed provided on each plot is often replaced by a larger structure, frequently constructed cooperatively out of recycled materials. With a carpet, a chair, and perhaps a place to brew tea, many of these simple structures come to symbolize "home"—a primal shelter, a place to rest or withdraw from the world, a place of security. Most clients visit their plots three times a week. The staff—a psychotherapist and a gardener—visit once a week. As the clients work alongside staff, they talk about their past: "Memories of terrible events are recounted as they struggle with couch grass and slugs and wind and rain. Being able to talk about their experiences in an open space, surrounded by trees and the sounds of nature, seems to help clients relax" (ibid., 71).

The psychotherapist uses metaphor and analogy to help clients get in touch with issues they have suppressed. "Parallels are drawn between the cycle of the natural world, with its successes and failures, and the world of the refugee client. . . . Many gardening words and expressions illustrate how steeped the language of cultivation is in the vocabulary of personal growth and nurture . . . : transplanting—uprooting—blossoming—putting down roots—cutting back—branching out—new growth—weeding out" (ibid., 42).

Typical participant responses include:

"It is the space and time I'm giving to myself on the land that has allowed me to clean my heart. . . . I believe that the work is holy."

"I call it my little bit of paradise. I lost everything—my country, my job in the hospital. . . . I was very sad. . . . When you work with fruit and vegetables you feel very glad, very calm. . . . It is better than medicine or tablets."

"This is our hospital, our hospital with a blue sky."

"Never in my life did I understand the meaning of the word "belong." My plot and shed belong to me. It is a palace, my shed, my room."

Clients remain in the project from one to six years. They learn more than the therapeutic act of gardening. They learn about number systems and vocabulary different from their own, forward planning, how to travel alone to their garden plot on public transportation, how to pay attention to TV weather forecasts, how to read and order from seed catalogs, and they gradually come to feel more at home in an initially alien land. At first, clients only want to grow crops from their home country, then often branch out to English varieties as they feel more settled. Clients remain in the project from one to six years.

The Buehler Enabling Garden, Chicago Botanic Garden, Glencoe, Illinois

Designer: Geoffrey Rausch, Architect

History of the Facility

For twenty years, a Learning Garden for the Disabled provided HT programs at the Chicago Botanic Garden, but it was located far from the main display gardens. In 1997 an interdisciplinary team was assembled to design an alternative space—the Buehler Enabling Garden—which opened in July 1999 (Chicago Botanic Garden 2013).

Design Philosophy

Guided by twenty years of experience with the Learning Garden and by the principles of Universal Design, the design team created an educational display garden to illustrate the best design for people of all abilities (Connell et al. 1999). The two-year planning process involved focus groups of

people with disabilities, HTs, and other caregivers to evaluate the design recommendations.

Description of the Garden

The Buehler Enabling Garden is located centrally within the Chicago Botanic Garden. As an educational display, the garden has three major components:

1. Physical features, plants, and a tool/equipment collection

2. Educational materials such as signs, brochures, and docent tours

3. Programs to increase understanding of how enabling gardens are used

The physical elements of the garden include three water features; a number of raised planting beds constructed of concrete with brick facing; five metal planting pans at various heights bolted to a brick wall; hanging baskets attached to pulley systems; a vertical wall planter; a raised planter with a metal grid overlay for use by the visually impaired; a tool shed; a small raised lawn designed for a wheelchair user to transfer onto the grass; a small, tucked away patio where staff can take a break or refreshments can be served to a visiting group; and brick paths (a minimum 5 feet wide) throughout the garden.

How the Garden Is Used

During spring, summer, and fall the colorful flowers and welcoming entry attract thousands of visitors into the garden, many of whom are not necessarily aware of its role as an educational exhibit space. Visitors also include people with disabilities who wish to continue (or start) gardening; they are either brought individually by family members or join a workshop or educational tour (fig. 15.3a).

A systematic evaluation of the use of the garden was conducted in 2001 (Rothert and Hammel 2002). Sixty-four subjects ranging in age from eighteen to ninety-one were recruited from local centers for independent living, senior centers, and the like throughout Chicago. Just under half reported physical impairments, approximately one-fourth reported a visual impairment, and another one-fourth had multiple impairments. All were independently mobile, including half who walked independently, one-fourth who used a mobility aid (cane, crutch, walker), and one-fourth who used a wheelchair or scooter.

On a 10-point scale, when participants were asked how important gardening was in their lives, the average rating was 7.2. The majority described themselves as moderately experienced or experts in gardening, but 70 percent reported they had given up some or all gardening activities. Reasons for wanting to garden included to take care of oneself (71 percent); to socialize (66 percent); to stay active (59 percent); to use/eat plants (57 percent); to relax (48 percent); and to maintain health (47 percent). The major barriers people reported that caused them difficulties in gardening were trouble stooping or kneeling (57 percent); trouble reaching (35 percent); trouble moving in the garden (34 percent); and issues with balance and fear of falling.

Those who did, or used to, garden remarked on its importance to them:

"If I couldn't garden I'd be depressed. . . . If I keep moving, my joints can't get stiff."

15.3a Raised beds and spring flowering bulbs at the Buehler Enabling Garden. The 10-inch wide sitting ledge proved uncomfortable for those who had to twist sideways to reach into the bed.
Photo by Clare Cooper Marcus

"I like the outdoors and the fresh air . . . just the beauty of it all. I think it's very good therapy . . ."

"It makes me feel alive and responsible and nurturing . . . and I like the results."

"I just like to be able to look outside and see something I had planted in the ground and watch it grow. To me that's an accomplishment . . ."

"Disability has made me very depressed . . . Gardening gave me a sense of accomplishment and it was therapy for me . . . It made me feel good about myself when I couldn't feel good about other things."

All subjects were asked to do simple gardening tasks using one or more of the enabling features. Each feature was found to have minor usability flaws. The significant findings were:

1. Raised beds with a 10″ wide sitting ledge proved uncomfortable for many who sat on the ledge or used a wheelchair and had to twist sideways to reach into the bed or stand and lean over the bed. Many found the bed too high (18″), which resulted in their feet not touching ground; or too wide (48″). However, the ledges on these beds were useful as seating by those who used the garden as a social space.

2. The metal pan beds at heights of 20″, 24″, or 27″ allowed for front sit/roll-under use, and fewer subjects reported problems with comfort or energy compared to the side-sit bed. But here the depth (front to back of the bed ranging from 34–48″) proved to be a problem in terms of reach and access. In addition, those using power wheelchairs or scooters could not completely roll under even the highest (27″) planting pan and had to sit sideways or bend forward (fig. 15.3b).

3. People appreciated the use of a hanging basket that could be lowered with a hand-crank mechanism to bring the plants up close. But some found getting the basket to the desired height difficult, especially when it was full.

4. A vertical wall planter 6′ × 6′ (and 1′ deep) with plants placed into holes in a plastic liner attached to lattice work evoked many positive responses. People found it novel and useful and enjoyed planting and relating to plants without the need to stoop or kneel. Wheelchair access was particularly easy, and those with visual impairments successfully used the grid as an orientation guide. The only problems related to reaching the top of the grid (62″ from ground level) or the bottom (14″ from ground level).

5. Seventeen people with visual impairments evaluated a 24″-high planting bed with a metal grid overlaying the 2′ × 13′ planting area into 1′ × 1′ squares. Some found the side-sit position uncomfortable but all enjoyed the grid-system planting. The majority was new to gardening and found the planting experience "fun" and "cool" (fig. 15.4).

6. The great majority appreciated the 5′ minimum brick pathways and sensory features of the garden, including the smell and feel of plants, and the accessible raised fountain beds and vertical water walls.

Of the features evaluated, most participants had never tried them before, and despite some problems most rated them as

15.3b Metal pan beds allow those using wheelchairs to roll under and work at planting tasks.
Photo by Clare Cooper Marcus

15.4 A metal grid overlaying a planting bed with 1-foot squares facilitates gardening for people with visual impairments.
Photo by Clare Cooper Marcus

easy to use. However, the majority said they would not try these features at home due to the expense, required space, or construction complexity. The study recommended information on features not as expensive or complex; more enabling gardens at community sites such as senior centers; and further research on user groups not included in the study, such as people with cognitive, developmental, and psychological disabilities, as well as children under eighteen.

It is understandable that many said they would not try similar enabling elements in their home garden. The design of the Buehler Garden appears rather grand and expensive, which makes for an attractive aesthetic but has limited its success as an educational display garden. To make up for this, raised beds and vertical wall systems that are available on the market and easy for the home gardener to obtain were added to the garden in 2013.

Certain features in the Buehler garden were not specifically evaluated in the 2001 study—some of which have been successful and some of which cause ongoing problems. Beds at 41" high with toe cutouts at the base have proved to be useful to optimize posture during stand-up gardening. Some of the raised beds are designed in an L-shape. The inside 90-degree angle makes it difficult to work in that area from any kind of wheelchair. The extreme contrast in color between limestone pavers denoting the three major areas of the garden and the predominant red brick is a problem for people with impaired or low vision who see the change in color as a depth change. The brick paving is a problem for other reasons: it gets slimy with algae around the base of the water walls, it absorbs heat and creates an "oven" effect in the garden in exceptionally hot weather, and staff constantly has to extract weeds out of the 11,000 square feet of cracks (Barbara Kreski, pers. comm., 2012).

CASE STUDY

Portland Memory Garden, Portland, Oregon

Designer: Brian Bainnson, Quatrefoil Inc., Portland, Oregon
By Patty Cassidy, HTR, president of the Friends of the Portland Memory Garden

Description and History

The Portland Memory Garden is a national demonstration garden project created as part of the "100 Parks, 100 Years" centennial celebration of the American Society of Landscape Architects (ASLA). Its creation was a collaboration involving the Oregon-Greater Idaho Chapter of the Alzheimer's Association, ASLA, the Center of Design for an Aging Society, Portland State University/School of Urban Studies and Planning, Legacy Health Systems, and Portland Parks and Recreation (PPR). Planning and design work began in 1998, and the garden was officially dedicated in 2002 (Friends of the Portland Memory Garden 2013).

Design Philosophy

The garden is designed specifically for people with Alzheimer's disease and other memory problems and is unique in that it is sited in a public park and is open to everyone. It is located in a low-income neighborhood of single-family houses. The site is relatively flat and is sited away from other park activity and significant traffic noise. One goal of the design was to allow caregivers respite while simultaneously providing a secure, sensorially stimulating, and peaceful environment for those with memory disorders who are brought to the garden.

Description of Outdoor Space

The quarter-acre garden is owned and partially maintained by PPR. Many mature Douglas fir trees on the site were preserved to provide shade and a sense of stability. The entry is marked by an attractive pavilion, and gates and fencing around the garden ensure that elderly visitors do not wander away. Tinted looped pathways offer a variety of ways to explore the garden. Six concrete raised beds at various heights are full of accessible plants, including herbs and annuals. Each bed is distinguished by an evergreen tree to give shape, color, and texture year-round (fig. 15.5). In-ground beds are planted with shrubs, perennials, and annuals, providing four-season color. At the far end of the garden, a clematis-covered arbor provides shade at a wheelchair-accessible picnic table—a good place for frail elders to have lunch and do crafts. Nearby are an accessible toilet and drinking fountain. Sturdy park benches offer places to rest, with a group of six in the inner circle of the garden for group conversation (fig. 15.6). An inner circle of grass provides for picnicking and barefoot walking.

How the Garden Is Used

Seniors and those with memory problems from both residential and day programs are brought on visits to the garden from late spring through early fall. A special grant offers free summer programs to senior communities by a horticultural therapist who provides appropriate activities and education in the garden. Typically, a group from a senior facility might come to the garden once a month and stay for an average of ninety

minutes. Family members with a relative with some form of dementia living at home also visit the garden.

Because it is a city park, the garden is open to everyone all year from dawn to dusk, and people come for picnics or quiet sitting. Neighbors who live in the vicinity use the garden

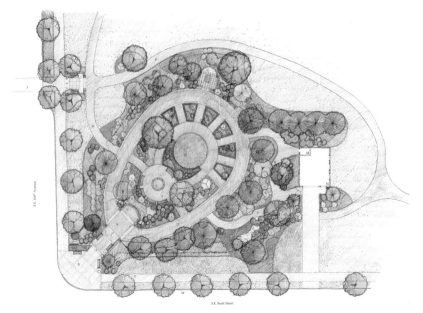

15.5 Portland Memory Garden site plan.
Image courtesy of Quatrefoil, Inc.

15.6 Raised beds at different heights encourage interaction with plants, while mature trees on the site were preserved to provide shade and a sense of stability. Comfortable benches offer a place for rest and socializing.
Photo by Clare Cooper Marcus

as part of their daily walking exercise. Dog-walkers use the space, and those who work in the nearby 911 call center often eat their lunch in the garden.

Since the garden is not staffed full-time, it is sometimes subject to vandalism, and dog-walkers do not always pick up after their pets.

The AIDS Memorial Grove, Golden Gate Park, San Francisco, California

History of the Grove

The creation of the National AIDS Memorial Grove (NAMG) had its beginnings in 1988, when six San Francisco area residents whose lives had been touched by AIDS conceived the idea of a living memorial (National AIDS Memorial Grove 2013). Discussions took place with the Recreation and Parks Department, which suggested the restoration of an existing area of Golden Gate Park—the De Laveaga Dell—as an appropriate site. Although overgrown with brambles and weeds, the site had great potential: its ravine-like topography created an enclosed setting, a central flat meadow provided a space where large gatherings might occur, and tall pines and redwoods provided a vegetative framework. An initial conceptual plan was developed by landscape architect William Peters, with input from the late Garrett Eckbo and local environmental consultants Isabel Wade and Alice Russell-Shapiro. Later a design charrette and then a master plan developed by landscape architects Michael Boland, Todd Cole, and Burt Tanoue and architect Ira Kurlander guided planting and construction. "We created the grove to be a vessel for a process as much as we were creating a place," says Boland. "Simply creating a beautiful landscape of contemplation and restoration was not enough. We actively sought to create a place where restoring a landscape also restored a community" (Cooper Marcus 2000).

After the official dedication of the site in September 1991, memorial services—both planned and spontaneous—began to occur. Certain areas became favorite places for these memorials, and small impromptu modifications, such as flowers or ribbons tied to trees, were left as personal marks on the landscape.

On Saturday mornings once a month, people came to the site to pull weeds, uproot brambles, plant shrubs, and share stories and food. Soon, in excess of five hundred people would show up. It was clear that people touched by the ravages of AIDS were keen to work on a project where their physical labor would help to assuage their anxiety and grief,

and where their work would result in the creation of a new public place where people could gather individually or collectively to reflect, remember, and mourn. Many community and school groups made the grove a focus of their service and volunteer programs, and the once-neglected valley became a place of activity and hope (fig. 15.7).

One of the few hotly debated issues in the design of the grove was whether or not to allow names to be displayed. At the early charrette, people felt strongly that this should not be a place where the names of those who had died would be recorded, but as the grove developed, with its own office, salaried staff, and board of directors, the need arose to raise funds, especially for a $1.5-milion endowment. Under the terms of an agreement with the city, the grove has to fund one gardener's salary in perpetuity and pay for annual repairs. "It seemed that the only way to raise money was to build structures . . . and to get people to pay for them," says William Peters. "I initially aimed for a softer approach, but in the end getting the grove established was what really mattered. This is not just a

15.7 Volunteers gather on a Saturday work day to help maintain the landscape of the AIDS Memorial Grove.
Photo by Clare Cooper Marcus

place to honor our friends, but a model of how to get part of an old city park restored" (ibid.).

In October 1996, by Act of Congress, the site was declared the National AIDS Memorial Grove. In 1999 it won the prestigious Rudy Bruner Award for Urban Excellence (see http://www.brunerfoundation.org/rba/index.php?page=1999/aidsmem).

In 2011, a one-hour documentary entitled *The Grove* received its premier in San Francisco and has since been shown on TV throughout the United States and at many film festivals.

Description of the Grove

Simple improvements and additions to the grove have created six subareas, each with its unique landscape features and experiences.

The Main Portal, at the meeting point of Middle Drive and Bowling Green Drive (two traffic arteries through the park) is marked by a seven-ton granite boulder with the words "AIDS Memorial Grove" inscribed into it, announcing the presence of the nearly hidden grove. A dirt and gravel path leads down a slope to the Meadow, while a concrete path with handrails provides an alternative route for those using wheelchairs or who are unsteady on their feet. This latter path leads into the Dogwood Crescent, a natural bowl at the eastern end of the grove that is marked by a semicircular, golden sandstone seating wall that embraces the Circle of Friends, where the names of friends and family who have died and those who have contributed to the grove's endowment fund are inscribed on flagstones in an ever-enlarging circle (fig. 15.8).

15.8 Names of those who have died of AIDS, and of donors, are inscribed in an ever-widening circle in the Circle of Friends.
Photo by Clare Cooper Marcus

A soft mulch path from the Dogwood Crescent leads past ferns and wild ginger into the Redwood Grove, where boulders and water-washed rocks mark the presence of a dry streambed. A tradition has developed of people taking rocks from the streambed and arranging them in delicately balanced sculptures on top of a number of granite boulders.

Throughout the grove there are places to sit and reflect, such as the Pine Crescent, situated halfway up the valley slope on its south-facing side. A set of stone steps leads to a semicircular sandstone seating wall where shrubs, trees, and the slope of the ravine all provide protection from the back, while the view is of a meadow below.

The grassy expanse of the Meadow, encompassing approximately one-fourth of the seven-acre site, provides the only flat, treeless part of the grove. Leading west from this space, two narrow dirt paths lead uphill, skirting both sides of a dry creek bed. A donation paid for the restoration of the stream and for the purchase of recycling pumps in 2011.

The two paths converge at the last of the grove's subareas, the Fern Grotto, a naturally bowl-shaped space that mirrors the Dogwood Crescent at the opposite end of the valley. Here, many elegant but decaying tree ferns had to be removed. A semicircular sandstone seating wall was added, and the slopes around the wall support a dense expanse of California live oaks and bay trees underplanted with native western sword fern and giant chain fern. A few of the old tree ferns and a massive fallen tree left in place create a sense of life and death in the primeval forest. The steps here, and at other locations in the grove, are built from recycled granite curbstones from the streets of San Francisco, some with faint traces of red-painted "No Parking" zones still visible.

How the Grove Is Used

Memorial gatherings are held at the Circle of Friends, where people also come for private reflection or to lay a flower over the name of a loved one. Monthly Saturday work days are a major activity, culminating in the noontime circle of remembrance in the Meadow, when people remember in silence friends and relatives who have died (fig. 15.9). This is followed by an informal picnic lunch. On World AIDS Day in early December, a large tent is erected in the Meadow for special ceremonies and fund-raising activities.

15.9 At the end of a workday people gather in the meadow to remember those who have died, while regular park activities—jogging, sunbathing, dog walking—continue alongside.
Photo by Mike Shriver

At other times people use the grove as they might any other park environment. On a mild August Sunday a young couple sits on a bench, talking softly while their baby sleeps in a stroller; two men groom a feisty golden retriever and then set off on a walk; a young woman with a backpack sits reading; a jogger pants by; an elderly couple, arm in arm, strolls slowly beside the Meadow; a woman sits eating a brown-bag lunch as a squirrel nearby waits for a handout; a young man on a bicycle stops at the Circle of Friends, stands reading the names for several minutes, and moves on; a group of seven young people spreads a blanket on the grass and settles down for a picnic. This is a place for everyone.

At no cost to the taxpayer, a public space has been beautifully renovated and reclaimed. While family or friends sometimes inter the ashes of a loved one at the grove, and inscriptions provide reminders of the AIDS epidemic, it is in no way a cemetery or a garden of remembrance. It is a seminatural setting, lush with ferns and redwoods, autumn-tinted maples, and spring-flowering bulbs. Its very creation and ongoing maintenance have provided participants with a restorative experience of collective action and a sense of purpose. The opportunity to make ephemeral modifications—notes tied to trees, small stacks of rocks, donated flowers—allows people to personalize this landscape in small but significant cathartic acts of healing.

CASE STUDY

Garden of Healing and Renewal, Clarkston, Michigan

Designer: Professional Engineering Associates, Inc. (PEA)
By Jeffrey T. Smith

Description and History

The Garden of Healing and Renewal is a four-acre public healing garden in Clarkston, Michigan, a northern suburb of Detroit. Although the garden is located on private property, it functions as a public space (PEA 2012). It is located within the McLaren Health Care Village, a 70-plus-acre healthcare campus that was master-planned to have a regional hospital for the McLaren Health Care Corporation, the McLaren Cancer Institute Cancer Center, and several medical office buildings.

Early concepts for a healing garden on the campus included providing a private patio-style garden connected to the cancer center or a courtyard garden within the future hospital. Neither of these early options was intended to be accessible to the general public.

During the planning process the landscape architect suggested that more effective therapeutic resources, benefiting a much broader user group, could be provided on a larger site than a patio or courtyard. Once it was decided to make the healing garden welcoming to the entire campus, it opened up the option to allow community access to the garden as well. In the end the decision was made to create a public healing garden for everyone to enjoy.

A prominent site within the campus was selected (fig. 15.10). This site had frontage on a public street and was connected to surrounding neighborhoods with a bike path and sidewalks.

The client did not want a lengthy design-by-committee process. The landscape architect prepared a concept for the garden, including a list of therapeutic resources, design solutions, and costs. This was presented to a panel of corporate executives; representatives from the marketing, legal, and facility departments; and representative doctors and nurses. The most significant change requested was a longer walking path for the staff. The local community planner requested a bike path through the site, but this was rejected in favor of a bike path to the entrance and the provision of bike racks. The response to the design in public hearings was largely positive and did not impact the final design. The Garden of Healing and Renewal formally opened to the public in the spring of 2009. The total cost was approximately $1 million ($750,000 for construction and approx. $250,000 for land), and funding came principally from the McLaren Health Care Corporation, which also maintains the park.

Design Philosophy

The design intent was to provide a restorative landscape to a broad user group, a welcoming feel to the public, and at the same time a safe, secure, and intimate place. Stress was the one ailment that everyone (hospital patients, visitors, and staff, as well as community members) would have in common, so the therapeutic resources provided were designed specifically for stress reduction.

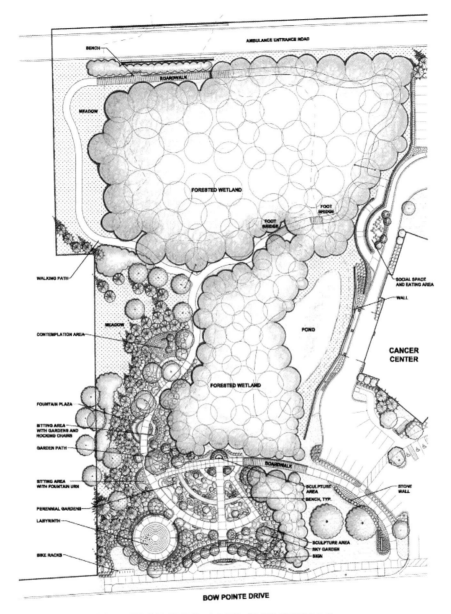

Labels within the site plan:

BENCH

AMBULANCE ENTRANCE ROAD

BOARDWALK

MEADOW

FORESTED WETLAND

FOOT BRIDGE

FOOT BRIDGE

WALKING PATH

MEADOW

CONTEMPLATION AREA

SOCIAL SPACE AND EATING AREA

WALL

POND

CANCER CENTER

FORESTED WETLAND

FOUNTAIN PLAZA

SITTING AREA WITH GARDENS AND ROCKING CHAIRS

GARDEN PATH

BOARDWALK

SITTING AREA WITH FOUNTAIN URN

SCULPTURE AREA

BENCH, TYP.

STONE WALL

PERENNIAL GARDENS

LABYRINTH

SCULPTURE AREA SKY GARDEN SIGN

BIKE RACKS

BOW POINTE DRIVE

GARDEN OF HEALING AND RENEWAL

Professional Engineering Associates, Inc.
Troy, Michigan / Howell, Michigan
Jeffrey T. Smith
Senior Landscape Architect
517-546-8583

15.10 Site plan of the Garden of Healing and Renewal.
Courtesy of Professional Engineering Associates, Inc.

Description of Outdoor Space

The four-acre garden site was originally a residential lot that contained wooded wetlands, upland forest, emergent wetlands, a small stream, and a pond. The house on the site was removed, and the natural features were incorporated into the design and utilized as part of the therapeutic resources. The site was designed as a series of "outdoor rooms" connected by pathways that wind through the landscape. The intent of each space is to provide a specific vehicle for stress reduction. The distinct spaces are spread out along a curved pathway designed to provide a visual link between each amenity area in order to continually draw people through the garden, thereby encouraging exercise. Seating and views are arranged so that dozens of people can utilize the garden at one time without losing a sense of privacy and intimacy (fig.15.11). The main public entrance to the site lies along Bow Pointe Drive and is well marked with a sign. It is 400 feet from the Clarkston Medical Group building and 200 feet from the front door of the cancer center, both of which have good views of the garden.

15.11 Hospital staff members enjoy walking in the garden during breaks or after work. Patients rest in the garden after a doctor visit. Families of patients and members of the public enjoy the colorful garden setting. *Copyright Jeffrey T. Smith*

How the Garden Is Used

The garden uses can be broken into categories based on the three primary user groups of healthcare providers (staff), patients and family members, and the community at large.

Healthcare providers

- Walk in small groups or alone, during breaks or before or after work. Some are clearly walking for fitness and some more for casual conversation.

- Eat lunch, alone or in groups, at the rocking benches by the main fountain.

- Gather for staff meetings at the tables and chairs located at a patio area adjacent to the cancer center.

Healthcare patients

- Walk the seven-circuit labyrinth or meditate in the garden before and after their chemotherapy or radiation treatment at the cancer center.

- Visit the garden to sit on the benches and relax after a doctor's visit. Healthcare providers inform patients about the garden, and they often visit after their appointments. Since these visits are usually unplanned, they are often quite short.

- Family members of patients will wait in the garden, sometimes even napping on the garden benches, while their loved ones are at their appointments.

Community members

- Local and regional garden clubs, landscape associations, and cancer support groups tour the garden.

- A group of local businessmen and women regularly eat lunch in the garden.

- A local resident who lives nearby walks the garden nearly every day with his dog.

- A group of seniors meet weekly in the garden to enjoy the plants. They walk the paths and then sit and visit.

- Photographers have used the gardens to take high school senior photos and family photos.

References

Chicago Botanic Garden. 2013. "Education: Horticultural Therapy Services: The Buehler Enabling Garden." Chicago Botanic Garden. www.chicagobotanic.org/therapy/buehler_garden.php.

Cleveland Botanical Garden. 2013. "Rejuvenate Yourself: The Elizabeth and Nona Evans Restorative Garden Lets You Feel the Gentle Healing Power of Nature." Chicago Botanical Garden. www.cbgarden.org/come-visit/collection-gardens/elizabeth-and-nona-evans-restorative-garden.aspx.

Connell, B. R., M. Jones, R. Mace, J. Mueller, A. Mullick, E. Ostroff, J. Sanford, E. Steinfeld, M. Story, and G. Vanderheiden. 1997. *The Principles of Universal Design.* Raleigh, NC: North Carolina State University, the Center for Universal Design.

Cooper Marcus, C. 2000. "Act of Healing: At the National AIDS Memorial Grove, Restoring a Landscape Has Helped Comfort and Restore Those Touched by AIDS." *Landscape Architecture Magazine* 90 (11).

Freedom from Torture. 2011. "Freedom from Torture: Medical Foundation for the Care of Victims of Torture." Freedom from Torture. www.freedomfromtorture.org.

Friends of the Portland Memory Garden. 2013. "Friends of the Portland Memory Garden." Portland Parks and Recreation. www.portlandmemorygarden.org.

Linden, S., and J. Brut. 2002. *The Healing Fields: Working with Psychotherapy and Nature to Rebuild Shattered Lives.* London: Frances Lincoln Ltd.

National AIDS Memorial Grove. 2013. "The National AIDS Memorial Grove: A Living Tribute to All Lives Touched by AIDS." National AIDS Memorial Grove. www.aidsmemorial.org.

Nature Sacred. 2013. Open Voices blog. Nature Sacred website: www.NatureSacred.org.

PEA (Professional Engineering Associates, Inc.). 2012. "Garden of Healing and Renewal: Independence Township, MI: Professional Engineering Associates, Inc. www.peainc.com/Project_Sheets/Garden_Healing.html.

Quiet Garden Trust. 2010. "Quiet Garden Movement." Quiet Garden Trust. www.quietgarden.org.

Rothert, E., and J. Hammel. 2002. *Evaluation of the Buehler Enabling Garden: Final Project Report.* Chicago: Chicago Botanic Garden.

CHAPTER 16

Horticultural Therapy and Healthcare Garden Design

Teresia Hazen, Coordinator of Therapeutic Gardens,
Legacy Health, Portland, Oregon

THIS CHAPTER PRESENTS AN OVERVIEW OF THE profession of horticultural therapy (HT), including the benefits of engagement in horticulture activities directed by a trained professional through horticultural therapy treatments, therapeutic horticulture activities, and vocational horticulture programs. Training requirements and work roles are described. Program settings and the four types of HT programs are described through sample programs from around the world (table 16.1). Interdisciplinary collaborations highlight the value of trained professionals in quality and value-added programming. Finally, design guidelines for the creation of gardens for HT are noted.

The American Horticultural Therapy Association (AHTA) recognizes that over the past decade, many people have become aware of the positive benefits of human interaction with plants and gardens. The recent surge of interest in this relationship, in combination with a substantial increase of horticultural activities in treatment programs, has resulted in numerous terms for these programs and activities, such as "therapeutic horticulture," "garden therapy," "social horticulture," and "therapeutic gardening," to name a few. Because these terms are used interchangeably, "horticultural therapy" has often been used as the catch-all phrase. However, there are some crucial differences between these terms. To increase understanding of the profession, AHTA (2007) developed definitions and terms associated with people-plant relationships and HT.

Types of Programs

AHTA recognizes four types of garden programs, three of which require trained professionals.

With programs in nearly every type of social service and healthcare setting, treatment approaches to meet the needs of patients, residents, and clients are also varied (AHTA 2007).

HTs lead, direct, and manage all of the above or a combination of types of programs in one facility/agency or multiple agencies, as employees or as private consultants.

Horticultural therapy is the "engagement of a client in horticultural activities facilitated by a trained therapist to achieve specific and documented treatment goals" (ibid., 1). This is a medical model and generally occurs in hospitals, rehabilitation centers, long-term-care nursing facilities, psychiatric programs, and special education programs (fig. 16.1).

Therapeutic horticulture (TH) is a "process that uses plants and plant-related activities through which participants strive to improve their well-being through active or passive involvement" (ibid.). In a therapeutic horticulture program, goals are not clinically defined and documented. However, the HT will have training in the use of horticulture as a medium for human well-being (ibid.). This type of program may be found in a wide variety of healthcare, rehabilitative, and residential settings and in day programs. TH programs are likely to serve the largest number of clients of all programs due to increased numbers of senior-living settings and resident history of gardening.

Vocational horticulture programs "focus on providing training that enables individuals to work in the horticulture industry professionally, either independently or semi-independently" (ibid., 2). These individuals may or may not have some type of disability. Vocational horticultural programs are found in schools, residential facilities, rehabilitation facilities, and correctional programs (ibid.). In school settings, students obtain prevocational and vocational skills. Sheltered workshops offer training and work opportunities in nurseries, greenhouse businesses, community gardens, food production, and sales. In prisons and correctional programs, inmates gain job skills.

Social horticulture, sometimes referred to as *community horticulture*, is a "recreational activity related to plants and

Table 16.1 Horticultural Therapy Program Types

Program Type	Leader	Models	Focus/Goal for Patient/Client
Horticultural therapy	Trained professional	Rehabilitation	Recovery from illness or injury
Therapeutic horticulture	Trained professional	Wellness	Quality of life, well-being
Vocational horticulture	Trained professional	Training	Employment
Social horticulture	Group or a member	Wellness, well-being	Leisure and recreational activity

gardening" (ibid., 1). No treatment goals are defined, no HT is present, and the focus is on social interaction and community engagement through horticulture activities. Therapeutic benefit is determined by participants' personal goals. Community gardens, local garden clubs, casual gatherings of gardeners, and garden workshops are examples of social horticulture settings.

Thrive, a national charity and gardening program in the United Kingdom, for example, promotes gardening to help improve the lives of people with disabilities. Thrive, in conjunction with over six hundred garden projects in the UK, provides social and therapeutic programs with a focus on the benefits of gardening to individuals and organizations. It also teaches techniques and practical applications so that anyone with a disability can take part in and enjoy gardening (Thrive 2012).

Professional Training

Horticultural therapists are trained professionals who involve the client in any phase of gardening—from propagation to selling products—as a means of bringing about improvement in the client's life. As members of treatment or care teams, HTs determine individual goals and create work plans to help clients improve their skills and maximize abilities (AHTA 2007). In 2008, AHTA outlined the first training core curriculum, consisting of three course areas for college course work.

Horticultural therapy specialization courses include HT techniques and special needs populations; HT programming (assessment, goal planning, activity planning, task analysis); program funding; and research and grant writing.

Horticulture sciences specialization courses include plant propagation; greenhouse or nursery production/management; botany; soil science; entomology; integrated pest management; plant pathology/physiology; and landscape design and floral design.

Human sciences include psychology, sociology, group dynamics, vocational rehabilitation, special education, recreation/therapeutic skills and services, anatomy/physiology, sign language, CPR, and crisis intervention college course work.

Upon completion of the core curriculum, HT students may apply for AHTA voluntary professional registration at a level of registered horticultural therapist (HTR). Licensing and certification are not currently required for one to be an HT; however, AHTA recently announced study goals regarding certification testing as part of the continued advancement of the profession (Starling 2011).

In the United States, many universities, colleges, and community colleges offer core classes for the HT curriculum, and some colleges offer degree programs. Thrive, in the UK, offers training workshops and college course work. The Asia Pacific Association of Therapeutic Horticulture (APATH) conducts training events and registers members. The Hong Kong Association of Therapeutic Horticulture provides course work and supervision of HT students. Since 2003, the Japan Society for Therapists of Horticulture NPO has trained students in HT and therapeutic and vocational programming.

Influences on the Development of HT

HT has evolved from its use by volunteer gardeners in the mid-twentieth century to become a recognized and respected therapeutic modality conducted by trained, registered professionals (Haller and Kramer 2006). In the 1940s and 1950s, garden club members served as activity leaders, paving the way for formation of the National Council for Therapy and Rehabilitation through Horticulture (NCTRH) in 1973. The name was changed to the American Horticultural Therapy Association in 1988.

16.1 Horticultural therapist Kirk Hines works with a client in the greenhouse at the geriatric facility Wesley Woods-Emory Healthcare in Atlanta, Georgia.
Photo courtesy of The Foundation of Wesley Woods. Billy Howard, photographer

The HT profession has borrowed from the principles and techniques of many disciplines, including psychiatry, rehabilitation, occupational therapy (OT), social work, psychology, recreational therapy (RT), environmental psychology, gerontology, human development, and others, to enrich the profession's scope (Davis 1998). A wide range of knowledge in many allied areas is essential to aid the HT in using horticulture, nature, and gardens for therapeutic purposes.

Roles of the Horticultural Therapist

Professional HTs perform numerous roles, including therapist, educator, consultant, designer, product developer, and writer (Relf 1999). They also engage the community through public and community relations and marketing strategies. As researchers and promoters of research, HTs help build the evidence base to support continued development of professional

16.2 Horticultural therapist Teresia Hazen teaches a patient to use a rake in order to strengthen her arms.
Courtesy of Legacy Health

services in health and human service settings. In the horticulturist role, professionals are responsible for well-maintained indoor and outdoor plant collections to support the therapeutic program. As fundraising team members, they help ensure program sustainability. Finally, HTs are pivotal as team members in promoting collaborative work and creative problem solving.

Program Settings

Indoor and outdoor settings are programmed by the HT for year-round use. Many successful HT programs utilize indoor spaces for activities such as craft projects, floral design, and plant propagation. A typical indoor treatment room might include a work table for individual and group work, doors for privacy, a counter or table with supplemental lighting for the houseplant collection, storage area for supplies, a sink, and a desk for staff (Airhart and Airhart 1998; Haller 1998). Outdoor garden settings evoke and reinforce a wide array of positive responses through growing, maintaining, harvesting, and observing plants and the garden through the seasons (Kavanagh 1998) (fig. 16.2).

Evidence Base for HT

Claims of the therapeutic value of horticulture can be found as far back as ancient Egypt (Shoemaker 2002). More recently, the positive effects of HT on mood and heart rate in patients participating in an inpatient cardiopulmonary

rehabilitation program were documented at New York University Medical Center (Wichrowski et al. 2005). Older adults in a horticulture activity program in Japan demonstrated a significant increase in "psychological well-being" in a group of long-term-care residents who participated in indoor horticulture activities (Yamane et al. 2004). A study in a psychiatric state hospital, Langenfeld Country Hospital in Germany, outlines the therapeutic benefits of the use of gardening in psychiatry, some of which include responsibility, communication skills, better response to work obligations, improved contact with others, continuity, perseverance, and stamina (Neuberger 2008). A corrections study reports the development of a horticultural program at a women's prison in South Korea and its effective impact on lowering measures of anger among female inmates (Lee, Suh, and Lee 2008).

Despite the growing research on healthcare gardens and HT, many knowledge gaps remain. Rigorous research on the clinical health benefits of gardens and HT programs is past due. In the meantime, research related to meaningful activity, motivation theory, pain management, exercise and movement, nature distraction, leisure benefits, quality of life, and therapeutic recreation make important contributions to support HT interventions.

Design Guidelines for the HT Garden

A purposeful horticultural therapy garden is an outdoor setting that provides distinct opportunities for the therapist to shape the therapeutic opportunities in the garden (HT modality) and for the patient to experience a variety of stimuli drawing from the richness of garden environments. As a specialized landscape, the HT garden may include different facilities and activities within its boundaries (fig. 16.3). However, the common goal of improving the physical, cognitive, psychosocial, and spiritual well-being of clients through horticultural activities and experiences suggests some common features (Kavanagh 1998). Healthcare design, research, and administrative professionals continue to define and establish HT and therapeutic garden "best practices" to this end.

There is no substitute for interdisciplinary input and collaboration if the garden program is intended as a therapeutic intervention for special-needs clients. Program and therapy leaders and the designer will engage in problem-solving issues as needed. Programs require very different elements and features to serve different users (e.g., hospitalized children, adult rehabilitation for patients in their twenties with brain injuries,

16.3 Beds and containers at various heights in the Stenzel Healing Garden, Good Samaritan Medical Center, Portland, Oregon, allow patients who are standing or who use a wheelchair to engage in simple gardening tasks.
Courtesy of Legacy Health

frail elders in a residential social-recreational program, or inmates in a prison vocational program for greenhouse production work). A checklist approach cannot substitute for collaboration with the site's specific interdisciplinary program team. Furthermore, one must design beyond the Americans with Disabilities Act (2010) Standards for Accessibility Design, which are only minimums and do not meet the needs of many special-needs clients. This advanced level of program-specific design is required to ensure client engagement and success.

Programming HT-specific environments
Required
1. **Use the AHTA Therapeutic Garden Characteristics (TGC) and Universal Design principles as guides in design work**. The board of directors of the AHTA adopted the TGC

guidelines in 1995. These descriptive characteristics identify the shared traits of gardens serving different special-needs populations in a variety of programs and climates. Topic areas include accessibility, programmed activities, boundaries, people-plant interactions, supportive conditions, and recognizable placemaking. Therapeutic gardens are most often intended to enable and serve people having a wide variety of abilities and disabilities. Such gardens are designed using the principles of universal design, which enable all garden visitors and users to share a common garden experience and to enjoy the garden at their own pace, on their own time, in their own way (Kavanagh 1998). The full text of each document can be found in Kavanagh (1998) and on the AHTA website (http://ahta.org/sites/default/files/attached_documents/TherapeuticGardenChracteristic_1.pdf).

2. **Raise some of the garden up to the gardener**. Raised beds of several heights can address the needs of a variety of client heights (in an adult group there may be a person 4′2″ tall seated in a wheelchair and a 6′8″ tall person using a front-wheeled walker). Heights of beds may range 12–48″ and will be determined by therapy goals and client needs and abilities. A person using a wheelchair may prefer an 18″ or 24″ wall height for improved reach. A patient while standing may find the 36–48″ raised bed more comfortable because she or he can lean against the wall for support. It is essential to provide a variety of raised bed heights in any single garden. Clients will generally be able to reach a maximum of 24″ into the bed for comfortable working. Roll-under beds are an option that allows the wheelchair user to wheel straight into a workstation; however, these beds are more expensive to construct. Roll-under beds usually allow for a few inches of potting mix, which will support only some shorter-height annuals. Unless the tray is properly sealed, a frequent issue is water drainage onto the client. Some roll-under beds have been constructed from metal; however, as temperatures increase, the bed is often hot to touch and may even be too warm for plant root growth. Sit-side beds are common, easy to construct, and meet client needs in most cases. Sit-side beds and groupings of containers tend to be more available when clients return home. Some rehabilitation clients dealing with spinal cord and other neurologic disorders may need to avoid twisting to the side. The client's physician will make these determinations and advise clients. In this case, working forward at containers of proper height for the patient should meet his or her needs. Another major variable to address is the wide range of sizes and heights of electric wheelchairs now being used.

3. **Containers in a variety of sizes and heights address program needs**. The garden population and program needs determine how many and what type of plants will be grown in containers. Material can range from wood to steel to plastic. For example, a day program in a senior residence may need several plastic containers for the patio; an adult physical rehabilitation setting might require six to eight differently sized containers of various materials to use as teaching pieces in educating the stroke patient in adaptive strategies for home. Since accessibility will be an issue, very large planters must be high enough to reach easily from a seated position or must be securely elevated on some type of structure that raises the pot to within the reach of a seated person. The Oregon Burn Center, Portland, Oregon, has two 48″ containers where patients stand to pick strawberries, harvest green peas on a teepee trellis, and interact with various herbs. Containers generally range 18–24″ high for seated work to 48″ high for standing work (Haas, Simson, and Stevenson 1998; Hazen 1997). **Locate containers in a grouping near the watering source and active work area**. Teaching recreational activities for meaningful leisure at home is an important program goal. Container gardens help promote this teaching (Hazen 1997; Haas, Simson, and Stevenson 1998).

4. **Vertical gardening options promote sitting and standing work**. These can be as simple as a teepee trellis in a container, a purchased trellis in a ground bed, or a constructed vertical wall garden (fig. 16.4). The Chicago Botanic Garden Horticultural Therapy Services is another resource for more detailed information about vertical gardening, raised-bed gardening, container gardening, paving alternatives, universal design, and other HT-related topics (www.chicagobotanic.org/therapy/).

16.4 A vertical gardening bed allows clients of varying heights to reach plants. Vertical gardens are also good design elements for creating privacy and shaping space within the garden. Designer: Hitchcock Design Group.
Photo by Naomi Sachs

5. **Ground-level planting supports physical engagement**, including plants to smell, touch, and grasp or pick from a wheelchair, recliner chair, or gurney. A blueberry plant or sunflowers at ground level at the hardscape edge support hands-on activity and may be the only option where raised beds are not yet available because of budget or other constraints. Ground bed plant materials are selected for visual, tactile, olfactory, and gustatory sensations and need to be sited for optimal engagement.

6. **Avoid toxic plants and other potential toxins**. While child patients are required to be supervised by adults (family or therapist), their creative discovery and exploration needs may put them at risk. For example, rhododendrons should not be used in a children's garden (see chapter 17 for a discussion of toxic plants). The plant world provides a rich and diverse palette from which to choose plants that are safe.

7. **A collection of well-maintained trees, shrubs, and flowers is necessary**. Four seasons of growth support the therapeutic program year-round. While clients participate outdoors, weather permitting, **seasonal plant materials** from the garden are essential for the indoor therapy program.

8. **Lockable storage** for gardening tools, hoses, carts, potting mix, pots, and other supplies should be located close to the group workspace. Program goals determine how the storage is organized.

9. **The work place for garden projects requires a table and appropriate chairs and seating area for a small group**. A **sink** is essential for hand washing, project work, and cleaning up. The work place requires adequate space to accommodate the group size and a variety of mobility devices, including four-pronged canes, manual wheelchairs, and a variety of power chairs. Occasionally, there may be a need to accommodate a standing frame for physical therapy co-treatment while engaged in a standing gardening activity. A current trend requires planning the space to include bariatric equipment (increased wheelchair size and chair size, for example). When the wheelchair does not align with the group table height, a bedside table or other adjustable table serves as an adaptive device. This type of problem solving is an assist to physical rehabilitation clients as they plan for return to their community and home setting. **The active HT treatment area may need to be located away from the main pathways** if the garden is used by visitors and employees at the same time as patient treatment activities.

10. Watering is a pleasurable and functional treatment activity. **The watering system should be easily accessible for client use**. Short hoses (25 feet or shorter and one-half inch in diameter) are easier, lighter, and safer to manage. Locate hose bibs to reduce the need for hoses to cross walkways. Otherwise, they may create trip hazards and limit wheelchair users. Install hose bibs on vertical risers because of decreased client ability to bend to the ground. Lever handles increase accessibility.

11. **Protection from sun, rain, and wind is essential** to client comfort and maximization of the garden setting for therapy Weather protection can be provided with wind sails, tents, pavilions, or other overhead covering.

12. **Access to restrooms and drinking water close to the therapy setting** maximizes therapy time and reduces client anxiety about restroom facilities.

13. Where possible, **plan and develop views out to the garden** from the indoors or a porch. This assists with supervision if clients are alone in the garden or if a therapist working with a group might benefit from additional oversight and assistance. Garden views help promote the program and may assist in motivating clients who experience emotional and social challenges.

14. **Safety and security for clients and program materials**: The garden design must protect vulnerable patients from wandering away. This may be achieved through the garden's location, by its arrangement of gates/doors, or by secure fencing or enclosure. Security for program materials, supplies, and furnishings must be addressed in the design.

15. **Maximize the garden investment**. It is possible to use a garden for therapy and at the same time as a restorative place for other clients, visitors, and employees. Well-designed gardens can meet many program needs. The Stenzel Healing Garden at Legacy Good Samaritan Medical Center, Portland, Oregon, was designed to be used concurrently by all rehabilitation therapists (PT, OT, SLP, HT, etc.), families, employees, and local neighbors. The Olson Family Garden at St. Louis Children's Hospital, St. Louis, Missouri is used extensively by patients, families, staff members, and for horticultural therapy activities (fig. 16.5).

16. **Design for as inclusive an area as the clinical program requires and allows**. For example, if grandchildren are encouraged to visit in a skilled nursing facility, an appropriate play area should be incorporated. Usually intensive-care and acute-care psychiatric units do not allow family members

16.5 A teenage patient in the Olson Family Garden at St. Louis Children's Hospital, St. Louis, Missouri, takes part in a horticultural therapy program.

Photo by Gary Wangler

on the medical unit or in the therapeutic garden area (which is a treatment area). They may be required to meet with the patient only in a specified family visiting room. In this case there would not be a need to design for a visiting children's play place.

Recommended

1. A **gathering space** for a large group activity, programs, celebrations, and social activities for clients as part of the therapeutic program.

2. A **greenhouse, atrium, conservatory, or screened porch** is a component for some programs. Greenhouses require a professional to maintain quality plant material, sanitation practices, and equipment and to plan the ongoing rotation and propagation of crops and plants. A conservatory or atrium may also require professional management. Short lengths of stay and the seriously acute condition of most hospital patients may not support active patient engagement in plant propagation in these more costly settings. A simple interior treatment room (plant room) close to patient rooms may meet program goals and work well when supplemented by the outdoor garden, weather permitting. Some populations and diagnoses require additional aspects of attention in design planning. Simson and Strauss (1998) dedicate a full chapter to each of several special needs populations regarding goals for programming, design, and adaptations for therapy.

Programming for children with special needs
Required

1. **Therapeutic garden enhancements for autism spectrum disorder in early childhood programs may aid in reducing stress**. The clinical team must be active leaders in collaborating with designers to help avoid causing additional distress to the children involved. There are specific design and program elements that address motivation and social needs (Flick 2012).

2. **Infection control and water-treatment protocols must be addressed** with the infection control officer to meet the safety requirements of the facility. For example, hospitals do not permit misting-fogging systems in most pediatric hospital garden settings because of the bacteria *Legionella pneumophila*, which can be aerosolized from contaminated water and cause Legionnaires' disease. Contact with soil and other water sources are determined by physicians when they write orders for patients to allow time outdoors, engagement in plant related activities, and other activities (fig. 16.6).

3. **Terminology is important for conveying safety meanings**. Avoid stating that "everything is edible or nontoxic" in the garden. Eating several pounds of lettuce or soil may cause distress. Standard safety protocol requires teaching children to check in with the supervising adult to "ask before putting anything in your mouth."

Programming for frail elders in long-term-care facilities
Recommended

1. **Site the HT activity area close to the building**, thus reducing amount of effort and time needed to get to the activity.

2. **Design for a range of simple but meaningful activities** such as long and short wheelchair loop walks through the garden, planting and tending tomatoes in a raised bed, deadheading the container flowers on the patio, or filling bird feeders (Hazen and McManus 2012).

3. **Safety and security**: A locked area protects patients from wandering away. Limit views to the street and busy activity to decrease distraction and opportunities for elopement.

4. **A simple, easily comprehended environment with limited choices supports the client in acute-care brain injury** medical stabilization and therapies. This stage requires one-to-one treatments (usually no groups) with the therapist.

16.6 Girls repotting plants in the garden at Rusk Institute of Rehabilitation Medicine, New York City.
Photo by Gwenn Fried

Funding

The funding of HT programs is as varied as the populations served. Experienced HTRs promote collaboration and creative problem solving to fund successful programs. However, there are challenges in funding HT programs since they are usually not reimbursable like physical, occupational, and speech therapies. At this time, programs in the United States are usually incorporated as part of the "package of services" and paid for by the healthcare agency from operating funds (usually including recreational, music, and horticultural therapies, social work, and other nonreimbursable services).

The experienced HT's leadership contributes to the success of gardens through the active use of landscape for therapy, increased publicity for the healthcare agency, and shared leading of fundraising efforts. HTs maintain therapeutic gardens to meet industry standards. This is a different and more detailed level of service than landscape maintenance "mow and blow" crews provide. Professional HTs are the interdisciplinary team members trained and skilled to help in the creative problem solving required to fund HT programs. For approaches to problem solving and funding, see chapter 19.

Collaboration among Therapies

HTs promote collaborative work with nurses, physicians, mental health professionals, and the full range of therapists (physical, occupational, speech, recreational, art, music, and pet). They encourage therapeutic use of gardens by all clinical staff for client programming as appropriate. At the Rehabilitation

Institute of Oregon, Portland, Oregon, for example, speech therapists often ask patients to talk about a plant to promote communication goals. Physical therapists engage their patients in balance activities while reaching to touch an iris or bending to smell a lily.

New York University Medical Center's Nancy Chambers, HTR, and Martha Sarno, speech and language pathologist, collaborated on a program for individuals with acquired aphasia, a communication impairment characterized by difficulty in speaking and understanding speech. The program consisted of structured activities designed to introduce plant care as a leisure-time activity. More than half of the patients reported that they continued to care for the plants they acquired in the project once they returned home. Participants were observed to increase their verbal behavior and social interaction, and their family members reported a noticeable improvement in patient mood (Sarno and Chambers 1997).

At Bryn Mawr Rehabilitation Hospital in Malvern, Pennsylvania, a 140-bed facility serving stroke, brain injury, and orthopedic patients, Karen Fleming, HTR, and Denise Odell Alford, OTR, prepared a program for a patient recovering from a viral infection. They collaborated with her to develop a treatment plan that included feeding the fish in the outside pond, harvesting ripe produce, collecting spent marigold blooms, and pulling petals from these blooms to be dried and used in potpourri (Fleming and Alford 1998). This patient met her treatment goals. She left the hospital with increased functional skills, which enabled her to return to her home and perform daily living activities with minimal assistance from family members. These examples demonstrate how creative clinicians promote collaborations and strive to create meaningful and functional treatments to enhance client outcomes and develop added value as a result of HT programs.

Conclusion

The major goal of this chapter has been to provide a knowledge base and support to designers, facility managers, and allied professionals who want to develop gardens for HT programs in healthcare settings. HT professionals are trained to manage this complex therapeutic modality.

Well-designed HT programs help to meet client needs, interests, and abilities across many health and human service settings (fig. 16.7). An understanding of the HT profession will help all those interested in developing HT programs to achieve better client outcomes and with more effective use of limited resources.

16.7 A veteran planting seeds in Gardening Leave's Victorian Greenhouse, the Stovehouse, Auchencruive, Scotland.
Photo courtesy of Gardening Leave Ltd.

The American Horticultural Therapy Association is a resource for agencies wanting to hire trained professionals. Health and human service allied professionals and administrators are encouraged to participate in AHTA meetings and conferences for networking, information gathering, and sharing.

References

AHTA (American Horticultural Therapy Association). 2007. *Definitions and Positions*. King of Prussia, PA: American Horticultural Therapy Association.

Airhart, D., and K. Airhart. 1998. "Inside Space and Adaptive Gardening: Design, Techniques and Tools." Pp. 317–54 in *Horticulture as Therapy: Principles and Practices*, edited by S. Simson and M. Straus. Binghamton, NY: Haworth Press.

Americans with Disabilities Act. 2010. *2010 ADA Standards for Accessible Design*. Washington, DC: US Department of Justice. http://www.ada.gov/regs2010/2010ADAStandards/2010ADAStandards.pdf.

Davis, S. 1998. "Development of the Profession of Horticultural Therapy." Pp. 3–20 in *Horticulture as Therapy: Principles and Practices*, edited by S. Simson and M. Straus. Binghamton, NY: Haworth Press.

Fleming, K., and D. O. Alford. 1998. "Case Studies, Physical Disabilities: Vanessa." *Journal of Therapeutic Horticulture* 9: 35–36.

Flick, K. M. 2012. "The Application of a Horticultural Therapy Program for Preschool Children with Autism Spectrum Disorder." *Journal of Therapeutic Horticulture* 22: 38–45.

Haas, K., S. P. Simson, and N. C. Stevenson. 1998. "Older Persons and Horticultural Therapy Practice." Pp. 23–56 in *Horticulture as Therapy: Principles and Practices*, edited by S. Simson and M. Straus. Binghamton, NY: Haworth Press.

Haller, R. 1998. "Vocational, Social and Therapeutic Programs." Pp. 43–70 in *Horticulture as Therapy: Principles and Practices*, edited by S. Simson and M. Straus. Binghamton, NY: Haworth Press.

Haller, R., and C. Kramer. 2006. *Horticultural Therapy Methods: Making Connections in Health Care, Human Service, and Community Programs*. Binghamton, NY: Haworth Press.

Hazen, T. 1997. "Horticultural Therapy in the Skilled Nursing Facility." Pp. 39–60 in *Horticultural Therapy and the Older Adult Population*, edited by S. Wells. Binghamton, NY: Haworth Press.

Hazen, T., and M. McManus. 2012. "Activities and Outside Space." Pp. 166–78 in *Designing Outdoor Spaces for People with Dementia*, edited by A. Pollock and M. Marshall. Sydney, Australia: HammondCare.

Kavanagh, J. 1998. "Outdoor Space and Adaptive Gardening: Design, Techniques and Tools." Pp. 287–316 in *Horticulture as Therapy: Principles and Practices*, edited by S. Simson and M. Straus. Binghamton, NY: Haworth Press.

Lee, S. M., J. K. Suh, and S. Lee. 2008. "Horticultural Therapy in a Jail: Correctional Care for Anger." *Acta Horticulturae* 790: 109–13.

Neuberger, K. R. 2008. "Some Therapeutic Aspects of Gardening in Psychiatry." *Acta Horticuturae* 790: 83–90.

Relf, D. 1999. "Living in America: The Role of Horticultural Therapists in Expanding Gardening in America." *American Horticultural Therapy Association Newsletter* 26 (1): 3–4.

Sarno, M. T., and N. Chambers. 1997. "A Horticultural Therapy Program for Individuals with Acquired Aphasia." Pp. 81–91 in *Horticultural Therapy and the Older Adult Population*, edited by S. Wells. Binghamton, NY: Haworth Press.

Shoemaker, C. A. 2002. *Interaction by Design: Bringing People and Plants Together for Health and Well-Being*. Ames, IA: Iowa State Press.

Simson, S., and M. Straus, eds. 1998. *Horticulture as Therapy: Principles and Practices*. Binghamton, NY: Haworth Press.

Starling, L. A. 2011. "The 3 C's: Credentialing, Certification, and Certificate Programs." *American Horticultural Therapy Association News Magazine* 40 (1): 4–5.

Thrive. 2012. "What Is Social and Therapeutic Horticulture?" Accessed March 10, 2012. http://www.thrive.org.uk/what-is-social-and-therapeutic-horticulture.aspx.

Wichrowski, M., J. Whiteson, F. Haas, A. Mola, and R. Mariano. 2005. "Effects of Horticultural Therapy on Mood and Heart Rate in Patients Participating in an Inpatient Cardiopulmonary Rehabilitation Program." *Journal of Cardiopulmonary Rehabilitation* 25 (5): 270–74.

Yamane, K., M. Kawashima, N. Fujishige, and M. Yoshida. 2004. "Effects of Interior Horticultural Activities with Potted Plants on Human Physiological and Emotional Status." *Acta Horticulturae* 636: 37–43.

CHAPTER 17

Planting and Maintaining Therapeutic Gardens

Marni Barnes

Introduction

Planting is perhaps the single most important aspect of a therapeutic garden. As they do in all gardens, the selection and placement of plants within the site provide functional and aesthetic qualities. Additionally however, in a therapeutic garden, plants carry the significance of providing respite, memory enhancement, and engagement, as well as being a stimulus for conversation. In the case of horticultural therapy gardens, plants also provide for a range of physical and social activities and the opportunity for users of the garden to demonstrate caring and nurturing behavior.

The aim of this chapter is twofold: First, it is to help the client achieve a space that will function as a therapeutic garden. It is not sufficient for an architect to simply declare an outdoor area to be "healing," nor, sadly, is every landscape architect able to create a space that is truly therapeutic. Many landscape architects have other agendas, and too many are emerging from their university training with a minimal knowledge of plants.[1] This chapter is intended to help both clients and designers understand and weigh the decisions that must be made with regard to planning, policy, and budgeting for planting and maintenance, and hence to be more assured of achieving a successful therapeutic garden. Second, it is hoped that this reminder of the importance of the subtleties and detailing of planting design and their integration with psychological principles will spur the landscape architect to work to the highest standard and create a beautiful garden that will thrive over time (fig. 17.1).

The definition of a "healing garden" is still evolving, and there are many different interpretations of what type of garden might be therapeutic. For example, a landscape architect may interpret a healing garden to be a physic garden, featuring medicinal herbs and plants used in traditional healing. While there is nothing wrong with this, there is no evidence that garden users in medical facilities are necessarily interested or soothed by seeing plants used in their medications.

In gardens for cancer patients, it may in fact be disturbing to see labeled plants from which chemotherapy drugs have been derived, especially if the patient has recently suffered uncomfortable side effects from that treatment. Other designers may base their plant selection strictly on the principles of color theory or aromatherapy. Although these philosophies are not without merit, they are, in the view of this author, narrow and, therefore, limiting in their approach. The emphasis of this chapter is on creating a garden that provides a holistic experience, one that supplies multisensory engagement, distracts users from stress and pain, and supports psychological equilibrium. To that end, the focus is on the principles and concepts that assist in the design of a therapeutic garden. Due to the range of climates in which readers will be working, offering specific suggestions or recommendations is not practical, so specific plant names are only used as examples or to illustrate a point.

17.1 Zebra swallowtail on butterfly weed (*Asclepias spp.*).
Photo from www.henrydomke.com

---

1. Jost (2012) notes that 48 percent of landscape architects surveyed self-described their knowledge of plants as "average."

17.2 Lush and varied planting in Anne's Garden, Northeast Georgia Medical Center, Gainesville, Georgia. Designer: The Fockele Garden Company.
Copyright, The Fockele Garden Company

Creating a Healthy Garden

Advance planning

Gardens are living systems. As such there are both initial requirements and ongoing needs that must be met. A designer must take into account basic conditions that will enable plants to thrive, such as the amount of sunlight, the depth and quality of the soil, and the amount of water and sufficient nutrients. These factors all play a role, and the appropriate needs of the plant species must be understood. It is therefore best if the garden area is planned during the earliest stages of site development and is designed by a landscape architect who is well versed in horticulture, preferably one trained specifically in therapeutic garden design. If an indoor garden is planned, it is essential that a specialist in interior planting and maintenance be on board from the beginning.

Policies to be addressed

Landscaped gardens, unlike any other type of designed space, are comprised of elements that are alive; because of this a garden will need constant attention throughout its entire existence. Therefore, in addition to advance planning, policies must be set in place to ensure that the garden receives what it needs to stay healthy and vibrant over time and that users continue to have access to that benefit (fig. 17.2).

All gardens should have a maintenance document that is written by the landscape architect in conjunction with the facilities manager, and it must be followed by those in charge of the garden. The maintenance manual for a therapeutic garden will differ from a typical landscape manual in that it needs to address specific maintenance practices that enhance the healing benefits of the garden. The details of such a manual are discussed later in this chapter.

The potential therapeutic benefit of the space is also impacted by operational policies such as the hours the garden will be open, the supervision of users, if required, and the potential for programmed activities. The intended use of the garden will affect these policy decisions, and they should be made at the time a garden is designed—as they, in turn, will impact the form and function of the garden.

Continued attention and adequate practice

To maintain a therapeutic garden at its highest level takes knowledge, a trained staff, and adequate funding. The selection of the people who will tend and maintain the garden needs to be given extensive consideration, as the highest level of competence and commitment is required to care for a garden that is intended to be therapeutic. Budgeting for the labor and on going materials cost for the garden must be sufficient to assure a continually thriving environment.

Basic Requirements for Plant Growth

The requirements of plants in a therapeutic garden are the same as any other landscape. However, in this situation, a healthy and attractive garden is *essential* for promoting the health and well-being of its users (clients, patients, residents, visitors, and staff). It is therefore critical that proper attention be paid to the basics in order to allow the garden to thrive over the long term. This will also save money over time.

In order to best promote the health of a therapeutic garden's users, its setting needs to be supportive of plant health and growth. This begins with selecting the location of the garden. Quite apart from the requirements that make a space available and attractive to potential users, the needs of the plants themselves must be considered. The landscape architect in charge of the project should address the following issues in the design process.

Sunlight

An adequate amount of sun in most of the garden will be required. The majority of the planting beds should receive direct sun for at least half of the day because most plants require that amount of sun or filtered light to thrive. There are plants that prefer shade, and it is possible to have an entire shade garden. However, the potential plant palette is limited by very shady conditions, and colorful blossoms in particular are less likely to thrive in deep shade. When there is a choice, it is best to select a garden site that provides as much sun exposure for the plants as possible, and the plants should always be selected to suit the sun conditions of the garden.

Soil

The quality and volume of the soil available is just as important for plant growth as the amount of light. Different plants thrive in different soil conditions, and for this reason the selection of plants needs to be matched to the soil conditions (degree of porosity, nutrient holding capacity, pH, etc.). The depth available for the root zone is especially relevant when the garden is set over a structure such as a building rooftop or an underground parking facility. If the garden is part of a major construction project, topsoil should be saved prior to demolition and moved back into the garden, as the subsoil exposed during construction usually does not provide adequate soil structure (fig. 17.3).

To a certain extent the soil can be modified to match the plants, but this is more difficult to achieve and harder

17.3 There are many opportunities to engage with nature on the roof garden of Clare Tower, a residence for older adults in Chicago, Illinois. Designers: Hoerr Schaudt Landscape Architects.
Photo courtesy of Hoerr Schaudt

to monitor and maintain over time. If plants with differing soil pH or porosity requirements are chosen, similar plants should be grouped into zones so that they can be tended efficiently.

Horticultural therapy (HT) gardens have additional soil requirements. Because clients are encouraged to manipulate the soil, planting beds that are used for activities should have light and friable soil that is easy to dig into and to place in pots. Also important is that there be no vermiculite or other soil amendments used that produce dust or otherwise release potentially carcinogenic particles into the air. "Sterile potting mix" is used in the nursery trade for propagation, and this is the best soil for hands-on activities in hospitals and other settings where clients may have compromised immune systems. New York University's Langone Medical Center has adopted a few simple procedures that address concerns about soil-borne microorganisms: (1) sanitize all work surfaces and pots between activities; (2) do not allow soil exchange between patients during group activities; (3) teach proper hand-washing technique, and have every patient wash before and after every activity; (4) as an extra precaution, provide masks for those patients who have pulmonary issues and may be sensitive to dust. The medical professionals within the various facilities and the facility's infection-control regulations will be the best guide for setting the appropriate policy for HT gardens. (For more details on HT gardens, see chapter 16.)

Water

Water needs vary between plants and will also change depending on the type of soil. Care needs to be given to grouping plants with like watering requirements together and to making sure that they have the soil that delivers the water to the roots at the rate that best meets their needs. This should be done for the health of the plants as well as for water conservation and ease of maintenance. Underground irrigation systems will be required in many regions, as healthy growth depends on the continuity of the water supply. A landscape architect who is well versed in horticultural practices and has local knowledge of plants should design the irrigation system and supervise the initial setting of the timing and sequencing of the valves.

Plants: Assets and Costs

In addition to the basic requirements mentioned above, plants of all types need attention from time to time. Plants can be categorized into six groups based on their growth habits and longevity:

- trees
- shrubs
- perennials
- grasses and herbaceous plants
- annuals
- groundcovers and vines

The assets as well as the maintenance implications for each of these plant groups are important to understand, as this awareness will directly affect the cost of installation as well as the ongoing budget. It is important that everyone involved with the planning process, as well as facilities management staff, understands the reasons behind planting and design choices—it is impossible to sustain therapeutic benefit through a process of "value engineering" if the therapeutic value remains unknown!

Trees provide a multitude of benefits. They can be as short as 15 feet or over 100 feet high. Often branching overhead, they can provide varying degrees of shade as well as screening from upper-story windows. A spreading canopy provides shelter and offers a sense of scale in a space that might otherwise be too large or be dominated by an adjacent structure. Their upright form adds an additional element to draw the eye through, then up and out of a space. Taller trees also provide an attractive view from windows on upper floors. The longevity of most trees makes them a wonderful asset for a garden, both aesthetically and because they can impart a symbolic meaning, representing a continuity of life that extends beyond our own existence (fig. 17.4).

A tree, especially a mature specimen, can be expensive to buy. However, purchasing an established tree might be a cost worth undertaking. A broad canopied tree is one of the best ways to achieve shade in a new garden, which is often critical for comfort and even for safety (people on various medications are more sensitive than others to UV light and glare). When a cost comparison is done with constructed shade structures (gazebos and shade sails, for example), a mature tree is often a good choice. Alternatively, buying a less mature tree costs less up front and will have the long-term benefit of the rapid growth that results from an unencumbered root system[2] (fig. 17. 5).

---

2. Studies from the University of California at Davis and others have shown that plants purchased in smaller container sizes will quickly catch up and outgrow the same species that has been planted out at a larger size.

17.4 Trees can provide structure, shade, and the symbolism of longevity in a garden.
Photo by Naomi Sachs

Ongoing costs to care for a tree are relatively minimal, although they vary according to species. Maintenance only becomes truly costly if the tree is planted in the wrong place. Some trees have weak crotches and are "self-pruning," meaning that they tend to drop large limbs with no warning (most eucalyptus have this characteristic). This can be expensive if the limbs cause damage as they fall. The most common issues with tree maintenance, however, are the size of the canopy and the (often overlooked) ultimate size of the root system. Either of these factors can cause a maintenance budget to skyrocket if structures are threatened with damage. Therefore, selecting the right tree for the right place is one of the most critical decisions in garden design (fig. 17.6).

Shrubs are woody plants that develop branches and generally reach maturity between three and twenty feet high (prostrate shrubs are categorized as groundcovers). They provide interest and screening, and they can direct the eye and create intimate settings. They are relatively long-lived (many for more than thirty years). Well placed, they can hold interest through the winter in a garden that otherwise might be lackluster. Shrubs can be used to create areas within a garden as well as soften or even hide unsightly elements such as vents and HVAC units. In addition to trees, shrubs can also provide an interesting overhead view for clients on gurneys or prone wheelchairs. Some shrubs require routine pruning, while others, once established, rarely need even that. They provide color, texture, form, and fragrance at relatively little cost.

In regions with long winters, shrubs play a particularly significant role in the garden. Evergreen shrubs and trees provide a green outlook all year long, while deciduous shrubs can be selected for attractive branching and winter interest, such as berries, colorful bark, and early bloom. Generally lower than trees, these features can be easily viewed from windows and can enhance what might be an otherwise dreary winter scene. Shrubs are a good investment in terms of both up-front cost and long-term maintenance and are considered the backbone of every garden.

Perennial is a term used differently by different professionals. Botanists refer to all plants (including trees and shrubs) that live over two years as perennials, while landscape architects, commercial nursery owners, and gardeners use *perennial* to refer to plants that either die back after flowering and remain dormant over the winter (herbaceous perennials such as iris and peony) or that generally begin to look unkempt after a few years (bushy perennials such as the sages and lavender). The definition that is commonly used in the landscape architecture profession is the one used in this book. Additionally, the two types of perennials (bushy and

17.5 This *Arbutus* "Marina" offers interest all year long. The rich color of the peeling bark contrasts with the deep green waxy leaves. The strong branching structure is attractive overhead and can hold the flowers in view of people who are reclining.

Photo by Marni Barnes

17.6 An elderly woman in a reclining wheelchair looks up into the branches of a tree while a visitor sits nearby.

Photo by Marni Barnes

herbaceous) are presented separately in this chapter because their function in the garden and their maintenance requirements are quite different. (Herbaceous perennials are grouped with grasses because many of their qualities and maintenance requirements are similar.)

Bushy perennials are available in an array of sizes, colors, forms, and shapes. They grow quickly and often are quite stunning during their first year in the ground. They can provide interest and sensory engagement (color, fragrance, and texture) in a garden. They tend to be small (over four feet high is rare) and fairly flexible, so they are often amenable to being touched and can be pulled closer for a good look or to catch a whiff of fragrance. Due to their prolific bloom, they also attract birds and butterflies and are a very important element in a therapeutic garden.

These perennials live only a few years because their primary reproduction is through seed, so they do not devote their energy to growing strong branches. Seeds are their survival mechanism, and they will increase blossom production if their flowers are cut, or "deadheaded," before they turn to seed. Perennials may be deciduous or evergreen, but most have poor shape and structure and are not adaptable to much corrective pruning. Many die back fully or partially after their bloom, creating areas in the garden that have an unsightly "down time." While this needs to be taken into account, it is usually not considered a significant drawback, especially in regions where winters are harsh and the garden is minimally used during the cold weather. Even in a year-round garden, the less attractive times can be balanced through good planning and design to minimize the impact of the unsightly phase of the perennial beds. A few perennials are invasive and will migrate around a garden if let go. Which species will do this depends on the local climate, so the landscape architect needs to have local knowledge if he or she is to exclude these from the garden.

Maintenance drawbacks of perennials include the additional time required to deadhead the spent flowers and that some need to be replaced every few years, which accrues material and labor costs. Despite this extra effort, perennials are a very important element of a therapeutic garden.

Perennials are especially useful in an HT garden. The color, fragrance, and "touchability" of these plants makes them appealing, and even the additional minor maintenance tasks, such as deadheading, can be an asset when they become a therapeutic activity (fig. 17.7).

17.7 Catmint (*Nepeta X faassenii*) is fragrant when touched. At Legacy Health Good Samaritan Hospital, Portland, Oregon, this recreational therapist is encouraging her client to enjoy the smell.
Photo by Marni Barnes

Ornamental grasses and herbaceous plants have much to offer a therapeutic garden. They are often considered as a group because one of their primary assets is the dramatic form of the foliage. The floppy leaves of Lily of the Nile (*Agapanthus*), the spiky colorful foliage of flax (*Phormium*), or the lush vegetation of bear's breeches (*Acanthus mollis*) can be used as a foil that contrasts well with other vegetation. Similarly, the wavy fronds of a tall grass are often used as a focal point because they contrast with the surrounding plants (fig. 17.8).

Bulbs such as daffodils and tulips, corms such as crocus, rhizomes such as iris, and tubers such as dahlias have colorful flowers as well as dramatic foliage. Unlike with bushy perennials, removing flowers and seed heads does not extend the bloom season for these plants. Indeed, some of their beauty lies in the ephemeral quality of their fleeting blossoms. They are often appreciated as harbingers of spring, with all of the psychological and symbolic benefit that designation can bring.

Grasses have striking forms and interesting seed clusters. They are light and wispy and prone to playing in the movement of a breeze. When grouped in massings, the sound of the grass rustling in the wind can be another pleasing aspect. Although some grasses self-sow or have invasive roots making them hard to control in a garden setting, ornamental grasses that do not have these characteristics are available in most climatic regions. Grasses can be particularly useful in a cold climate, as some of the more hardy varieties will hold their form under light frosts and new snow. Maintenance is minimal, usually consisting only of cutting back once a year so that the new growth will feature in the spring (fig. 17.9.).

Annual plants differ from region to region because the definition of an annual is that in a given climate zone it survives outdoors for less than a year. In other words, plants that are annuals in Northern California may well live for several years in the warmer climate of Mexico. Prized for their prolific color, beds of annual flowers are very attractive, provide high interest, and can make a section of the garden "pop" when they are in flower. They provide vibrant color for a season, then die back or begin to look unsightly after only a few months. So when selecting annuals, care should be taken that their peak flowering period overlaps with the seasons that the garden is most used or viewed.

Annual beds need to be dug up and replaced several times a year. (Because of the rapidity with which they need replacing, they are sometimes jokingly called "quarterlies.") Consequently, they are expensive to maintain and best limited to areas where high interest is worth the effort. Alternatively, planting in pots and tubs provides some structure and framing for these plants and has the added benefit that they can be moved to a spot where some attractive color is needed—for instance, near windows and doors during the winter months and perhaps further into the garden

17.8 This combination of perennials, grasses, and herbaceous plants in the Comfort Garden at San Francisco General Hospital, San Francisco, California, catches your eye as you walk along the path.
Photo by Marni Barnes

during better weather. In residential facilities or in HT gardens, planning and planting annual beds can be a therapeutic activity.

Groundcovers and vines may seem like opposites—one grows along the ground, the other often up a frame—but their habits are similar, and in their natural environment many vines tumble along the ground, so they are grouped together. From a design prospective, prostrate vines and shrubs, as well as rooting groundcovers, can serve as a resting place for the eye, giving relief to the upright form of many plants in the

17.9 Children love to run their hands through ornamental grasses.
Photo by Clare Cooper Marcus

17.10 The soft foliage of lamb's ears (*Stachys byzantina*) invites touch.
Photo by Clare Cooper Marcus

garden. They tend to visually recede and thereby create an openness that can feel expansive and provide an understated foreground to higher-interest plants in the distance. They can offer color and fragrance, and some have a touchable quality that begs to be investigated (fig. 17.10).

The longevity of different groundcovers varies greatly, as does the speed with which they establish and spread. For large expanses it is best to select those that are robust, evergreen in that climate region, and have a long life span. For smaller areas of filler, these characteristics are less important.

If vines are climbing up a structure, they serve as a strong design element and can provide screening of unsightly elements and blank walls. Their advantage is that they generally cover a large spreading area (whether high up or low to the ground) and other than a few rampant growers, which need frequent cutting back, they do not require maintenance beyond yearly trimming and occasional fertilizing. The initial cost is low, as they can be small when purchased and grow rapidly to cover a large area.

A relatively recent phenomenon is "living walls"—vertical structures planted with groundcovers and other small plants. These too are dramatic elements, in a garden or inside a building, and can be planted in a very artistic fashion. Unfortunately, the maintenance and water requirements of this mode of planting can be problematic. To get enough water to the plants, much more water needs to be applied than in a horizontal setting. The water then washes away nutrients from the soil, requiring the application of excessive

amounts of fertilizer. The end result is that the living walls often develop large dead spots that need constant replenishment. Because having healthy plants is the number one priority in a healing garden, the technology of the basic structure and the distribution of water need to be more fully developed before living walls can be recommended for a therapeutic garden. The only exception is in an HT garden, where the vertical wall provides easy access and can enable a patient to tend the plants. The plantings are usually changed during activities frequently enough to forestall the appearance of dead and dying areas.

Lawn is often called a groundcover, but technically it is not. In most regions a green lawn is achieved by weekly cutting, and it often needs to be watered and fertilized to excess to keep it struggling along. Different types of lawn grasses fare better in various climate regions, and this can mitigate the excessive maintenance. However, all lawns require substantial labor and material resources. The environmental issues concerning lawns and their required maintenance are covered in chapter 18, on sustainability. A good rule of thumb is that a lawn should only be planted where the space that it occupies doubles as an activity area. Proper groundcovers can provide the same aesthetic and therapeutic benefits that a lawn can—at less expense—if the surface is not to serve as an overflow patio area or for informal activities such as dining, sunbathing, or children's play. An additional consideration is the appropriate scheduling of irrigation. This can be problematic, especially if the soil is heavy. The grass must get enough water—which is a substantial amount—without creating a lawn that remains too soggy for people to walk, sit, and play on.

Plant Placement

Planting design in a therapeutic garden is largely determined by the intended function of a particular arrangement of plants. Outlined below are some of the functions that the planting must serve. Many of these will be familiar to the landscape architect, and it could be argued that these principles apply generally to good garden design. In therapeutic gardens, however, they are not optional. What makes a therapeutic garden a healing space is the degree of attention given to these refinements and their integration with the principles of environmental and social psychology as they apply to the user population.

Confidentiality and privacy

Confidentiality and privacy are two of the most significant factors that need to be addressed in medical settings. This is true for both legal and psychological reasons and has tremendous impact on planting design, especially when windows look onto the garden space. When people are in a therapeutic garden, they should feel that they are away from the interior of the buildings and not in plain sight of those within. Planting around the windows of common areas

of the building should provide masking and filtered screening of the seating areas of the garden. Consideration should also be given of the quality of the view out from the building, so the screening should provide interest and variety in both directions (fig. 17.11).

This is even more critical near windows in patient rooms and offices. Here thought needs to be given to sightlines and to sounds that may penetrate *into* the building, as well. To reduce disturbance to those within the building, larger buffer zones are necessary. Depending on the height of the window sill and the window covering inside the room, the physical and visual buffer outside residents' or patients' rooms may need to be as high as 10 feet if the garden can accommodate it. Mounding the soil and limiting the height of shrubbery can screen views while also allowing light to penetrate into the building (fig. 17.12).

Availability and proximity of seating

Availability and proximity of seating allows people to explore the garden with minimal exertion. Plantings near garden entries are important for three reasons: an appealing vista can draw people into the garden; entry patios are favorite socializing spaces; and because of mobility issues, a significant number of people do not venture further into the garden. Therefore, high-interest planting should abound near the entries. This is a good place for annuals if they are routinely

17.11 The planting outside these patient rooms at Legacy Health Good Samaritan Medical Center in Portland, Oregon, provides a good buffer for those inside and out. The planting is attractive from both directions and high enough to allow a degree of privacy.
Photo by Marni Barnes

17.12 The unimpeded view to a garden courtyard is welcome from a corridor or internal communal space but for privacy reasons would be inappropriate from a patient room.
Photo by Naomi Sachs

switched out when past their prime. Plants that have winter interest are also appropriate here, as this is where people may slip out for a few minutes on warmer days. Pots or sloping beds are particularly important near the entry. They increase the visibility of the plants for people who are sitting and can bring color and fragrance within reach of those with limited range of motion.

Attractive destinations

Attractive destinations encourage people to venture into the garden. The planting, in conjunction with other elements, should draw a person into and through the space. A sense of intrigue and wonderment can be created with hidden views and changing elements of interest. Well-planted destinations can serve as goals, and smaller areas of interest can cause one to pause and look again, to stop and reflect, to slow down and relax (fig. 17.13).

17.13 The planting and meandering pathway in this healing garden invite people to explore. St. Joseph Memorial Hospital, Santa Rosa, California.
Photo by Clare Cooper Marcus

Places to linger and semiprivate spaces

Places to linger and semiprivate spaces are important throughout a therapeutic garden. These can be subtly delineated by the canopy of a tree or more defined with plants that surround a space. As discussed under general design guidelines, in chapter 6, the variety, size, and character of the spaces is critical. Much of the quality of a space within a garden is determined by the proximity, density, and interest provided by the plants that surround it. The wispy branches of a willow tree can create a soft, permeable boundary to a patio underneath, while the density of a 4-foot-high clipped boxwood hedge would offer more seclusion and a feeling of protection. The planting near a seat can carry a particular significance. A shrub or a mature tree trunk can provide a feeling of comfort, or "prospect-refuge," because many people feel most secure when there is something sheltering their back. Conversely, in front and to the side of a bench, low, touchable, colorful, and mildly fragrant plants are an asset. These types of psychological influences should be a primary consideration when creating subspaces within the garden (fig. 17.14).

Areas for activities

Horticultural therapy gardens need areas for activities. These should consist of raised beds of varying heights, cantilevered beds, planting walls, hanging baskets on pulley systems, and other mechanisms that bring the soil for planting within easy reach of clients who need to sit, lean, or use other means of support while they work. A good HT garden will have shrubs and trees for structure, with annuals, perennials, and edible plants within arm's reach of the paths. Plant placement should take into account possible use by a physical or occupational therapist working with clients on range of motion, strengthening, and stretching exercises; as well as horticultural therapists who might use blooms and fruits for crafts and cooking; and speech pathologists who might invite clients to identify plants by color, recall memories, or read plant labels (for more details, see chapter 16) (fig. 17.15).

To ensure optimal use of the garden, placement of plants should take into account that growth may create hazards over time—for example, tree roots causing pathway paving to heave, groundcover growing over pathways, overgrown shrubs blocking window views, or rampant herbaceous growth swamping benches.

17.14 Tall bamboo creates a secluded seating space in the healing garden at Jupiter Medical Center, Jupiter, Florida.
Courtesy of Studio Sprout; photo by Michiko Kurisu

17.15 This HT garden at the Tzu Chi General Hospital, Taipei, Taiwan, has planting tables for both standing and seated patients. There are also 6-inch raised beds along the roof deck edge to offer opportunities for bending and squatting, and higher beds for small fruit trees.
Photo by Marni Barnes

Plant Selection: Plants to Avoid

Toxic and allergenic plants

A therapeutic garden needs to be a safe and healthy environment. So it might seem that the issue of toxic and allergenic plants hardly warrants a mention beyond the admonition "no toxic plants." However, an exhaustive list of plants that have the potential to cause some kind of adverse reaction in people is long. If a strict ban on all plants that are deemed toxic in any way is imposed, the plant palette becomes extremely limited.

Fortunately, toxicity is more nuanced than might first appear, and this can help in setting guidelines that are appropriate for a garden. There are differing types of toxicity, giving rise to differing symptoms. Some plants, for instance, cause dermatological symptoms. Others cause intestinal distress. Of greater concern is distress to the nervous, respiratory, or cardiac systems. There are also varying degrees of toxicity, which depend on dose or degree of exposure. Some plants are highly toxic, causing distress with minimal exposure, while others are moderately or mildly toxic. Additionally, although some plants are entirely toxic, others have only one or two toxic components (the roots or the seeds, for example). Knowing this can help in establishing which plants should be avoided in a given setting.

Some plants should be avoided in all settings—castor beans, for example, are extremely toxic. Eating two beans may be enough to kill an adult. Australian wattles (*Acacia* species) are known for their allergy-triggering—and asthma-inducing—pollen and are a common irritant to a large number of people. Trees and shrubs of all species that produce copious amounts of irritating pollen should be avoided in all therapeutic gardens. However, most plants are not as extremely or universally toxic as these examples, and every garden site should be looked at individually to create a specialized list of prohibited plants. The evaluation for designating which plants should be considered too toxic for a given site should be primarily based on who is likely to use the garden. The age, expected behaviors, cognitive ability, and medical condition of the users will determine how much concern a given plant might cause. The lowest common denominator—the most vulnerable user—becomes the limiting factor.

As an example, let us compare two plants that are toxic if ingested. The rhizomes of iris are toxic, and if eaten are likely to cause intestinal distress that can be severe but not serious.

Foxglove is also toxic (fig. 17.16). The leaves, if ingested, can cause nervous disorder—confusion and disorientation. If enough are eaten, they can cause cardiac arrest. Neither plant would be a good choice for a garden where the users may be cognitively or emotionally impaired and are at risk for eating plants that they find in the garden. However, let us look at these two plants in the context of a children's garden. Foxglove remains too high a risk: (1) the symptoms are extremely serious and sometimes fatal; (2) the effect is dose-dependent, and for a small person not many leaves need to be eaten to cause distress; (3) the leaves are low to the ground and are easily reached—even by a toddler; and (4) the plant has flowers that are bright and colorful and alluring to an inquisitive mind. What about irises? The poisonous part of the plant is below ground, and the level of distress caused by eating the roots is only mild to moderate. This plant deserves closer consideration and a second level of assessment. Can the same design intent be achieved in the garden without using iris? If so, a nontoxic alternative would be a better choice. If the benefit of using iris seems to outweigh the unlikely event that a child might eat enough of the rhizome to become symptomatic, then iris might be included in the children's garden. This is a judgment call, and it is best to include the owners or administrators in the decisions about toxic plants.

There are many sources for learning which plants growing in various regions can be toxic and how they affect humans. For North America, see Texas A&M University (2013), which has common name descriptions of symptoms of toxicity; the Canadian Biodiversity Information Facility (2009), which lists botanical and common plant names with links to details; the Pollen Library (2013), which lists pollen-producing plants by season and by US zip code; and the US Food and Drug Administration (2008), which has a searchable poisonous plant database. The local authority (such as, in the United States, a state's department of health) may require usage of a specific list. There are also books, though these often cover a specific region. Good references are Lampe and McCann (1985) and, for California, Ogren (2000) and James (1973).

Nuisance plants

There are other plants that are not toxic per se but should nevertheless be evaluated for appropriateness in a garden. Thorns are a commonsense hazard, and plants with long, sharp, or poisonous thorns need a compelling rationale for use in a therapeutic garden.

17.16 While the flowers of foxglove (*Digitalis grandiflora*) are bright and colorful, the leaves of are highly toxic.
Photo by Alberto Salvatore

Messy litter from trees and shrubs—especially large, hard seedpods or squishy berries—can be more of a hazard than one might think, especially on a pathway. It is equally important to consider fragrance. While light fragrance can be an asset, strong smells can be offensive to many who are not feeling well and can trigger allergic reactions even in those who are healthy. Even a "pleasant" smell can become an irritant when it is too strong. There are some settings, such as gardens for cancer patients and those in acute-care hospitals, where the use of fragrance should be carefully considered, since there may be people who are on medications that can induce nausea (see chapter 8). Other types of nuisances that need to be assessed are plants that are irritating to the touch and those that attract an inordinate number of stinging insects.

The same criteria—intended users' age, expected behaviors, cognitive ability, and medical condition—should be used to assess nuisance plants as toxic plants. Because the consequences are not as severe as with toxic plants, careful location of the plant can be a way to minimize potential drawbacks. For most gardens, spiny or thorny plants are acceptable if they are set back into a planting bed. Similarly, the intensity of a fragrance and concerns about fruit drop can be minimized by keeping the plant away from paths and patios. However, neither a garden for a psychiatric unit nor a garden for people who have severe dementia should have any nuisance plants anywhere.

Desirable Qualities of Plantings

Beyond applying the maxim of "do no harm," the principle guiding the formulation of a plant palette for a therapeutic garden should be that it provide physical and emotional comfort to users. Many plants can contribute to this goal. The following three concepts and descriptions can serve as a guide for formulating such a plant list.

Providing a place of respite

For example, retaining the existing trees on the site gives a sense of longevity to the garden and can symbolize permanence and stability. Differing types of shade create areas with differing psychological atmospheres. Deep shade feels more secluded and cozy, but it may make some feel threatened, so the psychological state of likely users should be considered. Filtered shade, on the other hand, provides an open, more expansive atmosphere while still offering protection. Selecting plants that are familiar to garden users or that have cultural significance can support a feeling of ease and sense of belonging. Color combinations and contrasting textures and forms are especially important and should be available year-round. It is this interest that activates "soft fascination" and provides mental respite (see chapter 3). In areas where the climate is harsh, the view from building windows is one of the primary benefits of the garden. It is especially important that these views offer qualities of respite.

Part of creating a refuge is to incorporate enchantment that gently engages the mind. Planting that draws the eye up to the sky or out of the site to a "borrowed landscape" can help to lift the spirit (fig. 17.17).

Wildlife such as squirrels and birds, as well as butterflies and other colorful insects, can attract attention and help to move one's thoughts away from serious things. Being ephemeral in nature, this kind of wildlife can also serve as a source of wonderment and perhaps be a reminder of spiritual or

17.17 The eye of this visitor to the healing garden at Kaiser Permanente Medical Center in Antioch, California, is being drawn up out of the courtyard space by the tall bamboo and the birds living in the canopy. *Photo by Marni Barnes*

religious connections beyond oneself. Using plants that have flowers and fruit can draw this kind of playful life into the garden. Additionally, blossoms and berries themselves, as well as fall color and the new growth of spring, add beauty and interest to the garden and can serve as a temporal anchor and as a reminder that life is cyclical and not static. Perhaps they can provide reassurance that something that is unpleasant right now may pass—or may need to be accepted as part of the fullness of life. Plants with unusual forms or delicate aspects can also inspire a sense of awe. Delicate shadow patterns bring interest to a garden, and often a breeze is noticed when the shadows of overhead branches move.

Color theory comes into play when creating places of respite. If the intention is to create a calming experience, then cool colors (blues, greens, and purples), whites, and pastel shades have been shown to be restorative. If, however, the goal is distracting the mind through stimulation, hot and vibrant colors such as bright reds, oranges, and yellows can be uplifting. Cultural beliefs relating to color must also be taken into account. For example, the Chinese associate white with death, so this color should be avoided if the predominant users of a garden have a Chinese background. Red, on the other hand, is associated in Chinese culture with good fortune and could be emphasized in plant choice (fig. 17.18).

The philosophies of feng shui from China and *vastu shastra* from India incorporate beliefs about geospatial relationships and colors that relate to harmonious energy flow—*chi* or *prana*—in the environment and in all living beings, and may influence how well a person feels. These ancient principles are too complex to summarize here, but there are numerous resources regarding these philosophies, and it is worth investigating which principles might be helpful in a given setting (Sparks, McCafferty, and LePorte 2012; Wydra 1997; Jayaprakash, n.d.; Ahsan 2004).

In all healthcare settings, especially those that are residential, with users perhaps spending a lot of time in the garden, planting should be arranged in forms reminiscent of a domestic garden rather than in large swaths of the same plant, often a hallmark of institutional and corporate settings. This is true for reasons of comfort and familiarity and because it increases the variety and interest that this smaller-scale planting provides.

Addressing all of the senses

Multisensory experiences are an essential part of a healing garden for aesthetic, and more important, therapeutic reasons. Vision is usually the most dominant sense, and every plant should have some form of visual interest, whether it be beautiful, unusual, or memory provoking. Beyond visual considerations, however, the therapeutic garden should have an array of sensual stimulation for the benefit of all users, and especially for those with differing physical and sensory limitations and who have developed a range of compensatory sensory dominances. Mild to moderate fragrances can be beneficial in several ways. They can act as an antidote to the unfamiliar or unwelcome smells that may permeate the interior of a facility. Because of the association in the brain between smell and memory, fragrances may also remind the client of other times and places. Plants that produce pleasant sounds with the movement of the air can bring soft attention to our surroundings, displacing other, perhaps troublesome, thoughts. Plants that appeal to the touch can bring a variety of experiences into the garden. Fine-textured foliage that is soft and easy to stroke, or woolly leaves that are pleasant to feel, can draw a person into the moment. On warm days the transpiration of smooth broad leaves causes their surface to be cooler than the air, and they are a treat to touch (fig. 17.19).

Similarly, by using plants that create canopies and capture the air, microclimates can be created by producing shade, capturing moisture, and creating sunny pockets. As one passes from one microclimate to the next, the whole skin of the body awakens and awareness of the present moment comes into focus.

Plants that are have fruit, leaves, or flowers that are edible directly from the plant can provide another sensory indulgence. Multisensory plants that can be discovered in the garden immerse all users in a richer, more beneficial environment.

Unusual plants and flowers such as this Turks Cap Lily can capture people's interest.
Photo from www.henrydomke.com

Inviting interaction

Whether it is the casual and spontaneous contact with plants in a restorative garden or the more active programmed interaction in an enabling or HT garden, all plants should be selected to be tolerant of—and even to invite—direct human manipulation. Plants may be pulled close for enhanced sensory experience—seeing, smelling, touching, and tasting. Flowers, fruit, and even branches are likely to be picked and

17.19 These broadleaf plants are cool to the touch on this hot day in the horticultural therapy garden at ALPHA, Awaji, Japan.
Photo by Marni Barnes

17.20 This huge hydrangea flower elicits a playful response from a horticultural therapist working with a patient.
Photo by Marni Barnes

foliage crushed for fragrance. The more that the plants are selected to encourage this behavior, the greater the degree of people's absorption in their surroundings and the potential for therapeutic benefit. Plants should be forgiving, have prolific blossom or repeat bloom seasons, be pliable so that they swing back rather than snap off, and be engaging in order to draw this kind of attention, with fun and unusual forms such as seedpods that shake or flowers that can be made to do tricks (such as the bunny-like mouth of a snapdragon that can appear to "talk" or sensitivity plants whose leaves close up when touched) (fig. 17.20, fig. 17.21).

Elements in the garden, including plants, often become the subject of conversation for garden visitors. The presence of an unusual plant can elicit comment. Labels or small signs with invitations such as "touch me" or "my flowers smell good" or literary quotations can also stimulate conversation and social connection. "Plant bingo" cards with pictures or drawings from the garden can entertain clients and visitors, especially children, in a garden—so plants with dramatic and recognizable characteristics are valuable as well (fig. 17.22).

Plant Selection: Desirable Plants

Plants for a horticultural therapy garden should have all of the above qualities and more, as they need to also provide for a range of activities and the opportunity for garden users to demonstrate caring and nurturing behavior. Plant materials need to support people-plant engagement outdoors (both independent activity as well as programmed events) during

17.21 A sign in the garden of Randall Children's Hospital, Portland, Oregon, encourages children to engage with what they can see in the garden.
Courtesy of Legacy Health

daily use of the garden. Gwenn Fried, horticultural therapist at New York University Langone Medical Center in New York City suggests a "rule of three" for all plants in an HT garden. Space is precious, she explains, so every plant in the garden needs

17.22 Plants with unusual features can attract people's interest in the garden.
Photo by Marni Barnes

to earn its spot. Rather than a limited recommendation of "good" and "bad" of plants, Fried selects plants that offer at least three qualities from the list below:

Sensory

   Color: bold or calming or contrasting (different effects for different user groups)

   Fragrance, or no fragrance

   Texture: pleasant or prickly to the touch

   Sound: stimulating, soothing

Flowers: prolific

Foliage: bold or soft, unusual color, captures/reflects light

Ease of propagation

Forcible blooms

Interesting bark, branching, habit

Container plant

Use in crafts, drying, wreath making

Familiarity in folklore

Ethnic uses

Nostalgic associations

Hardy and reliable

Medicinal uses

Multiple seasons of interest

Attracts birds, butterflies, bees

Noninvasive

Requires much or tolerates little maintenance (dead-heading, light pruning)

Long-blooming

Night-blooming

Educational

Produces seed pods or cones

Interesting habit

Culinary uses

Edible flowers

Easy to grow

Good in flower arrangements

Interesting shape/texture (for artistic rendering)

   There are many different ways in which plants can be used in therapeutic horticulture activities (see chapter 16), so a few of the qualities on the list are opposites (fragrant or not fragrant, for example). Which aspect is desirable in any given situation will depend on the client base and the needs and limitations of the users. It is especially important, therefore, that a horticultural therapist be involved in the selection and placement of plants within an HT garden.

If a plant meets three of the listed qualities, is not at all toxic, and can survive the predictable overwatering that will result from all of the care given by the clients, then it is a good choice for an enabling HT garden.

Special Healthcare Settings

The point has been made that all therapeutic gardens should be site-specific, with the basis for plant selection being the combination of the plant's requirements for health integrated with the needs of the users. It is important that the design team include medical professionals, patients, residents, family members, and maintenance staff. The comments that follow provide a quick overview of considerations regarding planting and maintenance for specific types of healthcare gardens. (See also chapters 7 through 15 for other design considerations.)

Gardens for inpatient psychiatric facilities

Plant selection for gardens in inpatient psychiatric facilities needs to be carefully considered. Because of the emotional instability and cognitive impairment that some patients may be experiencing, plants that can cause danger to oneself or others must be excluded. Unless supervision is provided by attendants in the garden or monitored cameras, even mildly toxic plants should not be used. Some patients may be oblivious to pain, while others may be seeking ways to hurt themselves, so any plants with spikes, thorns, or irritating sap should be avoided. Shade is important because photosensitivity is a side-effect of a number of psychotropic medications. Trees that are easy to climb or have low hanging limbs can present danger in these settings. Trees with higher branching structures, or ones that can be "limbed up," are a better choice. In addition to these precautions, the planting design and maintenance need to ensure that there are no hidden corners and that staff can monitor the whole space.

Visual and auditory distortions and delusions are common among psychiatric patients. In consultation with the medical staff, the garden designer should eliminate plants that have contorted forms, such as the Hollywood juniper. The areal roots of a banyan tree may appear

threatening or "nightmarish" and should also be avoided (fig. 17.23).

Special attention should be given to creating spaces within the garden that are of human scale. Areas that are too large, such as expansive lawns, can be intimidating. Patients may prefer to stick to the edges. Spaces that are too small or too dark can seem scary and claustrophobic and should be avoided as well (fig. 17.24).

On the other hand, there are plants that are especially beneficial in a psychiatric garden. Plants that go through seasonal change can provide a temporal reference for those suffering from confusion or disorientation. Plants that are common in residential gardens and therefore familiar or plants that have cultural meaning can also be reassuring. Bright complementary colors can be cheerful, while analogous colors in the cool range can be soothing. Also of great importance is a planting design that can be seen and enjoyed in all four seasons from the indoors, as many patients are not allowed to go outside.

Gardens for children

Some of the same concerns arise in pediatric settings. Through exuberance and lack of awareness or knowledge, children can get themselves into difficult situations. Moderately toxic plants, as well as scratchy, itchy plants, should be excluded from the garden completely. As a rule, trees should be limbed up—though a tree that has strong branches and is easy and safe to climb can be an asset in a children's garden if it is appropriately placed.

Physical and cognitive engagement is the goal in a children's garden. Often the users will include the well siblings of patients, so finding plants that provide opportunities for play and plant interaction is key. Flowers that can be picked or grasses that can be looped into necklaces provide fun activities. Children often like to give these as gifts. These plant materials allow children to give back, something that is often hard for youngsters to find a way to do. Counting petals, causing seedpods to burst and scatter, or blowing on seed clusters and launching them into the air are also time-honored activities. Touching, smelling, and collecting leaves is a pastime for many children. Therefore the more appealing the tactile and olfactory qualities of the plants, the more enjoyable the garden will be for children (fig. 17.25).

Smaller-scale places to explore can activate a child's imagination and may allow young people their own opportunity to safely "get away," physically and emotionally. Plants that are pendulous and can be used as forts, or bushes that are open inside and form mazes or create places for hide-and-seek

17.23 The contorted trunk of a banyan tree may make a psychiatric patient feel threatened.
Photo by Naomi Sachs

while retaining some degree of openness for adult supervision, are all welcome elements (fig. 17.26).

Gardens for the elderly and for dementia care

Dementia-care facilities, and to a lesser degree all senior-care facilities, also have special requirements. There is reason to be concerned about toxicity in these settings. In the later stages of Alzheimer's disease, people can revert to behavior akin to that of infancy—including putting everything in their mouths, which sometimes results in their ingesting plant material. Plant selection should be limited to those that are not toxic at any dose. For this same reason plants with thorns or irritating sap are best eliminated, but if they are included in the garden, they certainly should be away from paths and patios.

The garden design should support residents' limited spatial orientation abilities and be simply and clearly laid out so that they may enjoy the therapeutic setting even when on their own (see also chapter 10). Additionally, the planting and maintenance of gardens for dementia patients

17.24 The residents of this mental health facility in northern England spoke of the need to stay near the perimeter of the lawn, as its expansiveness made them feel uncomfortable.
Photo by Marni Barnes

17.25 A plant-covered Green House at the Huntington Library Children's Garden, Pasadena, California.
Photo by Naomi Sachs

should allow the staff to view the whole space from inside the building. Walkways need to be kept clear to limit the possibility that patients will trip, get scratched, get poked in the eye, or even be nudged off the path by a crowding plant.

What is most beneficial is providing clients with mild memory loss an atmosphere that is familiar and comforting. Memories may be stimulated by including typical residential plants from the period when the clients were young. Smells can also trigger memories, making fragrant plants especially welcome. In addition to providing familiarity, fragrances can spark conversations among the residents and their guests. Selecting plants that promote horticultural therapy activities can also provide added comfort and support (fig. 17.27).

As eyes age, they begin to lose their ability to dilate and contract. Transitions from dark to light can be painful, and changes from light to dark, dangerous. Providing filtered or high shade through the use of fine-textured canopies can help to ease these transitions. Similarly, as older patients develop cataracts, they are less able to see colors in the cool spectrum. These colors appear to fade to grey, while the brighter yellows and oranges retain most of their vibrancy. Liberal use of bright warm colors in these settings is recommended.

In all of the above settings it is important that the gardens be pruned and cared for to maintain the delicate balance between providing a degree of privacy to patients and allowing them to be supervised by staff. This is one of the subtleties that requires a sophisticated awareness on the part of the maintenance crew.

Maintenance

Much has been said throughout this book about the benefits of nature and the calming and rejuvenating aspects of being surrounded by plants. What needs also to be stressed is the potentially negative impact of a garden that has been poorly maintained. In a civic or residential setting, a dying or lackluster garden would be a disappointing backdrop. In a medical-care setting, it is much more than that. An unhealthy garden can exacerbate stress and perpetuate a negative outlook.

Individuals tend to see things in the environment that support the general state of their feelings and overlook the things that may run counter to these emotions. Psychologists refer to this phenomenon as "emotional congruence." A person in the throes of romantic love, for example, is apt to see beauty all around, while someone who is depressed may perceive only negative elements in the same scene. Beautiful, healthy plants are uplifting because of their vibrancy; sickly and dying plants are likely to evoke a strong negative reaction, especially for patients and visitors who are already stressed and are looking for reassurance that they, like the garden,

17.26 A child exploring the intriguing planting at the Huntington Library Children's Garden, Pasadena, California.
Photo by Naomi Sachs

will be well cared for. Under these conditions, an unhealthy garden will take on a symbolic meaning that goes beyond its physical properties. It thus becomes critically important that therapeutic garden spaces be kept healthy and attractive. (For further discussion of emotional congruence, see chapter 3.)

Maintenance of plants and all other landscape features (including paving, walls, benches, water features, and fixtures) is also critical for safety. Careful attention must be paid to (and the maintenance budget must address) anything that might harm any garden visitors, especially those made vulnerable by problems with mobility, vision, and the like (fig. 17.28).

Policies: personnel

One of the key considerations in achieving a healthy and vibrant garden is the quality of the gardening staff. They must be knowledgeable, experienced, and committed to keeping the garden in the best possible condition.

17.27 Old-fashioned flowers that may trigger memories are especially appropriate in gardens for those with memory loss. Fourth of July rose. *Photo by Clare Cooper Marcus*

17.28 Poor maintenance and inappropriate choice of planting render this bench in a hospital courtyard virtually unusable. *Photo by Clare Cooper Marcus*

There are three customary ways of securing a gardening staff: outsource the work to a gardening service, employ in-house gardening staff, or utilize volunteers. Larger institutions most commonly outsource the work. This brings the convenience of minimal supervision, decision making, or provision of materials involved. The gardeners come and go in a relatively short time, usually at a cost comparable to in-house staff. But there are drawbacks to this option, all revolving around the limited quality control inherent in outsourcing.

A good gardener has three crucial qualities: knowledge, experience, and commitment. With gardens in healthcare facilities, knowledge entails familiarity not only with the maintenance requirements of plants but also with their therapeutic uses and how the two are linked. Information about therapeutic benefit needs to be provided in a maintenance manual precisely because the typical gardener is not expected to have this knowledge. But with an outsourced gardening service, chances are high that persons actually working in the garden will never see the maintenance manual nor adequately understand the meaning of a therapeutic garden. Even if there is an initial review of the manual, there is a high likelihood that the importance of that information will be lost in the overall directive the workers receive. In terms of experience, it is relatively easy to determine the length of time a company has been in business. But turnover of the front-line workers is often high. In a regular garden this might not be critical; but in a therapeutic garden, where shape, form, and the feeling of maturity are so important, it is best not to have a neophyte lopping off the wrong branch!

Commitment is also compromised when gardening is outsourced. Some US municipalities are finding that the concept of "pride of ownership" plays an important role in quality of maintenance of city parks. To test this theory, the City of Sunnyvale, California, divided its gardeners into crews by task—a mowing team, an irrigation team, a pruning team, and so on—and rotated them from one park to the next. City officials soon found that the health and attractiveness of the parks deteriorated from the standard set by having a traditional gardener assigned to a specific location. The city reversed its decision and reassigned workers to their own parks, where they again took responsibility for all of the tasks, and the standard of care increased (Barnes 1983). With outsourcing there is no pride of ownership. Loyalty is to the gardening firm, and profit for the service provider may be at odds with appropriate care for a therapeutic garden. Furthermore, for purposes of efficiency and time management, power tools are used and plants are often sheared into balls and cubes rather than selectively pruned. As noted above, to achieve maximum therapeutic benefit from most plants, specific pruning instructions are necessary, most of which entail observing the plant, its growth habits, and the surrounding plants. It only takes a little more time, but for a company with a tight schedule of multiple gardens to service, this little bit extra is hardly ever done.

Additionally, the use of power tools creates far more noise and disturbance. Contract gardeners usually arrive with a team of several people, and there is little if any control over the scheduling of the crew. Having a crew there for two to four hours with lawnmowers, hedge-trimmers, and leaf-blowers during the time people would most like to be outside (during lunch or break times) makes enjoyment of the outdoor space almost impossible.

An alternative to contracting out the gardening service is to provide in-house gardening staff. This increases quality control by providing a knowledge base that enables the staff to benefit from increasing experience. This arrangement allows for pride of ownership and opens up the possibility of reward for service. Instead of the noisy "mow and blow" crew, an in-house gardener would spread those same person-hours across a longer period, the disruption would be far less, and the disturbance to clients would be kept to a minimum if rakes and hand shears rather than power tools were used. Additionally a regularly assigned gardener may become a known and welcome presence to the garden's users. Research in nursing homes and hospitals has shown that the gardener can become one of the aspects of a therapeutic garden that users comment on positively.[3] Similar to the "mayor" of a plaza or park, as described by William H. Whyte (1980) in his seminal work on open-space design, the gardener can accomplish his or her work while providing the added benefit of being a social catalyst.

---

3. Interviews during postoccupancy evaluations of four medical facilities in the San Francisco Bay area evoked comments on the pleasure derived from seeing the gardeners every day at San Francisco General Hospital and the comfort received from chatting with the strolling security personnel at Kaiser Permanente Medical Center, Walnut Creek, California (Cooper Marcus and Barnes 1995).

It is important to note that horticultural therapists have training and expertise well beyond that of the typical gardener. It is not a good use of their skills, nor do they have the time with a full caseload, to take on the responsibility for maintaining a garden. At the minimum, a part-time gardener should be assigned to an HT garden.

The drawbacks to having an in-house staff maintain the garden are more administrative (supervision of staff, provision of materials and equipment, for example) than cost-based. This option should be seriously weighed, with full consideration given to the increased quality of maintenance and the higher level of therapeutic benefit likely to be derived from seeing maintenance as providing for the well-being of staff and patients.

Utilization of volunteers is also a common way to maintain a garden. If volunteers can be vetted, trained, supported, and supervised, they can be a wonderful resource. At the Tippett House hospice in Needham, Massachusetts, the garden is maintained by the "Garden Angels," an enthusiastic group of volunteers. At Legacy Health System in Portland, Oregon, horticultural therapy students in their training program become part of the maintenance team as volunteers (see chapter 16). Some medical facilities include local gardening clubs in their maintenance program as well. As with all volunteer efforts, obtaining worthwhile results requires a paid employee to supervise the volunteers, and even then a backup plan needs to be in place to cover shortfalls in the labor force. If there is a strong volunteer component for other services within the institution, this can be a viable alternative (fig. 17.29).

17.29 Legacy Health System in Portland, Oregon, uses horticultural therapy student volunteers to help maintain its healing gardens.
Courtesy of Legacy Health

Policies: budget

The greater the designer's (and the healthcare organization's) understanding of the overall maintenance budget, the stronger the likelihood that the garden will continue to be maintained well throughout its life span. If the maintenance budget (for staff and/or materials) is low, a garden that requires less maintenance should be planned. The most beautifully planned garden will not function as a therapeutic environment if it is not well cared for.

When computing the running cost of a garden, a few items are commonly overlooked:

1. Overplanting: Best practice would dictate that the garden be initially planted to accommodate plants at their maturity. If a garden is overplanted, the initial cost for larger plants will be higher than necessary, and there will be an added cost for removing plants as they begin to crowd each other out. Though it is not ideal for overall plant health, some designers and healthcare facilities will nonetheless want the instant look of a lush garden. If this is the case, these costs should be factored into the budget and maintenance plan for when overcrowding begins. The use of perennials and annuals as filler is the most cost-effective way to achieve a full garden, as some of these plants tend to be shorter-lived and are relatively easy to remove. The spreading of fresh mulch in between plants makes a new garden look well manicured and cared for, even though the plants may be small.

2. Plant replacement: It is inevitable that some of the larger plants (trees or shrubs), as well as the annuals and perennials, will die and need to be replaced periodically. The cost of the plants, their availability at local nurseries, and the labor of planting should be taken into account.

3. Mulching, fertilizing, and pest control: Most gardens require fertilizing and pest control, whether organic or not, as well as repeated mulching. This is usually done more than once a year and is part of the running cost of a garden. In an appropriately designed garden, these costs will diminish over time. However, there will be a need for some additional tending throughout the life span of a garden.

4. Irrigation: In many regions an irrigation system will need to be installed—this should be maintained with regular checks, with funds allotted for the replacement of parts.

Practical considerations
Watering
In addition to an underground irrigation system, hose bibs should be set throughout the garden—for clean up as well as additional watering that needs to be done by hand (when a replacement plant is getting established, for example). In horticultural therapy gardens, hose bibs also serve as a therapeutic aid—an activity for clients who turn them on and off and water by hand.

Storage
The other necessary component is an appropriately placed tool shed. In a horticultural therapy garden, the shed must be located within the garden and be accessible to all. The closer and more available the tools are, the better the maintenance of the garden will be. Especially for gardens that are harder to access—such as interior courtyards and rooftops, for example—a tool shed within the garden space that is large enough for all of the necessary tools is recommended Where storage is not possible within the garden, it should be located nearby.

Maintenance manual
A manual or handbook is critical to ensure the long-term health of the garden. Created by the landscape architect and the facilities management team, the intent of this handbook is to preserve the therapeutic benefit of the garden. It is to be a resource for the supervising facilities staff as well the gardeners themselves. As such, it should have sections that cover theory and policies as well as practices.

A brief description of the intention of the garden and how natural environments can be restorative will lay the groundwork for understanding the tending and pruning practices contained later in the manual. Information describing the therapeutic benefits of being in the garden and having a view into it will explain the rationale behind many of the maintenance practices. Additionally, policies about access should be included in the manual, because gardens too often end up being kept locked—to reduce maintenance costs; because budget and staffing have not been provided to cover the supervision of clients' use; or because garden users are perceived as intrusive to those inside the adjacent building. Issues of this sort should be reviewed and documented in the maintenance manual. Administrative turnover and budgetary fluctuations affect garden policy, and it is critical that the significance of any policy changes be understood.

The section of the manual on plant maintenance should emphasize the significance of the natural environment and the importance of plants that thrive. Fertilization and pest-management practices (whether organic or not) need to be considered from the perspective of the impact they may have on garden users. Plant care that allows the display of seasonal

17.30 Appropriate and well-maintained planting at the entry can help assure patients that they, too, will be cared for Designer: Ten Eyck Landscape Architects Inc.
Photo by Bill Timmerman

changes, attractive form, and the movement and ephemeral features of plants should be described in the manual. There should be specific instructions on how to maintain the appropriate buffer between adjacent buildings and the garden, including attention to degrees of privacy, sound penetration, and views in and out.

The bulk of the manual will be a listing, by species, of all the plants and their requirements. If different treatment is required of the same species in different areas of the garden, the location of the species should be called out. For example, a shrub that is used as hedging in one area should be kept clipped, while the same species used as a freestanding shrub in another location should be more open. In such a case, that shrub should be listed twice, once for each location. In addition to notes on procedures required for plant health, preferred practices for supporting therapeutic benefits should also be addressed. Additional notes under

purple-leafed plum (*Prunus cerasifera*), for example, might read, "Keep the canopy open for filtered shade and views into the tree from the bench below. Selectively thin the branching only after the bloom has finished. If size reduction of the canopy becomes necessary, it should be done through drop-crotching, not through shearing."

A third section of the manual should contain a copy of the garden plans, with all sheets and specifications. If the installation differs from the original plans, the "as built" drawings should be attached. Similarly, subsequent modifications in the garden should be drawn up and added to the manual. Any new species introduced to the garden should be added to the plant list, along with recommendations for their maintenance. The list of prohibited toxic and nuisance plants should also be in this section, as this information needs to be preserved and will be important as the garden grows and changes.

In conclusion, a therapeutic garden can be successful only if two basic premises are kept in mind. First, the garden is a multitasking space, providing beauty at the same time that it meets the psychological and physical needs of the users. Second, it is a living, growing system, and as such it has needs and requirements that must be addressed throughout its life span. This chapter has outlined the whys and wherefores of these two premises. With this knowledge and the help of a landscape architect who has a strong horticultural background and training in healing garden design, the therapeutic benefit of the garden can be great indeed (fig. 17.30).

References

Ahsan, T. 2004. "The Indian Feng Shui." *The Llewellyn Journal*, January 27. www.llewellyn.com/journal/article/576.

Barnes, M. 1983. "Maintenance Standards as They Relate to Pride of Ownership amongst City Gardeners." Unpublished paper.

Canadian Biodiversity Information Facility. Canadian Poisonous Plants Information System. 2009. "All Poisonous Plants." Government of Canada. www.cbif.gc.ca/pls/pp/ppack.list?p_sci=sci&p_type=all&p_x=px.

Cooper Marcus, C., and M. Barnes. 1995. *Gardens in Healthcare Facilities*. Concord, CA: Center for Health Design.

James, W. R. 1973. *Know Your Poisonous Plants: Poisonous Plants Found in Field and Garden*. Healdsburg, CA: Naturegraph Publishers.

Jayaprakash. n.d. "Vaastu Shastra—Indian Feng Shui." Ayurveda Guide. www.dharmaayurveda.com/article/2408.html?a.

Jost, D. 2012. "Johnny Can't Plant." *Landscape Architecture Magazine*, April.

Lampe, K. F., and M. A. McCann. 1985. *AMA Handbook of Poisonous and Injurious Plants*. Chicago: American Medical Association.

Ogren, T. L. 2000. *Allergy-Free Gardening: The Revolutionary Guide to Healthy Landscaping*. Berkeley, CA: Ten Speed Press.

Pollen Library. 2013. "Allergens and Plants Research by Location." IMS Health Incorporated. www.pollenlibrary.com/.

Sparks, S., J. McCafferty, and C. LePorte. 2012. *Secrets of the Land*. Valley Village, CA: Harmony Gardens.

Texas A&M University. 2013. "Earth-Kind Landscaping: Common Poisonous Plants and Plant Parts." Texas A&M University. www.aggie-horticulture.tamu.edu/earthkind/landscape/poisonous-plants-resources/common-poisonous-plants-and-plant-parts/.

US. Food and Drug Administration. 2008. "FDA Poisonous Plant Database." US. Food and Drug Administration. www.accessdata.fda.gov/scripts/plantox/index.cfm.

Wydra, N. 1997. *Feng Shui in the Garden*. Chicago: Contemporary Books.

Whyte, W. H. 1980. *The Social Life of Small Urban Spaces*. New York: Project for Public Spaces.

CHAPTER 18

Therapeutic Landscapes and Sustainability

O NE WOULD ASSUME THAT IN HEALTHCARE, where the goal is to promote and restore human health, "healing," or "therapeutic," gardens would be landscapes that sustain both people and the environment. Examples do exist in which design for sustainability and for healing support each other, and an increasing numbers of designers and healthcare organizations are working to bridge and marry the two intentions. But unfortunately, there are still designed landscapes that do little to nurture either people or the environment, or that are sometimes harmful to both.

Much of the focus on sustainability in healthcare has been on water and energy conservation, avoidance of toxic chemicals, and waste reduction. As Kellert and Heerwagen (2008, 88) state, "These strategies . . . are necessary but insufficient . . . they fail to heal the breach between people and natural systems . . . The way most sustainable constructions and places might positively connect people with nature . . . has been neglected" (fig. 18.1).

Conversely, the majority of outdoor spaces in healthcare facilities, even those designed to be restorative, may have a green veneer but do little or nothing to address environmental

18.1 The retention pond at Jupiter Medical Center in Jupiter, Florida, also serves as a large water feature viewable from the Cancer Treatment Center.
Courtesy of Studio Sprout; photo by Michiko Kurisu

concerns. In some instances, the landscapes and the way they are maintained are actually harmful to the environment (and thus also to people, directly or indirectly). Maintenance practices such as application of fertilizer, pesticides, and herbicides; use of gas-powered lawn-mowing and leaf-blowing appliances; use of plants—including herbs and vegetables intended for consumption—that are not organically grown; waste of water and other natural resources; failure to adequately address stormwater management practices; use of materials that are not sustainable (stone from distant locations, wood from nonrenewable forests, and so on); and use of materials that harm others in production or as they break down (e.g., fences, play equipment, and furniture made from PVC) all detract from what could be a true environment for health. In *Sustainable Healthcare Architecture*, Jerry Smith and Jody Rosenblatt-Naderi (2008, 92) state, "Successful gardens tend to transport people away from the intensity of healthcare through contrasts and distractions. But, in doing so, they may, ironically, inadvertently displace nature with generic healing gardens. Tucked into the harsh landscapes of courtyards and hospital rooftops, these gardens can be an oasis, but are at risk of failing by being out of step with the ecology of the ambient landscape."

A strong business case is an excellent tool for convincing skeptical clients and team members of the value of creating landscapes that are both therapeutic and sustainable. The green industry has been successful at calculating positive return on investment (ROI) for projects, and proponents of evidence-based design (EBD) are developing similar models. Money saved, for example, on fossil fuels and labor hours for maintenance, as well as money earned through the competitive advantage of beautiful, "green" gardens that demonstrate the organization's commitment to a local and global environment of care, are all financial incentives. Awards, recognition, and increased communication strategies are helping hospitals see the value of publicizing their successes to set them apart. For example, at Lutheran General Hospital in Chicago, an attractive and informative exhibit in the main foyer explains how sustainable and therapeutic goals have been met in the facility's redesigned landscapes.

Complementary Approaches

Sustainable and therapeutic landscapes complement each other in myriad ways. In many cases, one strategy comes first and the other follows. Kent Hospital in Warwick, Rhode Island, for example, needed to address the Environmental Protection Agency's new MS4 stormwater runoff standards. This became the driver for implementing sustainable landscape practices throughout the site. The initiative created an opportunity, through the hospital's capital improvement plan, to build healing gardens that mitigated the stormwater runoff. A Serenity Garden replaced a parking lot next to the infusion center, and a rain garden replaced the lawn outside of the Breast Health Center (fig. 18.2).

Project landscape architect Thomas Benjamin explains that a "whole-site approach" enabled Kent Hospital to develop a new landscape language and emblem for themselves: "Sustainable design + a beautiful landscape = healing and health." Benjamin's last point is important. For many healthcare facilities, creating—and publicizing—gardens that are healthy for people *and* the environment shows a deep level of care that provides comfort, inspiration, and pride to patients, visitors, and staff. This patient- and environment-centered vision gives the healthcare facility an advantage over other institutions in a competitive market (Environmental Protection Agency 2012).

Regardless of which comes first—therapeutic or sustainable design—the examples that follow show how the two strategies can work together and reinforce each other:

- Window views of designed gardens and surrounding nature also bring daylight into buildings (or to look at it the other way, the provision of natural light creates an opportunity for views of nature). The Dell Children's Medical Center

18.2 The rain garden outside of Kent Hospital's Breast Health Center (formerly Women's Diagnostic Imaging Center) used to be a lawn. Warwick, Rhode Island. Designer: Wellnesscapes.
Photo courtesy of Thomas Benjamin, Wellnesscapes.com, on behalf of Kent Hospital

in Austin, Texas (designed by Karlsberger, with landscape architectural services by TBG), is part of a 700-acre mixed-use brownfield redevelopment. The hospital integrated numerous themed courtyards into the design of the structure that provide daylight to many of the buildings' interior spaces. The design uses local site materials, including native plantings irrigated with reclaimed water, stormwater treated in a centralized water quality lake, and one tree for every four parking spaces (Guenther and Vittori 2008, 100).

- Therapeutic gardens, landscaped grounds, and detention and retention ponds dovetail with stormwater management and other low-impact development (LID) practices.

- Green roofs reduce stormwater runoff and the heat island effect. The most successful rooftop healing gardens are often a combination of an *extensive* green roof, where the surface is covered with as much low-water use, low-maintenance plant material as possible, and an *intensive* green roof, designed for pedestrian traffic. At the Shady Grove Adventist Church in Baltimore, Maryland, a combination of extensive (27 percent) and intensive (73 percent) green roof was used, resulting in 74 percent greenscape and 26 percent paving (Scarfone 2012). Given that people prefer and benefit from a high ratio of plants to paving, the goals of a sustainable healing space are potentially well aligned. When physical garden access is not possible, extensive green roofs can provide views of greenery.

- Green facades help cool buildings and reduce the heat island effect.

- Trees shade buildings and pavement, reducing the heat island effect and the need for air-conditioning.

- Condensate from air conditioners, roof runoff, and gray water can be used to irrigate gardens.

- Gardens that are varied and support biodiversity encourage beneficial insects and wildlife (fig. 18.3).

- Integrated pest management practices encourage biodiversity and a healthy ecosystem.

- The use of native and adaptive plants puts the "right plant, right place" model into practice, reducing the need for chemical fertilizers and pesticides.

- Native plants can provide people with a sense of place.

- Growing or offering healthy food on-site encourages good nutrition, healthy eating, and sustainable farming practices (local, organic, non-GMO, hormone-free). Kaiser Permanente in California is one of several healthcare systems that offers on-site farmers markets for hospital visitors, staff, and members of the community. At Changi General Hospital in Simei, Singapore, the roof is planted with herbs for use in the kitchen and cherry tomatoes that yield an average of 440 pounds per year. In addition to cooling the roof and providing the most local food possible, a

18.3 Ruby-throated hummingbird. A rich tapestry of native plant life supports a diverse array of animals, including birds and butterflies. Such diversity is a classic example of how biophilic design can enrich people's experience of the outdoor world.
Photo courtesy of www.henrydomke.com

composting program uses kitchen and landscaping waste as a natural fertilizer that helps to remediate previously damaged soil (Guenther and Vittori 2008, 66, 170).

Progress

Sustainability and access to nature have been incorporated into healthcare guidelines through the US Green Building Council's (USGBC) LEED for Healthcare and the Sustainable Sites Initiative (SITES). LEED HC and SITES assign credits and give guidelines with specific measures for providing adequate daylight and visual and physical access to nature for mental restoration, opportunities for physical activity, and spaces for social interaction. The nonprofit organization Health Care Without Harm (HCWH) was founded in 1996 after the US Environmental Protection Agency identified medical waste incineration as the leading source of one of the most potent carcinogens, dioxin. HCWH applies the maxim "First, do no harm" by promoting the health of people and the environment. In 2002, HCWH and the Center for Maximum Potential Building Systems launched the Green Guide for Healthcare (GGHC), the foundation document for LEED for Healthcare. Based on the USGBC's LEED for New Construction and viewed through the lens and filter of health intent, GGHC was the healthcare sector's first sustainable design rating system—a toolkit that integrated enhanced environmental and health principles and practices into the planning, design, construction, operations, and maintenance of healthcare facilities. The ninety-six credit GGHC system includes credits such as SS-9.1, "Connection to the Natural World—Outdoor Places of Respite," and SS-9.2, "Exterior Access for Patients." The GGHC was accepted by the USGBC, reformatted as a LEED product, and launched in 2011 as LEED for Healthcare.

The Sustainable Sites Initiative (SITES) creates voluntary national guidelines and performance benchmarks for sustainable land design, construction, and maintenance practices. From its inception in the early 2000s, SITES recognized the salutary value of landscapes through their "human health and well-being" credit (the other four are hydrology, soils, vegetation, and materials).

> Site design sometimes ignores the human benefits of healthy, green environments and fails to provide opportunities for physical activity, restorative and aesthetic experiences, and social interaction. However, research indicates that the natural environment plays a much more important role in human health and well-being. In addition to performing biogeochemical functions, healthy ecosystems are the source of the many less tangible—but very real and measurable—benefits that humans derive from a relationship with nature. These benefits are especially important to the more than 80 percent of Americans who live in cities and towns. (SITES 2012)

Like the GGHC, the SITES rating system is based on LEED for New Construction. The USGBC is now a stakeholder in the initiative and anticipates incorporating SITES guidelines into the LEED Green Building Rating System in the near future.

CASE STUDY

The Lawn: Myth vs. Reality

The lawn is the epitome of a false economy landscape when it comes to the "triple bottom line" of social (health benefits), environmental (sustainability), and economic viability. At surface value, the lawn makes sense: It is perceived as a piece of nature that is easy and inexpensive to install and maintain. If views of greenery promote human health, a lawn is certainly more attractive than asphalt. Research indicates that visual or physical contact with any greenery, including an expanse of open grass is, indeed, preferred, and thus has greater positive health outcomes over urban scenes that have no nature whatsoever (Debajyoti, Harvey Jr., and Barach 2008; Hartig and Staats 2006; Kaplan, Kaplan, and Wendt 1972; Kuo 2010). However, preference, health benefits, and performance (productivity, test scores, and so on) all increase when the landscape is expanded from more than a simple lawn to one with trees, shrubs, and herbaceous plants (Appleton 1975; Heerwagen and Orians 1993; Kaplan, Kaplan, and Wendt 1972; Matsuoka 2010). Environmentally, lawn is more permeable and better at reducing the heat island effect than pavement. But the resources needed for maintenance are more harmful and expensive than is often taken into account. Lawns need more water, fertilizer, and other chemical treatment than most other plant material. Furthermore, they require frequent mowing (as well as weed-whacking and leaf-blowing), which uses fossil fuel (fig. 18.4). Garden equipment engines produce approximately 5 percent of US air pollution. In terms of volatile organic compounds (VOCs), one hour of mowing is equivalent to driving 350 miles, or to eleven new cars being driven for one hour (PPM 2008). For the water, material, and labor costs of traditional maintenance, a facility could instead have a far more interesting, sustainable, and cost-effective landscape. For example, the rain gardens at Kent Hospital do need more skilled maintenance than what a typical "mow-and-blow" crew would provide, but the care is less frequent (only about twice a year rather than weekly) and also less resource-intensive (clippers and rakes rather than gasoline and chemicals). Cost savings in landscape maintenance for the hospital over the past five years is estimated at between $20,000 and $40,000 (Novick 2012).

18.4 This lawn at a healthcare facility provides little visual interest for patients and passers-by and requires much higher maintenance than people usually account for. New additions to this Chicago hospital incorporate rain gardens, native planting, and other sustainable practices.
Photo by Clare Cooper Marcus

Conflicts and Solutions

Designers and healthcare facilities should strive to create environments that serve both people and planet. The ways in which these landscapes intersect and support each other far outweigh potential conflicts, but the conflicts, especially in the healthcare setting, are real. When a choice must be made, the ethical imperative in healthcare is to "do no harm"—to prioritize what supports patients, visitors, and staff. Some potential conflicts and possible solutions are:

Green roofs and rooftop healing gardens: Rooftop healing garden design must first consider the users' needs. Rooftops are often harsh environments that offer little protection from the elements. As discussed in chapters 3 and 6, physical comfort is essential for any successful therapeutic garden—the presence of trees for shade; plants of varying height and form for sensory interest; paths that are wide enough for wheelchairs, and even gurneys, to navigate; places for sitting; and protection from wind, rain, and snow. A rooftop healing garden that can accommodate, for example, mature shade trees will be considerably more expensive than an extensive green roof with 4 inches of soil and low-growing plant material. Early in the process, the design team must agree on and budget for the roof's intended use (fig. 18.5).

Water features: Research indicates that people respond positively to the presence of water in the landscape (Heerwagen and Orians 1993; Herzog 1985; Kellert, Heerwagen, and

18.5 The green roof at Mercy Medical Center in Baltimore, Maryland, provides a good ratio of greenscape to hardscape.
Photo by Patrick Ross, courtesy of Mahan Rykiel Associates

Mador 2008; Kellert and Wilson 1993; White et al. 2010). Qualitative—as well as some quantitative—evidence indicates that in healthcare settings, both natural and man-made water features are an important component of a restorative outdoor environment (Cooper Marcus and Barnes 1999; Ulrich et. al. 2008). Yet water is a precious resource. Most decorative fountains can be designed with recirculating water to reduce waste. In addition, and especially important in arid environments, water features should be designed with minimal spray to reduce evaporation (fig. 18.6). This also reduces the risk of slipping and of infection from aerosolized *Legionella* bacteria, discussed in the next section. Attractive stormwater management ponds and ephemeral streams that run during and after storms are additional ways to bring water into the landscape. In new construction, especially on greenfield sites, careful planning can take advantage of already existing water features near proposed buildings (see fig. 18.1).

Water and bacteria: With regard to outdoor water features, there is scant research on the infection risks posed by bacteria such as *Legionella*, and even less on water features such as ponds (natural and constructed) and wetlands. All water elements must be designed to reduce the growth and spread of harmful bacteria. Routine maintenance, including testing, is essential.

Water and insects: Mosquitoes in wetland areas, rain gardens, and biofiltration ponds are a concern in any landscape, but their presence becomes a serious health threat where people are immunocompromised. As with bacteria, proper design and regular maintenance are essential.

Pollen: Many people are allergic to flowering grasses, so native and ornamental grasses—as well as other flowering

18.6 A small recirculating bubbling fountain at Arizona Cancer Center in Tucson offers a sense of oasis in the desert. Native plantings are full, green, and lush, reinforcing the metaphor of the oasis as life. Designer: Ten Eyck Landscape Architects.
Photo by Christine Ten Eyck

plants—must be carefully researched. Furthermore, when a landscape is not properly maintained, plants such as the highly allergenic ragweed can take over.

Colored pavement: Many people in healthcare settings are sensitive to glare from sunlight. Thus, using darker paving, such as colored concrete, is recommended. However, dark paving absorbs and then emits more heat. A designer must carefully balance these two potentially conflicting design needs. Some manufacturers make colored concrete that is designed specifically to have higher solar reflectivity values even though it is darker than uncolored concrete.

Lawn: Despite all of the arguments against lawns cited above, a lawn is sometimes an important design element. In children's gardens, it can be used for running, playing, or picnicking. Lawns make good flexible spaces for informal seating, programmed activities, fund-raising events, and so on. Alternatives to thirsty sod such as Kentucky bluegrass are available and should be chosen based on location, type of soil, and light availability. Native and adaptive species usually require less water and fertilizing, and they often require less frequent mowing. Lawn areas should be kept as small as possible, but not so small as to create a maintenance or mowing problem. Best management practices such as integrated pest management, watering at short intervals at night, and less frequent mowing reduce the need for water, chemicals, and fuel (fig. 18.7).

Native and xeric (low water use) landscapes: The trend of landscapes designed with native plants continues to grow. Piet Oudolf's "New Wave" gardens in Chicago's Millennium Park and on New York City's High Line have successfully introduced a more natural, less manicured look to the mainstream. Landscapes with native and adaptive plants that require less water have becoming increasingly accepted, by businesses and homeowners alike, in desert regions like New Mexico and Arizona. This is an encouraging step toward sustainability.

However, the new aesthetic described above has not been universally embraced. For many people, a "native meadow" still looks like an overgrown, neglected tangle of weeds, and cactus growing amidst gravel and boulders is "zeroscape," not xeriscape. Most businesses have an identity and want their buildings and grounds to represent them, visually and functionally. For a healthcare facility, the message is usually, in effect, "We care about you, and we will take good care of you." Many people, when commenting on facility's gardens, state that an attractive landscape is reassuring for this very reason.

As with the Kent Hospital example cited above, savvy organizations can combine sustainable and therapeutic qualities in their landscapes to market themselves as caring for both people and the environment, locally and globally (fig. 18.8).

But what if the message is misunderstood? What if, in implementing, for example, a native meadow or a rain garden, people see a poorly managed landscape rather than one that is healing and environmentally responsible? Or if, even when they know, intellectually, that a water-wise landscape is good for the environment, they feel less nurtured than if they were surrounded by lush, verdant green plants? In "Influences of Passive Experiences with Plants on Individual Well-Being and Health," Ulrich and Parsons (1992, 96) discuss contemporary theories that explain why people benefit from interaction with nature. Evolutionary theory posits that biophilia, or attraction to life and living things, drives our instincts: "The long evolutionary development of humankind in natural environments has left its mark on our species in the form of unlearned predispositions to pay attention and respond positively to certain contents (e.g., vegetation, water) and configurations (e.g., prospect and refuge) that comprise those environments" (ibid., 96). Research over the past few decades has shown that people prefer water, and plants and animals that indicate the presence of water; a landscape that appears lush, with a higher ratio of greenscape to hardscape; and certain shapes and configurations of plantings and space. Native and drought-tolerant plants, as opposed to lush plantings, may conflict with preferences based on evolutionary theory

18.8 Native planting in the parking lot of the Medical Center of the Rockies in Loveland, Colorado, is an attractive, welcoming landscape that uses less water and conveys an image of care—for patients and the environment—as soon as people arrive. Designer: BHA Design. *Courtesy of BHA Design; photo by Jason Messaro*

(Cooper Marcus and Barnes 1999; Heerwagen and Orians 1993; Ulrich and Parsons 1992).

The theory of emotional congruence, discussed in chapter 3, may also apply to people's perception of the natural environment. When people feel strong and healthy, they may appreciate a native or xeric landscape for its natural beauty and environmental benefits, but when they feel sick, vulnerable, and in need of nurturing, they may yearn for a lush landscape that has its roots in genetic memory. Kellert and Heerwagen (2008, 87) point out that "biophilia is not a hard-wired instinct like breathing and eating. It is a 'weak' genetic tendency that must depend on experience, learning, and social support to become functionally manifest." Recent research indicates that our intellectual "nurture" brain can override the gut-level "nature" response. Education, interpretive signage, and certain visual cues—for example, symbols of order and care such as well-maintained pathways and attractive furnishings—can help people to understand and appreciate an otherwise less preferred landscape (Loder 2012) (fig. 18.9).

In a recent study of two offices in Chicago and Toronto with prairie meadow–style green roofs, Angela Loder found that employees associated green roofs with their overall well-being: "In addition to the expected benefits of viewing nature, participants also reported their sense of pride in the green roof, and

their sense of hope that some environmental action had been taken." Interestingly, "though participants did not always like the 'messy' aesthetic of the prairie-style green roofs, they were more fascinated by them, more likely to feel that they were part of nature, and more likely to mention how much it influenced their well-being." Furthermore, people reported a change in attitude and greater appreciation over time as they observed seasonal changes, increase in wildlife, and other positive attributes that overrode their initial (rather negative) aesthetic reaction (Gray, Loder, and Heerwagen 2011).

But in other settings, would clear pathways and attractive furnishings be strong enough cues to reassure people that this was not a neglected landscape? Would educational material in the garden about its ecological value mitigate potential

18.9 The courtyard at Scottsdale Healthcare in Scottsdale, Arizona, offers native and drought-tolerant plantings; shade provided by the buildings, an arbor, and palo verde trees; and a sculptural recirculating fountain. The effect is of a nurturing oasis. Designer: Ten Eyck Landscape Architects.
Photo by Nick Merrick

negative reactions? The question remains whether such a landscape is appropriate for a short-term healthcare setting such as a general acute-care hospital, where people (other than staff) may only experience the landscape and building once or over a short period of time.

Depending on the context and the population served, it may be best to err on the side of caution and implement a slightly less "wild" design. The landscape can still be comprised of native plants. It will still require less water and maintenance, and it will still support a greater degree of biodiversity. Since many POEs of therapeutic gardens indicate that users desire more color, shade, and privacy, perhaps focusing on these, as well as on sustainability, would mitigate people's concern about a "wild" aesthetic.

In most arid regions, drought-tolerant gardens can be created that feel lush and verdant. The palo verde tree, for example, is a green, native desert shade tree that for many may evoke the preferred savannah landscape of our ancestors (see fig. 18.9). But we know very little about people's preference for different types of plants (e.g., dark green vs. gray-green foliage, stiff and spiky vs. soft and delicate foliage). This is a critical time for research about which environments best support people, which might do more harm than good, and how one's physical and emotional state may affect preferences.

References

Appleton, J. 1975. *The Experience of Landscape*. London: John Wiley and Sons.

Cooper Marcus, C., and M. Barnes, eds. 1999. *Healing Gardens: Therapeutic Benefits and Design Recommendations*. New York: John Wiley and Sons.

Debajyoti, P., T. Harvey Jr., P. Barach. 2008. "Relationships between Exterior Views and Nurse Stress: An Exploratory Examination." *Health Environments Research and Design Journal* 1 (2): 27–38.

Environmental Protection Agency. 2012. "Connecting Wellness and Environmental Health: Rain Gardens and Other Sustainable Landscaping Practices for Stormwater Management." Online webinar. Environmental Protection Agency. http://mdh2e .org/2012/01/03/epa-webinar-connecting-wellness-and-envi ronmental-health-rain-gardens-and-other-sustainable-land scaping-practices-for-stormwater-mangement/

Gray, W. A., A. Loder, and J. Heerwagen. 2011. "Why Research Matters: New Approaches to Health, Stress and Productivity in Green Buildings." Research paper presented at Greenbuild, October 4–7, Toronto, Ontario.

Guenther, R., and G. Vittori, eds. 2008. *Sustainable Healthcare Architecture*. Hoboken, NJ: John Wiley and Sons.

Hartig, T., and H. Staats. 2006. "The Need for Psychological Restoration as a Determinant of Environmental Preferences." *Journal of Environmental Psychology* 26 (3): 215–26.

Heerwagen, J. H., and G. H. Orians. 1993. "Humans, Habitats, and Aesthetics." Pp. 138–72 in *The Biophilia Hypothesis*, edited by S. Kellert and E. O. Wilson. Washington, DC: Island Press.

Herzog, T. R. 1985. "A Cognitive Analysis of Preference for Waterscapes." *Journal of Environmental Psychology* 5 (3): 225–41.

Kaplan, S., R. Kaplan, and J. S. Wendt. 1972. "Rated Preference and Complexity for Natural and Urban Visual Material." *Attention, Perception, & Psychophysics* 12 (4): 354–56.

Kellert, S., and J. Heerwagen. 2008. "Nature and Healing: The Science, Theory, and Promise of Biophilic Design." Pp. 85–89 in *Sustainable Healthcare Architecture*, edited by R. Guenther, and G. Vittori. Hoboken, NJ: John Wiley and Sons.

Kellert, S., J. Heerwagen, and M. Mador, eds. 2008. *Biophilic Design: The Theory, Science, and Practice of Bringing Buildings to Life*. Hoboken, NJ: John Wiley and Sons.

Kellert, S., and E. O. Wilson, eds. 1993. *The Biophilia Hypothesis*. Washington, DC: Island Press.

Kuo, F. 2010. *Parks and Other Green Environments: Essential Components of a Healthy Human*. Executive summary for the National Recreation and Park Association. Ashburn, VA: National Recreation and Park Association

Loder, A. 2012. "Greening the City: Exploring Health, Well-being, Green Roofs, and the Perception of Nature in the Workplace." PhD dissertation, University of Toronto. http://hdl.handle .net/1807/33886.

Matsuoka, R. 2010. "Student Performance and High School Landscapes: Examining Links." *Landscape and Urban Planning* 97 (4): 273–82.

Novick, N. 2012. "Transition to Sustainability at Kent Hospital, Warwick, Rhode Island." Sustainability (blog), Ecological Landscaping Association. October 14. www.ecolandscaping. org/10/restoration/transition-to-sustainability-at-kent-hospi tal-warwick-rhode-island/.

PPM (People Powered Machines). 2008. "EPA Statistics: Gas Mowers Represent 5% of U.S. Air Pollution." People Powered Machines. www.peoplepoweredmachines.com/faq-environment .htm#environment.

Scarfone, S. C. 2012. "Hospital Rooftop Gardens Benefit Patients, Improve Environment." *Healthcare Design*, December 17. www.healthcaredesignmagazine.com/article/hospital-rooftop- gardens-benefit-patients-improve-environment.

SITES (Sustainable Sites Initiative). 2012. "Human Health and Well-Being." Sustainable Sites Initiative. Accessed March 23. www.sustainablesites.org/human/.

Smith, J., and J. Rosenblatt-Naderi. 2008. "Designing with Rhythm." Pp. 92–94 in *Sustainable Healthcare Architecture*, edited by R. Guenther, and G. Vittori. Hoboken, NJ: John Wiley and Sons.

Ulrich, R. S., and R. Parsons. 1992. "Influences of Passive Experiences with Plants on Individual Well-Being and Health." Pp. 93–105 in *The Role of Horticulture in Human Health and Well-Being and Social Development*, edited by D. Relf. Portland, OR: Island Press.

Ulrich, R., C. Zimring, X. Zhu, J. DuBose, H. Seo, Y. Choi, X. Quan, and A. Joseph. 2008. "A Review of the Research Literature on Evidence-Based Healthcare Design." *Health Environments Research and Design Journal* 1 (3): 61–125.

White, M., A. Smith, K. Humphries, S. Pahl, and D. Snelling. 2010. "Blue Space: The Importance of Water for Preference, Affect and Restorativeness Ratings of Natural and Built Scenes." *Journal of Environmental Psychology*, 30 (4): 482–93.

Organizations and Resources

Environmental Protection Agency: http://www.epa.gov/region1/topics/waste/greenscapes.html and http://www.epa.gov/region1/healthcare/

Health Care Without Harm: www.noharm.org

Practice Greenhealth: www.practicegreenhealth.org

Practice Greenhealth is a membership not-for-profit organization with over one thousand hospital members and over sixty business members nationwide. They have a learning community for sharing best practices on environmental stewardship in healthcare and their awards program results in the sector-only sustainability benchmark report.

Healthier Hospitals Initiative: www.healthierhospitals.org

Sustainable Sites Initiative (SITES): www.sustainablesites.org/human

USGBC LEED for Healthcare: www.usgbc.org

CHAPTER 19

The Business Case and Funding for Therapeutic Gardens

WHEN ROGER ULRICH'S OFT-CITED "VIEW through a Window" study was published in *Science* in 1984, the medical community began, for the first time, to consider the financial benefits of access to nature. If postsurgery inpatients who had views to greenery required fewer high-dose pain medications, went home sooner, and called the nurse less often, perhaps nature was not just an aesthetic frill but rather an investment that made good business sense. Perhaps providing access to nature would promote positive health outcomes not just for patients, visitors, and staff, but for the facility's financial status as well.

The sustainability movement has done an excellent job of making the business case for "green buildings." Proponents of evidence-based design (EBD) have made inroads in establishing a similar case for healthcare facilities. For access to nature, whose components are difficult to quantify, creating a business case is a more difficult, though not insurmountable, challenge.

Although it is impossible to estimate how many hospitals have incorporated what they refer to as "healing gardens" and other aspects of biophilic design into their buildings and campuses, there is evidence that construction and marketing of healing gardens has increased. LEED for Healthcare and the Sustainable Site Initiative (SITES) now assign credits for natural light, views, and "outdoor places of respite." In the 2014 *Guidelines for Design and Construction of Health Care Facilities*, "Views of and access to nature" is the eighth key element in the physical design component of the Environment of Care (a change from 2010).

The Center for Health Design conducted surveys of design research in healthcare settings in 2009 and 2010, and in both years, 33 percent of respondents indicated they always "implemented healing gardens," (Taylor 2009; 2010). In reviewing the facilities featured in *Healthcare Design* for the years 2007 through 2009, landscape architect Jerry Smith found that 30 to 40 percent mentioned "access to nature" or "views to nature" in the text or illustrations. With facilities receiving citations of merit in the Showcase issue of *Healthcare*

Design, mentions of "views to nature" increased from 66 percent (2007) to 100 percent (2009), while mentions of "access to nature" increased from 36 percent (2007) to 100 percent (2009). While these gardens or views of nature are not necessarily up to the standards discussed in this book, recognition in the medical design world that "nature"—in whatever form—is an asset is encouraging news.

Cost-benefit analyses of the extent to which nature might enhance a patient's recovery are difficult, given all the variables involved. Other EBD interventions such as single-patient rooms and patient lifts are easier to measure because they have fewer confounding variables. However, some viable estimates have been made regarding possible cost savings. A study of the economic benefits of biophilia states, "Over fifty studies have been published that associate biophilic elements as primary influences for faster recovery rates for patients, decreased dependency on medication, reduced staff and family stress. And improved emotional wellness as a result of natural daylighting and views to nature" (Terrapin Bright Green 2012, 15).

The business case, including return on investment (ROI) for access to nature and therapeutic gardens in healthcare facilities can be considered in three categories: improved patient health and well-being; stress reduction for patients, visitors, and staff; and improved patient/resident and visitor satisfaction (fig. 19.1).

Improved Patient Health and Well-Being

Findings from Ulrich's 1984 study revealed that patients with views to nature were released on average after 7.96 days, compared with those viewing a brick wall, who were released on average in 8.71 days—a decrease of 8.5 percent. A later study estimated that if all postsurgery patients in US hospitals were allowed to recover in rooms with views to nature, and the average hospital stay was reduced by roughly half a day, the nationwide saving per year from reduced hospital stay would amount to more than $93 million (Machlin and Carper 2007).

19.1 The Donor Tree in the PlayGarden at Rusk Institute of Rehabilitative Medicine, New York City, unobtrusively recognizes those who have supported the garden with monetary gifts.
Photo by Naomi Sachs

Windows that provide views to nature also allow in natural light. Dovetailing these design opportunities can potentially lead to significant cost savings. A number of studies have reported reduced hospital stays and lower cost of pain medication during hospitalization when patients are housed in sunny, daylit rooms, as compared with rooms without access to natural light. One study found that the mean length of stay for bipolar patients in rooms with direct morning sunlight was 3.67 days shorter, as compared with those who had none (Bendetti et al. 2011). Another study considered the cost of medication for patients recovering from lumbar spinal surgery. Those housed in rooms with 46 percent higher sunlight intensity than dimmer rooms perceived less pain and accumulated 21 percent less in pain medication costs for their length of stay (Walch et al. 2005). Studies have also found better sleep patterns and a reduction in aggression among patients with Alzheimer's disease and other forms of dementia after they spent a short time each day outdoors in natural light or sunlight (Calkins and Connell 2003; McMinn and Hinton 2000; Whall et al. 1997). Such reductions can lead to lower costs in staff time and necessary medications.

Stress Reduction

Stress has profound physiological and psychological effects on those served by a healthcare facility, as well as on the staff who care for them. Reduction in stress for patients/residents, visitors, and staff leads to measurable positive health outcomes and higher satisfaction. The evidence is clear that gardens and nature elements—plants, flowers, trees, water, wildlife—help in the reduction of stress by providing positive distractions, along with opportunities for exercise, social support, and a heightened sense of control (Ulrich 1999). When users of the gardens at four San Francisco area hospitals were asked how they felt after spending time in the garden, 95 percent reported a positive change in mood—more relaxed, less stressed, better able to cope (Cooper Marcus and Barnes 1995). Other studies have reported a similarly high percentage of people who experienced a positive change of mood (Whitehouse et al. 2001).

Studies documenting the use of gardens in hospitals—whether or not they are designated "healing gardens"—often report that staff members are the predominant users (Cooper Marcus and Barnes 1995; 2008). Healthcare is one of the few services that is stressful not only for the customer but also for the provider (Berry et al. 2004). There is a serious shortage of staff, particularly nurses, and an inordinate cost in hiring and training them. Stress and burnout lead to high turnover. Poor working conditions can lead to medical errors. A review of the literature reveals that EBD interventions such as improving ergonomic design, air quality, noise, and light can have significant impacts on staff health (Ulrich et al. 2008). It is worthwhile considering how a garden might assist in improving staff health, satisfaction, retention, and even reduction in medical errors. A study exploring the outcomes of exposure to views from nurse work areas found that of nurses whose alertness level remained the same or improved before and after a twelve-hour shift, 60 percent had exposure to exterior and nature views. Of those whose alertness levels deteriorated, 67 percent were exposed to no view or only a nonnature view. "Access to a nature view and natural light for care-giving staff could bear direct as well as indirect effects on patient outcomes" (Pati et al. 2008, 27) (fig.19.2).

Even relatively brief exposure to actual or simulated nature settings can elicit significant recovery from stress in as little as three to five minutes (Parsons and Hartig 2000; Ulrich1999). While it is difficult to put a dollar value on the reduction of stress, let us hypothesize that a hospital has installed a garden with positive therapeutic qualities, easily accessible from staff break rooms, at a cost of $500,000. Assume that there are 500 nurses and that 10 percent of them use the garden regularly. Assume also that this contributes to reducing work-related stress and that nurses are thus less likely to quit their job due to burnout. Estimates of replacing one nurse who works,

19.2 Staff at the Mount Hood Medical Center in Oregon were involved in the design and fund-raising for the new healing garden at that facility.
Courtesy of Legacy Health

for example, in an intensive care unit in the United States range from $35,000 to $100,000 for recruitment and orientation, depending on the area of the country (Ulrich 2002). Hypothesizing a replacement cost of about $60,000 for one nurse, the savings of not having to replace the fifty nurses who use the garden and are less stressed would be 50 × $60,000 = $3 million. If roughly half of the cost of their reduced stress resulted from use of the garden, then the cost of their replacement would still be approximately three times the cost of the garden. While this is only a hypothetical calculation, it provides some indication of the possible economic benefits to hospitals of investing in gardens (fig. 19.3).

Another way of calculating this is to hypothesize that the nurse turnover rate is reduced from 14 percent to 10 percent, as happened at Bronson Methodist Hospital, Kalamazoo, Michigan, after the hospital moved into a new building that

incorporated evidence-based design, including an interior garden. The hypothesized Fable Hospital was said to employ 391 nurses. If 39 nurses left (10 percent of 391) instead of 55 nurses (14 percent), there would be a saving of $328,000, or $20,500 per turnover, as assessed in this study. This scenario attributed 50 percent of the reduced nursing turnover to the design of the new facility, or $164,000 (Berry et al. 2004).

Improved Patient and Visitor Satisfaction

Another important argument for high-quality landscapes and gardens is the influence on patient, resident, and visitor satisfaction—the extent to which hospital patients are likely to be "return customers" and residents in senior facilities are likely to recommend them to others. For example, San Diego Children's Hospital (now Rady Children's Hospital) aimed to

19.3 Burnout and stress lead to high staff turnover and may contribute to medical errors. A garden located and designed to facilitate restful breaks may provide a significant return on investment.
Photo by Chris Garcia

gain a larger proportion of the market in pediatric services in its region when it inaugurated a healing environment program in 1993. Physical components of the program included improved interior and exterior building design, gardens, family spaces, and an art collection. As part of this program, the Leichtag Family Healing Garden was opened in 1997. Two years later, an extensive study of the garden revealed that 50 percent of users said that the garden "definitely" increased their overall satisfaction with the hospital; 72 percent reported that they would "definitely" recommend that other parents or staff visit the garden; 48 percent responded that the garden would "definitely" or "probably" influence whether or not they would recommend Children's Hospital to others. Finally, 90 percent of respondents (including those who had never been to the garden) expressed the view that it was important for hospitals to include gardens (Whitehouse et al. 2001).

Increasingly, procedures that used to require a hospital stay are being performed at outpatient ambulatory-care centers. As sedation is often required and a family member or friend has to wait, sometimes for hours, to take the patient home, it is possible that gardens will become an important component of these centers, and thus the design of these spaces may contribute to customer satisfaction and loyalty. A study of ambulatory facility design found that the physical attractiveness of a facility enhanced patients' satisfaction and perceived quality of care. "There is a strong correlation between patients' overall rating of care and their willingness to recommend a facility to others. . . . Customer loyalty translates into an increase in the

customer base, an important consideration for administrators responsible for growing market share and revenue" (Becker, Sweeney, and Parsons et al. 2008).

In 2011 the first of the baby boomers turned sixty-five, and the coming decades will see an enormous increase in the demand for senior living facilities. A study by Mather Lifeways found that in assisted-living centers for dementia patients, outdoor activity space was considered almost as important as the top-ranked overall feature, which was described as physical supports such as handrails and walking surfaces (Keane, Cislo, and Fulton 2003). *The Independent Living Report*, sponsored by the American Seniors Housing Association, found that the appearance of the outdoor space was almost as important as the location of the community, which ranked as the most important feature in their study (Wylde 2009). Far from being a frill, usable outdoor space may be one of the most cost-effective ways to upgrade an existing facility and to ensure that a new facility will be positively viewed by residents and visitors (Rodiek et al. 2013).

The marketing director of a retirement community in Illinois stated, "Definitely, quality outdoor space is an excellent investment. Families and residents appreciate the beauty and tranquility of quality gardens and the wildlife attracted by the flowers, water features, and greenery. From a marketing standpoint, quality outdoor space is a huge selling feature and draws many touring new prospects. Outdoor space encourages normalcy with residents and families struggling with the decision to move from a home to a facility. These same gardens and outdoor space become the backdrop for brochures and marketing materials distributed to outside communities" (D. McHale, Tabor Hills Premier Retirement Community, Naperville, IL, pers. comm., 2012).

It is estimated that, depending on the age of the community, from 14 to 41 percent of current residents in assisted-living facilities have moved there because of the recommendation of another current resident (Wylde et al. 2010). The same study found that "very satisfied" residents (97 percent) were far more willing/likely to refer others to their community than simply "satisfied" residents (31 percent). The quality of accessible outdoor space is a significant component of residents' overall satisfaction with a facility. Another study hypothesized that improving residents' satisfaction with outdoor space would increase the number willing to recommend the facility to others. The authors posited that since word-of-mouth referrals from existing residents constitute an important resource for recruiting new residents, improving the quality and accessibility of outdoor areas could generate an estimated increase of 4 percent in new residents, resulting in more than $170,000 in additional yearly revenue for a community of one hundred residents (Rodiek et al. 2013).

Access to nature may also help to attract staff. Some healthcare facilities take prospective employees to the healing garden not only to showcase that particular amenity but also to demonstrate their commitment to an overall high level of care.

In conclusion, it is significant that access to nature is starting to be recognized and incorporated into healthcare design as an essential component of the environment of care. Now is the time for more hard numbers to back up its value. Healthcare facilities are businesses that need to take care of the bottom line. The more that proponents of therapeutic outdoor spaces can cite research that supports their claims, the more their clients are likely understand the value of investing in such amenities. The more that proponents can make the business case for access to nature and therapeutic gardens, the more likely they are to make it past the schematic design phase.

Funding Therapeutic Gardens

There are probably as many approaches to funding therapeutic gardens and other nature spaces as there are gardens in healthcare facilities. Funding will vary significantly depending on the type of project, the client, and the people involved. In new construction, a garden is usually incorporated into the project from the beginning. With renovation projects, a garden is sometimes added or an existing outdoor space updated.

In an attempt to understand some of the complexities of this process, the authors solicited information on funding from a number of landscape architects, architects, and horticultural therapists. Their responses are summarized below and organized in terms of sources of funding, what to fund, timing of funding, and funding strategies (fig. 19.4).

Sources of funding

Sometimes creative solutions to funding are found by capturing money put aside for one project and redirecting it to fund a garden. This was the strategy used by one Chicago-area landscape architecture firm with two hospital gardens. In one case, $200,000 had been set aside to restore the landscape in a construction area after a new wing of a hospital was completed. The landscape architects proposed moving a planned garden to this location, and in this way obtained the $200,000 for construction of the garden. In a similar case at another site, the landscapes architects proposed that instead of reconstructing the whole of a driveway removed during hospital

19.4 Acknowledging the donors who helped fund the construction of an all-weather pavilion in the Stenzel Healing Garden, Good Samaritan Hospital, Portland, Oregon.
Photo by Clare Cooper Marcus

construction, part of the disrupted area be transformed into a garden. In this way $400,000 was captured for garden design and construction (Geoff Roehll, Hitchcock Design Group, pers. comm., 2013).

In some cases, all or most of the funding to create and staff a garden has come from a local philanthropic organization. This was the case at the Margaret T. Morris Center, a residential memory-care community in Prescott, Arizona. The one-acre site originally comprised wild grasses and a path. In 2004–2005, Adult Care Services (ACS) of Northern Arizona undertook a renovation of the site with wandering paths, native plantings, water features, and accessible planters. Funding came primarily as a grant from a local philanthropic organization, with matching funds from families and friends of the residents. The garden renovation was the impetus for ACS to create a full-time horticultural therapy position in 2005 that eventually became part of the annual operating budget. (A very limited part-time position had been in operation since 1991.) Maintenance of the garden is supported by a local foundation and individual donors.

In the case of a series of courtyards at Broadmead Lodge in Victoria, British Columbia—a facility for people with Alzheimer's and other forms of dementia—a large proportion of the residents were veterans and a significant amount of the funding came from Canada's Department of Veterans Affairs. The Graham Garden at Saanich Community Hospital in the same region received funds from an annual golf tournament organized by the hospital foundation. In both cases, designer Deborah LeFrank was paid for design development plans to aid in fund-raising, though payment for construction drawings was sometimes delayed until funding was in place.

Many healing gardens rely on private donors, often recruited through a hospital foundation or development office. For example, the Jacqueline Fiske Healing Garden at Jupiter Medical Center, Jupiter, Florida; Leichtag Family Healing Garden at Rady Children's Hospital, San Diego, California; and the Olson Family Garden at St. Louis Children's Hospital in Missouri were all funded by very large donations from individual local philanthropists ($1.9 million in the case of St. Louis Children's Hospital).

The horticultural therapist in charge of a healing gardens program at Alberta Children's Hospital, Calgary, Alberta, recognized the importance of private donors but observed, "I believe it is also important to find independent means of raising program funds. In addition to providing a certain level of autonomy with which to spend money, it also provides a means of validating the existence of healing gardens to organizations like a [hospital] foundation—in that we are able to raise some of our own funds independently. In this case, although the amount raised was modest (for example, $10,000 a year from plant sales), it provided an opportunity to engage staff, patients, and families in supporting the garden" (Becky Feasby, Alberta Children's Hospital, pers. comm., 2013).

Funding campaigns can consider involving employees in contributing money for part of a garden. This was a strategy used in the Johnny Appleseed program at Jupiter Medical Center in Jupiter, Florida, where a kickoff meeting described the healing garden to employees and invited payroll deductions or one-time gifts. Donations from 15 percent of the employees resulted in $17,000 being raised to fund a major portion of a rehabilitation garden.

It is important to consider looking to unusual sources for grants that may fund all or part of a garden. For example, a garden at a homeopathic hospital in Glasgow, Scotland, was funded by a grant from a UK forestry source. A pond that became a popular feature at the Pavilion, a nursing home at Jupiter Medical Center in Jupiter, Florida, was originally severely eroded. A grant from the Town of Jupiter Water and Stormwater Utitilies Department to "improve water quality" in the pond funded planting, bird habitat creation, and an aerating fountain.

Corporate sponsors are another potential source of funds. Wells Fargo Bank makes an annual contribution toward the upkeep of the AIDS Memorial Grove in Golden Gate Park,

19.5 Presentation of a check for $50,000 from Wells Fargo Bank toward the upkeep of the National AIDS Memorial Grove.
Photo by Clare Cooper Marcus

San Francisco, California (fig. 19.5; see also case study in chapter 15). Home Depot and other big-box stores often make grant contributions to a community if they meet certain criteria. Home Depot supports 501(C)(3) tax-exempt nonprofit organizations with grants of up to $3,000.

In some cases, the clients of healing gardens have saved considerable sums by having the garden designed and built by students as part of a class project. This has been the case in metropolitan Seattle, where a number of gardens have been designed and built by students from the University of Washington School of Landscape Architecture Design/Build Program, under the direction of Professor Daniel Winterbottom. These have included a rooftop garden for cancer patients and their families at Pete Gross House in Seattle (see fig. 8.2); several rooftop gardens at the Dorothy O'Brien Center in Seattle, which houses Cancer Lifeline, a resource center for cancer patients and their families (see figs.8.4, 8.5, and 8.6); and a garden replacement at Nikkei Manor, an assisted-living facility in Seattle serving primarily the Japanese-American community (fig. 19.6). In the latter case, the total cost of the garden was $75,000. It was estimated that the cost would have been $250,000 if the client had had to pay a licensed professional. The manager of Nikkei Manor reported, "The cost was minimal: two quarterly 'round donations' to the University of Washington of $15,000 to cover the teaching assistant's salary and transportation, plus the cost of materials (agreed upon prior to the 'build' phase) as a third 'donation'. . .We've had a handful of small donations ($1,000 or less) that have helped offset the initial costs.

19.6 The garden at Nikkei Manor—an assisted-living facility in Seattle, Washington—was designed and built by undergraduate landscape architecture students at the University of Washington under the direction of Professor Daniel Winterbottom, saving the facility approximately two-thirds of what it would have cost had they not used student labor.
Photo by Daniel Winterbottom

Otherwise, we planned the project as a capital expenditure and allocated the funds accordingly" (Lisa Waisath, Nikkei Manor, pers. comm., 2013). Winterbottom notes, "The design/build team did solicit and receive many donations in the form of services, materials, and in some cases reduced prices on services and materials. . . . The majority of the labor was donated, resulting in obvious reduction in costs" (Daniel Winterbottom, University of Washington, pers. comm., 2013).

What to fund

In the creation of a garden, there are three principal phases that have individual costs: planning and design, construction, and maintenance.

Some firms prepare a master plan that the client can use for fund-raising, with the agreement that the plan must be paid for whether or not the the necessary funds are raised. When the funds are raised, the client must reimburse the costs of the master plan and agree to compensate the designer for the necessary design documents and construction administration. "We have done this on numerous occasions to get a project started. It has been successful for all parties on each occasion" (Carter van Dyke, Carter Van Dyke Associates, pers. comm., 2013). In other cases, the preparation of initial plans to generate further fund-raising is paid for from a capital budget.

Once a garden is funded and constructed, there is also the question of maintenance. Funding for this is critical; without

it, the initial restorative intent of the garden may be compromised. In the case of the Olson Family Garden at St. Louis Children's Hospital (see chapter 7) and the AIDS Memorial Grove (see chapter 15), fund-raising for endowments that would cover maintenance salaries and supplies continued after the construction budget was assured.

Timing of funding

Some clients building healthcare gardens choose to finance the costs up front, even if this has to be done in phases, and then raise money to reimburse themselves after garden construction. This approach has the major advantage of allowing the client and designer to maintain control over the design and precludes donors from trying to donate items—such as sculptures, benches, or trees—that do not fit the design theme or are inappropriate for a healing garden. One landscape architect from the Midwest comments, "Our clients chose to only seek large contributions and only allowed rather insignificant donor plaques to be placed in the garden, as they felt corporate logos and frequent 'donated by' signs would detract from the garden. . . . If [funding up front] is not feasible, then the owner needs to be committed to sticking with the design during the fund-raising process even if it means losing some donors who will not accept not having their personal taste reflected in the design" (Jeffrey T. Smith, Professional Engineering Associates, Inc., pers. comm., 2013).

In the early stages of the budget discussion with clients, a Chicago-area landscape architecture firm that specializes in healthcare gardens recommends that construction of the garden "backbone"—including such elements as large water features—be financed with main capital funding and that donations be used for amenities (furniture, garden ornaments, and the like). This can result in problems, however, including the donation of items unsuitable to a particular garden. In one case, donations of a sculpture and plaques were made in memory of a family member who had died; their aesthetic clashed with that of the garden. The landscape architect who had designed the garden was brought back as a consultant and recommended that the donated items be replaced with a more appropriate water feature—an example of the costs and tensions that can occur when a proposed addition conflicts with the therapeutic intent of a garden design. A landscape architect reported that the Department of Defense wanted to donate artifacts from the World Trade Center to a tribute garden for wounded warriors at Walter Reed Medical Center, Bethesda, Maryland. The design team agreed unanimously that these were not suitable and turned down the donations. In another case, sculptures not originally planned were donated to gardens at a medical center and a school of medicine during the design phase and were incorporated into water features. "We would not have had a fountain without the donated sculpture. So you choose your battles," (Jerry Smith, Smith\GreenHealth, pers. comm., 2013).

At Legacy Health Systems in Portland, Oregon, where ten therapeutic gardens have been created across the system since 1991, construction of a garden does not take place until all the money for building and ongoing maintenance has been raised from the local community. The process starts with three one-hour design team meetings in which representatives of the staff, patients, and families collaborate to create the concept for a new garden with a landscape architect and the coordinator of therapeutic gardens (see chapter 5). Administration then directs the Legacy Foundation—Legacy Health's fund-raising arm—to raise the funds for construction documents, garden construction, supplies, and salaries. This can take anywhere from one to four years, after which ground is broken and construction begins (fig. 19.7).

Funding strategies

One strategy is to convince the client early on and let them be a champion of the project. Dublin Methodist Hospital, a large new hospital built on a greenfield site in Dublin, Ohio, was developed with a strong emphasis on evidence-based design. The entire design team and a very committed client were

19.7 Breaking ground for a healing garden at Mount Hood Medical Center, Legacy Health System, Portland, Oregon.
Courtesy of Legacy Health

convinced of the importance of views to nature and access to gardens, and these elements drove the design in terms of daylighting, wayfinding, and places of respite. The latter were in jeopardy, however, when the budget became strained and value engineering nearly reduced the gardens to light wells. In this case, the fact that the whole integrated design team and the president of the hospital had been advocates since the beginning led to the outdoor spaces being pulled out of the budget, presentation renderings being used in fund-raising, and all of the gardens and courtyards and garden areas installed and fully funded by opening day. "The take-home message would be to take the gardens out of the value engineering equation, if it comes down to cutting scope and quality in order to meet budget. These spaces are the easiest things to sell to donors, and it becomes a win-win. The key is to get the client committed and connected early on in the design process and let them be the champion voice of the garden" (Jerry Smith, pers. comm., 2013).

The experience of a New York City landscape architect who has created many restorative landscapes is that early and regular discussions on funding sources with the facility's development office are critical.

[These] might include planning grants, sustainability initiatives, and then, of course individual funders. We often develop concept plans for our gardens to encourage "seed money" from key donors. Such donors often encourage new funders, or hesitant ones, to step forward. Every garden needs a leader, and gardeners who are potential funders are often such leaders in our projects. For one, they understand the intrinsic value of nature and of garden design. They also understand that every garden

19.8 An amusing hypothetical appeal for funds in a healthcare garden.
Photo by Kirk Hines

requires maintenance and are often instrumental in the establishment of an endowment for long-term maintenance. Our discussions with development staff continue with special events, using our plans and sketches to generate interest, and with coffees or lunches to quietly discuss the project. It takes a particular level of commitment from the designer to directly engage in these efforts. It is often intense and, at times, personal. But the rewards are, of course, greatly satisfying. (David Kamp, Dirtworks, PC, pers. comm., 2013)

The strategy suggestion of a Florida firm that has designed a number of restorative gardens in healthcare is to encourage a champion within the healthcare facility to propose that a garden be initially funded from the capital budget:

Because there are no sales programs for healing gardens and [because] healthcare staff is usually too busy to consider such amenities, projects like these are often overlooked when yearly budgets are considered. The start-up costs for these projects make up a small percentage of the budget when compared to the cost of other major capital expenditures. There is considerable return on this small investment that provides alternative therapy modalities, benefits staff and caregivers, and improves public relations. . . . At a minimum, the capital budget can fund professional design fees to develop the

concept into a preliminary or conceptual plan or sketches." (Roy-Fisher 2007)

Facilities with healing gardens are often able to build on their initial investment through fund-raising events held in the garden. Cocktail parties, sit-down dinners, and even concerts can all reward past donors and attract future funders. A horticultural therapist involved in fund-raising noted that a garden is much easier for people to get excited and feel good about than a big piece of hospital machinery (fig. 19.8).

"How much will it cost?"

One frequently asked question pertains to the cost of a therapeutic garden. "How much per square foot should we budget? Will it be more than a regular garden?" Designer responses to these questions were varied. Several commented that a therapeutic garden, like any garden designed for more than—as one landscape architect put it—"parsley around the meatloaf," will likely be more expensive than no garden at all or simple foundation planting (lawn, a few trees, a row of shrubs). Most designers also said that since each project—facility and garden location, size, components, program, among other elements—is so different, any sort of hard number of hypothetical cost per square foot would be impossible to provide. However, designers echoed what has been stated in this chapter: For most facilities, the initial extra investment can have significant, long-lasting rewards.

References

Becker, F., B. Sweeney, and K. Parsons 2008. "Ambulatory Facility Design and Patients' Perceptions of Healthcare Quality." *Healthcare Environments Research and Design Journal* 1 (4): 35–54.

Bendetti, F., C. Colombo, B. Barbini, E. Campori, and E. Smeraldi. 2001. "Morning Sunlight Reduces Length of Hospitalization in Bipolar Depression." *Journal of Affective Disorders* 62 (3): 221–23.

Berry, L. L., D. Parker, R. C. Coile, D. K. Hamilton, D. D. O'Neill, and B. L. Sadler. 2004. "The Business Case for Better Buildings." *Frontiers of Health Services Management* 21 (1): 3–24.

Calkins, M., and B. R. Connell. 2003. "Mary, Mary, Quite Contrary: How Do You Get People to Use Your Garden?" Paper presented at the Joint Conference of the National Council on Aging and the American Society on Aging, Chicago, Illinois, March 16.

Cooper Marcus, C., and M. Barnes. 1995. *Gardens in Healthcare Facilities: Uses, Therapeutic Benefits, and Design Recommendations*. Concord, CA: The Center for Health Design.

———. 2008. *Post Occupancy Evaluations of Six Healthcare Gardens in the Chicago Area*. Unpublished manuscript.

Machlin, S. R. and K. Carper. 2007. "Expenses for Inpatient Hospital Stays." Statistical Brief No. 164. Rockville, MD: Agency for Healthcare Research and Quality, US Department of Health and Human Services. http://meps.ahrq.gov/mepsweb/data_files/publications/st164/stat164.shtml

McMinn, B. G., and L. Hinton. 2000. "Confined to Barracks: The Effects of Indoor Confinement on Aggressive Behavior among Inpatients of an Acute Psychogeriatric Unit." *American Journal of Alzheimer's Disease* 15 (1): 36–41.

Parsons, R., and T. Hartig. 2000. "Environmental Psychophysiology." Pp. 815–46 in *Handbook of Psychophysiology*, 2nd ed., edited by J. T. Cacioppo and L. G. Tassinary. New York: Cambridge University Press.

Parsons, R., R. S. Ulrich, and L. G. Tassinary. 1994. "Experimental Approaches to the Study of People-Plant Relationships." *Journal of Consumer Horticulture* 1 (4): 347–72.

Pati, D., Harvey Jr., T. E., and Barach, P. 2008. Relationships between Exterior Views and Nurse Stress: An Exploratory Examination. *Health Environments Research and Design Journal* 1 (2): 27–38.

Rodiek, S., M. Boggess, C. Lee, G. Booth, and A. Morris. 2013. "Can Better Environments Lead to Cost Benefits in Assisted Living Facilities through Increased Word-of-Mouth Referrals?" *Health Environments Research and Design Journal* 6 (2): 12–26.

Roy-Fisher, C. 2007. "Finding Funding Sources for Healing Gardens." Jupiter, Florida: Studio Sprout. http://studio-sprout.com/files/Finding-Funding-Sources-for-Healing-Gardens.pdf

Taylor, E. M. 2009. *Survey of Design Research in Healthcare Settings: The Use and Impact of Evidence-based Design*. Concord, CA: Center for Health Design.

———. 2010. *Survey of Design Research in Healthcare Settings: The Use and Impact of Evidence-based Design*. Concord, CA: Center for Health Design.

Terrapin Bright Green. 2012. *The Economics of Biophilia: Why Designing with Nature in Mind Makes Financial Sense*. New York: Terrapin Bright Green.

Ulrich, R. S.. 1984. "View through a Window May Influence Recovery from Surgery." *Science* 224 (4647): 420–21.

———. 1999. "Effects of Gardens on Health Outcomes: Theory and Research." Pp. 27–86 in *Healing Gardens: Therapeutic Benefits and Design Recommendations*, edited by C. Cooper Marcus, and M. Barnes. New York: John Wiley and Sons.

———. 2002. "Communicating with the Health-Care Community." Pp. 19–32 in *Interaction by Design: Bringing People and Plants Together for Health and Well-Being*, edited by C. A. Shoemaker. Ames, Iowa: Iowa State University Press.

Ulrich, R. S., C. Zimring, X. Zhu, J. DuBose, H. B. Seo, Y. S. Choi, X. Quan, and A. Joseph. 2008. "A Review of the Research Literature on Evidence-based Healthcare Design." *Health Environments Research and Design Journal* 1 (3): 61–125.

Walch, J. M., B. S, Rabin, R. Day, J. N. Williams, K. Choi, and J. D. Kang. 2005. "The Effect of Sunlight on Postoperative Analgesic Use." *Psychosomatic Medicine* 67: 156–63.

Whall, A. L., M. E. Black, C. J. Groh, D. J. Yankou, B. J. Kupferschmid, and N. L. Foster. 1997. "The Effect of Natural Environments upon Agitation and Aggression in Late Stage Dementia Patients." *American Journal of Alzheimer's Disease and Other Dementias* 5 (12): 216–20.

Whitehouse, S., J. W Varni, M. Seid, C. Cooper Marcus, M. J. Ensberg, J. R. Jacobs, and R. S. Mehlenbecket. 2001." Evaluating a Children's Hospital Garden Environment: Utilization and Consumer Satisfaction." *Journal of Environmental Psychology* 21: 301–14.

Wylde, M. 2009. *The Independent Living Report*. Washington DC: American Seniors Housing Association.

Wylde, M. A., E. Smith, D. Schless, and R. Bernstecker. 2009. "Satisfied Residents Won't Recommend Your Community, but Very Satisfied Residents Will." *Seniors Housing and Care Journal* 17 (1): 3–13.

CHAPTER 20

Evaluation of Therapeutic Gardens

WITH INCREASING NUMBERS OF HEALING gardens appearing in healthcare facilities, it is clear that the message regarding the restorative power of nature—now supported by plenty of research—is getting through. But we need to ask: What kind of nature? What kind of healing gardens? Where illustrations of gardens accompany featured facilities in professional publications such as *Healthcare Design*, they often depict recurring design problems: too much hardscape, not enough shade, few places to sit, not enough privacy, too little "nature." It is not sufficient to place a couple of benches and potted plants in an empty courtyard and call it a "healing garden." Perhaps the designers were unaware of the research suggesting what is essential for a truly restorative space. Perhaps the garden was designed by someone not trained in outdoor space design, such as an artist or interior designer. The only professional who should be designing gardens for healthcare is a landscape architect or landscape designer.

In some respects, healing gardens may be becoming too popular, to the detriment of the people who should most benefit from them. They are too often being used as a marketing tool, and perhaps as a way to attract the attention of judges of design awards. It may be appropriate for designers to push the envelope with an outdoor space for a corporate headquarters or a museum, but for healthcare facilities, design informed by evidence, with a solid understanding of the needs of the users, is essential. Unfortunately, too often healing gardens follow the latest fad. They are, in a word, fashionable.

We find ourselves in a similar situation to the sustainability movement, with people jumping on the green bandwagon, "greenwashing" design and construction. Those working to promote evidence-based design (EBD) face a similar challenge: people employ the term without understanding the ideas and scholarship behind it.

What is needed next is a better understanding of the available research; an increased use of postoccupancy evaluations (POEs) and other methods that expand our knowledge of what makes a landscape restorative; the sharing of excellent examples; presentation of useful design guidelines; and, ultimately, a system such as LEED or the Sustainable Sites Initiative (SITES) for rating and certifying healing gardens and other types of health-promoting outdoor spaces.

Evaluation

It is important to consider why and how some healing gardens succeed and others fail. Landscape architecture, like other design professions, has been lax in evaluating past work. Unless this happens in a consistent way, designers cannot learn from past mistakes, and the profession cannot move forward. It is true that a systematic evaluation costs money. This suggests the need for a line item in the budget for a garden that covers an evaluation—and fine-tuning—one to two years after implementation. Some of the resistance to evaluating built work and publishing the results is the fear, on the part of the designer or the client, of being perceived as having made mistakes. But any evaluation is an opportunity to learn, to improve an existing space, and to add to the fund of knowledge about design.

A problem for the evaluators of built environments is that designers rarely make their hypotheses explicit, and rarely record the goals of their design and how the resulting environment reflects those goals. The recording of this necessary information will light the way for POEs that truly reflect evidence-based design. Also essential is greater understanding by designers of how to read and interpret available research. A step in the right direction is the development of the Evidence-based Design Accreditation and Certification (EDAC), through the Center for Health Design. The program certifies individuals—designers, healthcare providers and staff (including facilities managers), and researchers—in the EBD process.

It is estimated that a comprehensive POE of a $150 million healthcare project would cost considerably less than 0.001percent of the project's budget (Watkins, Peavey, and Clarke 2012). The POE of a garden at such a facility would cost much less. Research suggests that what would have cost $1 to correct at the programming stage may cost $10 in schematic design, and $100 to correct during construction (Shepley 2011).

An unbiased, systematic evaluation of a healing garden two or three years after construction can document how well the intent of the garden and the needs of its users were understood; how well the original goals of the design were translated into physical form; how well the garden serves the users it was intended for—as well as those it was not planned for; how well the planting is doing; how well the space is being maintained; and what changes in physical design, maintenance, or policy need to be implemented. The POE is one of the best methods for this kind of analysis. While some designers will say that they routinely conduct POEs of their projects, these usually consist of a meeting with the client and a quick walk-through. While this can provide useful information for the designer and the client, it is neither a rigorous nor an objective evaluation.

The term POE covers a broad range of activities. The three most common types of POEs are indicative, investigative, and diagnostic (Cooper Marcus 2007) (fig. 20.1).

An *indicative* POE can be conducted in a short time (a few hours to a few days) and can include interviews with the staff and/or the designers and a walk-through evaluation (Anderzhon, Fraley, and Green 2007). More systematic is the use of an audit—a scored checklist of elements and qualities that should be incorporated into an ideal healing garden. Three or four individuals who are knowledgeable about therapeutic garden design but were not involved in the original design will evaluate the garden separately; then their scores are averaged so as to avoid any bias (Preiser, Rabinowitz, and White 1988; Cooper Marcus 2008). This form of evaluation can reveal a great deal about how well design details have been implemented—perhaps suggesting areas in need of change—but reveals nothing about who uses the space or their motivations.

An *investigative* POE is sometimes prompted by issues raised in an indicative POE. It covers issues in more depth, and the evaluation criteria may be explicitly stated—the relative design success of several gardens at the same facility, or how well shade or seating have been implemented.

A *diagnostic* POE is the most comprehensive evaluation and requires considerable time and budget. The use of multiple methods to provide reliable findings is essential. A diagnostic POE will ideally be carried out by a team of one or more social scientists familiar with the methods and one or more healing garden designers, but not the designers of the garden being

20.1 It doesn't require a costly POE to recognize that these behavior traces of well-worn short cuts through the landscaping should prompt a proposal for redesign.
Photo by Clare Cooper Marcus

studied or anyone responsible for it in any way, to avoid possible bias. The evaluation would include the following:

1. Project context—use of adjacent buildings, entries, views in and out of the space, etc.

2. Site analysis—sun and shade patterns, prevailing winds, etc.

3. Interviews with the designers and members of the design team to document the original goals for the garden, how those goals were translated into design, what had to be omitted or compromised because of budget constraints or other limitations.

4. Interviews with staff (clinical staff, administrators, facility manager, and gardeners, for example) to solicit their views on the space, problems related to design or access, changes they would like to see, and similar questions.

5. Observation of plant health and maintenance.

6. Behavior traces—visible clues as to what users do, or don't do, even when no one is present. Clues such as cigarette butts around a particular bench, a shortcut across a lawn, a raised gardening bed full of weeds—all tell a story (see fig 20.1).

7. Behavior mapping—systematic observation of actual use at different times of the day, different days of the week, with users recorded by age, gender, role, and activity. The data

recorded is quantitative and is much more accurate than asking people what they do. However, behavior mapping provides no information as to what people *feel*.

8. Interviews with users are essential to learn why they come to the space, how often they visit, what they like, what they would like to see changed or added, whether they feel different after spending time in the space, and so on. Interviewing users face to face and writing down the answers provides more

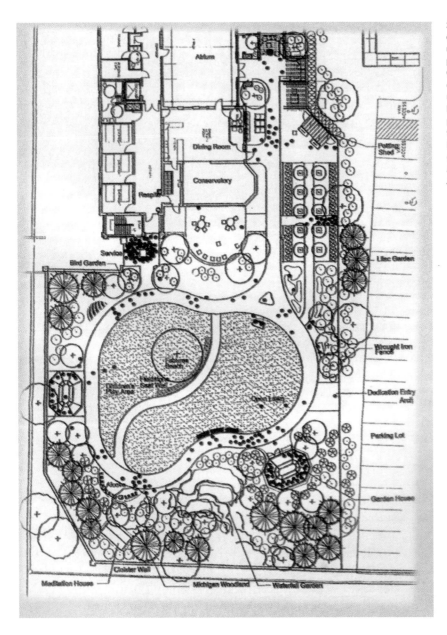

20.2 A behavior-mapping exercise: An aggregate map of the use of a garden for Alzheimer's patients in Grand Rapids, Michigan. Observations were made over five days in September 2001. People using the garden were plotted by location on a map for 10-minute periods at 20-minute intervals from 9:00 a.m. to 4:00 p.m., excluding the lunch hour. (See case study of this garden in chapter 10.)
PhD study by Charlotte Grant, College of Architecture, Georgia Tech.

accurate and reliable information than handing out question-naires and having people return them later. Sometimes it is desirable to interview nonusers to find out why they do not use the space.

Together these two basic categories of data—behavior mapping providing objective information about use, and interviews providing subjective information about motivation and feeling—offer a good overview of the success (or shortcomings) of the garden being studied (fig. 20.2).

Ideally, the results of any kind of POE are compared with the designer's original intentions; maintenance or construction changes since the garden was implemented; changes to the use of adjacent buildings; and changes of policy regarding who may use the garden, hours the garden is open, or similar isues. Particularly important would be the evaluation of a garden that used evidence-based design with specific desired outcomes. Did the design fulfill those? What could be done better next time, or what could be changed for future use? (fig.20.3).

Also important to consider is a *preoccupancy evaluation* (PROE) consisting of a systematic survey of the use of a space before redesign and feedback on proposals for change. These can serve as a baseline to compare with a POE conducted one to two years after the space has been reconstructed or changed (Naderi and Shin 2008). Among the references listed below under "Research Methods" providing in-depth detail on evaluation methods and techniques, the two most useful are Shepley (2011) and Zeisel (2006).

What We Can Learn from a POE

The results of a POE can provide valuable information on (1) the extent to which the design team's assumptions about how an outdoor space would be used were realized; (2) how the original goals of a garden were not fully understood by staff and users who were not involved in the original design process; (3) exemplary gardens that can serve as models of user-oriented design; (4) outdoor spaces intended to be therapeutic that have failed to live up to their promise; (5) needed changes in design and/or maintenance at a particular site; and (6) what to do differently next time at a similar site (fig. 20.4).

For example, investigative POEs plus behavior mapping at several Chicago healing gardens found very low use by children of a garden at a children's hospital because there was little there that engaged or interested them; and at an attractive garden at a facility for the elderly, lack of any seating along a looped pathway precluded use by those who needed to rest along the way (Cooper Marcus and Barnes 2008). An investigative POE of a garden for people with disabilities found problems with use because detailed knowledge of the heights and widths of planting beds was not available when the garden was designed (Rothert and Hammel 2002).

An excellent example of a series of indicative POEs can be found in *Design for Aging Post-Occupancy Evaluations*, published by the American Institute of Aging Knowledge Community (Anderzhon, Fraley, and Green 2007). An interdisciplinary team spent two days at each of a number of projects, touring the buildings and outdoor spaces, interviewing

20.3 A preoccupancy evaluation of the use of this trail through the campus of a Utah hospital could be compared with a postoccupancy evaluation after benches were added at regular intervals. Did this change result in more use overall, and in particular, by older individuals?
Photo by Chris Garcia

20.4 These pointed steel planters that leak, and the planting that does not provide privacy for adjacent patient rooms, may not have been the best choices for this hospital outdoor space.
Photo by Clare Cooper Marcus

20.5 Systematic behavior observations in the garden of this Chicago-area hospital recorded that these exposed benches were rarely used, whereas . . .

staff at all levels of the organization, talking with a few residents, and assessing how the project functioned in terms of its design. While not as rigorous (or time-consuming) as a diagnostic POE, these evaluations reveal much about the reality of these same projects versus designers' own descriptions and photographs submitted to the AIA's *Design for Aging Review* publications.

A diagnostic POE, which is more time-consuming, reveals more detailed findings than an indicative walk-through and is often carried out as an academic dissertation or consultant's report. A diagnostic POE of a rooftop rehabilitation garden in Tennessee revealed that clinical staff members, who had insisted on taking care of maintenance, did not understand the original intent of the planting design. They removed or severely pruned plants, rendering those in the garden and adjacent patient rooms overly exposed (Davis 2011). In a PROE of Texas hospital courtyard, nurses on short breaks

20.6 . . . this bench a few yards away, surrounded with colorful planting and close to a waterfall, was almost always in use.
Photos by Clare Cooper Marcus

complained of lack of privacy in a space with minimal greenery, as well as concrete benches that were either too hot or too cold to sit on (Naderi and Shin 2008). A diagnostic POE of gardens at three Texas children's hospitals found that lack of shade was a major deterrent to use by staff and families (Pasha, forthcoming; Pasha and Shepley 2013). Sometimes the POE will lead to changes being made. For example, a diagnostic POE of a children's hospital garden in San Diego found minimal use during the hottest months of the year because of a lack of shade. It also found that many nonusers did not know that the garden existed. As a result, the hospital added shade trees and put up more directional signs to the garden, in English and Spanish (Whitehouse et al. 2001) (fig. 20.5, fig. 20.6).

Even a brief walk-through can educate designers and researchers alike and can suggest possible problems that might be investigated later with a formal of POE. For example, a Canadian children's hospital roof area with large expanses of rubberized tile and nothing else but an occasional gazebo and potted conifer suggests little use of the space by sick children or their families. The same is true at new rooftop gardens at children's hospitals in Oregon and Arizona. Colorfully stylish plastic furniture may be appealing to adults, but there is a lack of anything likely to engage children's interest. A conversation with the director of a cancer resource center in Scotland revealed that no one—other than excited visiting children—used the outdoor space that consisted of two steep-sided mounds symbolizing cells in balance (see fig. 8.15). Observations over time at a cancer clinic's courtyard in Berkeley, California, revealed that very few people ever used it, probably because the exposed steel benches and minimal planting offered no privacy, and water leaking from planters created a slipping hazard.

Casual observations of garden-courtyards at many Publicly Financed Initiative (PFI) hospitals built for, and leased to, the United Kingdom's National Health Service (NHS) indicate that almost all of them are permanently locked, presumably to keep maintenance costs down. The courtyards at such hospitals in Glasgow, Edinburgh, and Norwich incorporate moderately attractive planting that can be viewed from adjacent corridors, but the spaces are never used. Casual conversations with staff at Hvidovre Hospital in Copenhagen, where the entire roof area of a spacious two-story building is covered with roof gardens, revealed that maintenance costs have led to many sections being closed. While such observations may not lead to any kind of POE, they can provide a useful base of knowledge for a designer or anyone with an interest in hospital outdoor space. The more gardens are visited with a questioning eye—even for short periods—the more a designer will be alerted to problems to be avoided and best practices to be emulated (fig. 20.7, fig. 20.8).

20.7 A comparative POE of the use of this outdoor space at a cancer center, with . . .
Photo by Clare Cooper Marcus

20.8 . . . a different designed space at another cancer center not far away, might yield some interesting results regarding people's preferences. Designer: Ten Eyck Landscape Architects.

Photo by Christine Ten Eyck

Finally, when a well-used and much-loved hospital garden is threatened with demolition, it does not take any kind of formal POE to raise awareness of its value and importance. A proposal to expand Boston Children's Hospital in Boston, Massachusetts, and eradicate the Prouty Garden, which has served the community since 1956, resulted in a vibrant online petition campaign to save it. Although an alternative roof garden was proposed, this replacement may not be an adequate substitute. Sometimes it is hard to argue the case that a garden is more important than additional patient rooms or an expanded emergency department. A garden may be seen as a soft option, but with more investigation (and user protests), an alternative site for expansion can sometimes be found (fig.20.9).

Next Steps

The research, observations, case studies, and evidence-based guidelines presented in this book provide tools to help translate existing research into good design. Guidelines are an important step in aiding designers and clients in making good decisions. The next steps towards improving the quality of outdoor spaces in healthcare are, first, to create, test, and implement a *standardized therapeutic garden evaluation* in the form of an audit, and, second, to develop a *certification program* comparable to LEED or SITES. The more that healthcare gardens can be evaluated and documented, the more we can learn and add to the growing fund of knowledge.

The authors are currently working with colleagues to refine a healthcare garden audit developed by Cooper Marcus and Barnes in 2008. While guidelines and evaluations help designers and clients understand what they should do, or should have done, only certification can hold stakeholders to certain standards. The certification program will likely grow out of the guidelines and the audit toolkit. Another useful step would be to institute healing or restorative garden awards, to be administered by the ASLA, the Academy for Design and Health, or a similar organization (Cooper Marcus and Sachs 2013).

20.9 Water collecting in these seats at an Oregon hospital suggest a poor design decision, considering that the region experiences frequent rain.
Photo by Clare Cooper Marcus

The authors look forward to continued research and advocacy for truly salutary healthcare design—design that is derived from a balance of knowledge and empathy and that nurtures, protects, and inspires patients, visitors, and staff.

Further Resources

Research methods

Bechtel, R. B., R. W. Marans, and W. Michelson. 1987. *Methods in Environmental and Behavioral Research*. New York: Van Nostrand Reinhold.

Cherulnik, P. 1993. *Applications of Environment—Behavior Research: Case Studies and Analysis*. Cambridge, MA: Cambridge University Press.

Cooper Marcus, C., and C. Francis. 1998. "Post-Occupancy Evaluation." Pp. 345–56 in *People Places: Design Guidelines for Urban Open Space*, 2nd edition, edited by C. Cooper Marcus and C. Francis. New York: John Wiley and Sons.

Preiser, W., H. Z. Rabinowitz, and E. T. White. 1988. *Post-Occupancy Evaluation*. New York: Van Nostrand Reinhold.

Shepley, M. M. 2011. *Health Facility Evaluation for Design Practitioners*. Myersville, MD: Asclepion Publishing.

Zeisel, J. 1981. *Inquiry by Design: Tools for Environment-Behavior Research*. Monterey, CA: Brooks/Col Publishing.

Zeisel, J., and J. B. Eberhard. 2006. *Inquiry by Design: Environment/Behavior/Neuroscience in Architecture, Interiors, Landscape, and Planning*. New York: W. W. Norton.

Examples of indicative POEs

Anderzhon, J. W., I. L. Fraley, and M. Green. 2007. *Design for Aging Post-Occupancy Evaluations*. Hoboken, NJ: John Wiley and Sons.

Cooper Marcus, C. 2003. "Healing Havens: Two Hospital Gardens in Portland Win Awards for Therapeutic Values." *Landscape Architecture Magazine* 93 (8): 85–91; 104–9.

———. 2005. "No Ordinary Garden: Alzheimer's and Other Patients Find Refuge in a Michigan Dementia-Care Facility." *Landscape Architecture Magazine* 95 (3): 26–39.

———. 2008. "For Burn Patients, a Place to Heal." *Landscape Architecture Magazine* 98 (4): 78–89.

Examples of diagnostic POEs

Anderson, B. J. 2011. "An Exploration of the Potential Benefits of Healing Gardens on Veterans with PTSD." Master of landscape architecture thesis, Utah State University. digitalcommons.usu.edu/gradreports/50.

Cooper Marcus, C., and M. Barnes. 1995. *Gardens in Healthcare Facilities: Uses, Therapeutic Benefits, and Design Recommendations*. Concord, CA: Center for Health Design.

Cranz, G., and C. Young. 2005. "The Role of Design in Inhibiting or Promoting Use of Common Open Space: The Case of Redwood Gardens, Berkeley, CA." Pp. 71–93 in *The Role of the Outdoors in Residential Environments for Aging*, edited S. Rodiek and B. Schwarz. Binghamton, NY: The Haworth Press.

Davis, B. E. 2011. "Rooftop Hospital Gardens for Physical Therapy: A Post-Occupancy Evaluation." *Health Environments Research and Design Journal* 4 (2): 14–43.

Heath Y., and R. Gifford. 2001. "Post-Occupancy Evaluation of Therapeutic Gardens in a Multi-Level Care Facility for the Aged." *Activities, Adaption and Aging* 25 (2): 21–43.

Hernandez, R. O. 2007. "Effects of Therapeutic Gardens in Special Care Units for People with Dementia: Two Case Studies." Pp. 117–52 in *Outdoor Environments for People with Dementia*, edited by S. Rodiek and B. Schwarz. Binghamton, NY: Haworth Press.

Shepley, M. M., C. Frohman, and P. Wilson. 1999. "Designing for People with AIDS: A Post-Occupancy Study at the Bailey-Boushay House." *Journal of Architectural and Planning Research* 16 (1): 17–32.

Sherman, S. A., J. W. Varni, R. S. Ulrich, and V. L. Valcarne. 2006. "Post Occupancy Evaluation of Healing Gardens in a Pediatric Cancer Center." Pp. 330–42 in *The Architecture of Hospitals*, edited by C. Wagenaar. Rotterdam, the Netherlands: NAi Publishers.

Sorensen, K. T. 2002. "Effect of Time Spent in a Hospital Garden on Satisfaction with Hospital Care." Master of landscape architecture thesis, University of Illinois at Urbana-Champaign.

Whitehouse, S., J. W. Varni, M. Seid, C. Cooper Marcus, M. Ensberg, J. Jacob, R. S. Melenbeck. 2001. "Evaluating a Children's Hospital Garden Environment Utilization and Consumer Satisfaction." *Journal of Environmental Psychology* 21: 301–14.

References

Anderzhon, J. W., I. L. Fraley, and M. Green. 2007. *Design for Aging Post-Occupancy Evaluations.* New York: John Wiley and Sons.

asha, S. and M. Shepley. 2013. "Research Note: Physical Activity in Pediatric Hospital Gardens." *Landscape and Urban Planning* 118: 53–58.

Cooper Marcus, C. 2007. "Post Occupancy Evaluation." Pp. 57–63 in *Landscape Architectural Graphic Standards*, edited by L. J. Hopper. New York: John Wiley and Sons.

———. 2008. "Alzheimer Garden Audit Tool." Pp. 179–91 in *Outdoor Environments for People with Dementia*, edited by S. Rodiek and B. Schwarz. New York: Haworth Press.

Cooper Marcus, C., and M. Barnes. 2008. *Consultant Report on Post Occupancy Evaluation of Six Hitchcock Design Healing Gardens in the Chicago Area.* Unpublished manuscript.

Cooper Marcus, C. and N. Sachs. 2013. "Gardens in Healthcare Facilities: Steps Towards Evaluation and Certification." *World Health Design*, July.

Naderi, J. R., and W. Shin. 2008. "Humane Design for Hospital Landscapes: A Case Study in Landscape Architecture of a Healing Garden for Nurses." *Health Environments Research and Design Journal* 2 (2): 82–119.

Pasha, S. Forthcoming. "Barriers to Garden Visitation in Children's Hospitals." *Healthcare Environments Research and Design Journal.*

Rothert, E., and J. Hammel. 2002. *Evaluation of the Buehler Enabling Garden.* Unpublished manuscript.

Shepley, M. 2011. *Health Facility Evaluation for Design Practitioners.* Myersville, MD: Asclepion Publishing.

Watkins, N., E. Peavey, and D. Clarke. 2012. "Research in Practice: Lesson 4." *Healthcare Design*, December 18. http://www.health caredesignmagazine.com/article/research-practice-lesson-4.

Whitehouse, S., J. W. Varni, M. Seid, C. Cooper Marcus, M. J. Ensberg, J. R. Jacobs, and R. S. Mehlenbeck. 2001. "Evaluating a Children's Hospital Environment: Utilization and Customer Satisfaction." *Journal of Environmental Psychology* 21: 301–14.

Index

Page numbers in *italic* type refer to illustrations.

academic training, horticultural therapy, 251
access
    accessibility, ADA and Universal Design, 57
    crisis shelters, 185
    dementia facilities, 155–56
    design guidelines, 71–75
        physical, 74–75
        visual, 62, 63, 69, 70, 71–74
    frail elderly facilities, 134–35
    hospice care, 170–71
    mental and behavioral health facilities, 182, 200
    to nature, defined, 4
    site planning, 66
    veterans hospitals, 214
activities of daily life, dementia facilities, 152
activity areas, 272. *See also* playgrounds
ADA (Americans with Disabilities Act), 57
ADHD. *See* attention deficit hyperactivity disorder
adolescent treatment center, Griffin Williamson
        Adolescent Treatment Center (Rockford,
        Illinois), 189–94
Advocate Hope Children's Hospital (Oak Lawn,
        Illinois), 69
Aegis Living (Napa, California), *154*
Aesclepion, Epidaurus, Greece, 6
aesthetic placebo theory, 31
aesthetics, 58. *See also* maintenance
aggression, mental health facilities, 179
AHTA Therapeutic Garden Characteristics (TGC),
        horticultural therapy, 254
AIDS Memorial Grove, Golden Gate Park (San
        Francisco, California), 243–46, *303*, 304
Alford, Denise Odell, 258
Alnarp Rehabilitation Garden (Alnarp, Sweden),
        194–98
allergenic plants. *See* poisonous plantings
ALPHA, Awaji Landscape Planning and
        Horticultural Academy (Awaji, Japan), *277*
Alzheimer's disease. *See* dementia facilities
    behavior mapping exercise, postoccupancy
        evaluation study, *310*
    characterization of, 148
    plantings, 280–81
American Horticultural Therapy Association
        (AHTA), 49, 250, 259
American Horticultural Therapy Association
        (AHTA) Therapeutic Garden
        Characteristics (TGC), horticultural
        therapy, 254
American Society for Healthcare Engineering
        (ASHE), 15–16
American Society of Landscape Architects,
        11–12, 241

Americans with Disabilities Act (ADA), 57
    horticultural therapy, 254
    veterans hospitals, 214
Anderson, Brock, 210
Anne's Garden, Northeast Georgia Medical Center
        (Gainesville, Georgia), *76, 262*
annual grasses and herbaceous plants, 267–68
anthroposophy, 11
antidepressant/antianxiety/antipsychotic
        medications, 182, 195, 215
antiquity, 6
Appleton, Jay, 23–24
architecture. *See* healthcare architecture
Arizona Cancer Center (Tucson, Arizona), *59,
        293, 314*
art, 27, 131
    abstract, 30
    preferences, 15-16, 23, 30,
    interactive features, design guidelines, 88, *89*
    research, virtual/real nature compared, 17
Asylum of Saint Paul de Mausole (Saint-Rémy,
        France), 179
asylums. *See* mental and behavioral health facilities
atrium gardens. *See* indoor gardens
attention restoration theory (ART), 28–29
Attention deficit hyperactivity disorder (ADHD),
        22, 235
Austin Health's Royal Talbot Rehabilitation Centre
        (Melbourne, Australia), *21*
Australia, *21,* 129, 152-153
autism, 235

backyard garden, location types, 39–40
Bainnson, Brian E., 216–20, 228–34, 241–43
Balconies, 65, 137
Baltimore Washington Medical Center (Glen
        Burnie, Maryland), *83*
Banfield Pavilion Roof-top Patio Garden,
        Vancouver General Hospital (Vancouver,
        British Columbia, Canada), 143–46
Banner Gateway Medical Center, Meditation
        Center (Gilbert, Arizona), *74*
Banner Gateway Medical Center, Women's Garden
        (Phoenix, Arizona), *82*
Barnes, Marni, 29, 261–87
behavioral health facilities. *See* mental and
        behavioral health facilities
behavior mapping exercise, postoccupancy
        evaluation study, *310*
being away, attention restoration theory, 28
benches. *See* seating
Bergeman, Jessy, 189-194
Biederman, Irving, 31

Bingen, Hildegard von, 6
biodiversity, sustainability, 290
biophilia, 57–58
    sustainability, 294–95
    theory, 23, 31
birds. *See* wildlife
Blairgowrie, Scotland, *150*
blood pressure
    as a measure of stress and health outcomes, 16,
        24, 27
    frail elderly facilities, 131
    scent, 17–18
Blue Shield, 11
bone density, frail elderly facilities, 129
bone health, sunlight, research, 19
Bonner Healing Garden, Bonner Community
        Hospice (Sandpoint, Idaho), *167, 168, 169,*
        172–76
borrowed landscape, location types, 36–37
boundaries
    children's hospitals, 97
    dementia facilities, 153
    design guidelines, 67
Bremerton Naval Hospital (Bremerton,
        Washington), 78
Bronson Methodist Hospital (Kalamazoo,
        Michigan), 300
Brooks Army Medical Center, Returning Heroes
        Home Healing Garden, Warrior and
        Family Support Center (San Antonio,
        Texas), 52–53
Bryn Mawr Rehabilitation Hospital (Malvern,
        Pennsylvania), 258
budgets. *See also* See costs; financing; funding
    design process programming, 60
    financing, 306
    maintenance, 285
Buehler Enabling Garden, Chicago Botanical
        Garden (Glencoe, Illinois), 238–41
Burn Center Garden (Portland, Oregon), 228–34
Burt, Virginia, *117*
business case. *See* budgets; costs; financing;
        funding
butterflies, design guidelines, 90

Caen, Herb, 121
California, University of, San Francisco Medical
        Center, Healing Garden: Mt. Zion, 120–22
Canada, *80, 132, 135,* 143–46, *150,* 152, *153, 157,
        158,* 158–59, 166, 181
Cancer Lifeline, Roof Gardens at, the Dorothy
        S. O'Brien Center (Seattle, Washington),
        117–200, 303

cancer center gardens, 115–28
  case studies, 117–27
    California, University of, San Francisco
      Medical Center, Healing Garden: Mt. Zion,
      120–22
    Dana-Farber Cancer Institute, Yawkey Center
      for Cancer Care (Boston, Massachusetts),
      122–25
    Dorothy S. O'Brien Center, Roof Gardens at
      Cancer Lifeline, 117–27
    Maggie's Centre Gardens (United Kingdom),
      126–27
  research findings, 115–17
Cannon, Walter, 24
Canuck House, children's hospice (Vancouver,
    British Columbia, Canada), 166
Cardiovascular Center, University of Michigan
    (Ann Arbor, Michigan), 45
Carman, Jack, 132, 211
Cassidy, Patty, 241–43
"Central Park" interior atrium, National
    Intrepid Center of Excellence (Bethesda,
    Maryland), 209, 209–10, 214
certification, horticultural therapy, 251
certification, therapeutic garden, 306
Chamberlain, Ann, 120–22
Chambers, Nancy, 111, 113, 258
Changi General Hospital (Simei, Singapore), 290
Chemainus Health Care Centre (Chemainus,
    British Columbia, Canada), 153
chemotherapy, cancer patients, 115, 116, 117
Chicago Botanic Garden (Glencoe, Illinois),
    85, 255
Chicago Botanic Garden, Buehler Enabling
    Garden (Glencoe, Illinois), 238–41
Chicago Botanic Garden, School of, 12
children
    crisis shelter, Danner's Garden (Copenhagen,
      Denmark), 184–205
    natural/urban environments compared,
      research, 21–22
    rehabilitation gardens, 227, 233
    special needs, 235
    special-needs, horticultural therapy design
      guidelines, 257
    plantings, 279–80
    veterans hospitals, 215–16
Children's Hospital (Albuquerque, New
    Mexico), 95
children's hospitals, 91–114
    case studies, 101–14
      Olson Family Garden, St. Louis
        Children's Hospital (St. Louis, Missouri),
        106–10
      Randall Children's Hospital at Legacy
        Emanuel Medical Center (Portland,
        Oregon), 101–5

Rusk Institute of Rehabilitation Medicine,
    The Children's PlayGarden (New York,
    New York), 111–14
  design guidelines, 96–100
  garden benefits and problems, 91–95
  hospice care, 165, 166
  multiple users, 95–97
The Children's PlayGarden, Rusk Institute of
    Rehabilitation Medicine (New York, New
    York), 96, 111–14, 258, 299
Chilgok County Geriatric Hospital (Korea), 51–52
cholera epidemics, 9
Christianity, 6
choice. See control
Church, Thomas, 120
cigarette smoking
    design guidelines, 70
    veterans hospitals, 216
city parks, borrowed landscape, location types,
    36–37
Clairvaux, Bernard de, 6
Clare Tower residence roof garden (Chicago,
    Illinois), 20, 43
Clark-Lindsey Masterpiece Gardens (University of
    Chicago), 294
Clement, Ann, 143–46
Cleveland Botanical Garden (Cleveland, Ohio),
    235, 236
cliffing, visual, 76–77, 135, 215. See also shadows
climate. See also season
    design guidelines, 60, 63, 70, 71, 74
    horticultural therapy, 253
    microclimate, 63,
    plantings, 265–68
Coastal Maine Botanical Garden, Lerner Garden
    of the Five Senses (Boothbay, Maine), 86
coherence, attention restoration theory, 29
color, plantings, 274–75
Combat Stress Garden (Leatherhead, UK),
    210, 210
comfort, 57
Comfort Garden, San Francisco General Hospital
    (San Francisco, California), 268
community, connection to.
    horticultural therapy, 252–53
    restorative gardens in public spaces, 235–249
    site planning, 66
    social horticulture, 250–51
compatibility, attention restoration theory, 29
complexity, attention restoration theory, 29
composting, sustainability, 291
conservatory, horticultural therapy gardens, 257
construction, design process programming, 60
control, stress reduction theory/theory of
    supportive gardens, 24–25, 77
cooking odors. See odors
cortisol, 18, 24

cost-benefit analysis, evidence-based design
    (EBD), 298
costs. See also See budgets; financing; funding
    Alzheimer's disease and dementias, 149–50
    research-informed design, 15
Cottage Grove Park (West Seattle,
    Washington), 235
Council of Landscape Architecture Registration
    Board (CLARB), 56
courtyards
    location types, 40–41
    mental and behavioral health facilities, 183
    site planning, 64
covered areas, design guidelines, 69, 70, 71
Crimean War (1854–56), 8
crisis shelter, domestic violence, Danner's Garden
    (Copenhagen, Denmark), 184–205
culture
    differences, 70, 71, 131, 133, 152–54
    organizational, 59–60
curbs, design guidelines, 76
curvilinear walkways, design guidelines, 76

Dana-Farber Cancer Institute, Yawkey Center
    for Cancer Care, The Thea and James
    Stoneman Healing Garden (Boston,
    Massachusetts), 63, 82, 122–25
Danish Museum of Design (Copenhagen,
    Denmark), 7
Danner's Garden domestic violence shelter
    (Copenhagen, Denmark), 184–89
David Evans Associates, 225–27
Daylighting. See also light
    frail elderly facilities, 129
    sustainability, 289–90
Dell Children's Medical Center (Austin, Texas),
    94, 289–90
delusions, mental and behavioral health facilities,
    182
dementia facilities, 148–64. See also frail elderly
    facilities
    case studies, 159–62
    design guidelines, 151–59
      access, 155–56
      boundaries, 153
      cultural differences, 152, 153, 154
      gardening opportunities, 154
      general considerations, 151–55
      lighting, 158
      maintenance, 158–59
      memory triggers, 152
      pathways, 157–58
      plantings, 158, 280–81
      play area, 155
      restrooms, 156
      seating, 156
      shade, shadows, 152

staff and design process,151
visibility from inside, 151
Portland Memory Garden (Portland, Oregon), 241
research results, 148–51
demography, frail elderly facilities, 129
design considerations, overarching
accessibility (ADA and Universal Design), 57
biophilia, 57–58
comfort, physical and emotional, 57
distractions, positive, 57
maintenance and aesthetics, 58
safety, security, and privacy, 56
sustainability, 58
design guidelines,
for specific patient/facility types
cancer care centers, 115–17
children's hospitals, 96–100
dementia facilities, 151–59
frail elderly facilities, 132–38
hospice, 165–72
mental and behavioral health facilities, 181–84
veterans and active service personnel, 213–16
general, 66–90. See also healthcare architecture
access, 71–75
physical, 74–75
visual, 71–74
general considerations, 66–71
interactive features, 87–89
lighting, 85
pathways, 75–78
planting, 80–83, 84. 261–81
programming and site planning, 57–65
other garden elements, 85–90
seating, 79–80
utilities, 83, 84–85
water features, 85–86, 87
wildlife, 90
lessons and future trends, 308–16
design, programming and site planning, 58–66
budget and funding, 60
construction, new vs. remodel, 60
environment of care (EOC) concept, 58–66
evidence-based design (EBD), 59
functional program, 59–60
interdisciplinary design team (IDT), 58, 60
location, 60
organizational culture, 59–60
patient needs, 60, 61
design process, participatory, 47–55
case studies
Chilgok County Geriatric Hospital (Korea), 51–52
Harrison Medical Center (Bremerton, Washington), 53
Returning Heroes Home Healing Garden, Warrior and Family Support Center,

Brooks Army Medical Center (San Antonio, Texas), 52–53
initiation of, 53
key elements in, 53–54
Legacy Health System, 48
lessons and future trends, 308–16
staff team benefits, 50–51
staff team organization, 48–50
destination points
design guidelines, 71,132
plantings, 271
Detweiler, Mark, 211
Dirtworks, PC, 5, 235, 236
disease theory, hospital design, 6, 9
distance markers, design guidelines, walkways, 77
distraction(s), positive, 24, 26–28, 57
children's hospitals, 97–98
dementia facilities, walkways, 157–58
natural, stress reduction theory/theory of supportive gardens, 26–28
dogs. See also pets
rehabilitation gardens, 224
service dogs, veterans hospitals, 216
domestic abuse/violence
abuse/sexual, substance, 235
crisis shelter, Danner's Garden (Copenhagen, Denmark), 184–205
donor recognition, 168, 299, 302
doors, access, design guidelines, 74. See also access
Dorothy S. O'Brien Center, Roof Gardens at Cancer Lifeline, (Seattle, Washington), 117–200, 303
Douglas Hills Associates, 159–62
Downing, Andrew Jackson, 9
drinking fountains, 85
Dublin Methodist Hospital (Dublin, Ohio), 305

Eden Alternative, 11
Edinburgh, Scotland, 8
Edinburgh Royal Infirmary (Scotland), 8, 37
Edward Heart Hospital (Naperville, Illinois), 65, 75
elderly. See frail elderly facilities
electrical outlets, 85
Elizabeth and Nona Evans Restorative Garden, Cleveland Botanical Garden (Cleveland, Ohio), 5, 235
elopement
dementia facilities, 153
mental and behavioral health facilities, 182
emotional congruence theory, 30–31, 281–82
empiricism. See research
enabling gardens
outdoor space, 3–4, 236–41
wheelchairs, 239–41
Buehler Enabling Garden, Chicago Botanical Garden (Glencoe, Illinois), 238–41

enclosure(s). See boundaries
engagement with nature (biophilia). See biophilia
England. See United Kingdom
entry garden
design guidelines, 64, 68
location types, 39
maintenance, 286
site planning, 64
environmental psychology, design staff team benefits, 51
environment of care (EOC) concept, 58–66
epidemiology, veterans hospitals, 206
Esserman, Laura, 120, 121, 122
evidence-based design (EBD), 1–2, 16, 32, 59. See also research
definition of, 16
design process, programming, 16, 59
horticultural therapy, 253
lessons and future trends, evaluation studies, 308–11
Evidence-based Design Accreditation and Certification (EDAC), 308
exercise
cancer patients, 115
design guidelines, 61, 64, 71, 77,
frail elderly, 129
green exercise, research, 17–19
mental and behavioral health facilities, 182
stress reduction theory/theory of supportive gardens, 26–28
exhaust vents, site planning, 63
extensive landscaped grounds, location types, 36

familiarity
hospice facilities, 165–66
veterans hospitals, 215
Family Life Center, The Living Garden at (Grand Rapids, Michigan), 159–62
Farmer Veteran Coalition (FVC), 211, 213
fascination, see soft fascination
fatigue, cancer patients, 115
fencing. See boundaries
Ferryfield House (Edinburgh, Scotland), 135
fight or flight response, 24
figure eight walkways, dementia facilities, 157
financing, 298–307. See also See budgets; costs; funding
budgeting, 306
funding sources, 302–4
funding strategies, 305–6
funding targets, 304
patient/visitor satisfaction, 300–302
research findings, 298–99
stress reduction, 299–300
timing, 304–5
Finland, 149

fishbowl effect, design guidelines, 40, 77
fish ponds, design guidelines, 90
fitness and nature trails, location types, 37–38
Fleming, Karen, 258
flexibility, veterans hospitals, 213–14
flight or fight response, 24
food odors. *See* odors
food services, sustainability, 290–91
forest bathing *(shinrin-yoku),* research, 18–19
fountains. *See also* water features
    mental and behavioral health facilities, *183*
    site planning, *65*
fragrances. *See* scents
frail elderly facilities, 129–47. *See also* dementia
    facilities
    case studies, 139–46
        Banfield Pavilion Roof-top Patio Garden,
            Vancouver General Hospital (Vancouver,
            British Columbia, Canada), 143–46
        The Pavilion, Jupiter Medical Center (Jupiter,
            Florida), 141–43
        Roger Smith Memorial Garden, Friendship
            Village (Schaumburg, Illinois), 139–41
    demography, 129
    design guidelines, 132–38
        access, 134–35
        atrium, 133
        balconies, 137
        destination points, 132
        gardening beds, 133
        general considerations, 132–34
        pathways, 135
        plantings, 138, 280-281
        seating, 135-6
        utilities, 138
    horticultural therapy design guidelines, 257
    research findings, 129–32
Fried, Gwenn, 277–78
Friends Asylum (Philadelphia, Pennsylvania),
    8–9
Friendship Village, Roger Smith Memorial Garden
    (Schaumburg, Illinois), 139–41
Fromm, Erich, 23
front porch, location types, 39
functional program, 60
funding. *See also See* budgets; costs; financing
    horticultural therapy, 258
    plantings, 263
    sources of, 302–4
    strategies, 305–6
    targets of, 304
    timing of, 304–5

Garcia, Chris, 141–43, 172–76
garden. *See also* nature; outdoor space
    defined, 5
    enabling gardens, 3–4

location types, 36–46
    restorative gardens, 3, *5*
gardening, research, 19
Gardening Leave (Scotland), *4, 207, 213,*
    214, 259
garden journal, 88
garden location, dementia facilities, 152
Garden of Healing and Renewal (Clarkson,
    Michigan), *28, 66,* 246–48
Garden of the Senses (Stockholm, Sweden), *159*
Gary Comer Youth Center (Chicago, Illinois), *22*
gates, dementia facilities, 153. *See also* boundaries
The Gathering Place, Norma's Garden at, cancer
    support group (Westlake, Ohio), *26,* 117
gazebo, design guidelines, 71
George Mark Children's Hospice (San Leandro,
    California), 170
germ theory, origins of, 9. *See also* disease theory
glare. *See also* light; lighting; shade
    design guidelines, 76, 78-9
    frail elderly, 135
    mental and behavioral health facilities, 182
    veterans hospitals, 215
Goethe, 8
Good Samaritan Hospital, Stenzel Healing Garden
    (Portland, Oregon), *223, 224*
government regulation, research-informed design,
    15–16
Graham Garden, Saanich Peninsula Hospital
    (Victoria, British Columbia, Canada), *80,*
    132, 135, 158
Grahn, Patrik, 194–98
grasses and herbaceous plants, 267–68
gray water, sustainability, 290
Greece (ancient), 6
green exercise, research, 17–19
greenhouse, horticultural therapy gardens, 257
green roofs. *See* roof gardens
greenways, borrowed landscape, location types,
    36–37
Griffin Williamson Adolescent Treatment Center,
    Rosecrance Healing Garden (Rockford,
    Illinois), 189–94
groundcovers and vines, 268–69
gurneys, 70, 171, 265

Haas Family Fund, 120
handrails, frail elderly facilities, 135
Hansen, Vi, 226
Harrison Medical Center (Bremerton,
    Washington), 53
Hazen, Teresia, 47–55, 250-260
Healing Forest Garden Nacadia, University of
    Copenhagen, Denmark, 198–204
healing garden, historical perspective, 6–13
Healing Garden: Mt. Zion, California, University
    of, San Francisco Medical Center, 120–22

healthcare architecture. *See also* design process
    defined, 3
    historical perspective, 6–13
    lessons and future trends, 308–16
    patient-centered approach, 1–2
    research-informed design, 14–15, 29
Health Care Without Harm, 291
Health Insurance Portability and Accountability
    Act (HIPAA), 56
Heavenston, Martha, 121
hedges. *See* boundaries
height to width ratio, site planning, 63–64
Helen House children's hospice (Oxford,
    England), *166*
Helgerson, Bryce, 48
herbaceous plants and grasses, 267–68
Hippocrates, 6, 10
Hippocratic Oath, 14
Hitchcock Design Group, 139–41, *65,* 69
HIV/AIDS, 179, 243–46
hole-in-a-donut garden, location types, 41
holistic design
    guidelines and, 56
    site planning, 60
homelike environment. *See* familiarity
horticultural therapy, 250–60
    academic training, 251
    design guidelines, 253–57, 264, 272
        frail elderly, 257
        special-needs children, 257
        specific environment programming, 254–57
    funding for, 258
    historical development, 251–52
    professionalism, 250
    program types, 250–51
    research findings, 253
    settings for, 253
    therapist role in, 252–53
hospice facilities, 165–78
    case studies, 172–78
        Bonner Healing Garden, Bonner
            Community Hospice (Sandpoint, Idaho),
            172–76
        San Diego Hospice (San Diego, California),
            176–78
    design guidelines, 165–72
        access, 170–71
        general considerations, 165–70
        maintenance, 172
        plantings, 171–72
    historical perspective, 165
    nature and, 165
hospital length of stay, surgical recovery time, 14
Hôtel Dieu (Paris, France), 8
Howard, John, 6
Huntington Library Children's Garden (Pasadena,
    California), *95, 281, 282*

Huntington Library Chinese Garden (Pasadena, California), *71*
HVAC systems, sustainability, 290

Illinois Cancer Care (Peoria, Illinois), *65, 116*
immunocompromised, 85, 117, 125, 163
Independent Gardening (UK), 208–9, 210
indicative postoccupancy evaluation, 309–16
indoor gardens, 44, *45,* 61, *63, 82,* 133, 159, 163, 183, 257. *See also* atrium gardens
    "Central Park" interior atrium, National Intrepid Center of Excellence (Bethesda, Maryland), *209,* 209–10, 214
    Dana-Farber Cancer Institute, Yawkey Center for Cancer Care, The Thea and James Stoneman Healing Garden (Boston, Massachusetts), *63, 82,* 122–25
infection control
    birds, 90, 168–70
    sustainability, 293
    water features, design guidelines, 85
insects
    design guidelines, 75
    sustainability, 293
interactive features
    design guidelines, 87–88, 96
    plantings, 276–77, 279
interdisciplinary design team (IDT). *See also* participatory design process; staff team
    process, 58, 60
    horticultural therapy, 258
    rehabilitation gardens, 222
    site planning, 60, 61, *62*
interiors
    dementia facilities, 151
    design guidelines, 67
    horticultural therapy, 253
    mental and behavioral health facilities, 183
    nature elements, 61, 63
    views from interior to outdoor space, 4, 61, *63, 64, 65, 69, 70,* 71–74, *83, 134, 271*
investigative postoccupancy evaluation, 309–16
irrigation. *See also* water features
    horticultural therapy, 256
    maintenance operations, 285
    sustainability, 290
    plantings, 264

James, William, 28
Jencks, Charles, 126
Johnson, Carol R., *63,* 122–25
Johnson Design Studio, 101–5
Joseph Weld Hospice (Dorchester, England), *67,* 165
journal (of garden, gift shop offering), 88
Jupiter Medical Center (Jupiter, Florida), *66, 71, 72, 80,* 141–43, *224, 288*

Kaiser Permanente, 11, 290
Kaiser Permanente Medical Center (Antioch, California), *275*
Kaiser Permanente Medical Center (Walnut Creek, California), *266*
Kaplan, Rachel, 28–29
Kaplan, Stephen, 28–29
Karlin, Bradley E., 47
Kemalyn, Nathan, 51
Kent Hospital (Warwick, Rhode Island), *3, 82,* 289, 294
Keswick, Maggie, 126–27
Kirkbride, Thomas, 9
Kübler-Ross, Elizabeth, 165
Kurisu, Hoichi, 189

labeling
    interactive features, 87–88
    plants, 100, 102–103, 117, 225, 227
    in horticultural therapy, 226–27, 231–33
labyrinths
    design guidelines, 78
    veterans hospitals, 211
Laguna Honda Hospital and Rehabilitation Center (San Francisco, California), 169
Lake Beauty Park, Orlando Health Medical Center (Orlando, Florida), 235, *237*
Lakeland Hospital (Niles, Michigan), 11
landmarks, walkways, dementia facilities, 157–58
landscape architect, site planning, 60
landscaped setback, location types, 38–39
Landscape Forms, Wellspring benches, *79*
Lane, Sandy, 211
lawns
    for events, *72*
    plantings, 269–70
    sustainability, 291–96
Lee, Hun Hyang, 51–52
LEED for Healthcare (United States Green Building Council), 291
LeFrank, Deborah, *157, 158*
Legacy Campus Children's Medical Center of Dallas (Plano, Texas), 93–94
Legacy Emanuel Medical Center, Randall Children's Hospital at (Portland, Oregon), *77, 92,* 95, *96, 97, 98, 99,* 101–5, *277*
Legacy Health Good Samaritan Hospital (Portland, Oregon), *69, 270, 284*
Legacy Health system
    design process, 48–51
    funding, 305
legibility (of garden space), 29, 67, 132, 157, 181, 183
Leichtag Family Healing Garden, San Diego Children's Hospital, Rady Children's Hospital (San Diego, California), 91–93

length of stay, surgical recovery time, 14
Lerner Garden of the Five Senses, Coastal Maine Botanical Garden (Boothbay, Maine), *86*
lessons and future trends, 308–16
    evaluations, 308–11
    postoccupancy evaluation studies, 311–16
Lewis, Kenyon, 121
licensing, horticultural therapy, 251
light. *See also* shade
    frail elderly facilities, 129
    hospital design, 6, 8
    site planning, 63–64
    visual access, 71–74
    sustainability, 289–90
lighting, *75,* 85
    dementia facilities, 158
    visual access, 74
Lindheim, Roslyn, 10–11
Lister, John, 9
The Living Garden at the Family Life Center (Grand Rapids, Michigan), 159–62
location
    design process programming, 60
    site planning, 62–64
location types, 36–46
    atrium garden, 44, *45*
    backyard garden, 39–40
    borrowed landscape, 36–37
    courtyard, 40–41
    entry garden, 39
    extensive landscaped grounds, 36
    front porch, 39
    hole-in-a-donut garden, 41
    landscaped setback, 38–39
    nature and fitness trails, 37–38
    peripheral garden, 43–44
    plaza, 42
    roof garden, 42, *43*
    roof terrace, 42–43
    "tucked away" garden, 40
    viewing garden, 44, 46
Loder, Angela, 295
Lodge at Broadmead, The (Victoria, British Columbia, Canada), *157*
Lorenz, Christian Cay, 6–7
low-impact development (LID), sustainability, 290
Lugumira, James, 211
Lundström, Sarah, 194–98
Lygum, Victoria L., 184–205

Maggie's Centre Gardens (United Kingdom), 126–27
Mah, Ron, 225–27
Maintenance
    and aesthetics, 58
    dementia facilities, 158–59
    hospice facilities, 172

Maintenance (*cont.*)
    manual, 285–87
    plantings 281–87
    storage for equipment and tools, 81, 100, 253, 256, 285
    sustainability, 290–95
    user's manual, 151, 185–86
markers, walkways, dementia facilities, 157–58
Martin Luther Alzheimer Garden (Holt, Michigan), 148–49
Massachusetts General Hospital, Ulfelder Healing Garden (Boston, Massachusetts), *68*
McKay Dee Hospital (Ogden, Utah), *3, 27, 81*
McKee Medical Center (Loveland, Colorado), 18
Medical Center of the Rockies (Loveland, Colorado), *294*
medical model, horticultural therapy, 250
meditation gardens
    Meditation Center, Banner Gateway Medical Center (Gilbert, Arizona), *74*
    Banner Gateway Medical Center (Gilbert, AZ), *74*
    Cottage Grove Park (West Seattle, Washington), 235
memorials, commemorative, hospice care, 168, *178*
memory triggers
    dementia facilities, 152, 154, 158
    scent, *17*
    plantings, *283*
mental and behavioral health facilities, 179–205
    case studies, 184–204
        Alnarp Rehabilitation Garden (Alnarp, Sweden), 194–98
        Danner's Garden domestic violence shelter (Copenhagen, Denmark), 184–89
        Healing Forest Garden Nacadia, University of Copenhagen, Denmark, 198–204
        Rosecrance Healing Garden, Griffin Williamson Adolescent Treatment Center (Rockford, Illinois), 189–94
    design guidelines, 181–84
    enabling gardens, 4
    historical perspective, 8–9
    research findings, 179–81
    staff, 164
    plantings, 279
    water features, 163
Mercy Medical Center (Baltimore, Maryland), *292*
Michigan, University of, Cardiovascular Center (Ann Arbor, Michigan), *45*
microclimates, site planning, 64
Middle Ages, 6, *7*
military hospitals, antiquity, 6
Mirka, Alar, 48
monastic gardens, 6
Monklands General Hospital (Scotland), 126

moral treatment, mental health hospitals, 8
morbidity and mortality, hospital design, 8
mortality. *See* morbidity and mortality
Mount Hood Medical Center (Gresham, Oregon), *300, 305*
multiple use
    adolescent treatment center, 192–93
    cancer hospitals, 117–18, 121–22
    children's hospitals, 95–96, 96–97, 108–9
    dementia facilities, 153, 162
    design guidelines, 70, *72*
    frail elderly facilities, 140, 142–43, 145
    horticultural therapy gardens, 256–57
    hospice facilities, 174, 177–78
    rehabilitation gardens, 226–27, 230–33
    restorative gardens in public places, 203, 239–41, 241–43, 245–46, 248
    veterans hospitals, 215–16, 220
Murray, Dorinda Wolfe, 208–9, 210
Myers-Thomas, Judy, 11
mystery, attention restoration theory, 29

Nacadia, Healing Forest Garden, University of Copenhagen, Denmark, 198–204
National Council for Therapy and Rehabilitation through Horticulture (NCTRH), 251–52
National Health Service (NHS, UK), 47
National Intrepid Center of Excellence, "Central Park" interior atrium (Bethesda, Maryland), *209,* 209–10, 214
native landscapes and planting, sustainability, 59, *83,* 290, 293, 294, *295,* 296
Natural Growth Project (London, England), 237–38
nature. *See also* garden; outdoor space
    Alzheimer's disease and other dementias, 148–51
    defined, 4
    engagement with (biophilia), 57–58
    hospice facilities, 165
    mental and behavioral health facilities, 201
    patient-centered approach, 1–2
    urban environments compared, research, 19–22
nature and fitness trails, location types, 37–38
nature-based therapy, 198, 203,
New York University Medical Center (New York, New York), 258, 277–78
nightime access, design guidelines, 74
Nightingale, Florence, 8
Nikkei Manor assisted-living facility (Seattle, Washington), 303, *304*
Nojima, Cenri, 121
Normas's Garden at The Gathering Place, cancer support group (Westlake, Ohio), *26, 117*
Northeast Georgia Medical Center (Gainesville, Georgia), *2, 76, 262*

nuisance plants. *See* poisonous plants
nursing homes. *See* frail elderly facilities

O'Brien Center, Roof Gardens at Cancer Lifeline, (Seattle, Washington), 117–20
occupational therapy (OT), historical perspective, 9, *62*
odors, unwanted (cooking, exhaust, food), 61, 63, 121,
Olson Family Garden, St. Louis Children's Hospital (St. Louis, Missouri), 23, *72,* 93, *94,* 95, *99,* 106–10, *257, 304*
Oregon Burn Center, Legacy Emanuel Medical Center (Portland, Oregon), 48–51, *63,* 228–34
organizational culture, 59–60
Ospedale Maggiore (Milan, Italy), 6
Östra Psychiatric Hospital (Gothenburg, Sweden), *180*
outcomes (health), 14, 16–17, 24–25, 32, 60
oxytocin, 31, *224*

Pacific Presbyterian Medical Center (San Francisco, California), 10
pain control, research, 17–22
Palo Alto Veterans Administration Hospital (Palo Alto, California), *82*
Parkins, Michelle, 208
parks. *See* public parks
participatory design process, 47–55. *See also* design process; interdisciplinary design team (IDT)
Pasteur, Louis, 9
pathways. *See* walkways
patient-centered approach
    design process, 60
    historical perspective, 1, 10–11
    site planning, 60–61
patios, 64, 69
The Pavilion, Jupiter Medical Center (Jupiter, Florida), *66,* 141–43
pavilion hospital
    germ theory, 9
    outdoor space, 7–8, *10*
Pearson, Dan, 126–27
perennial grasses and herbaceous plants, plantings, 267–68
perennial shrubs, plantings, 265–66
perfumes. *See* scents
pergolas, 67, 69, 71,
peripheral garden, location types, 43–44
personal safety. *See also* safety
    Alzheimer's disease and dementias, 150
    crisis shelters, 185–86
    horticultural therapy, 256
    mental and behavioral health facilities, 181–82

security and privacy, 56
veterans hospitals, 214–15
pest management, sustainability, 290
Pete Gross House (Seattle, Washington), *116, 303*
pets. *See also* dogs
hospice care, 170
rehabilitation gardens, *224*
physical access. *See* access
physical challenge, 158, 214. *See also* exercise,
physical therapy
physical movement, stress reduction theory/theory
of supportive gardens, 26–28
physical therapy (PT) – *Also see* chapters 13 and 14
historical perspective, 9
Pinel, Phillipe, 8
Planetree model, patient-centered approach,
10–11
Plantings, 261–287
adolescent treatment center, 190–91
assets and costs, 264–70
cancer patients, 117, 124–25
children's hospitals, 100
color theory, 275, 281
dementia facilities, 158
design guidelines, 80–83, *84*
desirability factors, 274–79
destination point, 271
fascination, 274
frail elderly facilities, 138
horticultural therapy, 256, 264, 272
hospice facilities, 171–72
interaction with, 276–77, 279
maintenance, 281–87
budgets, 285
centrality of, 281–82
operations, 285–87
personnel policies, 282–84
native. *See* native landscapes and planting
overview, 261
placement, 270–72
planning in advance, 262
plant growth requirements, 263–64
planting desirability factors, 274–79
planting selections, 264–70
grasses and herbaceous plants, 267–68
groundcovers and vines, 268–69
lawns, 269–70
shrubs, 265–66
trees, 264–65
policies, 262
privacy, 272
rehabilitation gardens, 230
shade, 274, 279, 281
special settings, 279–81
children, 279–80
frail elderly facilities, 280–81
psychiatric facilities, 279

staff and funding, 263
sustainability, 290
toxic/nuisance plants, 273–74, *See also*
poisonous plants
views, 274
wildlife, 274
playgrounds
children's hospitals, 96–97
crisis shelters, 186
frail elderly facilities, 133
hospice care, 168, *169*
veterans hospitals, 215–16
plaza, location types, 42
Plaza at Twin Rivers (Arkadelphia, Arkansas), *136*
pleasure, nature and, theory, 31–32
poisonous plants
children's hospitals, 100
dementia facilities, 158
horticultural therapy, 256
mental and behavioral health facilities, 182
toxic, allergenic, and nuisance plants,
273–74, 293
policy, research-informed design, 15–16
pollen, sustainability, 293
porches
design guidelines, *71, 134,* 136
horticultural therapy gardens, 257
Portland Memory Garden (Portland, Oregon),
241–43
positioning. *See* solar orientation
positive distraction. *See* distractions
postoccupancy evaluation (POE)
examples, 91–94, 139–43, 315
methods, 306–11
lessons and future trends, 311–13
posttraumatic stress disorder (PTSD), veterans
hospitals, 206–7
Princess Alice Hospice (Esher, England), 165
privacy
cancer patients, 115
design guidelines, 63–64, 67, 71, 77
frail elderly facilities, 136–37
hospice care, 168
mental and behavioral health facilities, 182
plant placement, 270, 272
refuge, 274–75
site planning, *65*
stress reduction theory/theory of supportive
gardens, 24–25
veterans hospitals, 215
Professional Engineering Associates, Inc.,
246–48
professionalism, horticultural therapy, 250
professional staff
enabling gardens, 3–4, 103
site planning, *62*
programming. *See* design process, programming

prospect-refuge
design guidelines, 79
theory, 23–24
veterans gardens, 215
psychiatric facilities. *See* mental and behavioral
health facilities
public parks
borrowed landscape, location types, 36–37
restorative gardens in, 235–49

Quatrefoil, Inc, *63,* 216–20, 228–34, 241–43
Quiet Garden movement, 235

Rady Children's Hospital, San Diego Children's
Hospital, Leichtag Family Healing Garden
(San Diego, California), *69,* 91–93,
300–301
Randall Children's Hospital at Legacy Emanuel
Medical Center (Portland, Oregon), *77, 92,
95, 96, 97, 98, 99,* 101–5, *277*
Rasmussen, Eiler, 198
ratio
building, height to width, 63–64
plants (softscape) to hardscape, 28, 81
Rausch, Geoffrey, 238–41
real nature, virtual nature compared, 17
recovery time, research, 14
reflection, veterans hospitals, 215
refuge, plantings, 274–75
rehabilitation gardens and rehabilitation hospitals,
222–34
case studies, 225–34
Oregon Burn Center, Legacy Emanuel
Medical Center (Portland, Oregon),
228–34
Stenzel Healing Garden, Good Samaritan
Hospital (Portland, Oregon), 225–27
enabling gardens, 4
historical perspective, 9
interdisciplinary design team (IDT), 222
research findings, 222–24
stress-related disease, 194–98
veterans hospitals, 214
research, 14–22. *See also* evidence-based design
(EBD); theory
on benefits of nature, 16–17
evidence-based design (EBD), 16, 32
hospital recovery time, 14
importance of, 14–16
lessons and future trends, evaluation studies,
308–11
natural/urban environments compared, 19–22
virtual/real nature compared, 17
restorative gardens in public places, 235–49
case studies, 237–48
AIDS Memorial Grove, Golden Gate Park
(San Francisco, California), 243–46

restorative gardens in public places (*cont.*)
   Buehler Enabling Garden, Chicago Botanical
      Garden (Glencoe, Illinois), 238–41
   Garden of Healing and Renewal (Clarkson,
      Michigan), 246–48
   Natural Growth Project (London, England),
      237–38
   Portland Memory Garden (Portland,
      Oregon), 241–43
   examples of, 235–37
Retreat at York (England), 9
Returning Heroes Home Healing Garden, Warrior
      and Family Support Center, Brooks Army
      Medical Center (San Antonio, Texas),
      52–53
ritual, veterans hospitals, 215
Roger Smith Memorial Garden, Friendship Village
      (Schaumburg, Illinois), 139–41
Roman Catholic church, 6
Romanticism, hospital design, 8
Rome (ancient), 6
roof gardens, 68, 72, 73, 94, 95, 222, 263,
   green roofs, sustainability, 290, 292, 295
   location types, 42, 43
   Children's PlayGarden, Rusk Institute of
      Rehabilitative Medicine (New York, New
      York), 110–14
   Olson Family Garden, St. Louis Children's
      Hospital (St. Louis, MO), 106–10
   Roof Gardens at Cancer Lifeline, the Dorothy
      S. O'Brien Center (Seattle, Washington),
      117–20
roof terrace, location types, 42–43
Roosevelt, Franklin D., 210
Rosecrance Healing Garden, Griffin Williamson
      Adolescent Treatment Center (Rockford,
      Illinois), 189–94
Rothschild Garden, senior center (Evanston,
      Illinois), 70
Rousseau, Jean-Jacques, 8
Royal Chelsea Hospital (London, England), 6
Royal Horticultural Society, Hampton Court
      Palace Flower Show, 2010, 210
Royal Infirmary (Edinburgh, Scotland), 77
Roy-Fisher, Connie, 141–43
Runa, Tom, 172–76
Rusk Institute of Rehabilitation Medicine, The
      Children's PlayGarden (New York, New
      York), 96, 111–14, 258, 299
Russia, 154

Saanich Peninsula Hospital, Graham Garden
      (Victoria, British Columbia, Canada), 132,
      135, 158
Safety. *See also* security
   Alzheimer's disease and dementias, 150
   crisis shelters, 185–86

design guidelines, 56–57
horticultural therapy, 256
mental and behavioral health facilities, 181–82
veterans hospitals, 214–15
St. Christopher's Hospice (London, England), 165
St. Joseph Memorial Hospital (Santa Rosa,
      California), 78, 89, 271
St. Louis Children's Hospital, Olson Family
      Garden (St. Louis, Missouri), 23, 72, 93, 94,
      95, 99, 106–10, 257
St. Nicholas Hospice (Suffolk, England), 165
St. Richard's Hospice (Worcester, England), 165
St. Thomas' Hospital (London, England), 8
Salem Veterans Administration Medical Center
      (Salem, Virginia), 210–11, 212
Salt Lake City Veterans Administration Medical
      Center GEM Court Garden and
      Purtkwahgahm (Healing Ground) (Salt
      Lake City, Utah), 215
Sanders, Dr. Cicely, 165
San Diego Children's Hospital, Rady Children's
      Hospital, Leichtag Family Healing Garden
      (San Diego, California), 69, 91–93,
      300–301
San Diego Hospice (San Diego, California), 44, 61,
      169, 171, 176–78
San Francisco General Hospital, Comfort Garden
      (San Francisco, California), 268
San Francisco Medical Center, Healing Garden:
      Mt. Zion, University of California,
      120–22
San Juan Medical Center (Farmington, New
      Mexico), 166
Santiago de Compostela, Spain, 7
Sarno, Martha, 258
satisfaction, patient/resident/staff/visitor, 298-300
scale
   children's gardens, 279–80
   frail elderly facilities, 132, 138
   human, 63, 82
   mental and behavioral health facilities, 183
scents
   plantings, 136, 267, 275
   rehabilitation gardens, 229
   research, 17–22
   restorative garden, 235
Schaal, Herb, 106–10
Scotland. *See* United Kingdom
Scottsdale Healthcare Healing Garden (Scottsdale,
      Arizona), 75, 84, 295
screening
   design guidelines, 75
   horticultural therapy gardens, 257
Scutari military hospital (Constantinople
      (Istanbul), Turkey), 8
season, water features, design guidelines, 86. *See
      also* climate

seating
   behavior mapping exercise, postoccupancy
      evaluation study, 312
   cancer patients, 115, 124, 126–27
   children's hospitals, 98–100
   design guidelines, 68, 70, 76, 77, 79–80, 82
   frail elderly facilities, 135–37
   plant placement, 270–71, 272
   rehabilitation gardens, 229
   site planning, 64
   water features, design guidelines, 85, 87
security, 56. *See also* safety
   adolescent treatment center, 190
   mental and behavioral health facilities, 182
   sense of, 24, 29, 56, 67, 74,
Seirei-Mikatagahara Hospital Hospice (Shizuoka
      Prefecture, Japan), 166
senior. *See* frail elderly
sensory experience
   dementia facilities, walkways, 157–58
   plantings, 275–77
   research, 17–22, 201
   veterans hospitals, 215
The Serenades by Sonata (Longwood, Florida),
      149, 150
service dogs, veterans hospitals, 216
sexual abuse, restorative gardens, 235
shade
   cancer patients, 115, 117, 121
   dementia facilities, 152
   design guidelines, 66-67, 81
   mental and behavioral health facilities, 182
   planting, 274, 279, 281
   rehabilitation gardens, 229, 231
   site planning, 63–64, 67
   veterans hospitals, 215
shadows, visual perception, 76, 77, 152, 215. *See
      also* cliffing, visual
Shady Grove Adventist Church (Baltimore,
      Maryland), 290
Sharp Mesa Vista Hospital (San Diego,
      California), 183
shinrin-yoku, forest bathing, research, 18–19
shrubs, 265–66, 272
Siegmund, John, 172–76
Signage. *See also* wayfinding
   access, design guidelines, 74, 75
   site planning, 61
   walkways, 77
Singapore Botanical Garden, restorative garden,
      235
site planning, 60–66
   recommendations, 64–66
   requirements, 60–64
sleep patterns, Alzheimer's disease and dementias,
      149–50
slip hazards, water features, design guidelines, 85

Smilow Cancer Hospital, Yale-New Haven Hospital (New Haven, Connecticut), *73*

Smith, Jeffrey T., 246–48

Smith, Jerry, 298

Smith, Shelagh, 143–46

smoking areas
    design guidelines, 70
    veterans hospitals, 216

Snow, John, 9

social horticulture, described, 250–51

social support
    crisis shelters, 185
    horticultural therapy gardens, 257
    mental and behavioral health facilities, 182
    stress reduction theory/theory of supportive gardens, 25–26
    veterans hospitals, 215

Society of Friends (Quakers), 8

soft fascination, attention restoration theory, 28, 81, 274,

soil, 263–64

solar orientation. *See also* shade; sunlight
    dementia facilities, 152
    hospice care, 166–67
    site planning, 64

sound(s)
    adolescent treatment center, 192
    design guidelines, site planning and programming, 62–63, 71
    hospice care, 167–68
    natural/urban environments compared, research, 19–22
    research, 17–22
    veterans hospitals, 215
    water features, design guidelines, *65, 71, 85*–86
    wind chimes, 71

Spellman Brady and Company, *64, 65, 116*

Spalenka, Rick, 216

special-needs children, horticultural therapy design guidelines, 257

staff
    children's hospitals, 97,103
    dementia facilities, 151, 152
    maintenance, plantings, 263, 265, 282–84
    mental and behavioral health facilities, 181, 184, 194,
    separate spaces for, 60–61, *63, 72,* 184
    turnover and burnout in, *301*
    visual access, 71

staff team, 48–51. *See also* interdisciplinary design team (IDT)

Stauchnitz, Frederik, 194–98

Steiner, Rudolf, 11

Stenzel Healing Garden, Good Samaritan Hospital (Portland, Oregon), *223, 224,* 225–27

Sternberg, Esther, 17, 31

Stigsdotter, Ulrika A., 194–98

Stigsdotter, Ulrika K., 184–205, 198–204

Stoneman Healing Garden, Yawkey Center for Cancer Care, Dana-Farber Cancer Institute (Boston, Massachusetts), *63, 82,* 122–25

storage, for maintenance equipment and tools, 81, 100, *101,* 253, 256, 285

stormwater management, sustainability, 290

stress reduction
    evidence-based design (EBD), *16*
    funding, 299–300
    Planetree model, 11
    research, *16,* 17–22, 31–32
    theory, 24–28

stress-related disease, rehabilitation garden, 194–98

subspaces, design guidelines, 70, 272

substance abuse, restorative gardens, 235

Summerley, Victoria, 127

sundowning, dementia facilities, 152

sunlight. *See also* shade; solar orientation
    design guidelines, 67, 76
    plantings, 263
    research, 19
    site planning, 64
    veterans hospitals, 215

supervision, access, design guidelines, 74

surface coverings, pathways, 107

surgical recovery time, research, 14

sustainability, 58, *59,* 288–97
    complementarity concept, 289–91
    lack of, 288–89
    progress in, 291

Sustainable Sites Initiative (SITES), 291

Swan, Katsy, 120–22

tables
    design guidelines, 80

temperature, research, 19

Ten Eyck Landscape Architects, *59, 75, 84, 293, 286, 295,*

terraces, site planning, 65

Texas Children's Hospital (Houston, Texas), 93–94

Texas Medical Center Hospice (Houston, Texas), 165

texture, plantings, 274–75

theory, 22–32. *See also* research
    aesthetic placebo, 31
    attention restoration theory (ART), 28–29
    biophilia, 23
    emotional congruence theory, 30–31
    flight or fight response, 24
    of supportive gardens, 24–28
    pleasure, 31–32
    prospect-refuge theory, 23–24
    stress reduction, 24–28

therapeutic horticulture, described, 250

Thieriot, Angelica, 10

Thomas, William, 11

thresholds, door, access, design guidelines, 74

Thrive (gardening program, UK), 251

time-of-day
    dementia facilities, 152
    mental and behavioral health facilities, 184

Tippet House hospice (Needham, Massachusetts), 284

TKF Foundation, restorative garden, 235

Tomt, Gene, 172

toxic plants. *See* poisonous plantings

trails, nature and fitness trails, location types, 37–38. *See also* walkways

transcendence, hospice facilities, 166

traumatic brain injury (TBI), veterans hospitals, 206

trees
    design guidelines, 67, 82
    plantings, 264–65

Trinity Hospice (London, England), 165

trip and slip hazards, water features, design guidelines, 85

"tucked away" garden, location types, 40

Tuke, William, 8

Tyson, Martha, 159–62

Tzu Chi General Hospital (Taipei, Taiwan), *272*

Ulfelder Healing Garden, Massachusetts General Hospital (Boston, Massachusetts), *68, 88*

Ulrich, Roger, 11, 14, 24–25, 28, 298

United Kingdom (UK), 6
    Edinburgh Royal Infirmary (Scotland), 8, *37*
    Ferryfield House (Edinburgh, Scotland), *135*
    Gardening Leave (Scotland), *4, 213, 214, 259*
    horticultural therapy, 251
    hospice care, 165
    mental health facilities, 179
    participatory design process, 47
    Royal Infirmary (Edinburgh, Scotland), *77*
    Scotland, 8, 150

United Nations (UN), 184

United States Department of Defense (DOD), 208

United States Environmental Protection Agency (EPA), 291

United States Green Building Council (USGBC), 291

Universal Design Principles, 57, 254

urban environments, nature compared, research, 19–22

utilities
    children's hospitals, 100
    design guidelines, 83, 85

Vadnais, Gretchen, 101–5

Valleroy, Marie, 48

Vancouver General Hospital, Banfield Pavilion Roof-top Patio Garden (Vancouver, British Columbia, Canada), 143–46

van Gogh, Vincent, 179
ventilation, hospital design, 6, 8
vertical gardening bed, horticultural therapy
    design, 258
Veterans Administration (VA), 208
Veterans Administration Greater Los Angeles
    Healthcare System (California), 211
Veterans Administration Hospital (Palo Alto,
    California), *82*
Veterans Administration New Jersey Health Care
    System (VA NJHCS, East Orange, New
    Jersey), 211
veterans hospitals, 70, 206–21
    built gardens, 209–13
    case study, Warrior and Family Support Center
        Therapeutic Garden, Returning Heroes
        Home (San Antonio, Texas), 216–20
    design guidelines, 213–16
    epidemiology, 206
    posttraumatic stress disorder, 206–7
    research findings, 208–9
    research limitations, 207–8
    restorative garden, 235
    traumatic brain injury, 206
Vidar Clinic (Järna, Sweden), 11
viewing garden, location types, 44, 46
views
    dementia facilities,151, 153,
    design guidelines, 67, 68, 69, 80-83
    frail elderly facilities, 131, 133–134,
    from interior to outdoor space, 4, 61, *63, 64, 65,*
        69, 70, 71–74, *83, 134, 271*
    healing and, 14, *15*
    horticultural therapy, 256
    hospice care, 170
    mental can behavioral health facilities, 185,
        193, 200,
    plantings, 274
    site planning, 61, 64–65, 69
View Through a Window study (Ulrich), 24, 298
vines and groundcovers, plantings, 268–69
violence, dementia facilities, 150, 155
virtual nature, real nature compared, 17
visibility, dementia facilities, 151–52
visitor's book, 88, 110, 231
visual access, design guidelines, 71–74
visual sense, research, 17–22
vitamin D
    frail elderly facilities, 129
    sunlight, research, 19

vocational horticulture, described, 250
volunteers, maintenance staff, 284

Walking. *See also* excercise
    frail elderly facilities, 129
    research, 18–19
walking surface coverings, pathways, 107
walkways
    adolescent treatment center, 190–91
    cancer patients, 115
    children's hospitals, 98, *104,* 107
    dementia facilities, 157–58
    design guidelines, 75–78
    frail elderly facilities, *130,* 135
    hospice care, 167–68
    peripheral garden, *44*
    rehabilitation gardens, 229
    restorative gardens (healing, therapeutic
        gardens), *202, 271*
    site planning, 65
    trails, nature and fitness trails, 37–38
wall art, research, virtual/real nature compared, 17
wandering, dementia facilities, 155
Wangler, Gary, 109
Warrior and Family Support Center Therapeutic
    Garden, Returning Heroes Home (San
    Antonio, Texas), *216,* 216–20
Washington, University of, Peter Gross House
    (Seattle, Washington), *116*
water features. *See also* irrigation
    adolescent treatment center, 190–92
    dementia facilities, 154–55
    design guidelines, *65,* 71, *73,* 85–86, *87*
    hospice care, 170
    infection control, 85, 293
    mental and behavioral health facilities,
        183, *183*
    restorative garden, 235
    restorative gardens (healing, therapeutic
        gardens), 198, 202
    site planning, *65*
    sustainability, 292–93
    veterans hospitals, 290
wayfinding
    design guidelines, 67–68, 69
    mental and behavioral health facilities, 183
    signage, 67-68, *74,* 75, 77
weather. *See also* climate
    design guidelines, 70, *71,* 74
    horticultural therapy, 253

plantings, 265–68
Wellspring benches, Landscape Forms, *79*
Wesley Woods (Atlanta, Georgia), *252*
Wheatley-Miller, Mariane, 1
wheelchairs
    design guidelines, 70, 77
    enabling gardens, 240
    horticultural therapy, *254*
Wildlife (including birds, butterflies)
    biodiversity, sustainability, 290
    design guidelines, 90
    hospice care, 168–69, 170
    infection control issues, 90, 168–69, 170
    plantings, 138, 274–75
Wilheit-Keys Peace Garden, Northeast Georgia
    Medical Center (Gainesville, Georgia), *2*
Willard Middle School (Berkeley, California),
    restorative garden, 235
Wilson, Edward O., 23
wind chimes, 71. *See also* sound(s)
windows
    daylighting, sustainability, 289–90
    operable, 65–66
    outdoor space, 4, 61, *63,* 71–74
    site planning, 63, 65–66. *See also* interiors
wind, site planning, 64
Winterbottom, Daniel, *116, 303, 304*
women, crisis shelter, Danner's Garden
    (Copenhagen, Denmark), 184–205
Women's Garden, Banner Gateway Medical Center
    (Phoenix, Arizona), *82*
World Health Organization (WHO), 179, 184
World War I, 9
World War II, 9
Wren, Christopher, 6

xeric landscapes, sustainability, 293, *294*

Yale-New Haven Hospital, Smilow Cancer
    Hospital (New Haven, Connecticut), *73*
Yawkey Center for Cancer Care, Dana-Farber
    Cancer Institute, The Thea and James
    Stoneman Healing Garden (Boston,
    Massachusetts), *63, 82,* 122–25
York, England, 8

Zaragosa, Spain, 8
Zen stone garden, adolescent treatment
    center, 190
Zimmer Gunsul Frasca, Architects, *63,* 122–25